D0524916

Democracy and Development

'And I will give unto thee the keys of the kingdom of heaven: and whatsoever thou shalt bind on earth shall be bound in heaven: and whatsoever thou shalt loose on earth shall be loosed in heaven.'

Matthew 16:19

Democracy and Development

Theory and Practice

EDITED BY ADRIAN LEFTWICH

Polity Press

First published in 1996 by Polity Press in association with Blackwell Publishers Ltd.

2 4 6 8 10 7 5 3 1

Editorial office:
Polity Press
65 Bridge Street
Cambridge CB2 1UR, UK

Marketing and production:
Blackwell Publishers Ltd
108 Cowley Road
Oxford OX4 1JF, UK

Blackwell Publishers Inc.
238 Main Street
Cambridge, MA 02142, USA

ISBN 0–7456–1266–0
ISBN 0–7456–1267–9 (pbk)

A CIP catalogue record for this book is available from the British Library and the Library of Congress.

Typeset in 10.5 on 11 pt Sabon
by Graphicraft Typesetters Ltd, Hong Kong
Printed in Great Britain by Hartnolls Ltd, Bodmin, Cornwall

This book is printed on acid-free paper.

Contents

List of Tables

Notes on the Contributors

Svante Ersson holds a PhD for research on electoral support for communist parties in Western Europe. He is Lecturer in the Department of Politics in the University of Umea. He is co-author, with Jan-Erik Lane, of *Comparative Political Economy* (Pinter, 1990) and *Comparative Politics* (Polity, 1994).

Geoffrey Hawthorn teaches Sociology and Politics at Cambridge University, and is a Fellow of Clare Hall.

John D. Holm is Professor of Political Science at Cleveland State University and Associate Dean of the Ohio School of International Business. He has conducted field research and written widely on political development in Botswana since 1970. He is a co-founder of the Democracy Project at the University of Botswana.

Sudipta Kaviraj is Reader in Politics at the School of Oriental and African Studies, University of London. He has taught previously at the University of Burdwan and the Jawaharlal Nehru University, New Delhi. His main fields of interest are political theory and Indian politics. His study on Indian nationalist discourse, *The Unhappy Consciousness*, was published by Oxford University Press, Delhi, in 1995.

Yong-Cheol Kim is a full-time lecturer in the Department of Political Science, Chonnam National University. He wrote a doctoral dissertation on the state and labour in South Korea at the Ohio State University. He has published articles in *Pacific Focus* and *Korean Observer*. Dr Kim is currently working on the politics of labour management in South Korea.

Peter Larmour is Senior Lecturer in the Department of Political Science at the University of Tasmania, and is currently on secondment to the National Centre for Development Studies at the Australian National University, where he is director of the graduate programme in Development Administration. He has worked previously at the University of Papua New Guinea and at the University of the South Pacific in Fiji.

Jan-Erik Lane is Professor of Political Science at the University of Oslo and Adjunct Professor in Administration at the Norwegian School of Management: BI. He has published extensively in the fields of political theory, comparative politics and public policy. His most recent book, co-authored with Svante Ersson, is *Comparative Politics* (Polity, 1994).

Adrian Leftwich is Senior Lecturer in Politics at the University of York, England. He specializes and publishes in the politics of development. He authored *Redefining Politics: People, Resources and Power* (Methuen, 1983) and has edited a number of books on aspects of the discipline of politics. He is currently completing a comparative study of *States of Development* to be published by Polity Press in 1995.

Tom Lodge is Associate Professor in the Department of Political Studies at the University of the Witwatersrand and is the author of *Black Politics in South Africa since 1945* (Longman, 1983) and many other publications on politics in South Africa.

Chung-in Moon is Professor of Political Science at Yonsei University, Seoul. He previously taught at the University of Kentucky, the University of California, San Diego, and Williams College. He has published over 50 articles in edited volumes and such scholarly journals as *World Politics, International Studies Quarterly, Journal of Asian Studies,* and *Millennium.* His books include *Arms Control on the Korean Peninsula, The U.S. and the Defense of the Pacific, Rethinking the Korean Peninsula* and several other volumes. He is currently working on two books, one on the political economy of defence industrialization in South Korea, and the other on the politics of democratic transition in South Korea.

Jenny Pearce lectures in the Department of Peace Studies, University of Bradford. She is author of a number of books on Latin America, including *Promised Land, Peasant Rebellion in Chalatenango, El Salvador* (Latin American Bureau, 1986) and *Colombia: Inside the Labyrinth* (Latin American Bureau, 1990). Since 1993, she has been part of a two-year ESRC-funded research project on the transition to democracy in Chile.

Peter Rutland is an Associate Professor of Government at Wesleyan University in the United States and a Fellow at the Harvard University Russian Research Center. His publications include *The Myth of the*

Plan (Hutchinson, 1985) and *The Politics of Economic Stagnation in the Soviet Union* (Cambridge University Press, 1993).

Paul Seabright teaches Economics at Cambridge University and is a Fellow of Churchill College.

Richard L. Sklar is Professor Emeritus of Political Science at the University of California, Los Angeles, and has also taught at universities in Nigeria, Uganda, Zambia and Zimbabwe. His publications include *Nigerian Political Parties* (Princeton University Press, 1963), *Corporate Power in an African State* (University of California Press, 1975), *Postimperialism: International Capitalism and Development in the Late Twentieth Century* (Lynne Rienner, 1987, with three co-authors) and *African Politics and Problems in Development* (Lynne Rienner, 1991, co-authored with C. S. Whitaker). His current research includes further investigation of 'developmental democracy' in addition to the role of the traditional authorities in African polities and a collaborative project on 'postimperialism' as an approach to the study of world politics.

Gordon White is a political scientist and Professorial Fellow at the Institute of Development Studies, University of Sussex, working on the socio-political dimensions of development, with particular focus on China. His most recent books are *Riding the Tiger: The Politics of Economic Reform in China* (Macmillan, 1993) and (with Paul Bowles) *The Political Economy of China's Financial Reforms: Finance in Late Development* (Westview, 1993).

Acknowledgements

I should like to thank a number of people who helped greatly in shaping this book. First, David Held at Polity took an interest in the idea from the start. His suggestions about content and structure were invaluable in the early stages of the work when crucial decisions needed to be taken. His encouragement and the speed and decisiveness of his comments made it easier to keep things moving at a steady pace. Second, all collections of essays of this kind depend on the cooperation of the contributors and they have all been as good as their word. They have delivered interesting and important chapters within the broad timeframe we set ourselves and have thus helped to create what I believe is a timely and valuable set of essays on questions of central importance in the modern world. Finally, Katy Fellows in the Politics Department at the University of York acted as an administrative and secretarial anchor for this project. Her reliability, speed and accuracy in preparing the manuscript for the publisher made my editorial task very much easier. I am grateful to all these people for their assistance.

Adrian Leftwich
Department of Politics
University of York

PART I
Theory and Controversy

1

On the Primacy of Politics in Development

ADRIAN LEFTWICH

INTRODUCTION AND OVERVIEW

Democracy, and especially democratization, is once again on the move. On all continents, north and east and west and south, democratic regimes are emerging or reemerging. Samuel Huntington has referred to this as the 'third wave' of democratization (starting with the 1974 overthrow of the Portuguese dictatorship). He distinguished this from the first wave, which commenced with the French and American revolutions at the end of the eighteenth century, and the second wave, which arose out of the allied victory in the 1939–45 World War (Huntington, 1991). The percentage of formally democratic states in the world grew from a bare 25 per cent in 1973 to 45 per cent in 1990 and to 68 per cent in 1992 (Huntington, 1991: 26; Freedom House, 1992) and is still on the increase. It is of course true that already there has been slippage, or democratic reversal, in the early 1990s (as in Algeria and Nigeria). More reversals must be anticipated in the 1990s especially in Africa and Latin America. But, despite this, it is clear that there has been a significant increase in the number of formally democratic polities.

Where there is resistance to democratization – as, for instance, in Cuba, Myanmar (Burma), China and in many parts of sub-Saharan Africa – considerable direct or indirect international pressure is allegedly being brought to bear on regimes to change their ways. As the British Foreign Secretary observed in 1990: 'In practical terms, it means that we ... will reward democratic governments and any political reform which leads to greater accountability and democracy. The corollary is that we should penalise particularly bad cases of repression and abuse of human rights' (Hurd, 1990: 4).

This general line has been adopted by most Western governments and by many international development agencies, intergovernmental organizations and regional groupings. These include the European Communities, the Commonwealth, the Organization for Economic Cooperation and Development and the Organization of African Unity (Leftwich, 1993: 611; IDS Bulletin, 1993: 7–8). They all appear united in their belief that democracy is a good thing. And most would endorse S. M. Lipset's observation in 1960 that 'democracy is not only or even primarily a means through which different groups can attain their ends or seek the good society; it is the good society itself in operation' (Lipset, 1960: 404). The more speculatively-minded theorists of this view, such as Francis Fukuyama, portray liberal democracy, broadly speaking, as the teleological terminus of history, seeing 'the universalization of Western liberal democracy as the final form of human government' (Fukuyama, 1989: 4).

But liberal democracy is not only seen as the high point of human civilization: in a certain sense that has always been the formal and highly Eurocentric position of much of the West since the nineteenth century. Now a new orthodoxy prevails in official Western circles which systematically connects democracy to the question of development in an entirely new way. It is now claimed that democratic good governance is not an outcome or consequence of development, as was the old orthodoxy, but a necessary condition of development (Hurd, 1990; Chalker, 1991). Contrary to some of the very best work on left and right in political analysis (Hyden, 1985; Huntington, 1987; Sandbrook, 1990), this general view about the developmental efficacy of democracy appears to assume that there are no tensions between the many goals of development such as growth, democracy, stability, equality and autonomy. Furthermore, the new orthodoxy implies that democracy can be inserted and instituted at almost any stage in the developmental process of any society – whether Rwanda or Russia, Chile or China – irrespective of its social structure, economic condition, political traditions and external relations, and that it will enhance development.

In many fundamental respects, the new orthodoxy turns on its head an older view which prevailed in the bulk of Western social theory and also in much of its imperial practice. This older view held that many parts of what used to be called the 'undeveloped', 'backward' or colonial world were not 'ready' for democracy and that a considerable amount of economic and social progress, plus political tutelage, was required before the institutions and processes of democracy would stick (Lee, 1967: 171–3; Larrain, 1989: 22–7).

From a narrowly academic point of view, therefore, what is

interesting about the current orthodoxy (and the debate it has generated) is that it both universalizes and brings dramatically into focus a very long-standing question in political science: what are the conditions for sustainable democracy? But it does more than this. It serves the purpose of bringing critical problems of development (by which, at least for the moment, I mean primarily economic growth and its distribution into individual and social welfare) into much closer alignment with some of the central concerns of political science. Put another way, it puts politics at the core of development studies and, at the same time, shows that the question of development is at the heart of political science.

The essays in this book all look at the democracy–development relationship in distinctive ways and in diverse theoretical and empirical contexts, from South Africa to South Korea and from Chile to China. Is democracy a condition for steady economic development or do the causal processes run the other way? That is to say, is a certain minimum level of economic development necessary for democracy to flourish? And what is the historical and contemporary evidence for such a claim? What are the prospects for stable democracy in societies which are undergoing rapid development and change? And what are the prospects for rapid and sustained development in democratic societies? What kind of theory can help to answer these questions and predict where both democracy and development might succeed together and where they could not?

In the final chapter of this book I shall try to pull together threads and comparative conclusions which emerge from the richness of these individual case studies and theoretical contributions. But for present purposes, three important questions immediately arise.

1 Why has the contemporary preoccupation with democratic governance as a condition of development emerged now?
2 What does democratic governance mean?
3 And is the question of governance, that is the *form of government*, really the right question to focus on when considering the appropriate political arrangements and institutions for the effective promotion of development?

In addressing these questions I will argue in this and the final chapter that, contrary to the current orthodoxy, what matters for development is not the system of government, or regime type – that is, whether it is democratic or not – but the type of *state*. The distinction is fundamental. Crucially, moreover, it is not its technical and administrative arrangements which determine the character and competence of the state, but the politics which both generates and sustains that state, *irrespective* of whether the state is democratic or not. Analytically and in practice, the centrality of politics and the state in development, not governance and democracy, forms a major theme of the final chapter of the book.

Since the notion of politics plays such a central role in the argument here, it would be as well to spell out briefly what I mean by the term. I start from the assumption that human societies are characterized by a diversity of interests, preferences, values and ideas. Each of these directly or indirectly involves the use of resources, or ways of doing things with resources, which individuals or groups seek to promote or protect. In general, also, people prefer to get their way. But they also have to live together and cooperate if they are to prosper, and so constant war and outright victory in dispute is not a viable long-term solution to the problem of diversity of interests, though it often happens. With one possible exception (de Waal, 1982), the human species is the only one to have evolved a set of conscious processes for trying to sort out or resolve these differences. These processes are what I call politics, which may be defined to mean *all the activities of conflict, cooperation and negotiation involved in the use, production and distribution of resources, whether material or ideal, whether at local, national or international levels, or whether in the private or public domains* (Leftwich, 1983: ch. 1). And of course achieving cooperation and negotiation has always been much harder to attain where the differences between the interests, ideas and preferences have been sharp and hence less compatible.

It will be clear from this definition why all 'development' is therefore inescapably political, not managerial or administrative in the current technicist sense. For at any point in any developmental sequence what is crucially at issue is how resources are to be used and distributed in new ways and the inevitable disputes arising from calulations by individuals and groups as to who will win and who will lose as a result. For as Hugh Stretton observed in a different context: 'People can't change the way they use resources without changing their relations with one another' (Stretton, 1976: 3).

The new orthodoxy overturned much of the mainstream social theory on left and right about change and development which prevailed from the nineteenth century to modern times. The bulk of that theory may be loosely described as modernization theory. And it is worth recalling just how wide-ranging and systematic these theories were, especially in their attitude to democracy as an outcome, rather than as a cause or condition, of development.

MODERNIZATION THEORY AND DEMOCRACY

As indicated earlier, the belief that democracy should, could and would spread to what was then the colonial or 'backward' world, was in many respects integral to both main-stream social theorizing and the imperial ideology of the west, especially in Europe. In one form or another it was present in the broad thrust of nineteenth-century theories of modernization and in their twentieth-century successors (Apter, 1965; Harrison, 1988; Larrain, 1989). At the heart of these theories was the essential claim that the structures and processes of human societies develop from simple forms of traditionalism to complex expressions of modernity. In political terms, according to the general theory of modernization, these processes have involved a shift from non-democratic to democratic forms of government, or at least from various forms of authoritarian rule to arrangements involving wider popular control.

For Herbert Spencer, writing in 1876, this implied a change from simplicity to complexity, involving progress with respect to 'size, coherence, multiformity, and definiteness' in the structure of society (Spencer, 1969: 155). In terms of legal development, this movement from traditionalism to modernity was characterized in 1861 by Sir Henry Sumner Maine, in his classic study *Ancient Law*, as a shift 'from status to contract' in the legal principles, processes and institutions of 'progressive societies' (Maine, 1908: 151). For the German theorist, Ferdinand Tönnies, writing in 1887, law emerged through a process of modernization from its origins in customs and folkways to its expression as formal legislation. This occurred, he argued, as the structural basis of societies shifted progressively from community (*gemeinschaft*), in which what he calls 'natural will' predominated, to association *(gesellschaft)*, in which 'rational will' predominated (Tönnies, 1955). Durkheim, writing in 1893, saw the essential difference between traditional and modern societies as being characterized by their respective 'mechanical' and 'organic' forms of solidarity (Durkheim, 1964). In the early years of the twentieth century Max Weber conceived of modernity, at least in terms of its politico-administrative arrangements, as being expressed in the rational-legal basis of the modern state which had emerged from prior forms of political traditionalism such as gerontocracy, patriarchy and patrimonialism. In these traditional political systems, power and authority had been highly personalized and unaccountable, not institutionalized or subject to forms of popular control as in the modern state, which had evolved in the course of capitalist economic development (Weber, 1964).

But perhaps no theorist of the nineteenth century had a sharper conception of the distinction between 'traditional' and 'modern' societies than Marx. And no theorist was more dedicated to their modernization than he. For Marx was a modernizer, of a special kind, as the whole thrust of his writing on history and change illustrates, and especially his conception of the trajectory of revolution-punctuated progress from feudalism to communism. Central to Marx's theory of politics, moreover, was the fundamental postulate that the 'stage of development' of the 'economic structure' of society constituted the basis, or substructure, from which arises the 'legal and political superstructure'; or, in other words, 'the mode of production of material life conditions the social, political and intellectual life-process in general' (Marx, 1958b: 363; Callinicos, 1984). In short, each mode of production both shaped and set limits to the forms of political life possible within it. A representative democratic politics was therefore unthinkable for Marx in a largely peasant society or in one in which the feudal means and forces of production predominated. Bourgeois democracy, a purely 'political' form of democracy, was thus the limited form of democracy made both possible and necessary by advancing industrial capitalism. Despite its many limitations, bourgeois democracy might nonetheless be used by workers to promote the next stage 'in the course of development', true democracy (Marx, 1958d: 54). This 'true democracy' (Avineri, 1969: 31–43) in turn was only possible in communist society, itself based on an industrial or post-industrial order in which class distinctions and property had been abolished. Such a society would be governed by the principles of science and secularism, where the control of production was in the 'the hands of a vast association of the whole nation . . . in which the free development of each is the condition for the free development of all' (Marx, 1958d: 54). Only this could liberate the human species from the wheel of nature by 'replacing the domination of circumstances and chance over individuals by the domination of individuals over chance and circumstances' (Marx, 1977: 190).

Both bourgeois and true democracy thus presupposed advanced stages in the development of the economic structure for Marx, a view which is entirely at one with the deepest assumptions of modernization theory. And it is hardly surprising therefore that the traditional and primarily agrarian economic structure of mid-nineteenth-century French society embodied for Marx the 'idiocy of rural life' (Marx, 1958d: 38) in which he likened the French peasantry to a 'sack of potatoes' (Marx, 1958a: 334). Worse still was his castigation of the economic structures of traditional Asian society in which the masses were steeped in an 'undignified, stagnatory and vegetative life' under regimes of 'oriental despotism', which 'restrained the human mind, making it the unresisting tool of superstition . . . depriving it of all grandeur and historical energies' (Marx, 1958c: 350).

While Marx nowhere provided a clear template of socialist or communist society, it is not hard to infer its structural principles from his writings (Leftwich, 1992). In their modernity they stand in direct contrast to the traditionalism of agrarian France or 'Asian' society. Unlike Lipset and Fukuyama, the teleological conclusion of history for Marx was not liberal democracy, but communist society, which *would be* true democracy, and in which the distinction between economics and politics would be collapsed. But, just as other nineteenth-century modernizers assumed in their own accounts of progress, Marx also saw that this would be based on the technological potentials of an industrial or post-industrial economic basis, and therefore would broadly follow the pattern of the West. In short, 'The country that is more developed industrially only shows to the less developed, the image of its own future' (Marx, 1976: 91).

Whether liberal or democratic-socialist in their approaches, the-orists of the modernization school of the 1960s drew on all these traditions, both in their conceptions of modernity and in their ana-lyses of the trajectories of change towards it. S. N. Eisenstadt, for instance, defined modernization as:

> the process of change towards those types of social, economic and political systems that have developed in western Europe and North America from the seventeenth century to the nineteenth century and have then spread to other European countries and in the nine-teenth and twentieth centuries to the South American, Asian and African continents. (Eisenstadt, 1966: 1)

Politically, Eisenstadt argued, modern societies are 'in some sense' (ibid: 4) democratic societies, in which the formal ideal (if not al-ways the practice) of political equality had been established. This had generally been a consequence of structural change in the eco-nomic and social systems, as a result of which the power, legitimacy and control of traditional rulers had been eroded by the emergence and spread of wider or popular power and the requirements of some degree of institutional accountability. In a comparable approach, Neil Smelser identified structural differentiation as the central pro-cess of social change brought about by and accompanying economic development, and it is reflected as much in the political institutions as in the more narrowly economic and social structures of a society in the course of modernization (Smelser, 1968). For David Apter, one of the most thoughtful analysts of modernization, the move towards modernity involved a shift from a society based on what he called the sacred-collectivity model to one based on the secular-libertarian model (Apter, 1965: 28–33). The politics at the heart of the latter model, democratic politics, presupposed for Apter – as it had for Marx – the predominance of an 'ethic of science' (ibid: 461) which in the West had arisen from industrialization, commercializa-tion, urbanization and bureaucratization and in which the funda-mental principles of individualism had become firmly established.

Equally, in the twentieth century, some Western Marxists in the classical tradition of that school, such as Paul A. Baran (1957), Bill Warren (1980) and Gavin Kitching (1983), and those influenced by this tradition (Hyden, 1985), have developed these same central themes and have applied them explicitly to the developing world. As Kitching has observed, 'materially poor societies cannot produce the democratic life which is an essential pre-requisite for the creation of socialist democracies' (Kitching, 1983: 54). Only economic growth – through industrialization – can provide the platform on which democratic values, institutions and processes can be sustained. Most recently, Dietrich Rueschemeyer, E. H. and J. D. Stephens (1992) have explored the relationship between capitalist development and democracy, focusing on the changing balance of class power and its significance for democratization. In questioning the central role given to the middle classes in promoting democracy, their comparative studies suggest that capitalist socioeconomic development also enhances the size and power of the working class as a democratic force, and diminishes the size and power of the anti-democratic social groups. And since the struggle for democracy is essentially a struggle for power, the role of the working class in promoting democracy is critical (Rueschemeyer, et al., 1992: ch. 3).

Much of nineteenth-century modernization theory, with its evolutionary and diffusionist assumptions, has been criticized as arrogant, Eurocentric and wrong. Likewise, many of the post-war theories of modernization received intense criticism in the 1960s and 1970s (O'Brien, 1972; Tipps, 1973). The roots of this critique go back, at least, to Lenin's modification of classical Marxism and also to the theories of radical nationalists in the developing world, notably India in the 1920s and Latin America in the 1940s and 1950s (Warren, 1980; Harrison, 1988). Why then deal with them at this length here? I do so for two main reasons. First, I wish to suggest that they require sympathetic re-evaluation and reformulation in the light of global developmental trends in the second half of the twentieth century. The weak record of democracy in so much of the developing world suggests that preconditions have not been present and that modernization theories, on left and right, have much to contribute by way of explanation. But, second, I also want to emphasize the contrast which the new orthodoxy in official Western thinking now poses to the earlier tradition and to ask why official Western policy now runs counter to its earlier theory and practice. The starting point for doing this is to look at its origins.

ORIGINS OF CONTEMPORARY CALLS FOR DEMOCRATIC GOVERNANCE

It needs immediately to be said that in the post-war world, under US leadership, the West has long maintained a formal commitment to promoting democracy and human rights, as one of its foreign policy goals. This reaches back at the very least to President Truman's programme of assistance for Greece and Turkey in 1947 as part of the evolving policy of promoting democratic regimes against the communist challenge (Packenham, 1973: 25–49). Later, in the early 1960s, President Kennedy sought to give this concrete expression in Latin America through the Alliance for Progress (Furlong, 1980). But it is important to note that even in this programme it was assumed that socioeconomic growth was the essential basis for a secure democratic politics, and it was recognized that democratization without well-distributed economic and social development would have little chance of success. But in the event, the democratic commitment was 'one of words rather than actions or deeds' (ibid: 181). The policy goals of the Alliance failed as a rash of military governments took over in Latin America from the mid-1960s (there were fewer democracies by 1980 than there had been in 1960). Moreover, as the Cold War intensified and the fear of communism grew, the US and Western governments seemed oblivious to the abuses and incompetence of many non-democratic governments in the developing world. Aid and support continued to flow to them so long as they remained loyal to US interests. In acknowledging American support for such friendly but odious regimes, one US president made the essential political point when he was alleged to have said: 'They may be sons of bitches but at least they are *our* sons of bitches.'

Indeed throughout the 1970s and 1980s, official development assistance (ODA), not to mention military aid, flowed freely to non-democratic regimes, such as El Salvador, Honduras, Zaïre, Kenya, Pakistan and the Philippines under Marcos, most of them with appalling human rights records. Calculated as a percentage of their GNP, total ODA (from both bilateral and multilateral sources) to those countries in 1986 was as follows: El Salvador 9.2 per cent, Honduras 8.5 per cent, Zaïre 8.0 per cent, Kenya 6.9 per cent, Pakistan 2.9 per cent, and the Philippines 3.2 per cent (OECD, 1984; Humana, 1987; World Bank, 1988: table 22).

So although the commitment to democracy and improving human rights is not new, it is clear that it has always been provisional, and apparently always subject to considerations of regional or global security and economic interests.[1] But why has this renewed push for democracy come about now? And why are regimes which were previously supported now being told to change their ways? I think there are four main reasons, and they are all political: the legitimization of conditionality (or 'leverage') as an instrument of policy; the ascendancy of neo-conservative or neo-liberal theories and ideologies of political economy in the West; the collapse of the Soviet Union and its client states; and the growth of democratic pressures in some developing countries.

Legitimizing conditionality

In the twenty years after the first oil crisis of 1973, economic progress in much of the developing world has been very poor. With some notable exceptions – for example Botswana, Mauritius, Thailand, Indonesia and of course the East Asian 'tigers' – growth was negligible and, in many cases, negative. Overall, between 1965 and 1990, the average annual rate of growth of GNP per capita was negative in many African countries, and also in Jamaica, Bolivia, Peru and Venezuela (World Bank, 1992a: table 1).

Western development institutions, notably the International Monetary Fund (IMF), the World Bank and their major members attributed these poor records to the prevailing policies and strategies of development which had been pursued in the post-war era (Landell-Mills, 1992; World Bank, 1991). The major flaw in these strategies, they argued, had been the degree of state involvement in economic affairs and the curtailment of free markets and liberal trade regimes. Reducing the economic power and role of the state therefore became a central strategic objective. The means adopted by the West for achieving this in the 1980s was to develop a new breed of policy-based loans, 'structural adjustment lending' as it came to be known, which involved a high degree of conditionality.

'Structural adjustment' was the generic term used to describe a package of economic and institutional measures which multilateral and bilateral aid donors – singly, but more often together – sought to persuade many developing countries to adopt in return for loans (Mosley, et al., 1991: ch. 1). The aim of adjustment lending was to promote open and free competitive market economies, supervised by minimal states. Loans were offered in return for the transformation of economic policies, structures and institutions through varying doses of deregulation, privatization, slimming down of allegedly obese and inefficient public bureaucracies, reducing subsidies and encouraging realistic prices to emerge as a stimulus to greater productivity, especially for export (Mosley and Toye, 1988: 403–41).

Though the net long-term effects of adjustment are as yet far from clear, the important point for our purposes here is that the process of adjustment lending legitimated the practice of openly imposing quite severe conditions on developing countries. Although conditionality – sometimes euphemistically described as 'policy-dialogue' – has long been part of the armoury of the international institutions, especially the IMF but also the World Bank, it now became much more explicit and invasive in Western aid practices generally. As the British aid minister was able to say in 1991, after a decade of adjustment lending: 'The idea of conditionality attached to aid in support of economic reform is well established' (Chalker, 1991: 3). More important, as analysis of their results came to be made, it became clear that *politics* was crucial in determining the success or failure of adjustment programmes (Nelson, 1990). In particular, Western aid and development institutions came to realize that the coalitions of vested interests which dominated mainly the non-democratic states (but also some democratic ones) could and did prevent economic adjustment taking place (Toye, 1992). If effective adjustment was to take place, these coalitions would have to be broken up or circumvented. And while reducing its role in the economy was one means of stripping the state of its power (through a variety of structural adjustment processes), democratic accountability through electoral politics came to be seen as another crucial means for doing so.

Neo-conservative hegemony

The promotion of economic adjustment programmes in the third world, and later Eastern Europe, was not simply a technical or theoretical shift in development thinking. It also represented the *political* ascendancy of neo-conservatism (or neo-liberalism) in Western politics, economics and public policy from the late 1970s (Toye, 1987) with its emphasis on markets, deregulation, privatization, supply-side economics, individualism, competition and the 'enterprise' culture.

However, neo-conservatism is not only an economic theory. It also has strong *political* dimensions which are both normative and functional in relation to politics and the state. Its normative features are well known (Green, 1986; Leftwich, 1993) and celebrate, *inter alia*, individual political freedom, personal responsibility, rights and liberties, freedom of choice and responsibility. However, neo-conservatism also has a functional theory of politics, one strand of which links its concern with markets and economic growth to its concern with democracy. For it assumes that democratic politics is not only desirable but also *necessary* for a thriving free-market economy, and *vice versa*, and that the two are inextricably implicated with each other (Friedman, 1980; Hurd, 1990). Neo-conservative developmentalists claim that both poor records of economic growth and failures in adjustment programmes have often been the direct consequence of political factors such as authoritarian rule or deficient democratic practice, arising from excessive state or political involvement in economy and society (Bates, 1981; Lal, 1983). They thus argue that *political* liberalization through democratic reform would both reduce and redistribute this central power. Democratization in the context of a free economy would thus compel governments to be more accountable, less corrupt and hence more efficient developmentally, for they would be judged on their performance and thrown out if they did not deliver public goods effectively. This aspect of the dominant theory and ideology of political economy in the West became influential in shaping overseas aid and development policy and especially its most recent concern in the 1990s with democratization.

The collapse of communism

The collapse of Eastern European communist regimes from the late 1980s, accompanied by the demise of many of the official Marxist-Leninist regimes in the developing world, meant the end of the structure of bipolar international political relations which had dominated the world since the end of the Second World War (Gills and Rocamora, 1992; Hawthorn and Seabright, in this volume). Invasive economic and, now, political conditions could thus be imposed on recipients of aid without fear of chasing client, allied or even non-aligned states into the arms of the Soviet camp. But the end of the communist regimes also confirmed neo-liberal and neo-conservative economic theory that non-democratic communist states were unable to produce sustained economic growth. Moreover, not only did their political structures prevent economic change but their lack of demo-cratic politics directly promoted corruption, economic mismanage-ment, inefficiency, stagnation and decline.

Political liberalization in the form of democratization was thus seen as a necessary condition for economic liberalization and growth. This confident linkage of economic and political liberalism is nowhere better illustrated than in the articles of agreement of the new Euro-pean Bank for Reconstruction and Development (EBRD), established in 1991 to help restructure the Eastern European and former Soviet economies. Unlike the World Bank, it has combined explicit economic and political objectives which are to 'promote multi-party democracy, pluralism and market economics' (EBRD, 1991: article 1).

The impact of the pro-democracy movements

Finally, indigenous pro-democracy movements in Latin America, Korea, the Philippines and latterly Eastern Europe in the 1980s stimulated similar movements elsewhere (Huntington, 1991). In Africa, between 1989 and 1992, a mixture of internal and external pressures prompted steps in the direction of democratization in a host of countries, from Nigeria to Mozambique and from Guinea to Kenya, not to mention the momentous recent events in South Africa (1989–94), though this seldom occurred without profound resist-ance from incumbent regimes, or constituent parts of their coalitions (Sandbrook, 1990; Riley, 1991; Tordoff, 1994; Woodward, 1994). Democratization in Asia – though stalled in China and Myanmar, for example – has advanced in the Philippines, South Korea, Tai-wan, Bangladesh and even to some extent in Nepal. The West has drawn legitimacy for its pro-democracy policies from these move-ments around the world and can thus claim to be supporting genuinely popular and intellectual demands in those societies (Ake, 1991).

What is important to recognize is that each and every one of these reasons is in some respects *political* or, at least, their provenance lies in politics and political change, not in theoretical advance. That is to say, the reversal of the earlier putative sequential relationship between development (first) and democracy (later) in both modern-ization theory and in official aid and foreign policy theory and prac-tice has not simply been a consequence of theoretical or technical discoveries about the processes of development. It is true, of course,

that a long and distinguished tradition in neoclassical political economy (Bauer, 1981; Hunt, 1989) has always argued the theoretical
case for liberal and democratic capitalist development – more in economics than in political science. But its emergence as the new orthodoxy from the prior 'misconceptions of development economics', as
Lal (1988) described the earlier orthodoxy, has essentially been a
political process.

DEMOCRACY AND GOOD GOVERNANCE

If, for a combination of all these political reasons, democratic good
governance is now held to be a necessary condition of development,
what precisely is meant by this notion in official circles? I suggest
that there are really two fundamental meanings associated with this
idea: the first is narrow, the second is broad.

Good governance as sound 'development management'

This somewhat narrow administrative, or managerial, notion of
good governance is associated primarily with the official position of
the World Bank (1992b). The bank's articles of agreement (International Bank for Reconstruction and Development, 1989) formally
prohibit it from making political judgements in its operations and
from being partisan with respect to the internal politics of its members (Shihata, 1991: ch. 2). As a consequence, according to one of
its recent presidents, the bank does not impose 'political condition-
alities' in its work (Conable, 1991: 8), although it has referred to the
desirability of a 'pluralistic institutional structure', at least for Africa
(World Bank, 1989: 60). In practice, the prohibition on political
considerations also appears to have stopped the bank from incor-
porating the evaluation of politics in development in its theoretical
and analytical work. At least this has been so in public, although in
private some of its senior staff have advanced some important ideas
about the relevance of politics, and democratic politics in particular,
for development (Landell-Mills, 1992). Instead, in its concern to
promote 'good order' (Shihata, 1992: 85), the bank has focused on
mainly technical, administrative and managerial issues of 'governance' (not politics, note).

Briefly, a system of good governance in this limited administrative sense, therefore, would consist of a set of rules and institutions
(that is, a legal framework for development) and a system of public
administration which is open, transparent, efficient and accountable.

Such a system would provide clarity, stability and predictability for the private sector which would constitute the essential engine of economic development, not the state, in a 'market friendly' development strategy. Despite the formally apolitical stance of the bank on this question, there is little doubt that underlying even this limited vision of good governance is a Western model, ringing with Weberian echoes, with its emphasis on free markets, individualism and a neutral but efficient public administration, subject to a legitimate government (Williams and Young, 1994).

Good governance as democratic governance

The broader meaning of good governance includes all of the above, but goes one major step further in insisting that good governance also involves democratic politics. Broadly speaking, this has been the position of most Western governments and has become a more or less explicit feature of their official bilateral relations with recipients of aid. The position is best illustrated by the policy of the British government, as expressed by its overseas development minister, Mrs (now Lady) Lynda Chalker. Arguing that the introduction of market forces and competition is crucial for the efficient use of resources and that governments must 'level the playing field for the private sector and individual enterprise so that they can act as engines of growth', she went on to say that:

> a major new thrust of our policy is to promote pluralistic systems which work for and respond to individuals in society. In political terms this means democracy ... And we firmly believe that democratic reforms are necessary in many countries for broad-based sustainable development. (Chalker, 1991: 2–3).

While Western governments have not specified the form which democracy should take, or the institutional arrangements which should be instituted, it is clear that a democratic polity for them means one in which the following minimal characteristics prevail: competitive party systems, regular and fair elections, an independent judiciary, a free press and the protection of human rights.

It should be clear, then, that this broader notion of good governance which combines administrative competence, probity and accountability with democratic politics in a market economy is not simply a new *technical* answer to the difficult problems of development, but a *political* one. For the barely submerged structural model and ideal of politics, economics and society on which the notion of good governance rests is nothing less than that of liberal (or social) democracy – the focal concern and end-point of much modernization theory.

GOVERNANCE, DEMOCRACY, POLITICS, THE STATE –
AND DEVELOPMENT

But why quibble at such an ideal? Who could possibly be against
good governance, in either its narrow administrative sense or in its
broader democratic sense, as Richard Sklar's chapter in this volume
so elegantly reminds us? For is it not the case that any society –
whether liberal or socialist – must be better off with a public service
that is both efficient and honest, open and accountable, and with a
judicial system that is independent and fair? Even in the most
unpromising third world circumstances, good governance in this
limited administrative sense must be better for development than its
opposite, bad governance. And is it also not the case, from a liberal
or socialist point of view, that the consolidation, extension and
protection of human rights (in political *as well as social and economic terms*, as Gordon White reminds us in his chapter on China
in this volume) must be preferred to their erosion or limitation?
Finally, as the painstaking statistical work of Lane and Ersson (also
in this volume) shows, there is a clear and positive relationship between democracy and an improving quality of life.

What is at issue here therefore is not the definition or desirability
of democracy (even in its most limited forms). What is at issue is
the naïveté and analytical shallowness of the current orthodoxy in
assuming not only that democracy can somehow be made to hap-
pen, but also that it will work on a sustained basis *and* that it will
also promote growth. Nowhere in the official thinking of Western
governments or the multilateral institutions does there appear to be
any recognition of the fact that good or, more broadly, democratic
governance is not something that can simply be had to order. In
other words, Western governments and institutions do not seem
to appreciate that good governance and democracy are not mere
components which can be inserted into any society at any point in
its development, like a sprocket or valve. On the contrary, both
good governance and democracy depend crucially on the character
and capacity of the *state* which, alone, can institute and insist on
it. And the capacity of a state to deliver good governance and protect democracy is in turn a function of its politics and its developmental determination. For example, to expect that heavy doses of
externally imposed conditionality will yield either good governance
in the managerial sense or stable democracy in the liberal pluralist
sense – let alone sustained economic development – in societies like
Haiti, Zaïre, Myanmar or China seems naïve, to say the least. The
only social process that can both institute and sustain both good governance and democracy is the process we know as politics which I
defined earlier as consisting of all the processes of conflict, cooperation and negotiation involved in the use, production and distribution
of resources.

It is precisely for this reason that development cannot simply be managed into motion by some idealized system of good governance, evacuated from the world of politics. For neither democracy nor good governance are independent variables which have somehow gone missing in the developing world: they are dependent ones. And whatever their relationship with economic growth and development may be, both are the product of particular kinds of politics and can be found only in states which promote and protect them. Indeed, they *are* a form of politics in themselves, not simply a set of institutional arrangements and rules. To illustrate the point concretely, until societies such as Haiti, Zaïre and Myanmar (Burma) – and countless others to varying degrees – are able to evolve a politics that is not characterized by the predatory (Lundahl, 1992), patrimonial (Medard, 1982) or cronyist (Haggard, 1990) patterns which currently define them, there is no hope for either good governance or democracy in almost any sense imaginable. Indeed, to insist on democratic institutions and practices in societies whose politics will not support them and whose state traditions (or lack of them) will not sustain them may be to do far greater damage than not insisting on them. Moreover, the kind of political turbulence which such insistence may unleash is bound to have explosive and decidedly *anti-developmental* consequences (Leftwich, 1993).

In short, the current focus on governance and democracy as necessary ingredients of development misses the point that it is politics and the character of the state alone which will give rise to them and keep them in place. It is politics that will determine the kind and quality of governance and the effectiveness of its developmental capacity. And it is politics, too, which will determine the kind of state which is able both to spur and shape development.

My central thesis here is that, from a developmental point of view, it is the primacy of politics and the character of the state that has to be the focus of our attention, not the form of government (democracy or not) or the institutional ideal of good governance, although the latter (but not democracy) is indisputably necessary for development. And it is their politics and their states which explain the sustained and successful developmental performances over the last 25 years of societies as different as Botswana and Korea, or Mauritius and Thailand, *not* their regime types (since half are democratic and half are not). Likewise, it is their politics and their states which explain the negative or weak developmental records of societies as different as Jamaica and Zaïre, or India and Venezuela, not their regime types (since half are democratic and half are not).

Many of the chapters which follow underline this notion of the primacy of politics and the state in development – and some do so in deeply uncomfortable ways. For instance, as Jenny Pearce argues, the turn-around in Chile's economic fortunes from the mid-to-late 1980s appears to have been a direct consequence of the destruction of traditional patterns of politics by an extremely ruthless and cruel state, itself a product of the turbulent politics of the late 1960s and early 1970s in that country. Gordon White suggests that in the case of China, the post-Maoist developmental drive towards a freer economy could only have been undertaken by an authoritarian state providing a stable political context for the transition to a mixed economy. Conversely, as becomes clear in Peter Rutland's chapter, the political turbulence of the post-Soviet era in Russia makes the prospects for a successful and simultaneous transition to democracy *and* a free economy there appear grim. And, as John Holm's chapter on the developmental success of Botswana shows, the institutions and practices of good governance (including a high degree of expatriate involvement) have been a direct consequence of the political dominance and developmental determination of the *de facto* one-party rule of the Botswana Democratic Party (BDP) and its leadership – all of which has been almost unique in Africa. Although we do not deal with them in this volume, this is equally true of the two other major examples of successful *democratic development*, Singapore and Malaysia. In both cases, the politics of democracy has been the politics of *de facto* one-party rule. In the South African case, as Tom Lodge points out, the declining rates of growth in the last decades of apartheid must be traced primarily to the politics of white dominance and the conflicts this generated, as must the dramatic changes that were generated from 1989. Likewise, the enormous developmental tasks now to be achieved in South Africa and the prospects for an enduring democracy will depend critically on the politics of balancing the diverse and distinctive demands of very different interest groups. Everything will depend on politics and the capacity of the state both to broker these demands and, where necessary, rise above them. The same is true for the developmental future of India, despite its strong democratic tradition and record of (at least relatively) good governance. For, as Sudipta Kaviraj points out, that huge society is increasingly faced by centrifugal political tensions of a regional and ethno-religious kind which do not augur well for a secular, national and democratic multi-party system as hoped for by Gandhi and Nehru. Finally, Peter Larmour's material from the South Pacific suggests that the politics associated with turbulent transitional episodes and processes between low and high levels of economic development, that is when growth and structural change are occurring rapidly, are the most threatening to democracy. This is indicative, at least, of some deep structural incompatibility between at least some phases of development and democracy.

The question, then, as to whether democracy is a condition of development or not appears far too blunt. Successful developmental outcomes, both historically and in the modern era, seem to have depended less on whether regimes have been democratic or not and more on such factors as internal stability (of a democratic or non-democratic kind); on acceptability in international economic *and* political markets; on positive relations with dominant economies;

on the relative autonomy of the state in both democratic and non-democratic polities; on sound infrastructure and competent administration; on low levels of corruption; on a critical minimum degree of consensus between groups and regions about the objectives of growth and the rules of the game for achieving it (Przeworksi, 1988); and on an increasing degree of both regional and social equality in the distribution of the costs and benefits of that growth.

All these are a function of politics. That is they flow from, or in fact are expressions of, the typical patterns of cooperation, conflict and negotiation in the use, production and distribution of resources in any society. Their delivery depends on the state and its character, competence and commitment; while this, in turn, is a function of the politics which establishes and sustains the state (Leftwich, 1995). For this reason there is a need to bring not only governance but *politics* back centrally into the study of development, from which it has been extruded for too long. But what kind of state is most likely to provide the optimum medium for development, whether democratic or not? And what kind of politics is most likely to generate it? I return to these questions in the final chapter of this volume in the light of the fascinating and insightful chapters which follow.

CONCLUSION

The primacy of politics in development should not, it seems to me, be disguised any longer behind a technicist language about governance and management. For while no one would deny the importance of institutions and rules, it is political processes which bring them into being and, crucially, which sustain them. No institution, constitution, convention or rule is likely to withstand for long the determined threat of the bayonet, the march of the jackboot or the rumble of the tank. Institution building for development, in the language of the current orthodoxy, which is essentially external in provenance or imposed or insisted on as a condition of aid or support, and which is not integral to an endogenous politics, is bound to fail. More to the point, sustained economic development which can bring clean water, regular food supplies, schools, roads and a generally enhanced expectancy and quality of life will fail too. Until and unless the politics of a society can devise and sustain a stable democratic system, other non-democratic systems may in practice be preferable if at least some of the material objectives of development are not to be lost for another generation, or more.

The question, therefore, is not what institutional arrangements and procedures define good governance and democracy, nor whether or how they can be insisted upon through tough forms of conditionality, nor even the nature of their relationship with development.

The question is what kind of politics makes each of them – that is democracy, good governance and development – possible at all? Moreover, does one kind of politics make them all possible or may their requirements differ? And, in any event, what brings such politics into being?

These are essentially the core questions which all strands of modernization theory (however inadequately named) sought to address. They remain good questions. And the history of developing societies in the last 30 years suggests that it would be foolhardy to ignore some of the insights of that large body of theoretical and empirical scholarship on modernization in trying to answer them. For whatever its many limitations, modernization theory in general terms assumed the intimacy of politics with other social and economic processes, especially in the course of change, not its extrusion from them. And if we are to understand the intensely complex relations of democracy and development in diverse societies, then it is with this intimacy of politics in these processes that we must start. The chapters which follow provide some vital illuminations.

ACKNOWLEDGEMENTS

I am grateful to my colleague Neil Robinson for astute and helpful comments on this chapter. Responsibility for it, however, remains mine.

NOTES

1 Even the contemporary commitment to democracy and human rights promotion appears less sure than at first sight. In May 1994 President Clinton reversed US trade policy in relation to China and granted that country Most Favored Nation status, despite that regime's failure to improve on human rights conditions.

REFERENCES

Ake, C. 1991: Rethinking African Democracy. *Journal of Democracy*, 2, 32–44.
Apter, D. 1965: *The Politics of Modernization*. Chicago: University of Chicago Press.
Avineri, S. 1969: *The Social and Political Thought of Karl Marx*. Cambridge: Cambridge University Press.
Baran, P. A. 1957: *The Political Economy of Growth*. New York: Monthly Review Press.

Bates, R. C. 1981: *Markets and States in Tropical Africa*. Berkeley: University of California Press.

Bauer, P. T. 1981: *Equality, The Third World and Economic Delusion*. London: Methuen.

Callinicos, A. 1984: Marxism and Politics. In A. Leftwich (ed.), *What is Politics? The Activity and its Study*, Oxford: Basil Blackwell, 124–38.

Chalker, L. 1991: *Good Governance and the Aid Programme*. London: Overseas Development Administration.

Conable, B. B. 1991: *Africa's Development and Destiny*. Address to the 27th Session of the Organization of African Unity (OAU) Assembly of Heads of State and Government, held in Abuja, Nigeria, on 4 June 1991.

de Waal, J. 1982: *Chimpanzee Politics*. London: Cape.

Durkheim, E. 1964: *The Division of Labour in Society*. New York: Free Press.

Eisenstadt, S. N. 1966: *Modernization: Protest and Change*. Englewood Cliffs, NJ: Prentice Hall.

European Bank for Reconstruction and Development (EBRD), 1991: *Agreement Establishing the European Bank for Reconstruction and Development*. London: EBRD.

Freedom House Survey Team, 1992: *Freedom in the World. Political Rights and Civil Liberties, 1991–1992*. New York: Freedom House.

Friedman, M. and R. 1980: *Free To Choose*. Harmondsworth, Penguin.

Fukuyama, F. 1989: The End of History? *National Interest*, Summer 1989, 3–18.

Furlong, W. L. 1980: Political Development and the Alliance for Progress. In H. Wiarda (ed.) *The Continuing Struggle for Democracy in Latin America*. Boulder, Colo.: Westview Press, 167–84.

Gills, B. and Rocamora, J. 1992: Low Intensity Democracy. *Third World Quarterly*, 13, 501–23.

Green, D. C. 1986: *The New Right*. Brighton: Harvester.

Haggard, S. 1990: The Political Economy of the Philippine Debt Crisis. In J. Nelson (ed.) *Economic Crisis and Policy Choice*. Princeton, NJ: Princeton University Press, 215–55.

Harrison, D. 1988: *The Sociology of Modernization and Development*. London: Unwin Hyman.

Humana, C. 1987: *World Human Rights Guide*. London: Pan.

Hunt, D. 1989: *Economic Theories of Development*. Brighton: Harvester.

Huntington, S. P. 1987: The Goals of Development. In M. Einer and S. P. Huntington (eds) *Understanding Political Development*, Boston: Little Brown, 3–32.

Huntington, S. P. 1991: *The Third Wave: Democratization in the Late Twentieth Century*. Norman: University of Oklahoma Press.

Hurd, D. 1990: Promoting Good Government. *Crossbow*, Autumn 1990, 4–5.

Hyden, G. 1985: *No Shortcuts to Progress. African Development Management in Historical Perspective*. London: Heinemann.

IDS Bulletin, 1993: The Emergence of the 'Good Government' Agenda: Some Milestones. *IDS Bulletin*, 24 (1), 7–8.

International Bank for Reconstruction and Development, 1989: *Articles of Agreement*. (As amended, effective February 16, 1989). Washington: The World Bank.

Kitching, G. 1983: *Rethinking Socialism*. London: Methuen.

Lal, D. 1983: *The Poverty of 'Development Economics'*. Hobart Paperback, 16. London: Institute of Economic Affairs.

Lal, D. 1988: The Misconceptions of 'Development Economics'. In H. Wiarda (ed.) *The Political Economy of Development and Underdevelopment*, 4th edn, New York: Random House, 28–36.

Landell-Mills, P. 1992: Governance, Civil Society and Empowerment in Sub-Saharan Africa. Paper delivered at 1992 Annual Conference of the Society for the Advancement of Socio-Economics, Irvine, California.

Larrain, G. 1989: *Theories of Development. Capitalism, Colonialism and Dependency*. Cambridge: Polity Press.

Lee, J. M. 1967: *Colonial Development and Good Government*. Oxford: Clarendon Press.

Leftwich, A. 1983: *Redefining Politics: People, Resources and Power*. London: Methuen.

Leftwich, A. 1992: Is there a Socialist Path to Socialism? *Third World Quarterly*, 13, 27–42.

Leftwich, A. 1993: Governance, democracy and Development in the Third World. *Third World Quarterly*, 14, 605–24.

Leftwich, A. 1995: Bringing Politics Back In: Towards a Model of the Developmental State. *Journal of Development Studies'*, 31, 400–27.

Lipset, S. M. 1960: *Political Man*. London: Heinemann.

Lundahl, M. 1992: *Politics or Markets? Essays on Haitian Underdevelopment*. London: Routledge.

Maine, H. S. 1908: *Ancient Law*. London: John Murray.

Marx, K. 1958a (1853): The Eighteenth Brumaire of Louis Bonaparte. In *Selected Works*, Vol. 1. Moscow: Foreign Languages Publishing House, 243–344.

Marx, K. 1958b (1859): Preface to A Contribution to the Critique of Political Economy. In *Selected Works*, Vol. 1. Moscow: Foreign Languages Publishing House, 360–5.

Marx, K. 1958c (1853): British Rule in India. In *Selected Works*, Vol. 1. Moscow: Foreign Languages Publishing House, 345–51.

Marx, K. 1958d (1888): Manifesto of The Communist Party. In *Selected Works*, Vol. 1. Moscow: Foreign Languages Publishing House, 33–65.

Marx, K. 1976: *Capital*, I. Harmondsworth: Penguin.

Marx, K. 1977: *Selected Writings*, (ed.) D. McLellan. Oxford: Oxford University Press.

Medard, J.-F. 1982: The Underdeveloped State in Tropical Africa. Political Clientelism or NeoPatrimonialism? In C. Clapham (ed.) *Private Patronage and Public Power*. London: Pinter, 162–92.

Mosley, P. and Toye, J. 1988: The Design of Structural Adjustment Programmes. *Development Policy Review*, 6, 395–413.

Mosley, P., Harrigan, J. and Toye, J. 1991: *Aid and Power. The World Bank and Policy-based Lending*, 2 vols. London: Routledge.

Nelson, J. (ed.) 1990: *Economic Crisis and Policy Choice. The Politics of Adjustment in the Third World*. Princeton, NJ: Princeton University Press.

O'Brien, D. C. 1972: Modernization, Order and the Erosion of a Democratic Ideal. *Journal of Development Studies*, 8, 49–76.

OECD (Organization for Economic Cooperation and Development), 1984: *Development Cooperation Review 1984*. Paris: OECD.

Packenham, R. A. 1973: *Liberal America and the Third World*. Princeton, NJ: Princeton University Press.

Przeworksi, A. 1988: Democracy as a contingent outcome of conflicts. In J. Elster and R. Slagstad (eds) *Constitutionalism and Democracy*. Cambridge: Cambridge University Press, 59–80.

Riley, S. P. 1991: *The Democratic Transition in Africa*. Conflict Studies, 245. London: Research Institute for the Study of Conflict and Terrorism.

Rueschemeyer, D., Stephens, E. H. and Stephens, J. D. 1992: *Capitalist Development and Democracy*. Cambridge: Polity Press.

Sandbrook, R. 1990: Taming the African Leviathan. *World Policy Journal*, VII, 672–701.

Shihata, I. 1991: The World Bank in a Changing World, *Selected Essays*. London: Martinus Nijhoff.

Smelser, N. J. 1968: Toward a Theory of Modernization. In his *Essays in Sociological Explanation*. Englewood Cliffs, NJ: Prentice Hall, 125–46.

Spencer, H. 1969: *Principles of Sociology,* (ed.) S. Andreski. London: Macmillan.

Stretton, H. 1976: *Capitalism, Socialism and the Environment*. Cambridge: Cambridge University Press.

Tipps, D. C. 1973: Modernization Theory and the Comparative Study of Societies: A Critical Perspective. *Comparative Studies in Society and History*, 15, 199–226.

Tönnies, F. 1955: *Community and Association*. London: Routledge and Kegan Paul.

Tordoff, R. 1994: Political Liberalization and Economic Reform in Africa. *Democratization*, I, 100–15.

Toye, J. 1987: *Dilemmas of Development*. Oxford: Basil Blackwell.

Toye, J. 1992: Interest Group Politics and The Implementation of Adjustment Policies in Sub-Saharan Africa. *Journal of International Development*, 4, 183–97.

Warren, B. 1980: *Imperialism. Pioneer of Capitalism*. London: Verso.

Weber, M. 1964: *The Theory of Social and Economic Organization,* (ed.) Talcott Parsons. New York: Free Press.

Williams, D. and Young, T. 1994: Governance, the World Bank and Liberal Theory. *Political Studies*, XLII, 84–100.

Woodward, P. 1994: Democracy and Economy in Africa: The Optimists and the Pessimists. *Democratization*, I, 116–32.

World Bank, 1988: *World Development Report 1988*. New York: Oxford University Press.

World Bank, 1989: *Sub-Saharan Africa. From Crisis to Sustainable Growth*. Washington: The World Bank.

World Bank, 1991: *World Development Report 1991*. New York: Oxford University Press.

World Bank, 1992a: *World Development Report 1992*. New York: Oxford University Press.

World Bank, 1992b: *Governance and Development*. Washington: The World Bank.

2
Towards a Theory of Developmental Democracy

RICHARD L. SKLAR

INTRODUCTION

Democracy and development are frequently paired as universal goals for national communities in the latter twentieth century. Yet these terms are also used by theorists to represent conditions, or means, of collective action, rather than values or ends-in-themselves. The phrase 'developmental democracy' implies an end–means relationship; but its meaning will be ambiguous unless the question 'Is it an end or a means?' is answered for each of these two terms. In this exposition, democracy is considered to be a means, while development signifies an end, to wit, the realization (to any degree) of valued outcomes.

In our day, the paramount goals of development for people everywhere are largely derived from the philosophical idea of progress. Formulated by European philosophers in the seventeenth century, this idea means that time's proverbial arrow slopes ever upward toward improvement in the quality of human life (Bury, 1932).[1] In seventeenth-century Europe, absolute monarchy and the remnants of feudalist inequality were identified by progressives as formidable impediments to social improvement. Hence progressive reformers subscribed to the values of personal freedom and equality of individual opportunity. At present, however, these individualistic conceptions of freedom are disputed by a growing number of progressive thinkers who assert the primacy of alternative values – for example, personal security, human survival, physical well-being, social justice and organizational efficiency in the performance of essential tasks.

Plainly stated, the idea of development, defined to mean improvement in the quality of life, can be disengaged from the old doctrine of progress with its value premise of personal freedom. If the plagues of poverty, famine, pestilence and unemployment continue to ravage the lives of increasing millions of people, remedial actions and counter-measures will surely be taken with little regard to their effects on individual freedom. That tendency is exemplified by China's notorious policy of compulsory abortion and sterilization to terminate and prevent unauthorized pregnancies. Ultimately, public support for personal freedom, as a value premise of development, depends mainly on its merit as a means of human survival and economic progress rather than its worth as an end-in-itself.

Political science is not moral philosophy; it does not prescribe the ends of political action (Catlin, 1962: 43–64). If development is understood to signify a complex goal pursued by national communities, its specific content of related values will vary among countries. Political scientists are not qualified by virtue of their professional expertise to prescribe universal values of development. However, political scientists ought to be able to clarify relationships between the ends and means of political action.[2] When the goals of development have been determined by a national (or other) community, political scientists should be able to provide professional guidance for their realization in addition to estimates of social benefit and cost. A theory of developmental democracy would demonstrate the efficacy, as well as the probable limitations, of democratic methods in pursuit of development.

IMAGES OF DEMOCRACY

Like development, the concept of democracy is associated with various core values. When it is conceived as a means, rather than an end, democracy signifies a form, or method, of social control. The literal, classical meaning of *democratia* is 'power of the people'. As a practical matter, however, 'the people' cannot exercise power on a continuing basis. Binding political decisions are normally made by political elites and office-holders. In all but a few tyrannical dictatorships, such persons are held accountable from time to time, if not at regular intervals, for their performance in positions of public trust. Surprisingly, political theorists have scarcely charted the dimensions of accountability. This principle may be so integral to the concept of democracy that the utility of isolating it for purposes of separate analysis has rarely been recognized.

For the purpose of this analysis, we shall take accountability to mean the obligation to answer, or account, for one's conduct toward other persons who are entitled to judge it. Two principal forms of accountability should be distinguished: first, the accountability of leaders to followers, of rulers to those who are ruled, of office-holders to the citizenry, or people. This is democratic accountability, properly so called, because it acknowledges an ultimate 'power' of the people.[3] A second form of accountability consists in the obligation of office-holders to answer for their actions, or decisions, to one another. This kind of relationship is properly denominated constitutional accountability. In the idiom of sport, democratic accountability is 'deep', while constitutional accountability is 'lateral'. And while these two types of accountability involve distinct, and very different, forms of obligation, they are also mutually reinforcing in their effects: in practice, constitutionalism and democracy are inseparably related.

In this discussion, accountability, like democracy, is conceived as a means, rather than an end or ethical ideal. Although the existence of deep, or democratic, accountability is relatively easy to substantiate, its significance is by no means equivalent to that of the much broader concept of democracy. Accountability is a relatively mechanistic conception, whereas democracy is a far more complex idea about power in human relations. Yet the very presence of accountability in a political relationship is presumptive evidence of either democratic or constitutional practice, depending on the form that it takes.

There is a world of difference between research designed to discover forms of democratic political behaviour and research undertaken to determine whether one, or more than one, whole political system measures up to a prescribed democratic standard. This is equally true for research on the subject of constitutional government. The forms of democratic behaviour range from the minimal criteria of deep, or democratic, accountability to referendums and other manifestations of direct popular control over leaders and office-holders. No practical system of government could ever be entirely democratic; every system is an Aristotelian mixture of democracy (power of the people) and oligarchy (rule of the few). Invariably the political systems of countries that are regularly cited as democratic models have distinctly undemocratic features. Thus, in capitalist countries, the political advantages enjoyed by those relatively few people who are independently wealthy, as a result of their wealth, is a conspicuously undemocratic feature of political life.

Despite the timeliness of ancient, Aristotelian, wisdom, most contemporary scholars in the field of comparative government continue to believe in the existence of whole-system democracies. From that standpoint, they are wont to classify some countries as democratic, others as partially democratic and others still as undemocratic. The virtue of simplicity, by itself, does not account for the persistence of this simplistic analytical procedure. The deeper reason is methodological: most political scientists still exclude 'economic' and 'social' institutions from their conceptions of the political system, or the state. Mostly, they classify political systems on the basis of criteria selected in accordance with preconceived disciplinary canons and specifications rather than the realities of power. This questionable method of analysis minimizes the extent of democratic practice in many countries where historic forms of popular control coexist with regimes that are otherwise largely autocratic. For example, in Indonesia, parliamentary government continues to evolve in accordance with a Hindu-Javanese political tradition that emphasizes persuasion and consensus, rather than divisive voting, to resolve questions of public policy (Keyfitz, 1988). In Indonesia, as elsewhere, the fluid mixture of democracy and oligarchy cannot be encapsulated within a static, whole-system analytical category.

As categories of political thought, democracy and oligarchy are idealized, abstract conceptions, rather than representations of concrete realities. A specifically democratic pattern of behaviour can be established or eliminated, enlarged or reduced, strengthened or weakened, but it cannot be separated, or experienced apart, from other, concurrent aspects of political life. Analytically speaking, democracy is manifest in prescriptive norms, or rules of conduct. Metaphorically speaking, democracy is constructed in parts, or fragments, which complement one another. A theory of developmental democracy would demonstrate that increments of democratic change are likely to produce positive developmental effects (Sklar, 1987: 714).

Cogent objections to the idea of developmental democracy arise from at least two bodies of thought, representing the concerns of economists and sociologists, respectively. First, political economists often perceive a need to choose between popular, distributive policies associated with democracy and satisfactory levels of capital accumulation based on wage restraint and related pressures on the labour force. In the advanced capitalist countries, political stability is conditioned on the occurrence of various 'trade-offs' between the values of 'equality and economic efficiency' (Okun, 1975). However, it is far more difficult to strike stabilizing balances between productive investment and mass consumption in poor countries, where capital is scarce. During most of the twentieth century, oligarchic solutions to the problem of scarcity have been chosen by the leaders of such countries. In scholarly treatments of this subject, two generic concepts – 'bureaucratic-authoritarianism' (O'Donnell, 1973) and 'developmental dictatorship' (Gregor, 1979) – encapsulate the two main forms of developmental oligarchy. The former refers to regimes that seek to minimize popular political initiatives; the latter to mass-mobilizing, avowedly revolutionary, dictatorships.[4] Although the mass-mobilizing variant has nearly faded from sight in our day, 'neo-authoritarian' oligarchy does appear to be a viable option for numerous countries, including China and Indonesia.

However, neo-authoritarians everywhere, almost without exception, now appear to place their faith in market economies, meaning that people are free to become entrepreneurs, to seek employment in occupations of their choice and to shop where they please for goods of their choice. Invariably, market economies stimulate political activity, including pressures for democracy. The contradictions between capitalism, under any flag (including the red flag, as in China), and dictatorship are volatile, more so, it would appear, than those between state socialism and dictatorship. Furthermore, it is unmistakably clear that the basic values of democracy, including political liberty and equal rights for all citizens, appeal to most people in all countries. Hence, it is important to show that democratic government is a viable developmental alternative to neo-authoritarian oligarchy. Otherwise, dictatorships may be countenanced mainly for the sake of keeping order in societies that seethe with discontent and suffer in despair.

Dismal, and self-fulfilling, prophesies of dictatorship flow from a second objection to the idea of developmental democracy. Political sociologists, following Lipset (1960: 45–76), suggest that democratic political development is dependent upon a combination of economic, social, and cultural 'requisites' that are unlikely to exist in countries with underdeveloped economies. From this perspective, the notion 'that democracy, itself, may be the mainspring of development appears to put the proverbial cart before its horse' (Sklar, 1987: 690).[5] Just as the case for neo-authoritarian oligarchy can be sustained on empirical grounds with reference to episodes of economic development in various countries, so too can numerous setbacks for democracy be attributed, plausibly if not conclusively, to the social and cultural consequences of economic backwardness or stagnation. But it does not follow, as a logical consequence, that democratic political experiments are doomed by the absence of propitious economic, social and cultural conditions. Specific relationships between democratic or dictatorial methods, on the one hand, and developmental outcomes, on the other, are affected by many and diverse variables of history and personal politics, among other things. In this century, the methods of dictatorship have not been more regularly developmental in their effects than those of democracy. Since many relationships between democracy and development have been reciprocal, rather than one way, the idea of developmental democracy would appear to complement, or refine, standard theories concerning the requisite conditions of democracy.

Now that market-based, as opposed to state-centred, economic principles have gained near-universal acceptance; and now that the principle of democratic representation, implying freedom to form political parties and compete for office in elections that are both free and fair, appears to be a political goal for people everywhere, pessimists and sceptics are more than ever inclined to proclaim the existence of cultural impediments to the universal advance of democracy. Among those alleged primordial perils, one particular spectre should be exorcised, namely the shade of traditional, including religious, culture. These days, scarcely a month passes without one or another religion having been identified as a source of anti-democratic intolerance, or by zealots as a good reason for rejecting toleration in the name of higher values. No matter that, for each religion so defamed or acclaimed, countervailing evidence of service to the cause of human dignity is readily at hand. Thus, for every Tehran of 1983 (aggressive Islamic fundamentalism) there is a Sarajevo of 1993 (embattled Islamic secular humanism); for every Ayodhya of 1992 (Indian Hindu fanaticism) there is a comparable and offsetting reaffirmation of Hindu humanism in India. And Tiananmen Square, 1989: was that not a testament to the aspiration of many Chinese to create democratic political institutions? As China's Sakharov, Fang Lizhi, wrote in the aftermath of Tiananmen, 'China's students, intellectuals, and ordinary citizens do not accept the standard of "Chinese characteristics" [deplored by Fang as a 'double standard' detrimental to respect for human rights]. Their dreams and aspirations are no different from those of any other people. Their values are no exception to the values held by the rest of the human race' (Fang, 1991: xlii). Misperceived as a nemesis of democracy, or obstacle to it, traditional, especially religious, culture is a phantom of the academic *opera buffa*.

In addition to the market economy and democratic representation, people in the various societies and cultures of the world, not only those in 'Western' societies, believe in the rule of law, which is generally understood to mean that no political authority is superior to the law itself. Where the rule of law prevails, the rights of citizens are not dependent on the will of rulers; such rights are established by law and protected by independent courts. Whenever rulers can disregard the law and decide for themselves whether or not their own actions are lawful, then the form of government is not properly constitutional.

However, the real world of constitutional government, like that of democracy, does not exist in pure form. Heads of state everywhere lay claims to the exercise of extra-constitutional, or 'prerogative', powers both to cope with perceived emergencies and to defend alleged public interests against avowedly exceptional threats.[6] In many countries, crucial norms of constitutional government have been preserved during periods of autocratic, typically military, rule. For example, the judicial system in Nigeria has been respected by civilian and military regimes alike. All but one of the several military governments that have ruled Nigeria for most of its existence as an independent country have been dedicated (or pledged) to the systematic restoration of fully constitutional government; all but one have preserved, and attempted to improve, that country's federal system of government. In no part of the world does the conception of a judicial culture correspond to the reality of social conflict resolution more thoroughly than it does in Africa, where courts regularly harmonize concurrent systems of statutory, religious and customary law.

This conception of a world made up of imperfect or quasi-constitutional governments may be contrasted with H. W. O. Okoth-Ogendo's judgement that African states have 'constitutions without constitutionalism'.[7] In comparative studies of constitutional government, whole-system categories of analysis are no more valid than they would be in comparative studies of democracy. They are too crude to measure the effects of constitutionalist fragments, such as judicial independence, federalism or ombudsman-type institutions that often coexist with arbitrary forms of rule. In comparative studies of democracy, whole-system categories are narrowly and plainly ideological; invariably, they disregard some of the most fundamental relationships of power in society.

SOCIAL JUSTICE

Fairly or not, theories of liberal democracy have been criticized by socialists and even by many social democrats on the ground that they justify economic institutions that perpetuate social inequality.[8] Since the socialist débâcle of the 1980s, disparaging views of liberal democracy have fallen into disrepute. Any number of erstwhile anti-liberals have 'seen the light' and now bear witness to the virtues of liberal democracy. However, the intelligentsia is no less fickle than the general public. Given the persistence of human misery, based on economic conditions, throughout the world, and the inevitable growth of disillusionment with liberal-capitalist societies, socialists could easily revert in desperation to doctrinaire criticisms of liberal democracy. Hence it may be useful to criticize the most cogent negative assessments of liberal democracy made from a socialist or social-democratic standpoint lest the tragedy of twentieth-century socialism be repeated.

In my opinion, C. B. Macpherson (1973) has constructed the strongest anti-liberal argument on democratic-socialist foundations.[9] Briefly, he contends that in modern capitalist societies, democratic forms of government enable citizens to increase their freedom to participate in the enjoyment of those material benefits that accompany economic development. Yet capitalism tends to undermine democracy because it compels most people to transfer their natural powers of self-development to economic overlords who control capital and other resources. The ongoing 'net transfer' of power from a majority of the people to a minority results in both social inequality and political domination by the capitalist class. In this circumstance, he argues, the developmental principle of democracy is vitiated by the extractive principle of capitalism.

During the early stages of Western capitalist industrialization, human values were readily and routinely sacrificed to the needs of economic productivity. As a result, Macpherson avers, the 'ontological' (irreducibly essential) assumptions of democracy were contradictory:

the desire to realize personal economic aims ('maximize individual utilities') could not be reconciled with the democratic ideal of the greatest possible self-fulfilment for everyone. Furthermore, he believed that technological advances of the past century have finally rendered this contradiction of democratic capitalism obsolete and therefore intolerable; it is no longer necessary, that is ethically justifiable, to countenance the transfer of human powers from the many to the few. At present, the continuation of this practice is merely conservative and unjustifiably exploitative.

Macpherson also presumed that the acquisition of advanced technology by communist countries would probably result in their political liberalization while the capitalist countries would become ever more militaristic and repressive. Therefore, he warned, the main threat to Western civilization arises from the use of technological power to forestall the ontological evolution of democracy. In effect, what Macpherson said was that technology would liberalize the communist countries but militarize and tyrannize the Western countries. Despite its tendentious appearance in his own work, his impression of 'a fateful race between ontological change and technological change' was similar to the alarm of many democratic, humanistic and progressive thinkers during the era of the 'silent generation' in America, corresponding roughly to the time of the Truman and Eisenhower presidencies. Nothing since then has confuted the dissenting wisdom of social critics who challenged the prevailing orthodoxies of those complacent years.

But it was plainly mistaken, if not illogical, for Macpherson to believe that technological change would have a more liberating effect under communist auspices than it appeared to have in the West. That opinion minimized the evident reality of repressive rule by privileged elites in the communist countries. It was also naïve for Macpherson to conclude that technological advance necessarily 'assists' democratic ontology in the non-Western countries. For instance, the extraordinarily fruitful 'green revolution' of the 1960s and 1970s brought food self-sufficiency to India; but it also worsened the plight of tens of millions of poor farmers and dispossessed peasants, many of whom subsist fatalistically in abject poverty. It is not realistic to presume that technological modernization itself will lead inexorably to democratic humanism; and it is reckless to justify dictatorships on the basis of that assumption.

In any case, Macpherson expected the non-Western countries to be governed by anti-capitalist, popular dictatorships, anchored in egalitarian, general-will ideologies that are reminiscent of the pre-Marxist and pre-liberal, radical traditions of the Western world (1973: 156–69). He forecast a prolonged era of 'heavy reliance on ideology' by political elites who would be 'at once the intelligentsia and the political leaders'. While it is still too soon to conclude that this platonic image of development for most of the world is illusory, its specific ideological content does not accord with the revival of capitalist and liberal thought in Africa, South Asia and Latin America during the 1980s, not to mention countries in the former Soviet sphere. Nor does it resemble China's embrace of capitalism in the name of socialist industrialization. While the pro-democratic intent of Macpherson's theory of development is not in question, his identification of capitalism versus socialism as the most important question for social theory greatly diminishes the explanatory power of his analysis.

Macpherson's economistic (capitalism versus socialism) theory of democratic development is the inverted, or mirror, image of a constricted theory of democracy that simply disregards the effect of social inequality on citizenship. These familiar alternatives make similar mistakes from opposite angles of scientific vision. Perhaps the most sophisticated refutation of the idea that distributive, or social, justice is an essential component of democracy is contained in the works of Friedrich August von Hayek, who repudiated that idea as a dangerous 'myth', the pursuit of which is inimical to constitutional liberty.[10] A more mundane theory of democracy, erected on purely liberal foundations, has been projected onto the screen of world history by Francis Fukuyama (1989, 1992), whose thesis on 'the end of history', like Hayek's conception of the democratic ideal, excludes the question of social justice from the register reserved for issues of world-historical importance. No other statement of this rigorously liberal position appears to me to coincide with the issues of world development as completely as that of Fukuyama.

Briefly, Fukuyama (1989: 3) contends that the late twentieth century has witnessed 'an unabashed victory of economic and political liberalism'.

> What we may be witnessing is not just the end of the Cold War, or the passing of a particular period of postwar history, but the end of history as such: that is, the end point of mankind's ideological evolution and the universalization of Western liberal democracy as the final form of human government. (ibid.: 4)

Evidently, he uses the word 'history' as a metaphor for the history of ideas; and within the history of ideas, he confines his argument to the subject of government. Inverting the standard Marxist view that social justice is the master question for historians, he relegates it to relative insignificance. He is also careful to differentiate his idea from a similar thesis, known as 'the end of ideology', which had been propounded by liberal thinkers during the latter 1950s and early 1960s. While he indicates his belief that his own thesis is more fundamental than 'the end of ideology', he neglects to say that social justice was central to the thought of most, if not all, of the thinkers who were associated with the latter conception. Most of them probably believed that 'acceptance of a Welfare State' was part of the Western intellectual consensus (Bell, 1962: 402).

The 'end of ideology' thesis captured the attention, but not the universal endorsement, of Western scholars who subscribed to the theory of modernization, an explanation of the economic, familial, legal, political and social transformations that define the rise of industrial civilizations. Unlike Fukuyama, or Hayek, the modernization theorists were deeply interested in the question of social justice. In a seminal essay on the 'political aspects' of modernization, James Smoot Coleman (1968: 397) identified equality as 'the ethos of modernity'. Twenty years later, Leonard Binder observed that 'the still dominant paradigm' of modernization 'links democratic legitimacy with high levels of participation and with egalitarian distributive outcomes' (1988: 24).

Despite its egalitarian ethos, the modernization paradigm of mid-century social science had been erected on functionalist and pluralist analytical foundations that were inhospitable to class analysis. Functionalist modes of analysis postulated the integration and persistence of existing social systems; pluralist thought contemplated conflicts of interest that would have outcomes other than social revolution. These analytical approaches, favoured by the most influential social scientists of that era, were evasive with respect to many problems arising from the effects of social inequality and imperialism alike. Inevitably, many dissenting scholars were attracted by Marxist theories which focus on social inequality but either disregard or minimize the political causes of exploitation and repression. During the 1980s, egalitarians and socialists in all parts of the world belatedly recognized the inadequacy of political theories derived mainly from Marxist or similar expositions of economic exploitation. The precipitous flight of intellectuals from Marxism to liberalism created a favourable climate of opinion for Fukuyama's alternative one-dimensional theory of democracy, derived from the simple postulate of choice between authoritarian and liberal types of government. To my mind, neither of these one-dimensional perspectives, that of Marxism or of Fukuyama, encompasses the multi-dimensional reality of several basic issues for humanity, among them belligerent nationalism, environmental depredation and cultural imperialism, in addition to the doctrinal staples of economic exploitation and political repression.

At the end of the day, modernization theory prevails against economistic theories of capitalist exploitation and strictly libertarian theories of repressive government. In its revised, triumphal form, modernization theory is no longer wedded to modes of analysis that evade the revolutionary implications of social and national inequality. It has been enriched by Marxist ingredients, including class analysis, and infusions of cultural relativism that balance, and thereby enhance, its claim to universal acceptance. Apart from the unhistorical 'postmodernists', few social scientists can reasonably fault Lucian Pye's recent contention that the worldwide 'crisis of authoritarianism' signals 'the vindication of modernization theory' (1990: 7), as well as the emergence of universal standards of political conduct that the leaders of residual dictatorships cannot defy without shame and disgrace in their own national abodes.

Contrary to either Fukuyama's nuanced liberalism[11] or the concerns of libertarian constitutionalists, modernization theorists care deeply about social justice; they believe that democracy accompanied by extremes of poverty and wealth is democracy *manqué*, or deeply flawed. Where the neo-modernization theorists fall short of realism is in the treacherous vicinity of whole-system classifications, strewn with their ideological traps. Even Pye, who acknowledges the need for 'richer typologies' to assort political systems that are 'part authoritarian and part free', postulates a 'continuum from authoritarianism to democratization' (1990: 13), as democracy is patented in the West. Evidently, we need to revive and strengthen the intellectual tradition that diagnoses and seeks to arrest the pathologies of capitalist democracy before they produce a new cycle of political disillusionment and global insecurity.

DEVELOPMENTAL ESTATES

The term 'developmental democracy' was proposed by C. B. Macpherson (1977: 44–76) to mark a stage in the evolution of liberal democracy characterized by particular concern for 'individual self-development' as a universal right. Macpherson attributed this ideal, which had never been approximated in practice, to the thought of John Stuart Mill and his intellectual heirs, including L. T. Hobhouse, A. D. Lindsay and Ernest Barker in Britain; Woodrow Wilson, John Dewey and R. M. MacIver in the United States. Despite his appreciation for the idealism of this conception, Macpherson did not recommend it as a goal for democrats because he believed that it minimized the undemocratic implications of class inequality while it greatly exaggerated the democratic effects of political and social pluralism.

In 1982, I adopted the concept 'developmental democracy' to connote collective, and specifically national rather than individual, self-development (Sklar 1983: 19–20). The analogy between personal and social development that may be implied by this formulation was merely coincidental and without organicist intent, although it may have heuristic value. In his classic exposition of 'organic solidarity', Emile Durkheim, maintained that moral imperatives, manifest in norms of human conduct, do foster cooperative attitudes among differentiated groups that perform complementary social functions (Durkheim, 1984: 329–41). He identified 'organic' (the polar opposite of 'mechanical') solidarity as a basic condition of efficient social organization in complex, modern societies. Analogously, I suggest that developmental democracy is founded on a powerful norm of political conduct, namely accountability, which is manifest in two distinct ways: first, organized groups of all kinds – social, economic, political, professional, administrative and others – are accountable to one another in accordance with settled rules of inter-active conduct; second, groups promote the interests of their members when leaders are accountable to followers by whom they are chosen. I have referred to broad categories, suitable for the classification of groups that contribute to national development, as 'developmental estates of the realm' (Sklar, 1987: 713). In all countries, the inventory of such 'estates' would include, but not be limited to, the following categories: organized workers, economic entrepreneurs, artisans, farmers, members of the learned professions (including clergy) and managers of bureaucratic (including military) organizations.

Symbiotic relationships, involving both cooperation and competition, among developmental estates attest to the practice of democracy in, at least, a part of the polity in question. Democratic practices may even flourish in a part of the polity despite the absence of a democratically accountable government, as in the case of China to-day, where some elements of economic democracy coexist with political oligarchy. Whole-system theorists tend to stumble over this idea because they are hampered by a highly restrictive conception of political organization, one that simply excludes from notice various oligarchic institutions in societies classified as democratic. For example, business corporations are routinely excluded because they are assigned to the category of economic, rather than political, institutions. Whole-system theorists then advertise their gradations of simplified political systems from more to less democratic. Were the arena of politics defined to encompass relationships of power in all social institutions, it would be far more difficult, if at all possible, to grade the universe of nation-states on a linear scale, because each one would be appraised more accurately as an Aristotelian mixture of democracy and oligarchy. In such mixtures a large or small amount of democracy may coexist with either a large or small amount of oligarchy. So conceived, national political systems might be ranked in order of their graded democratic content, but not as they are currently in conventional rankings; and no country, or political sector of the world, could plausibly claim to have an exclusive patent on democracy, which is being forged in a multitude of political workshops throughout the world, but in pieces and parts, not in its entirety.

A broad, inclusive view of democracy would take into account the norms of accountability for leaders of the estates. Obviously, autonomy disappears when officials of the constituent organizations of estates are appointed and controlled by external authorities. For example, the autonomy of organized labour, as an estate, depends on the rights of workers both to control their unions and to choose representatives for bargaining with employers. These rights, which are essential to the maintenance of a modern democracy, cannot be secured in the absence of basic political liberties for all citizens. In modern times, the contributions of organized labour to national struggles for constitutional liberty have been monumental; but with few exceptions, notably in the case of Poland, such contributions in the latter twentieth century have not been researched deeply. Too often, political studies of organized labour have been guided by one-dimensional theoretical precepts that emphasize social justice but minimize the independent significance of political liberty.

Among the recent national struggles for political freedom in which organized workers have assumed a leading role, two concurrent cases in southern Africa demonstrate the close relationships between democratic labour movements and developmental democracy. In South Africa, the contributions of organized black workers to democratization are second to no other segment of the freedom movement. Opportunely, in 1991, Cyril Ramaphosa, the general secretary of the National Union of Mineworkers was elected secretary-general of the African National Congress, destined to become the leading force in South Africa's first non-racial government. Also in 1991, Frederick Chiluba, a former chairman of the Zambia Congress of Trade Unions was elected president of the republic in Zambia's first free election after two decades of one-party rule. This trade unionist turned statesman stands for capitalism and multi-party democracy, while his South African counterpart is a democratic socialist. The difference between them highlights this undeniable reality: organized workers, like people in all other walks of life, perceive their interests to coincide with either capitalism or socialism, regardless of their class identifications. There are no iron laws of appropriate ideology for either social classes or the functional estates of society. Everywhere, mixed ideologies, like mixed economies, are required to cope with the challenges of our time. A developmental democracy would combine a reasonable measure of social justice, defined as fairness in the distribution of wealth, with economic and political freedom, neither of which has ever been secure in the midst of deprivation, misery and poverty.

The natural complementarity of developmental estates has been minimized by those neoclassical market theorists who evince negativity toward the labour movement and view it as an obstacle to economic growth, rather than an asset.[12] Occasionally, union members have been reviled by populist thinkers as self-serving 'labour aristocracies', or privileged workers who exploit poor people by creating inflation; hence it has been alleged that vigorous collective bargaining and minimum wage laws are detrimental to the interests of unorganized workers, the unemployed and their families. That view is open to challenge. Researchers have found that vigorous trade unionism does promote overall economic development in two main ways: first, strong unions negotiate contracts which provide for the delivery of 'basic human needs', including health care, housing and canteens for nutrition. A 'full basket of basic needs' can do wonders for the productivity of labour where disease, hunger and malnutrition are rife. Second, the wage gains of unionized workers do spill over into the wider society; for example, small businesses often depend on the purchasing power of workers and their families. Many such businesses are conducted outside the so-called formal sectors of national economies, where economic activity is regulated by such legally enforceable devices as contracts and licences. The so-called informal sectors are not isolated arenas of economic activity to which people 'withdraw' in desperation in order to survive. On the contrary, they are integral parts of unified economic systems: formal-sector firms depend on informal-sector producers and traders to supply many of their needs and buy some of their products. The symbiotic interaction of these two entrepreneurial sectors is a basic fact of economic life in all countries at early stages of industrialization, as are the various relationships between labour unions in the formal sector and small businesses in the informal sector. Not only do strong unions generate a demand for goods and services obtainable from suppliers in the informal sector, but wage-earners also invest their savings in small businesses on a family or cooperative basis. Nor should we neglect to mention that strong labour unions, by virtue of their capacity for effective bargaining, increase the flow of wealth from transnational corporations to the people of a host country. It bears repeating that, by definition, strong unions are controlled by their members, not the government; they are founded on the democratic principle that leaders are accountable to the rank and file.[13]

Recent studies of democratization have retrieved the old concept of 'civil society' from the works of Hegel, Marx and Gramsci, using it to describe and explain 'transitions from authoritarian rule' (O'Donnell and Schmitter, 1986: 48–56).[14] This concept affords a conceptual linkage to the role of functional estates in societal development. Representative examples from recent research on democratization include these topics: anti-authoritarian and anti-statist initiatives by entrepreneurs in Brazil (Cardoso, 1986) and Venezuela (Becker, 1990); the union democracy movement in both Brazil (Kech, 1989) and Mexico (Middlebrook, 1989); the spontaneous summoning of a Rural Estates General by farmers in Mali (Bingen, 1994); the formation of pluralistic agrarian 'demand groups' in India (Rudolph and Rudolph, 1987: 333–401); the political dilemmas of professional engineers in Egypt (Moore, 1980); the emergence of anti-authoritarian managerial ideologies in Peru (Becker, 1983: 270–3) and South Africa (Lipton, 1985).

The complementarity of estates in modernizing societies does not imply social harmony without conflict. As Durkheim remarked, 'The role of solidarity is not to abolish competition but to moderate it.' Hence, he reasoned, 'the more complex an organization is, the more the necessity for extensive regulation is felt' (1984: 302–3). Regulation, he observed, is the specific function of government.

When the governments of modern societies regulate the complementary estates equitably and in accordance with the wishes of their members, democracy can be upheld as an efficient form of social organization for development. Conversely, repressive regulations that subjugate the estates and drain them of their vitality deviate from democracy, regardless of their impact on development. The former, collaborative, type of regulation is known in American political thought as 'positive government', which should be differentiated from those corporatist, or 'corporativist', conceptions which imply statist economic management.[15] However, 'democratic corporatism', a variant that has flourished in Western Europe, Japan and several countries in other parts of the world during the latter twentieth century has also enhanced the quality of life in those countries, as well as their economic performance.[16] Both 'positive government' and 'democratic corporatism' signify realistic alternatives to *laissez-faire* market liberalism, which is as unrealistic as it is unrelated to any of the vaunted examples of successful industrialization in East Asia.[17] Whatever else one may think of his inflationary fiscal policies, developmental democrats might warm to the words of Viktor S. Chernomyrdin, prime minister of Russia, on 20 January 1994, when he declared: 'The period of market romanticism has ended for us.' Would that it were so for all of us!

Market economies do stimulate the political organs of society. The suppression of markets in favour of administrative determination of incomes, prices and supply, almost always results in the de-politicization of society. This evidently causal relationship may be identified as the ultimate irony of Leninist communism's 'political' strategy of development. At the other extreme, markets beyond the reach of purposeful public regulation are, at best, utopian dreams; at the very least, they are fraught with hazards to public health, welfare and safety. Democracy implies the public management and nurture of markets so that they will flourish with affordable fairness in the distribution of opportunities, services and wealth.

IN BRIEF

This essay proposes an alternative to the cruel choice between *laissez-faire* liberalism without social justice, on the one hand, and dictatorial forms of state-centred economic development, on the other.[18] It draws attention to the 'developmental merits' of democracy as a form of government and, more broadly, a system of power in society.[19] Yet the basic purpose of this essay is not to advocate developmental democracy, but to indicate its robust existence in all regions of the world, contrary to a common opinion that cultural, religious and social barriers obstruct the progress of democracy in 'non-Western' countries.

Although democracy can be posited as an abstract end-in-itself, a theory of developmental democracy would be predicated on the idea that democracy is a means to effectuate improvement in the over-all quality of human life. In all countries, democracy is manifest in diverse forms, or fragments, which reinforce one another in the production of developmental effects. This conception of democracy 'in parts' is an alternative to whole-system conceptions of democracy that are neither realistic nor scientific, as opposed to ideological. The parts, or fragments, of democracy are incorporated into economic and social institutions as well as the institutions of sovereign governments. They include freedom of the press and the autonomy of professional organizations as well as judicial independence; guaranteed health services and welfare benefits as well as equal protection of the laws; elements of industrial democracy as well as electoral democracy.

These, and other democratic practices foster collaborative and mutually beneficial relationships between the occupational interest groups of society. In this essay, such groups have been identified as developmental estates of the realm. The term, to be sure, is borderline archaic. In the 1840s, Marx had already declared that emergent classes were sounding death knells for the historical estates in all developing countries (Marx and Engels, 1947: 59).

Class is a powerful idea because it implies that the division of labour in society is unjust. Its neglect almost invariably results in the evasion of social problems in all modern societies, regardless of the form of economic organization. However, the thick, refractive lens of class analysis also minimizes the significance of functional and occupational specialization as a condition of social progress. Perhaps a renovated concept of estate can compensate for that analytical deficiency in class. In the idiom of Marxist thought, the recovery and restoration of this concept by democratic theorists would fruitfully negate a negation and facilitate new thinking about the problems of societal development.

NOTES

1 See Gellner (1964) for a pioneering application of the idea of progress to the question of world development in the current era; and Almond, Chodorow and Pearce (1982) for a global survey.
2 For classic statements of this position, see Brecht (1959), especially the preface and chapter 3 and Catlin (1962).
3 This form of accountability coincides with the conception of democracy advanced by Plamenatz (1973: 38–9 *et passim*).
4 For a valuable survey of these and related concepts and themes, see Perlmutter (1981), who also demonstrates the convergence of these types in practice as well as in theory.
5 In a judicious reassessment of Lipset's durable thesis on the 'requisites

of democracy', Diamond (1992: 487–8) observes that Lipset (1960: 47) allowed for the anomaly of 'a "premature" democracy', one that survives by fostering conditions that are 'conducive to democracy'.

6 On the problem of extra-constitutional executive power in the United States, see Adler (1988).

7 In his insightful contribution to a pioneering symposium on comparative constitutionalism, Okoth-Ogendo (1993: 66) identifies this paradox: 'the simultaneous existence of what appears as a clear commitment by African political elites to the idea of the constitution and an equally emphatic rejection of the classical or at any rate liberal democratic notion of constitutionalism'. In another contribution to this symposium, Okoth-Ogendo's idea is endorsed by Borón (193: 339–53) for application to the record of constitutional government in Latin America.

8 For a classic statement of this kind of criticism, see Macpherson (1966).

9 C. B. Macpherson (1973), particularly essays I, II, III and VIII.

10 See Gray (1986) for an authoritative exposition of Hayek's theory of liberty.

11 Fukuyama maintains that both social democracy and group rights can be accommodated 'under the tent of liberal democracy', although the challenges of relativism and particularistic identities should not be minimized (1992: 294, 332–5).

12 Elsewhere I have observed, with respect to the World Bank, that 'there is nary a word on organized labour in its current blueprint for African economic development, and little, if anything, more in the entire series of reports on African development issued by the World Bank over the course of a decade' (Sklar, 1992: 404).

13 This paragraph is partly derived from Sklar (1987: 710–12), where sources for the 'informal sector', and its relationship to trade unionism are also cited. Two other studies are fundamental: MacGaffey (1987) and De Soto (1989); the latter work, previously published in Spanish, applauds popular entrepreneurship as 'the invisible revolution in the Third World'.

14 See Bottomore, (ed.) (1983: 72–4) for Anne Showstack Sassoon's precise comparisons of Hegel's, Marx's and Gramsci's conceptions of 'civil society'.

15 For the concept of positive government as an alternative to statist command in the thought of Woodrow Wilson, see M. J. Sklar (1988: 33–40, 401–12, 436). Wilsonian liberalism 'affirmed the principle of administered markets under the primary management of the corporations and other private parties engaging in contractual relations, subject to secondary government regulation. On that basis, positive government, in both regulatory and distributive functions, supplementary to and corrective of market relations, might develop to the farthest limits, and might in the process modify property rights in the interest of expanded human rights, depending on the times and circumstances. Society would still retain the decisive initiative and continue to render the state its servant' (ibid.: 37).

16 Schmitter (1983) and Katzenstein (1985) differentiate clearly between democratic and undemocratic variants, and epochs, of corporatism. The negative historical connotations of this conception should not be allowed to discourage its appreciation by democratic theorists.

17 See Schatz (1987a), Robison (1988) and Amsden (1989).

18 Denis Goulet's felicitous formulation of a 'cruel choice' between economic efficiency and social justice in Latin America is as timely today as it was two decades ago (Goulet, 1971).
19 For the concept of 'developmental merits', see Schatz (1987b: 197–8).

REFERENCES

Adler, D. G. 1988: The Constitution and Presidential Warmaking: The Enduring Debate. *Political Science Quarterly*, 103(1), 1–36.
Almond, G. A., Chodorow, M. and Pearce, R. H. (eds) 1982: *Progress and its Discontents*. Berkeley/Los Angeles: University of California Press.
Amsden, A. H. 1989: *Asia's Next Giant*. New York/Oxford: Oxford University Press.
Becker, D. G. 1983: *The New Bourgeoisie and the Limits of Dependency*. Princeton, NJ: Princeton University Press.
Becker, D. G. 1990: Business Associations in Latin America: The Venezuelan Case. *Comparative Political Studies*, 23(1), 114–38.
Bell, D. 1962: *The End of Ideology*, rev. edn New York: Free Press.
Binder, L. 1988: *Islamic Liberalism: A Critique of Development Ideologies*. Chicago/London: University of Chicago Press.
Bingen, R. J. 1994: Agricultural Development Policy and Grass-Roots Democracy in Mali. *African Rural and Urban Studies*, 1(1).
Borón, A. A. 1993: Latin America: Constitutionalism and the Political Traditions of Liberalism and Socialism. In D. Greenberg et al. (eds) *Constitutionalism and Democracy* New York/Oxford: Oxford University Press, 339–53.
Bottomore, T. (ed.) 1983: *A Dictionary of Marxist Thought*. Cambridge, Mass.: Harvard University Press.
Brecht, A. 1959: *Political Theory*. Princeton, NJ: Princeton University Press.
Bury, J. B. 1932: *The Idea of Progress*. New York: Macmillan.
Cardoso, F. H. 1986: Entrepreneurs and the Transition Process: The Brazilian Case. In G. O'Donnell, P. C. Schmitter and L. Whitehead (eds) *Transitions from Authoritarian Rule: Comparative Perspectives*. Baltimore/London: Johns Hopkins University Press, 137–53.
Catlin, G. E. G. 1962: *Systematic Politics*. Toronto: University of Toronto Press.
Coleman, J. S. 1968: Modernization: Political Aspects. In D. Sills (ed.) *International Encyclopedia of the Social Sciences*. New York: Macmillan.
De Soto, H. 1989: *The Other Path: The Invisible Revolution in the Third World*. New York: Harper and Row.
Diamond, L. 1992: Economic Development and Democracy Reconsidered. *American Behavioral Scientist*, 35(4/5), 450–99.
Durkheim, Emile 1984 (1893): *The Division of Labor in Society*, trans. W. D. Halls; intro. L. A. Coser. New York: Free Press.
Fang Lizhi 1991: *Bringing Down the Great Wall*. New York: Knopf.
Fukuyama, F. 1989: The End of History? *National Interest*, 16 (Summer), 3–18.
Fukuyama, F. 1992: *The End of History and the Last Man*. New York: Free Press.

Gellner, E. 1964: *Thought and Change.* Chicago: University of Chicago Press.
Goulet, D. 1971: *The Cruel Choice*, New York: Atheneum.
Gray, J. 1986: *Hayek on Liberty*, 2nd edn. Oxford: Blackwell.
Gregor, A. J. 1979: *Italian Fascism and Developmental Dictatorship.* Princeton, NJ: Princeton University Press.
Katzenstein, P. J. 1985: *Small States in World Markets.* Ithaca/London: Cornell University Press.
Kech, M. E. 1989: The New Unionism in the Brazilian Transition. In A. Stepan (ed.), *Democratizing Brazil.* New York/Oxford: Oxford University Press, 252–96.
Keyfitz, N. 1988: The Asian Road to Democracy *Society,* 26(1), 71–6.
Lipset, S. M. 1960: *Political Man.* Garden City, NY: Doubleday.
Lipton, M. 1985: *Capitalism and Apartheid.* Totowa, NY: Rowman & Allanheld.
MacGaffey, J. 1987: *Entrepreneurs and Parasites: The Struggle for Indigenous Capitalism in Zaïre.* Cambridge/New York: Cambridge University Press.
Macpherson, C. B. 1966: *The Real World of Democracy.* Oxford: Clarendon Press.
Macpherson, C. B. 1973: *Democratic Theory: Essays in Retrieval.* Oxford: Clarendon Press.
Macpherson, C. B. 1977: *The Life and Times of Liberal Democracy.* Oxford: Oxford University Press.
Marx, K. and Engels, F. 1947: *The German Ideology*, ed. R. Pascal. New York: International Publishers.
Middlebrook, K. J. 1989: Union Democratization in the Mexican Automobile Industry. *Latin American Research Review,* 24(2), 69–93.
Moore, C. H. 1980: *Images of Development.* Cambridge, Mass.: MIT Press.
O'Donnell, G. A. 1973: *Modernization and Bureaucratic-Authoritarianism: Studies in South American Politics.* Berkeley: Institute of International Studies, University of California.
O'Donnell, G. and Schmitter, P. C. 1986: *Transitions from Authoritarian Rule: Tentative Conclusions about Uncertain Democracies.* Baltimore/London: Johns Hopkins University Press.
Okoth-Ogendo, H. W. O. 1993: Constitutions without Constitutionalism: Reflections on an African Political Paradox. In D. Greenburg et al. (eds) *Constitutionalism and Democracy* New York/Oxford: Oxford University Press, 65–82.
Okun, A. M. 1975: *Equality and Efficiency: The Big Tradeoff.* Washington DC: The Brookings Institution.
Perlmutter, A. 1981: *Modern Authoritarianism.* New Haven, Conn.: Yale University Press.
Plamenatz, J. 1973: *Democracy and Illusion.* London: Longman.
Pye, L. W. 1990: Political Science and the Crisis of Authoritarianism. *American Political Science Review,* 84(1), 3–19.
Robison, Richard 1988: Authoritarian States, Capital-Owning Classes, and the Politics of Newly Industrializing Countries: The Case of Indonesia. *World Politics,* 46(1), 52–74.
Rudolph, L. I. and Rudolph, S. H. 1987: *In Pursuit of Lakshmi: The Political Economy of the Indian State.* Chicago/London: University of Chicago Press.

Schatz, S. P. 1987a: Laissez-Faireism for Africa? *Journal of Modern African Studies*, 23(1), 129–38.

Schatz, S. P. 1987b: Postimperialism and the Great Competition. In D. G. Becker, J. Frieden, S. P. Schatz, and R. L. Sklar, *Postimperialism*. Boulder, Colo./London: Lynne Rienner, 193–201.

Schmitter, P. C. 1983: Democratic Theory and Neocorporatist Practice. *Social Research*, 50(4), 885–928.

Sklar, M. J. 1988: *The Corporate Reconstruction of American Capitalism, 1890–1916*. Cambridge/New York: Cambridge University Press.

Sklar, R. L. 1983: Democracy in Africa. *African Studies Review*, 28(3/4), 11–24.

Sklar, R. L. 1987: Developmental Democracy. *Comparative Studies in Society and History*, 29(4), 686–714.

Sklar, R. L. 1992: The Future of Socialism in Africa. *Dissent*, 39(3), 399–405.

3

Democracy and Development: A Statistical Exploration

SVANTE ERSSON AND
JAN-ERIK LANE

INTRODUCTION

A democratic regime has intrinsic value, because its political norms celebrate the active participation of the people in government. Moreover, democratic states meet certain criteria of political decency, such as the institutionalization of human rights, which is considered to be intrinsically valuable in public international law as well as in several constitutions.

In the early 1990s democracy has been widely recognized as the best political regime yet invented, because its citizens are both treated with respect or dignity and have some say in political decision-making. But we must also consider the extrinsic value of democratic rule. Do democracies in the long run tend to deliver other favourable outcomes, such as presenting their citizens with a high level of social and economic development? If this was not the case, then one might start searching for other types of regime which could lead to a higher level of affluence or sustained economic growth over a longer time period.

In this chapter we use statistical methods to explore the second part of the argument favouring democratic regimes, that is the extrinsic merits of democracy. Is it true that democracies generally deliver better outcomes than other kinds of political systems? Is social or economic development more favourable in democracies than in non-democracies?

It is not enough merely to look at the overall performance of democratic states. One must also try to pin down the causal link between democracy and development, if indeed there is such a connection. The occurrence of a democratic regime in an affluent society could be accidental, or it could result from the impact of socio-economic development upon democracy. Is income equality higher in democratic countries than in authoritarian regimes, and if so, why?[1]

THE DISCOURSE

One may identify a number of different approaches which focus on the relation between democracy and development. One tradition starts with the concept of democracy, asking first how to measure democracy and then rank regimes as more or less democratic, in order to proceed then to look at what consequences democracy may have for development. This position has been taken by political scientists or sociologists (Bollen, 1980; Bollen and Jackman, 1985, 1989; Muller, 1988). Another tradition looks at a variety of factors which may have an impact on development, among which institutional factors in politics are included. Here we mostly find economists or political economists (Scully, 1988, 1992; Pourgerami, 1988; Grier and Tullock, 1989).

Starting from the recognition of a factual association between levels of affluence and degrees of democracy, the problem was how to interpret such empirically given relationships. The classic argument that development is conducive to democracy was put forward by Seymour Martin Lipset (1959) and, later, by others (Rueschemeyer et al., 1992; Diamond, 1992; Lipset et al., 1993). 'Development' here has usually meant the level of affluence as measured, for instance, in terms of GNP per capita. A high level of affluence, it was argued, would enhance democratic institutions by creating a broad middle class with cross-cutting cleavages, thus tempering conflicts and enhancing the practical politics of bargaining. However, nothing excluded the contrary hypothesis that democracy could foster economic development. Still another possible interpretation was that democracy and affluence could accompany each other or interact, reinforcing each other reciprocally.

What is at stake here is the precise question about politico-economic causality, that is whether democracy is or is not conducive to social and economic development (Sirowy and Inkeles, 1990; Pourgerami, 1988). We will test a number of models that somehow claim that democracy has direct consequences for socioeconomic development. 'Development' is a general concept that stands for various things such as economic growth and level of affluence, or even social development as measured by a complex set of indicators. In this chapter we are particularly interested in any evidence that supports the hypothesis that the direction of causality is from democracy to development, and not the other way around.

One may state that in the social science debate about democracy and development one finds three different arguments about their relationship (Sirowy and Inkeles, 1990). We look first at three sets of relevant models that advance such theoretical arguments. After that we examine more closely the measurement of the key concepts: economic growth, affluence, quality of life or human development, income inequality and democracy.

Conflict models

One set of arguments states that democracy is not conducive to development, interpreted as either economic growth or as improvements in quality of life. This position not only claims that democracy has no positive impact upon development but, in addition, often argues that democracy may have a negative impact upon socioeconomic development (Leftwich, 1993). This view seems to receive considerable support from developments in South East and East Asia, where rapid economic development has taken place within three more or less authoritarian regimes, as in South Korea, Taiwan and Singapore. There are two versions of the negative argument.

First, it is asserted that democracy has a lot of dysfunctions, particularly in new democracies which face problems in establishing stable government that may pursue effective and consistent policies. In particular, such political instability can hamper economic and social development in the new democracies of the third world (Myrdal, 1957; Myrdal, 1968).

Second, there is another argument, relevant for older democracies, that takes as its starting point the need for governments in countries with a democratic regime to win support from a majority of the voters. In order to secure such popularity, governments must respond with policies that meet demands for more welfare spending in the form of redistribution that is not conducive to economic growth. Democracies harbour strongly organized interests which tend to take care of their own special interests at the expense of the general interests of the nation, or public interests, such as economic growth (Olson, 1982). The stronger the organized interest groups, the less favourable are the conditions for economic development (Olson, 1990).

The different conflict models argue that democratic regimes are forced to focus almost exclusively on questions of redistribution at the expense of matters related to investment and capital accumulation. Democracy is based on pork-barrel 'politicking' which results in myopic policies that reduce overall effectiveness in the economy. Democracies tend to favour equality ahead of efficiency in the trade-off between policies which stress allocation and which enhance growth, on the one hand, and policies with redistributive aims, on the other. An empirical test supporting the conflict model is provided by Weede, who concludes; 'The overall effect of political democracy on economic growth is negative, but rather weak' (Weede, 1983: 35).

Compatibility models

The compatibility models put forward two kinds of arguments for the hypothesis that democracy is conducive to development, or, in a softer version, that democracy at least does not decrease affluence or economic growth. On the one hand, it is stressed that a market economy, involving special institutions, tends to go hand in hand with institutions that safeguard civil and political rights, that is with political democracy (Olson, 1993). If a market economy is expected to operate well, then it requires the kind of social institutions that tend to be available only in democracies. If democracy is a precondition for a functioning market economy, then it may also be conducive to development in the form of economic growth.

Thus, democracy indirectly promotes economic development, because it strengthens the market economy which tends to outperform other economic systems (such as the planned economy) on development criteria which include growth, quality of life or level of human development (Vorhies and Glahe, 1988; Spindler, 1991; Scully and Slottje, 1991).

On the other hand, there is an argument which starts from the tendency of a democracy to rely on the cooperation of the people (Wittman, 1989). In order to achieve such broadly based cooperation among citizens, it is necessary to develop social conditions that meet the needs of the population. This implies that social inequalities tend to be less pronounced in societies with a democratic regime.

In the long run, democracies enhance economic development as well as promote social equality, since they act to foster a community of well-educated citizens, who in turn produce highly qualified industrial outputs, further strengthening both cooperation and growth. A study supporting this version of the compatibility model is to be found in the *World Development Report* of 1991: 'The results of regression analysis do not go as far as to suggest that liberties contribute positively to income growth, but they imply that they do not hold growth back' (World Bank, 1991a: 50).

Sceptical models

The sceptical argument admits that it may well be the case that democracy and development go together in the long run. But it stresses that democracy in itself has little direct impact upon development for there are many intervening factors that may have an impact on the interaction between them. This sceptical view is strengthened by several empirical studies on the relationships between democracy and development which are inconclusive: some support the conflict model, while others support the compatibility model (Przeworski, 1992).

This sceptical standpoint is to be found in many studies (Sorensen, 1992). For example, Barsh concludes an article as follows: 'Democracy does not appear to "cause" growth, but economic differentiation certainly creates demands for democratic participation, which governments must then meet in the interests of further economic growth and political stability. Democracy is neither a "quick fix" for development problems, nor a substitute for resources. Over the long run, however, democracy and development can become reinforcing' (Barsh, 1992: 133). The same conclusion is to be found in another study whose authors state: 'We find that indexes of revolutions and coups (REVC) and civil liberties (CIVL) are not robustly correlated with GYP (i.e. average annual growth rate of GDP per capita)' (Levine and Renelt, 1992: 957). In a recent article Przeworski and Limongi say that we simply do not know 'whether democracy fosters or hinders economic growth' (1993: 64). A similar conclusion is offered by Weede (1993).

We evaluate the evidence for these three models in this chapter. The conflict model argues that democracy and development tend to clash; the compatibility model states that democracy may enhance social and economic development; and finally the sceptical model hints that democracy and development may accompany each other, but that it is hardly the case that democracy is a major cause of socioeconomic development, at least not in the short run. But, first, we introduce our empirical tools and, second, we test a number of models related to the three arguments outlined above.

Method and data

In order to assess carefully the relationship between democracy and development we rely on a data-set covering states with a population of more than one million in 1990.[2] This means that we cover some 130 contemporary states. In some instances we look also at the new states created after 1990, but our analysis will mainly focus on the period prior to 1990.

The states included may be classified in many different ways, but for present purposes we use five groups: (a) OECD + Israel, (b) former socialist states, (c) the Americas, (d) Africa and (e) Asia. The rationale for this classification is that we wish to inquire into the stability of estimates over various parts of the world, divided into sets of states.

The same rationale explains our choice of different time periods. Our main analysis will focus on relationships during the 1980s, but in order to test for the stability over time of our estimates we will also cover time periods from the early 1950s and forward.

As a starting point for our analysis we will rely on correlation analyses and regression analyses using OLS estimates. And in order to test for the robustness of the estimates made they will be applied to various measures for different periods of time (see Appendix of Statistical Terms, pp. 67–9). Thus, in our analysis, we try to inquire into the stability and robustness of estimated relations between democracy and development that take into account possible variation in space and in time. Our choice of variables and indicators included in the analyses is presented in the following sections.

DEMOCRACY

The term 'democracy' may be defined in various ways. One may stress political democracy, economic democracy or social democracy. In the present context we focus on what is most commonly labelled as 'political democracy', which implies the existence of extensive political rights and civil liberties, in addition to contestation between parties, as suggested by Dahl in his discussion of polyarchy (Dahl, 1971; Bollen, 1990). Although there is some consensus about what this interpretation implies with regard to the referents of the concept, that is the countries that are to be designated as 'democracies', there remain issues where opinions differ, for example what the concept of democracy implies beyond the political sphere.

When mapping democracy in the present world one crucial issue to resolve is whether it is possible to characterize democracy in terms of properties that are categorical or continuous. One line of argument holds that democracy is an inherently categorical variable: that is, it is only meaningful to distinguish between democracies and non-democracies. Democracy in this sense is indivisible; either a state is democratic or it is not, although there may also be something called 'semi-democracy' (Huntington, 1991: 11).

The other line of argument claims that it is meaningful to distinguish between states that are more or less democratic, meaning thus that democracy is a measurable property (Bollen, 1980; Bollen and Jackman, 1989; Bollen, 1990 and 1993). Following this idea, a series of indicators of democracy, or proxies for democracy, have been constructed, from Lerner (1958) and Lipset (1959) down to Bollen (1980) and Humana (1992).

We adopt the second position, arguing for the utility of constructing continuous measures of democracy, which make it possible to map the variation in democracy between nations, in space as well as time. This does not mean that it is an easy task; some may even argue that this is more or less impossible, since such indicators tend to be biased towards Western political culture (Barsh, 1993). But even though it is problematic to use such measures, we find that they allow for a much more systematic analysis of problems related to democracy which are highly relevant today.

We explicitly focus on indicators of political democracy that try to capture the extent of political rights and civil liberties available to the citizens of given polities. This means that we reject the inclusion of measures referring to economic democracy or economic freedom (Spindler, 1991). At a conceptual level, political democracy must be distinguished from economic democracy or economic freedom, although empirically there may be interrelations between indicators of these concepts.

Measures of democracy

There are now a lot of measures available for democracy, human rights or similar concepts (Bollen, 1986). The first systematic attempt to measure democracy was made by Bollen (1979, 1980), constructing widely used scores for the years 1960 and 1965. He was preceded by others such as Cutright (1963), Neubauer (1967), Adelman and Taft Morris (1967), Smith (1969) and Jackman (1975). Gastil and Freedom House have worked on such measures from 1973 and other attempts in this direction have been reported by Perry (1980), Humana (1983, 1986, 1992), Pourgerami (1988), Coppedge and Reinecke (1990), Vanhanen (1990, 1992), Gurr (1990), Arat (1991), Hadenius (1992) and Bollen again (1993). Most of these measures cited are only available for one or two different periods of time, but there are two exceptions: Gurr (1990) and the Gastil/Freedom House contribution.

The time period covered by Gurr is considerable, since it starts with 1800 and ends with 1986. Gurr employs two indicators that are relevant for measuring democracy, namely AUTOC = institutionalized autocracy, and DEMOC = institutionalized democracy. These two indicators covary, yet they are not identical, which means that combining the two indicators (DEMOC minus AUTOC) results in a measure that allows for more variation in the low range as well as the high range of democracy. This new measure has then been normalized, meaning that a highly democratic regime has a score of 10 and a highly non-democratic regime has a score of 0.

The indices constructed by Gastil and Freedom House cover the period from 1973 to 1994. They give yearly scores for two indices, one for political rights and one for civil liberties. Analyses of these indices have proved that they are highly correlated, therefore one of them may be said to be redundant (Banks, 1989). This makes it reasonable to add the two scores and combine them to one democracy score, since the two main components of political democracy are political rights and civil liberties. This new democracy measure has been arrived at through adding the scores, and normalizing the democracy scores so that a highly democratic regime gets the score 10 and a highly non-democratic regime gets the score 0.

We therefore have access to different sets of measures for democracies. Gurr and Gastil/Freedom House cover longer periods, while others (Bollen, Perry, Vanhanen, Coppedge and Reinecke, Hadenius) cover only short time periods. The next step is to test the reliability of these indices by means of a series of correlation analyses. Do they roughly measure similar phenomena that might be called 'democracy', or the extent of democracy?

Correlating indices of democracy

The most useful indices are the Gurr and Gastil/Freedom House measures, because together they cover the post-war period till now. How well do they match other indices? And how well do they covary themselves? In order to clarify this, a set of correlations are explored. First, there are tests for different periods of time from 1960 up to 1990. The Gurr measures and the Gastil/Freedom House measures are correlated with the measures constructed by Bollen, Perry, Vanhanen, Coppedge and Reinecke and Hadenius, as well as the Gurr measures and the Gastil/Freedom House measures. Secondly, these correlations are tested for the five subsets of nations outlined earlier. Is there an internal consistency between the different measures when applied to the same periods of time and tested on the total set and the various subsets?

Looking at the total set, the correlations are generally high enough to justify the conclusion that these indicators do indeed measure similar phenomena. It is important to note that the Gurr index correlates quite well with the Bollen index for 1960, 1965 and 1980. Gurr's index also correlates highly with the Coppedge and Reinecke index for 1980. The Gastil/Freedom House index covaries highly with the Bollen index for 1980 and the Hadenius index for 1988. The correlations with the Perry index and the Vanhanen index are somewhat lower, but still acceptable. The Gurr index and the Gastil/ Freedom House index also coincide strongly for the years 1975, 1980 and 1985 with the lowest correlation coefficient of .87.

The overall finding is the same, if one looks into the five subsets, but there are some exceptions. The African political systems are not as easy to classify as the systems on other continents. This also applies to the socialist political systems. To sum up, it seems reasonable to conclude that the Gurr index and the Gastil/Freedom House indices measure phenomena which are similar enough to interpret as democracy. These indices seem to be reliable in terms of different time periods as well as in terms of different subsets. Consequently, these two indices will be used as our indicators measuring the degree of democracy in the post-war world.

Variation in democracy in time and space

Based upon these two democracy indices, it is now possible to present an overview of the variation in democracy in time and in space. Let us first look at the scores for the two indices over time and the variation for the different subsets. These data are given in table 3.1.

The scores for the two indices differ somewhat, depending on the number of countries included and the particular time point looked at. Still, the rankings of the subsets are similar, and very stable.

The OECD countries rank first, followed by the Americas, Asia, Africa and the socialist states. This pattern holds true for all periods of time except the first (1950) and the last (1992), where the socialist subset has risen from last to third position. This is also the case when one looks at the development over time. Democracy has been on the rise from the mid-1970s till now, whereas it went down from a higher level in 1950 to the lowest level in 1975. This pattern differs from one subset to another. That this is the case is also apparent from a correlation analysis where developments over time are estimated.

In general, the correlation coefficients for the total set are high, ranging from lowest at .68 (GU50–GU80, GU50–GU85, and DEM75–DEM92) to the highest at .97 (DEM85–DEM88) and .92 (GU80–GU85). The larger the time interval covered, the lower the coefficients due to changes taking place in between. The rise of the Castro regime as well the processes of democratic transition after 1989 are evident when looking to the socialist subset. In a similar manner the transition from authoritarian regimes to democratic regimes in the Mediterranean in the mid 1970s is revealed in the OECD subset.

So far we have mapped one crucial independent variable: democracy. The next step is devoted to the analysis of the dependent variable: development.

DEVELOPMENT

The concept of development, too, has many meanings. It is relevant to distinguish between development as a process (rate of change)

Table 3.1 Democracy scores

Index	N	Total	Africa	Americas	Asia	Socialist	OECD	E^2
GU50	(82)	5.21	4.75	4.18	4.26	2.04	8.85	.50
GU60	(101)	5.08	3.63	5.48	4.12	2.04	8.78	.40
GU70	(124)	4.55	3.00	5.29	4.04	1.73	8.76	.41
GU80	(128)	4.66	3.00	5.55	3.81	1.92	9.50	.50
GU85	(128)	4.86	2.89	6.64	3.84	1.88	9.76	.61
DEM80	(129)	4.21	2.46	5.48	3.17	1.15	9.35	.64
DEM85	(129)	4.27	2.12	6.51	3.17	1.03	9.42	.69
DEM88	(129)	4.48	2.26	6.79	3.47	1.35	9.53	.69
DEM92	(128)	5.26	3.47	6.75	3.56	4.93	9.57	.50

The set of socialist countries covers the former communist states before and after the 1989 regime transformations. GU = Gurr's index; DEM = Gastil/Freedom House index. The numbers 50, 60 and so on refer to estimates for 1950, 1960 etc. The indices are normalized: 0 (minimum) means non-democracy and 10 (maximum) stands for democracy.

and development as a condition (or level) (Riggs 1984: 133). When democracy is considered a cause or a partial cause of development, then the way the concept is being used must be clarified. Either development describes some rate of change, like economic growth; or it stands for a general level of socioeconomic welfare or social equality. Both interpretations require the construction of indices that measure economic growth, quality of life and income inequality. Let us look into these two meanings of 'development': process versus condition.

Development as economic growth

Within mainstream economics development stands for economic growth, that is growth in output as indicated by standard measures like GNP/GDP, often expressed on a per capita basis. As these measures can cover longer or shorter time periods, we rely on two different sets of data in order to map economic growth. One set refers to estimates of average annual growth rate of GDP per capita in various editions of the World Development Report covering the periods 1950/60, 1960/70, 1970/81 and 1965/89 (World Bank, 1983, 1991a).

The other set refers to estimates constructed from Summers' and Heston's data bank covering roughly the same periods of time from 1950 to 1985 (Summers and Heston, 1988). Growth rates are computed for the relevant time period and averaged by the number of years included. This data set is preferred to the later 1991 data set, because it includes estimates for the former communist states. The data refer to growth per capita and the time periods covered include three short-term periods (1950/60, 1960/70 and 1970/80) and one long-term period (1960/85).

In order to test the reliability of these measures a new set of correlation analyses has been devised. These correlations refer to four different time periods and two sets of economic growth data.

These two measures of economic growth do covary, although there is a distinct difference between the period 1950/60 with $r = .90$ and the period 1965/89–1960/85 with $r = .76$. This also holds true for the subsets, but there are instances where the reliability is low, as within the OECD subset for the period 1965/89–1960/85. The discrepancies may be explained by differences in the measurement procedure and the time periods covered. These differences are also displayed when mapping the records of economic growth for the various time periods and the different sets of nations.

The figures based on the World Development Report exhibit in general lower estimates than the figures based on Summers and Heston – see table 3.2.

The growth figures for the socialist states reported are high, probably too high. Excluding these states the pattern is fairly clear. In the

Table 3.2 Economic growth rates (%)

Time	N	Total	Africa	Americas	Asia	Socialist	OECD	E^2
EG50/60	(81)	2.30	1.51	2.08	2.39	4.40	3.33	.11
EG60/70	(103)	2.80	1.83	2.41	3.13	5.23	4.34	.29
EG70/81	(114)	1.80	0.58	1.95	2.92	4.43	2.34	.13
EG65/89	(97)	1.62	0.86	1.01	2.43	4.45	2.60	.17
G50/60	(64)	3.60	1.17	2.39	4.15	5.98	4.30	.29
G60/70	(112)	3.65	2.48	3.33	3.97	4.55	5.36	.14
G70/80	(116)	2.72	1.43	2.58	4.26	3.80	3.26	.11
G60/85	(111)	3.40	2.08	2.08	5.24	5.02	4.81	.13

Growth rates refer to per capita growth; G = Summers' and Heston's series; EG = World Bank series; EG = yearly growth rates reported in World Development Report; 50/60, 60/70 etc. = growth rates for 1950–60, 1960–70 etc.; N = number of countries included in the calculation of average growth rates for the various subsets like Africa, Americas etc.

1950s and the 1960s the OECD countries in general, and Japan in particular, experienced the highest economic growth, while other Asian states took the lead during the 1970s and 1980s. The African states had the lowest growth rates, while the Americas came somewhere in between.

The pattern of economic growth over time is not stable. The 1950s comes close to the 1960s but the 1970s differs from the 1960s, and growth in the 1950s has no implications for growth between 1960 and 1985, while this long-term growth goes hand in hand with growth in the 1960s and the 1970s. The conclusion that might be drawn from these findings is that high economic growth during one period of time does not imply a high growth rate during another period.

Development as human development

One criticism of the interpretation of development as economic growth is that it only captures an economic dimension. Development is something else, or something more complex which ought to be related to the quality of life of mankind (Doyal and Gough, 1991; Inkeles, 1993). As a response to this criticism a lot of indices have been constructed that try to cover these complex aspects of human development and human well-being.

One of the innovators of this field is Morris (1979) who invented a Physical Quality of Life Index (PQL) that took account of life expectancy and infant mortality. Since 1990 the United Nations Development Programme has presented a Human Development Index (HDI) that combines an adjusted GDP/capita estimate, life expectancy, infant mortality and level of literacy. Slottje et al. (1991a, 1991b) have constructed rankings of indices of quality of life that capture a wide range of indicators from socioeconomic ones to political ones. The problem with these rankings is that they often generate counter-intuitive conclusions. Although there are a lot of other indices as suggested in the literature (Dasgupta and Weale 1992; Lind 1993) we will rely on PQL and HDI as measures of human development.

It is evident that these indices measure similar phenomena. Although they cover various periods of time, they do covary to a very high degree. This is also true, if one looks into the five subsets, even though the covariation is somewhat lower for Africa, Asia and the socialist subsets. The level of human development differs quite sharply between the five subsets. As may be expected, the highest level is to be found in the OECD subset, while the socialist states rank second, although a decrease is noticeable there in the 1990 scores; among the other subsets, the Americas rank third, Asia fourth and Africa last, as detailed in table 3.3.

Table 3.3 **Human development scores**

Index	N	Total	Africa	Americas	Asia	Socialist	OECD	E^2
HDI70	(107)	.485	.211	.600	.385	.812	.823	.79
PQL	(125)	57.8	31.0	68.8	50.8	86.5	91.4	.74
HDI87	(127)	.574	.296	.694	.505	.801	.950	.66
HDI90	(125)	.553	.284	.667	.495	.737	.941	.66

HDI = Human Development Index   PQL = Physical Quality of Life
Sources: Morris 1979; UNDP 1990, 1991, 1993

Development as income equality

Another aspect of development that has been related to democracy in many analyses is the degree of income equality within a society (Hewitt, 1977; Simpson, 1990). Low or moderate inequalities are associated with a higher level of development, while large inequalities go hand in hand with lower levels of development (Kuznets, 1955).

There are a lot of measures available for income distributions. The data we rely on refer to total household income for various income groups (World Bank, 1991b). We mainly use estimates of the income share of the top 20 per cent of households, that is the larger the share of incomes of this group, the more unequal the income distribution tends to be. These distributions are reported for three different periods of time, roughly equal to 1960, 1970 and the late 1980s. In addition, two summary measures have been created in order to increase the number of cases, one for the top 10 per cent of households, and another for the top 20 per cent of households. As might be expected these summary measures of income inequality covary to a rather high degree.

These measures do covary quite well for the whole set indicating that they isolate a similar phenomenon. The low number of cases makes some of the correlations for the subsets irrelevant, but it is important to note that the two summary measures (TOP10 and TOP20) correlate well for the whole set as well as for all the subsets.

The pattern of income distribution disclosed in table 3.4 indicates that the most even income distribution was found in the former communist states. Even though one may raise some question marks around this fact, there are reports that give this picture a certain plausibility (Alexeev and Gaddy, 1993). Disregarding the socialist states, it is evident that the OECD states reveal the most equal distribution, while inequalities seem to be most pronounced in the Americas.

Table 3.4 Income inequality

Index	N	Total	Africa	Americas	Asia	Socialist	OECD	E²
TOP2060	(29)	48.8	45.6	59.6	49.2	38.5	46.9	.51
TOP2070	(46)	50.9	54.9	59.8	48.8	35.7	44.0	.54
TOP2089	(33)	44.9	49.0	52.7	45.1	36.7	40.6	.57
TOP10	(48)	29.8	32.1	36.8	32.5	22.3	24.9	.53
TOP20	(62)	48.3	51.7	56.2	46.3	36.7	42.9	.41

TOP2060 = share of total income of the rich 20 per cent of the population around 1960; TOP10 = share of total income of the rich 10 per cent of the population
Sources: World Bank (1991b)

The data indicate that income inequalities have hardly changed over a period of roughly 30 years since the early 1960s. For Africa the data indicate an increase in income inequality which reflects the overall weak economic performance of this continent.

DEMOCRACY AND DEVELOPMENT

Thus far, we have presented a few apparently reliable measures of democracy and such different aspects of development as economic growth, human development and income distribution. In order to be able to say something about what effect, if any, democracy has on development, we adopt the following path of analysis. First, we establish the bivariate or surface relations between these two phenomena with no conclusion about the direction of the interaction; second, we try to model the deeper interaction between democracy and development, taking into account some of the factors generally suggested in the literature as relevant for explaining the variation in socioeconomic development.

Democracy and development: the bivariate case

Speaking generally, one may argue that a simple model of a bivariate relation between two phenomena tends to be under-specified. Still, it is also the case that the bivariate relation revealed tends to remain valid also in other better specified models. To look at the bivariate relation is thus a relevant step in the inquiry into a causal relationship, if indeed one exists. The correlation analyses commented upon below will cover several periods of time and involve one total set of states and five subsets of states.

Democracy and economic growth

Two democracy indices (Gurr, Gastil/Freedom House) will be relied upon, as well as two different estimates of economic growth (World Bank, 1991a; Summers and Heston, 1988). A correlation analysis of the relation between these measures has been made.

Criteria for a robust relation between democracy and economic development would be that the different measures show significant relations for the whole set as well as for the different subsets. There is no instance where all these criteria are met. However, it is evident that in the short-run periods, for instance the 1950s, 1960s and 1970s, the covariation is weak and most often not statistically significant for the whole set.

Significant and weakly positive relations are to be found *only* when looking at the long-run periods. In particular this is true when the democracy scores are averaged for longer periods of time. This is, however, not the case when going into the different subsets. Thus, one may conclude that this relation is not invariant over either time or space. Thus, only by looking at the whole set of nations, may one conclude that there seems to be a positive but weak relation between democracy and economic development in the long run. The data so far support the argument that democracy has little impact upon economic growth.

Democracy and human development

The next step in the analysis of bivariate relations concerns another aspect of development that covers development as a more complex phenomenon, that is human development. A correlation analysis following the same outline as that in the preceding analysis has been employed.

Whatever democracy index used, time period chosen or subset of nation selected, there seems to be a stable positive relationship between democracy and human development. There are some deviations from this general pattern as, for example, the OECD nations in the early 1970s, the socialist states in the early 1980s and Asia in the 1980s. Still, one may conclude that there is a robust positive relationship between democracy and human development. These data thus support the compatibility argument.

Democracy and income distribution

The third aspect of development to be scrutinized is income distribution. One problem in the analysis of income distribution, ignoring for the moment the problems of measurement, is the lack of estimates for most nations of the world. This means that breaking down an

analysis for the different subsets of nations is not always meaningful. A correlation matrix of the relation between democracy and
measures of income distribution must take into account that the low
number of cases makes such an undertaking precarious. In most
instances it is evident that no significant relations are available. One
of the exceptions refers to the relation between the averaged democracy scores (GU, DEM) and the summarized measure of the income
of the top 20 per cent households (TOP20). Here, a significant negative relation is to be reported for the whole set, while the African
subset has another sign. Democracy seems to covary positively with
an equal income distribution if one takes a long-run perspective. The
data here again support the compatibility argument.

MODELLING DEMOCRACY AND DEVELOPMENT

Moving from bivariate relationships to model estimations it is important to specify models that satisfy reasonable demands for theoretical relevance. Let us first look at models relating democracy and
economic development.

Models of democracy and economic development

When the sources of economic growth are researched within a cross-
sectional framework a set of important factors having clear impact
has been identified (Levine and Renelt, 1992; Mankiw et al., 1992;
Barro, 1991; Kormendi and Meguire, 1985). The so-called convergence thesis emphasizes the starting-point or the initial per capita
income as countries with a low output at an early stage tend to catch
up with rich countries, given the same growth potential as determined by access to human capital (enrolment in secondary schools),
physical capital and technology. Other relevant economic factors include the size of the public sector, growth of the working-age population and the openness of the economy or the economic system.
Non-economic factors considered are cultural factors like religion,
age of political regimes but also the character of the political regime
such as the degree of democracy.

We try to estimate models relevant for explaining the variation in
long-term economic growth, that is for 1960–85 (G6085) and for
1965–89 (EG6589). Four different measures are used to capture
the impact of democracy on economic development: two average
measures, and two measures referring to the mid-1980s. Two of the
models estimated are presented in table 3.5.[3]

It is striking that economic factors like investment in physical
capital as well as access to human capital have a positive impact on
economic development. Economic growth is also negatively related

Table 3.5 Regression models for economic growth 1965–1989

Factors	Model 1: growth 60–85 (G6085)			Model 2: growth 65–89 (EG6589)		
	B	t-stat	Beta	B	t-stat	Beta
AVEDEM	.285	1.58	.26	.074	.66	.12
LNGNPC60	−6.098	−.85	−1.63	−3.791	−.85	−1.83
LNGNPC60sq	.193	.38	.74	.214	.68	1.49
INVEST	.214	3.67	.47	.128	3.48	.51
SECSCO	.421	2.80	.41	.085	.88	.15
OPEN80	−.006	−.56	−.06	.003	.48	.06
ECOSYST	−.496	−1.71	−.16	−.398	−2.14	−.23
CORE	.627	.64	.13	−.663	−1.10	−.25
PROT	−1.590	−1.09	−.12	−1.740	−1.94	−.23
SCLER	−.007	−.78	−.12	−.009	−.58	−.29
CONSTANT	42.304	1.35		32.081	1.59	
R^2A	.36				.25	

AVEDEM = average of democracy scores 1973–88 (Gastil/Freedom House); LNGNPC60 = the logarithm for GNP/cap in international US dollar 1960 (Summers and Heston, 1988); LNGNPC60sq = the square of 1n for GNP/cap in international US dollars; INVEST = investments as a percentage of GDP on an average 1960–85 (Mankiw et al., 1992); SECSCO = share of working-age population in secondary school on an average 1960–85 (Mankiw et al., 1992); OPEN80 = import and export as percentage of GDP in 1980 (Summers and Heston, 1988); ECOSYST = type of economic system ranging from free market to planned economy (Gastil, 1987); CORE = position in the world economy (Terlouw, 1989); PROT = percentage of the population with Protestant creed (Barrett, 1982); SCLER = consolidation of modernized leadership (Black, 1966)

to the initial per capita income as predicted by the convergence or maturity hypothesis. This is more or less the general pattern, but our interest is primarily focused on the impact of democracy. What is the finding with regard to this factor?

Among 16 parameters estimated, four meet our criteria of statistical significance, while one comes very close. Among the other 11, ten show the expected sign, but they are not significant, meaning that chance factors may have influenced the estimates. There are also differences depending upon choice of dependent variable since in no instance is the variable EG6589 associated with a significant effect from the democracy variable. That is, the differences in estimates are primarily due to the choice of dependent variable and not caused by the choice of democracy measure. However, the conclusion one may draw from this is that there is no robust, significant and positive relationship between economic growth in the long run and the degree of democracy in a nation. To claim a robust relationship would imply

Table 3.6 **Regression models for economic growth 1950–1981**

	B	t-stat	Beta	R^2A
EG50–60				
(1) GU50	.217	2.05	.41	.07
(2) GU50	.206	2.05	.38	.13
G50–60				
(1) GU50	.307	2.31	.44	.13
(2) GU50	.293	2.31	.42	.18
EG60–70				
(1) GU60	−.087	−1.07	−.16	.34
(2) GU60	−.094	−1.18	−.17	.33
EG70–81				
(1) DEM75	.106	.89	.14	.13
(2) DEM75	.148	1.30	.19	.14
G70–80				
(1) DEM75	.106	.69	.11	.12
(2) DEM75	.107	.69	.11	.13

See Tables 3.1 and 3.2 for the abbreviations. (1) = original model; (2) = modified model

significant estimates irrespective of the choice of the crucial dependent and independent variables.

The preceding analysis will now be applied to economic growth in the 1950s, the 1960s and the 1970s. Similar models will be tested, but somewhat modified due to availability of relevant data. The purpose of the analysis is once again to inquire into the robustness of the impact of the democracy variable within various model specifications. In table 3.6 only the estimates of the democratic variables are displayed.

Three periods of time are selected with various specifications of the models: (1) the original model and (2) the modified model. Looking to the 1950s one can establish that there is a robust positive relation between democracy and economic development. However, this is the only set of robust estimates arrived at. For the 1960s as well as for the 1970s there are no such significant relationships to report, and this is so irrespective of what measures are used for the independent or the dependent variables. Thus, only for the 1950s is it possible to say that the impact of democracy on economic development is positive. In most other instances there is no significant relationship between democracy and economic development.

The finding is that democracy has no stable impact upon economic development, it is neither negative nor positive for economic growth. Other factors are of much greater importance: investment in physical capital and access to human capital on the one hand, and the starting-point of economic development on the other hand. Thus, we may also conclude that it is not the case that democracy is an obstacle to economic development.

Models of democracy and human development

If development is given a more complex meaning it might equal human development. According to the bivariate analyses reported on earlier, democracy seems to be positively related to human development. Is this also true when this relation is tested within the framework of different model specifications?

The general model attempted is roughly the same as the ones attempted in the analysis of economic growth, that is in addition to democracy measures the independent variables contain information on investment in human capital, level of economic development, economic system, openness of the economy and non-economic factors like strength of Protestantism, time of political modernization. Two measures on human development are used as the dependent variables: the Human Development Index of 1990, and the Physical Quality of Life Index close to 1980. Four measures of democracy are used, two average measures and two measures referring to 1980. The findings of these estimations with respect to the democracy measures are reported in table 3.7.

Even when taking into account the effect of the level of initial economic development and access to human capital there remains a stable positive relationship between democracy and human development. This holds true irrespective of which human development measure is used or which democracy measure it is tested against. This seems to be a case of a robust positive relationship. Democracies are to be found in societies where the human development scores are high and vice versa. Which is cause and which is effect?

Models of democracy and income distribution

Our final indicator of development is income distribution. One may expect a negative relationship between democracy and our measures of income distribution: the more democracy, the more equal the distribution of income, that is the lower scores on our measures TOP10 and TOP20. The form of presentation of the analysis follows the same pattern as in the preceding analyses. Only estimates for the democracy measures are reported in table 3.8.

There are some differences between the two independent variables, the impact of democracy being positive on TOP10 and negative on TOP20. Still, none of these estimates are significant. All the

Table 3.7 **Regression models for human development level**

	B	t-stat	Beta	R^2A
HUMD90				
(1) AVEDEM	20.86	3.16	.22	.88
(2) AVEDEM	22.09	3.67	.24	.88
(1) AVEGU	16.30	3.20	.18	.88
(2) AVEGU	17.77	3.63	.20	.88
(1) DEM80	11.23	2.04	.12	.87
(2) DEM80	13.44	2.60	.15	.87
(1) GU80	10.18	2.32	.12	.87
(2) GU80	11.85	2.83	.14	.87
PQL				
(1) AVEDEM	3.13	5.65	.37	.89
(2) AVEDEM	3.19	6.15	.38	.89
(1) AVEGU	2.14	4.81	.27	.88
(2) AVEGU	2.16	5.08	.27	.88
(1) DEM80	1.79	3.71	.27	.88
(2) DEM80	1.92	4.25	.24	.87
(1) GU80	1.44	3.71	.19	.87
(2) GU80	1.46	3.98	.20	.87

AVEDEM = average score for the Gastil/Freedom House index measures
1973–88; AVEGU = average score of the Gurr index measures 1973–86

democracy measures meet with insignificant estimates, irrespective
of what model specification is chosen. It is thus not possible to say
that democracy is conducive to a more equal income distribution,
but neither can one say that inequality is a consequence of democracy. The relations estimated simply say that democracy is more or
less irrelevant for the kind of income distribution found in society.

CONCLUSION: DEMOCRACY AND DEVELOPMENT

When inquiring into the relationship between democracy and development we have tried to use reliable measures of democracy and of
development that are available for different periods of time after
the Second World War. We have also identified three dimensions of

Table 3.8 Regression models for income inequality

	B	t-stat	Beta	R^2A
TOP10				
(1) AVEDEM	.695	1.14	.31	.36
(2) AVEDEM	.380	.64	.17	.34
(1) AVEGU	.351	.68	.13	.34
(2) AVEGU	.254	.68	.13	.34
(1) DEM80	−.194	−.38	−.09	.34
(2) DEM80	−.504	−1.05	−.23	.25
(1) GU80	.079	.22	.04	.26
(2) GU80	.050	.15	.03	.29
TOP20				
(1) AVEDEM	−.24	−.32	−.08	.32
(2) AVEDEM	−.20	−.29	−.06	.32
(1) AVEGU	−.37	−.77	−.14	.32
(2) AVEGU	−.27	−.61	−.10	.33
(1) DEM80	−.24	−.42	−.08	.29
(2) DEM80	−.13	−.24	−.04	.29
(1) GU80	−.30	−.73	−.12	.30
(2) GU80	−.19	−.48	−.08	.30

(1) = original model; (2) = modified model

development, namely economic development, human development and income distribution. The purpose of the inquiry is to evaluate whether democracy is conducive to development or not. We are looking for a robust relationship, meaning a relationship that is stable over time and valid irrespective of reliable measures that are used.

The findings imply that the answer to the democracy–development causation problem depends upon what is meant by 'development'. There is only one robust relationship that we have been able to identify, and that concerns democracy and human development. The positive finding concerns the interaction between democracy and quality of life, which is stable over time and also independent of what measures we have relied upon.

The negative findings are that it has not been possible to establish a stable relation between democracy and economic growth or between democracy and degree of income equality. There is evidence for the existence of a positive relation between democracy and economic growth for certain measures and certain periods, but it is not stable. The same applies even more to the evidence of an impact of democracy upon income distribution.

The first positive conclusion that we may draw is that democracy tends to go together with human development. Thus, democracy is strongly connected with human development. But it is premature to conclude that this is a one-way causal relationship, since we have not excluded the possibility that the level of human development may be conducive to democracy. The second positive conclusion is that democracy is not an obstacle to economic growth or a fair income distribution.

NOTES

1 The nature of the link between affluence and democracy has been discussed by political scientists, sociologists and economists in an effort to explain why there is this positive – though not perfect – correlation between the two entities. One may point out that affluence and democracy are distinct from an analytic point of view. The first entity refers to *economic output*, or the level of national income in a country, whereas the second entity stands for *rights*, in particular the implementation of civil and political rights. Surely, it is conceivable that output may be high in a country at the same time as human rights may not be enforced. Evidently, the direction of causality between output and rights, if any, must be that the former comes first and the latter after, because the mere introduction of civil and political rights will not bring about affluence, as many countries have experienced since 1989.
2 Data utilized in this publication were made available by the Inter-university Consortium for Political and Social Research. The data for *Polity II: Political Structures and Regime Change, 1800–1986* were prepared by Ted Robert Gurr. Neither the collector nor the Consortium bears any responsibility for the analysis presented here.
3 Our design for estimating the models has been quite simple. First we included all the potentially relevant explanatory variables in the model (the original model). Second, another model (the modified model) has been estimated that includes the democracy index together with those variables that meet the criteria of statistical significance at a reasonable level, that is that the t-statistics should roughly be +/– 2 or larger. This adds up to a total of sixteen models estimated, since they are applied to two measures of economic growth and four measures of democracy; only two of them were reported in detail in table 3.5.

APPENDIX OF STATISTICAL TERMS

OLS = Ordinary Least Squares estimates, which amount to a method for determining the parameters in a regression equation, including the regression coefficient B, by means of estimators that minimize the sum of squares of deviation of the observed scores from the linear equation.

Correlation = The extent to which two or more properties (variables) are related ('co-related') to one another, which is expressed as a correlation coefficient.

Correlation coefficient = A number showing the degree to which two variables are related. Such coefficients range from −1.0 to +1.0. If there is a perfect negative correlation (−1.0) between A and B, whenever A is high, B is low, and vice versa. If there is a perfect positive correlation (+1.0) between A and B, whenever one is high or low, so is the other. A correlation coefficient of 0 means that there is no relationship between the variables.

Pearson's Correlation Coefficient = Pearson's product-moment correlation coefficient, Pearson's r. The statistic shows the degree of linear relationship between two variables measured on interval or ratio scales.

r = Symbol for a Pearson's correlation which is a bivariate correlation (between two variables).

R = Symbol for a multiple of the between-group variance to the within-group variance.

R^2 = The 'R-squared' symbol stands for a coefficient of multiple determination between a dependent variable and two or more independent variables.

Adjusted R^2 = An R-squared adjusted to give a true (smaller) estimate of how much the independent variable in a regression analysis explains the dependent variable. The adjustment is made by taking into account the number of independent variables.

Eta-squared (E^2) = The ratio of explained to unexplained variance in an analysis of variance, that is, the ratio of the between-group variance to the within-group variance. The higher the Eta squared score, the larger the between-group variation is and the smaller the within-group variation.

Between-Group Differences = Usually contrasted to differences within the groups.

Mean = The average. To get the mean, one adds up the values for each case and then divides the total by the number of cases. Often symbolized as M.

Regression analysis = Methods of explaining or predicting the variability of a dependent variable using information about one or two more independent variables. Regression analysis asks: 'What values in the dependent variable can we expect given certain values of the independent variable(s)?'

B = Regression coefficient indicating the values of a dependent variable associated with the values of an independent variable or variables. A regression coefficient is part of a regression equation.

Beta coefficient = It indicates the difference in a dependent variable associated with an increase (or decrease) of one standard deviation in an independent variable when controlling for the effects of other variables, called the standardized regression coefficient or beta weight.

Significance = The degree to which a research finding is meaningful or important.

Significance level = The probability of making a Type I Error, or incorrectly concluding that two variables are related when they in fact are not. The lower the probability, the higher the statistical significance.

t-test = A test statistic, also used to test the significance of correlation coefficients and regression coefficients. The higher the t-statistic, the higher the statistical significance.

N = Number of case studies (for example, countries or states).

REFERENCES

Adelman, I. and Morris, C. T. 1967: *Society, Politics and Economic Development*. Baltimore: Johns Hopkins University Press.
Alexeev, M. and Gaddy, C. G. 1993: Income Distribution in the USSR in the 1980s. *Review of Income and Wealth*, 39, 23–36.
Arat, Z. F. 1991: *Democracy and Human Rights in Developing Countries*. Boulder, Colo.: Lynne Rienner.
Banks, D. L. 1989: Patterns of Oppression: An Exploratory Analysis of Human-rights Data. *Journal of the American Statistical Association*, 84, 674–81.
Barrett, D. B. (ed.) 1982: *World Christian Encyclopaedia: A Comparative Study of Churches and Religions in the Modern World*, AD 1900–2000. Nairobi: Oxford University Press.
Barro, R. J. 1991: Economic Growth in a Cross Section of Countries. *Quarterly Journal of Economics*, 56, 407–43.
Barsh, R. L. 1992: Democratization and Development. *Human Rights Quarterly*, 14, 120–34.

Barsh, R. L. 1993: Measuring Human Rights: Problems of Methodology and Purpose. *Human Rights Quarterly*, 15, 87–121.

Black, C. 1966: *The Dynamics of Modernization*. New York: Harper and Row.

Bollen, K. A. 1979: Political Democracy and the Timing of Development. *American Sociological Review*, 44, 572–87.

Bollen, K. A. 1980: Issues in the Comparative Measurement of Political Democracy. *American Sociological Review*, 45, 370–90.

Bollen, K. A. 1986: Political Rights and Political Liberties in Nations: An Evaluation of Human Rights Measures, 1950 to 1984. *Human Rights Quarterly*, 8, 567–91.

Bollen, K. A. 1990: Political Democracy: Conceptual and Measurement Traps. *Studies in Comparative International Development*, 25, 7–24.

Bollen, K. A. 1993: Liberal Democracy: Validity and Method Factors in Cross-national Measures. *American Journal of Political Science*, 37, 1207–30.

Bollen, K. A. and Jackman, R. W. 1985: Political Democracy and the Size Distribution of Income. *American Sociological Review*, 50, 438–57.

Bollen, K. A. and Jackman, R. W. 1989: Democracy, Stability and Dichotomies. *American Sociological Review*, 54, 612–21.

Coppedge, M. and Reinicke, W. H. 1990: Measuring Polyarchy. *Studies in Comparative International Development*, 25, 51–72.

Cutright, P. 1963: National Political Development: Measurement and Analysis. *American Sociological Review*, 28, 253–64.

Dahl, R. A. 1971: *Polyarchy: Participation and Opposition*. New Haven, Conn.: Yale University Press.

Dasgupta, P. and Weale, M. 1992: On Measuring the Quality of Life. *World Development*, 20, 119–31.

Diamond, L. 1992: Economic Development and Democracy Reconsidered. *American Behavioral Scientist*, 35, 450–99.

Doyal, L. and Gough, I. 1991: *A Theory of Human Need*. Basingstoke: Macmillan.

Freedom House 1992: *Freedom in the World: Political Rights and Civil Liberties 1991–1992*. New York: Freedom House.

Freedom House 1993: The Comparative Survey of Freedom: 1993. *Freedom Review*, 24, 1, 3–22.

Gastil, R. D. 1987: *Freedom in the World: Political Rights and Civil Liberties 1986–1987*. New York: Greenwood Press.

Gastil R. D. 1990: The Comparative Survey of Freedom: Experiences and Suggestions. *Studies in Comparative International Development*, 25, 25–50.

Grier, K. B. and Tullock, G. 1989: An Empirical Analysis of Cross-national Economic Growth, 1951–80. *Journal of Monetary Economics*, 24, 259–76.

Gurr, T. R. 1990: *Polity II: Political Structures and Regime change, 1800–1986* [Computer file]. Boulder, Colo.: Center for Comparative Politics [producer], 1989. Ann Arbor, MI: Inter-university Consortium for Political and Social Research [distributor], 1990.

Hadenius, A. 1992: *Democracy and Development*. Cambridge: Cambridge University Press.

Hewitt, C. 1977: The Effect of Political Democracy and Social Democracy on Equality in Industrial Societies: a cross-national comparison. *American Sociological Review*, 42, 450–64.

Humana, C. 1983: *World Human Rights Guide*. London: Hutchinson.
Humana, C. 1986: *World Human Rights Guide*. London: Economist Publications.
Humana, C. 1992: *World Human Rights Guide*. New York: Oxford University Press.
Huntington, S. P. 1991: *The Third Wave: Democratization in the Late Twentieth Century*. Norman: University of Oklahoma Press.
Inkeles, A. 1993: Industrialization, Modernization and the Quality of Life. *International Journal of Comparative Sociology*, 34, 1–23.
Jackman, R. W. 1974: Political Democracy and Social Equality: A Comparative Analysis. *American Sociological Review*, 39, 29–45.
Jackman, R. W. 1975: *Politics and Social Equality: A Comparative Analysis*. New York: Wiley.
Kormendi, R. C. and Meguire, P. G. 1985: Macroeconomic Determinants of Growth: Cross-country Evidence. *Journal of Monetary Economics*, 16, 141–63.
Kuznets, S. 1955: Economic Growth and Income Inequality. *American Economic Review*, 45, 18–25.
Leftwich, A. 1993: Governance, Democracy and Development in the Third World. *Third World Quarterly*, 14, 605–24.
Lerner, D. 1958: *The Passing of Traditional Society: Modernizing the Middle East*. New York: Free Press.
Levine, R. and Renelt, D. 1992: A Sensitivity Analysis of Cross-country Growth Regressions. *American Economic Review*, 82, 942–63.
Lind, N. C. 1993: A Compound Index of National Development. *Social Indicators Research*, 28, 267–84.
Lipset, S. M. 1959: Some Social Requisites of Democracy: economic development and political development. *American Political Science Review*, 53, 69–105.
Lipset, S. M. 1960: *Political Man: the Social Base of Politics*. Garden City, NY: Doubleday.
Lipset, S. M. Seong, K.-Y. and Torres, J. C. 1993: A Comparative Analysis of the Social Requisites of Democracy. *International Social Science Journal*, 45, 2, 155–75.
Mankiw, N. G. et al. 1992: A Contribution to the Empirics of Economic Growth. *Quarterly Journal of Economics*, 57, 407–37.
Morris, M. D. 1979: *Measuring the Conditions of the World's Poor: the Physical. Quality of Life Index*. New York: Pergamon Press.
Muller, E. N. 1988: Democracy, Economic Development, and Income Inequality. *American Sociological Review*, 53, 50–68.
Myrdal, G. 1957: *Economic Theory and Underdeveloped Regions*. London: Duckworth.
Myrdal, G. 1968: *Asian Drama*, 3 vols. New York: Pantheon.
Neubauer, D. 1967: Some Conditions of Democracy. *American Political Science Review*, 61, 1002–9.
Olson, M. 1982: *The Rise and Decline of Nations: Economic Growth, Stagflation and Social Rigidities*. New Haven, Conn.: Yale University Press.
Olson, M. 1990: *How Bright are the Northern Lights?* Lund: School of Management.
Olson, M. 1993: Dictatorship, Democracy, and Development. *American Political Science Review*, 87, 567–76.
Perry, C. S. 1980: Political Contestations in Nations: 1960, 1963, 1967 and 1970. *Journal of Political and Military Sociology*, 8, 161–74.

Pourgerami, A. 1988: The Political Economy of Development: A Cross-national Causality Test of the Development-democracy-growth Hypothesis. *Public Choice*, 58, 123–41.

Przeworski, A. 1992: The Neoliberal Fallacy. *Journal of Democracy*, 3, 3, 45–59.

Przeworski, A. and Limongi, F. 1993: Political Regimes and Economic Growth. *Journal of Economic Perspectives*, 7, 51–69.

Riggs, F. W. 1984: Development. In Sartori, G. (ed.) *Social Science Concepts: A Systematic Analysis*. Beverly Hills, Cal.: Sage, 125–203.

Rueschemeyer, D., Stephens, E. H. and Stephens, J. D. 1992: *Capitalist Development and Democracy*. Cambridge: Polity Press.

Scully, G. W. 1988: The Institutional Framework of Economic Development. *Journal of Political Economy*, 96, 652–62.

Scully, G. W. 1992: *Constitutional Environments and Economic Growth*. Princeton, NJ: Princeton University Press.

Scully, G. W. and Slottje, D. J. 1991: Ranking Economic Liberty Across Countries. *Public Choice*, 69, 121–52.

Simpson, M. 1990: Political Rights and Income Inequality: A Cross-national Test. *American Sociological Review*, 55, 682–93.

Sirowy, L. and Inkeles, A. 1990: The Effects of Democracy on Economic Growth and Inequality: A Review. *Studies in Comparative International Development*, 25, 126–57.

Slottje, D. J. 1991a: Measuring the Quality of Life Across Countries. *Review of Economics and Statistics*, 73, 6, 84–93.

Slottje, D. J. et al. 1991b: *Measuring the Quality of Life Across Countries: A Multidimensional Analysis*. Boulder, Colo.: Westview Press.

Smith, A. K. 1969: Socio-economic Development and Political Democracy: A Causal Analysis. *Midwest Journal of Political Science*, 13, 95–125.

Sorensen, G. 1992: *Democracy and Authoritarianism: Consequences for Economic Development*. Aarhus: Institute of Political Science.

Spindler, Z. A. 1991: Liberty and Development: A Further Empirical Perspective. *Public Choice*, 69, 197–210.

Summers, R. and Heston, A. 1988: A New Set of International Comparisons of Real Product and Price Levels Estimates for 130 Countries, 1950–1985. *Review of Income and Wealth*, 34, 1–25.

Terlouw, C. P. 1989: World-system Theory and Regional Geography: A Preliminary Exploration of the Context of Regional Geography. *Tijdschrift voor Economische en Sociale Geografie*, 80, 206–21.

United Nations Development Programme (UNDP) 1990: *Human Development Report 1990*. New York: Oxford University Press.

United Nations Development Programme (UNDP) 1991: *Human Development Report 1991*. New York: Oxford University Press.

United Nations Development Programme (UNDP) 1993: *Human Development Report 1993*. New York: Oxford University Press.

Vanhanen, T. 1990: *The Process of Democratization: a Comparative Study of 147 States, 1980–88*. New York: Crane Russak.

Vanhanen, T. 1992: *Strategies of Democratization*. Washington: Crane Russak.

Vorhies, F. and Glahe, F. 1988: Political Liberty and Social Development: An Empirical Investigation. *Public Choice*, 58, 45–71.

Weede, E. 1983: The Impact of Democracy on Economic Growth: Some Evidence from Cross-national Analysis. *Kyklos*, 36, 21–39.

Weede, E. 1993: The Impact of Democracy or Repressiveness on the Quality of Life, Income Distribution and Economic Growth Rates. *International Sociology*, 8, 177–95.

Wittman, D. 1989: Why Democracies Produce Efficient Results. *Journal of Political Economy*, 97, 1395–424.

World Bank 1983: *World Tables*. 3rd edn, Baltimore: Johns Hopkins University Press.

World Bank 1991a: *World Development Report 1991*. New York: Oxford University Press.

World Bank 1991b: *Social Indicators of Development 1990*. Baltimore: Johns Hopkins University Press.

4

Governance, Democracy and Development: A Contractualist View

GEOFFREY HAWTHORN AND PAUL SEABRIGHT

INTRODUCTION

The existence of an international financial system with the capacity for good and bad effects of a major kind on the lives of the citizens of sovereign states, but whose agents are not directly accountable to those citizens, has throughout the post-war period posed a problem – politically, legally and ethically – for the sovereignty of states that has underpinned the international order. The problem has been especially acute for those institutions such as the International Monetary Fund (IMF) and the World Bank that have been established by governments to pursue public rather than entrepreneurial goals. From its inception the IMF has imposed conditions on its lending to member states to limit these states' freedom to pursue independent macroeconomic policies. The World Bank has (like any bank) imposed conditions on the projects to which it lends. More significantly, since the 1980s it has also imposed conditions on the sectoral and macroeconomic policies of its borrower countries. These conditions have until recently been presented as strictly economic in character, not impinging on the social policy or the more general political discretion of borrowers. But a sharp distinction between economic and social policy has always been difficult to sustain. Since the later 1980s (especially since the end of the Cold War) the World Bank, like the aid agencies of individual governments, has come under pressure to concern itself more directly with social and political conditions in borrower countries. And the new European Bank for Reconstruction and Development (EBRD), established in 1990 to assist ex-communist countries in central and Eastern Europe, has actually had the promotion of liberal democracy written into its charter. How should the international institutions and borrower governments react to these developments?

In this paper we shall be concerned with four aspects of this problem. Our first question is: are international financial institutions justified in seeking to influence social and political conditions in formally sovereign states? Granted that some such influence will always be exercised, should the institutions nevertheless seek to minimize its extent? Or should they deliberately wield it to further certain ends? We shall consider only those international institutions established to serve public ends, but what we say may have implications for the question of whether restrictions should be put on the behaviour of private international banks whose actions also have significant effects on the citizens of sovereign states. Second, if there is a justification for trying to influence sovereign states, what should such influence seek to achieve? Third, how are the answers to these questions affected by the lack of direct accountability of the institutions concerned? Fourth, if, as we believe, influence on the 'internal affairs' of sovereign states can sometimes be justified, how might this affect the principle of national sovereignty?

CONSEQUENCES OR CONTRACTS?

That national sovereignty is no longer so widely assumed always to trump any reason that an external agency might have to influence social and political conditions in sovereign states owes much to the end of the dual superpower structure that characterized the Cold War (though not only to that, as we discuss below). This structure, held in place by nuclear weapons, meant that the United States and the Soviet Union had to find other means with which to pursue their rivalry. One of these was to seek client states. This led the superpowers to put the stability of such clients before any consideration of how far the governments of these states represented the wishes of their citizens. And the governments themselves had an interest in resisting the use of the policies of international agencies for such rivalrous ends. They were protected by their patrons, and suspected that to be subject to politicized international agencies might serve to increase the influence of the rival superpower. Those that wanted to remain unaligned would find doing so more difficult if they were to be subject to political pressure from the international bodies. These considerations, together with the near impossibility of distinguishing attempts in good faith to influence a country's internal affairs for the better from covert subversion (and the fact that both the United States and the Soviet Union often used humanitarian aid as a cover for such activities), made all parties wish the multilateral agencies to be formally committed to an apolitical stance. Decolonization had also made many in the South unwilling to allow former colonizers to continue to exercise their influence by other means. And a certain post-war optimism about the possibility of a technocratic approach to economic policy formulation encouraged a belief in the possibility of apolitical international institutions. Even those who were inclined to criticize the IMF and World Bank as an extension of colonialism by other means did so on the understanding that it was possible to envisage an international economic order in which national sovereignty was respected.

All this has changed. The end of the Cold War, as well as the evident nastiness of many of the regimes that benefited from it, has undermined the prudential justification for treating national sovereignty as trumping other considerations. Fading memories of colonization have weakened the disposition to accept that previously colonial territories should have an unconditional right to determine their own affairs, all the more so as it has become clear how few of the populations of these new states have been able to decide the fate of their governments. Olympian technocracy has been dethroned by a more justly cynical view of policy-making. And an increasing economic interdependence, dissolving the fantasy of insulation from the world economy, has made it plain that if the influence on the internal affairs of sovereign states is not managed well, it will be managed badly. Nevertheless, even if 'de-linking', as it was sometimes called in third world circles, has now been discredited by many in the South itself, national sovereignty, as one value among others, has not been (or not self-evidently). Its proper place is our final question.

In addition to the changes in the economic and political environment in which the international financial institutions operate, there have in recent years been changes also in the intellectual foundations of thinking about the responsibilities of public policy-making. The technocratic conception of the actions of the state was grounded in an essentially utilitarian approach to public action. The goal of such action was taken to be the maximization of some (perhaps weighted) sum of individual welfares.[1] Such a view has made it difficult to understand the asymmetry of duties implied by claims of national sovereignty. To be sure, national governments have often been in a better position to influence the lives of their citizens than external agencies. But when external agencies do have an influence, a utilitarian approach to public action will require them to use it to enhance the sum of individual welfares. Paradoxically, therefore, the heyday of national sovereignty since 1945 has coincided with a philosophy of the state in which the idea of such sovereignty was all but unintelligible.

The influence of utilitarianism has declined in recent years (Sen and Williams, 1982). As part cause and part effect of this process, there has been a renewed interest in alternative conceptions of ethical and political responsibility: in particular in a number of more or less contractualist theories – of the foundations of ethics (Scanlon, 1982), of substantive conceptions of justice (Rawls, 1971) and, in a more applied context, of the role of the state in economic development (Dasgupta, 1993). Such theories base obligations to act upon some actual or hypothetical relation between the parties rather than solely on the consequences of the actions concerned. They accordingly provide a rationale for the view that the duties of a state to its citizens may differ from those of an external agency for reasons more fundamental than the pragmatic ones of proximity and information. By providing an account of the duties of the state to its citizens, they also, as we shall suggest, provide a way of thinking about the legitimacy of external influence upon the state's discharge of those duties. And since a contractualist conception allows for the domain of public action to be less than the whole sphere of human welfare and concern, it opens the way for pluralism, in the sense of delimiting a sphere of public policy that is compatible with widely varying conceptions of the good life, and which need not therefore involve an imposition of one set of cultural values on all citizens (Seabright, 1993).[2]

This is not to claim that contractualism is the metaphysically most attractive foundation for ethics or that it can ground a comprehensive moral theory. It is merely to say that where, as in the international relations of development, no moral framework exists, contractualism is consistent with one's minimal intuitions about what such a framework requires, and suggests the obligation that it could impose.[3]

THE CONTRACT TO DEVELOP

States, we suggest, exist to enhance the benefits of cooperation between their citizens. This is to say that their justification – as distinct from their explanation, which is far more complex – is to regulate and perhaps also to institute kinds of cooperation that citizens could not (or could not so effectively) regulate or institute themselves. What these are will depend on the condition of the country and the prevailing political opinion within it. The governments of all modern states accept that they are responsible for organizing the security of the state itself and, in principle, that of its citizens also. All accept also, in principle, that they have some responsibility for arranging education and health. Many have taken a degree of responsibility for other matters, for communications, for instance, for information (especially radio and television), for aspects of cultural life and for one or other of the conditions of effective production, distribution and trade. Occasionally, states will meet all the costs of cooperation from their own revenue; more often, they require the citizens to supplement these costs. The more benefits of cooperation that a state can provide, the more 'developed' it is. For this reason we also suggest that those international institutions that are charged with 'development' exist to help governments provide such benefits. By extension, therefore, an international institution of this kind can be seen to have an implicit contract with a borrower state in the same way in which and for the same reason as a state has a contract with its citizens.

This contract can be understood in one or other of three ways. In the first, the international institution can be seen to have a contract solely with the government of a borrower state. In this case, it is for the institution and the government in question to agree on whatever conditions for a loan they have a mind to. In the second, the institution can be seen to have a contract with the government of the borrower state in the latter's capacity as the representative of the citizens of that state. In this case, it is for the lending institution and the citizens (or a majority of the citizens) of the borrowing state to agree on whatever conditions these parties have a mind to. In the third, the international institution can be seen to have a contract with the government in question as the agency responsible for enhancing the benefits of cooperation within the borrower state. In this case, agreement between the two will depend on whether either has good reason to dispute that this condition, and this condition only, is met.

This is, to be sure, very general. But it does discriminate. Since the Bretton Woods Act, the international financial institutions have standardly been concerned with outcomes, have usually had clear ideas about how the outcomes they want can be achieved and have tried to avoid questions of politics. In principle, they have been consequentialist. In practice, however, they have proposed an implicit contract. This has been to support a potential recipient if and only if that government agrees to implement a specified set of policies. This has been a contract of the first of our three kinds: with a government itself, rather than with the citizens of the state it governs or with government as an agent of social cooperation. An increasing number of bilaterals, however, together with the EBRD and the more established international institutions, now require outcomes to be realized under explicitly political conditions. These ask the government of the recipient state to accept what the West thinks of as 'democratic' rules of rule.[4] This would seem to be a contract of the second kind: with a borrower government in its capacity as the representative of the wishes of its citizens. Or at least, it would seem to be a contract of this kind unless the institutions are assuming that it is only under democratic rules of rule that the benefits of social cooperation can be enhanced. If this is so – if enhancing the benefits of social cooperation is the institution's ultimate end – the contract is of the third kind.

As they stand, however, none of these three kinds of contract is well grounded. If the contract is solely with the government, rather than with the government as the representative of the citizens' preferences or the agent of social cooperation, it is perfectly possible for the two parties to agree on policies which serve the purposes of each but which do not do as much as could (in the circumstances) be done to enhance the benefits of social cooperation. This would also seem to be the case if the contract is with the government as the representative of the citizens' preferences. Such preferences, as Sunstein explains, are 'shifting and endogenous rather than exogenous, are ... a function of current information, consumption patterns, legal rules, and general social pressures', and are not therefore prior to politics (Sunstein, 1991: 10). The citizens, to put it simply, may either not know their own best interests or not be in a position to articulate them. And if the contract is with the government as the agent of social cooperation, the conditions that the international institutions have been minded to impose in the later 1980s and 1990s may be unacceptably pre-emptive. This is more likely to be true, as we explain later, of conditions other than those of a strictly banking kind. It is most likely to be true of political conditions. A borrower government and the citizens it serves may be able reasonably to claim that (in the circumstances) the benefits of cooperation are not best enhanced by a competitive multi-party democracy of the kind that those who guide the international institutions (mostly Americans and West Europeans) now have firmly in mind.

Such denials exist. President Mobutu, for instance, like other African leaders, has persistently claimed that to allow competitive democracy in Zaïre would be to license disorder. The claim may be strained; like President Moi's in Kenya in 1992, it has certainly been self-serving. But in the years after the civil war in what was then Congo-Kinshasa between 1960 and 1965, indeed until the late 1970s, it was not self-evidently absurd. Likewise, factional disputes within the Democratic Party in the short-lived but politically more open Second Republic in South Korea in 1960–1 made it impossible for Prime Minister Chang to form stable cabinets and govern effectively, and thereby made it easier for army officers to justify the coup that they had initially planned against Syngman Rhee before the First Republic fell (by other hands) in 1960. Exploiting the discredit into which political competition had fallen under Chang, the soldiers made a tacit bargain with the citizens to forsake open democratic competition in favour of security and prosperity. Certainly, one can argue that the risks of competitive electoral politics were in each case overstated. The conflict in Congo-Kinshasa was exacerbated by the fact that the United States and the Soviet Union decided to contest each other there. Internal rebellions continued to erupt until 1967, and Zaïrean exiles invaded economically important areas of the south in 1977 and again in 1978. The United States continued until the late 1980s to see Mobutu as crucial to their policy in southwestern Africa. Yet it is possible that the conviction in Washington that the choice was 'Mobutu or chaos' was exaggerated. In Korea, Chang did manage to secure the redirection of economic policy on which the subsequent success of the Park regime depended, and given that success, it might in retrospect seem that there was no reason why, with political will and some skill, the country could not have moved more quickly than it did to democracy.

These, however, are the judgements of hindsight. It is much less easy persuasively to claim, looking forward from Kinshasa in 1978, let alone 1965, or from Seoul in the early 1970s, let alone 1961, that open political competition would have been practicable. In each country, the United States was usually pleased to agree with the ruling group that external and internal security was at a premium. And what experiments in democracy there had been in each country had proved self-defeating.[5]

By the later 1980s, however, the world, the West believed, had changed. External threats (real or imagined) to the integrity of most nation-states had disappeared, and governments predicated on 'national security' were no longer thought to be defensible. In many parts of the post-Cold War world, including most of central and Eastern Europe, this may have been correct. But internally generated disorder, or the threat of such disorder, is still widespread: in the former Yugoslavia, in the republics of the former Soviet Union, in Turkey, Iraq, Afghanistan, India, Sri Lanka, Myanmar (Burma), Cambodia, Indonesia, Guatemala, the Dominican Republic, Peru and throughout much of Africa from Algeria to Angola. If Przeworski is correct, that democracy is about the rules of rule, not outcomes, and that competing parties will only accept defeat by such rules if they can be sure that those in power will continue to observe them and allow the chance of victory in the future (1991: 26–34); if Schumpeter also was right, that a 'democratic government will work to full advantage only if all the interests that matter are practically unanimous not only in their allegiance to the country but also in the allegiance to the structural principles of the existing society' (1950: 296); then it may be asking too much of governments (or indeed citizens) in the circumstances that prevail in such places readily to endorse rules of this kind.

Instability, disorder and insecurity, moreover, are not incidental to the course of development itself. In its earlier stages, which are often prolonged, development is uneven. It disproportionately benefits one sector, class or region, and actively disbenefits others. It exacerbates old divisions and excites new ones. It can indeed be pursued, and sometimes has been, as a tacit civil war. It requires decisions about how to allocate (or more painfully to reallocate) existing assets and new resources. For this reason, and because such decisions, to be effective, require action over the long term, they are not always best arrived at by governments which have to subject themselves to competition in regular elections or to acknowledge established interests and compromise with them. Such decisions may be better taken outside the arenas of open political contest altogether. If it is possible to argue that a government in a non-democratic regime is in the medium or long run enhancing the benefits of social cooperation, it may not make sense for donors to insist that it open itself to political defeat. The demands of financial stabilization and structural adjustment, in which heads of state and ministers of finance have been asked by the donors to assume exceptional powers, are the most recent cases in point.[6] Even if a government is governing under a formally democratic constitution, and thus acceptable to those international institutions for whom constitutional democracy is a desirable pre-condition, it can work its constitution in such a way as to stay in power without effective opposition. Yet the benefits of its rule may be sufficiently promising to justify external support. This might now be said both of some of the new states in central and Eastern Europe (Ascherson, 1992a, 1992b) and of many of those in the south. In Mexico, for instance, where despite the vigour of its other reforms and its endorsement of the North American Free Trade Agreement in 1993, the ruling group is still resisting pressure to open the Institutional Party of the Revolution to open competition. It might be said also of Japan and Singapore, of South Korea since 1990 and of the two Chinese republics as many of their citizens, as well as their political classes, would like them to be. If, moreover, there is anything in the argument that overcoming the unevennesses of early 'development' is itself a pre-condition for a publicly competitive politics, support for a non-democratic regime may in time produce what is, to democrats, a more acceptable one.

What we are suggesting, in short, is that the international institutions exist to help states enhance the benefits of social cooperation between their citizens. Donors and recipients can accordingly be seen to be parties to a contract to enhance such benefits. Each party may reasonably ask the other to consider conditions it believes to be conducive to this end, and some of these conditions may be political. But since there is no necessary connection between what can reasonably be said to be a necessary (or indeed sufficient) condition of social cooperation and an openly competitive multi-party politics, donors have no reason to claim that this kind of 'democracy' is an essential condition of their assistance. Some kind and degree of democracy may be desirable for other reasons, but under the contract we here suggest between donors and borrower states, these are not the donors' concern.

ACCOUNTABILITY

How are the arguments we have advanced affected by the accountability or lack of accountability of the international financial institutions themselves to the citizens whose lives they affect? To be sure,
institutions such as the IMF and the World Bank are not entirely
autonomous. They are subject to the control of boards of directors
appointed by their principal shareholders, in this case the political
authorities of the main industrial countries. These authorities enjoy
voting rights in proportion to their shareholdings. To a first approx-
imation, therefore, we can say that the accountability of the institutions is that of an ordinary bank. This is subject to the qualification
that the IMF and the World Bank's shareholders, being political authorities, exercise their rights not on their own behalf but on that of
the citizens whose taxes they appropriate. The accountability to the
ultimate shareholders may be indirect and imperfect; but since many
shareholders even in ordinary banks are themselves financial institutions, pension funds, for instance, and unit trusts (mutual funds)
exercising their rights on behalf of clients whose portfolios they manage, this contrast should not be exaggerated.

Whether this accountability is adequate is therefore a question to
be addressed in several stages. First, are ordinary banks accountable
enough for the exercise of their banking functions? Second, in so far
as institutions like the IMF and World Bank perform such functions,
are there any significant differences (in their size, for instance) that
might warrant their being held more or differently accountable from
ordinary banks? Third, and most important, to what extent do these
institutions perform their functions differently from those of banks,
and to what extent should they? In particular, do the arguments we
have suggested for exercising an influence on the internal affairs of
sovereign states suggest that this influence should be exercised through
institutions that also perform certain banking functions? And what
do these arguments also suggest for the nature and degree of accountability of instititions that exercise such influence?

Are ordinary banks accountable enough? They are, like any other
legal company, formally accountable to shareholders. Through the
normal provisions of bankruptcy legislation, they are accountable also
to their creditors. But there are two practical differences between the
accountability of banks to their creditors and that of ordinary non-
bank firms. The first is that banks, unlike non-bank firms, typically
have large numbers of dispersed small creditors (the depositors).
They are likely to face significant problems of collective action in
organizing to represent their interests (akin to those of small shareholders in non-bank firms). The other is that because there is a fear
of systemic banking crises, in which actual or rumoured problems
of solvency at one bank cause liquidity crises at other healthy institutions, political authorities in almost all countries have been more

heavily involved in the regulation of the banking system than in the regulation of non-bank firms. This has taken the form of various kinds of crisis intervention (lender-of-last-resort facilities, deposit insurance, *ad hoc* rescue operations of various kinds), as well as of *ex ante* regulation of banks' behaviour – the latter designed primarily to alleviate the distorted incentives, what theorists call the 'moral hazards', caused by the former.

Banks are not, however, accountable to their borrowers except through the law of contract. Nor, for that matter, are other firms in a private-ownership economy liable to their customers except through the law of contract. One can say that the law of contract is the mechanism of accountability of firms to the parties with whom they transact. This position is a little simple, of course, since the law of contract is heavily qualified in many economies, at least with regard to labour transactions. Arguments for qualifying the law of contract in this way (that is, for setting restrictions on the kinds of contract between consenting parties that the state will honour) usually rest on the position of dependence that can result between partners to a transaction that continues over time, and the highly unequal bargaining position of the partners in such a position (management and labour, for example, in an employment relation that can last many years). There are certainly analogies with credit relations: the threat to foreclose can place a borrower in a weak position where there is significant collateral at stake. For our purposes, however, there is no need to ask whether appropriate means of redress are to be found in legal safeguards to a relation that remains essentially contractual, or in some more formal mechanism of accountability of firms to those with whom they transact. International sovereign debt differs from private debt in that there is no collateral at stake, and the issue of unequal bargaining does not therefore arise. (Or at least, it does not arise in this form.) The reason why sovereign borrowers can find themselves under great pressure to repay previous loans is that they fear loss of access to loans in the future. Their claim to a right of control over lending institutions, which is based on the effects on them of decisions taken by these institutions, is therefore on a par with that of all potential future borrowers.[7] And it must be said that it would be hard to find reasons why firms in a private-ownership economy should be formally accountable to their potential customers.

In so far therefore as the international financial institutions act as banks, there is no case for their being subject to a greater or different form of accountability than that provided by the system of contract law. But even as banks, these institutions are unusual. In the first place, they are larger. Their decisions to lend or not accordingly have more impact on the welfare of those to whom they lend. Also, they have been set up not to transact the same kind of business as orthodox banks, but to lend in precisely those areas where loans can be expected to be worth undertaking from the point of view of social welfare but where they might not be attractive to private lenders: that is, where loans are large or very risky; where the greater clout of the international institutions acts as a stronger incentive against wilful default; where environmental or other externalities lead to a divergence between private and social rates of return; where the possible impact on poverty makes them worthwhile even if their profitability in an accounting sense is marginal.[8] One can think of the mandate of such institutions as analogous to that of a regulatory agency within a nation-state, charged with alleviating some of the failings of the operation of the private enterprise economy and answerable to government for its discharge of that mandate.

The relationship of regulatory agencies to government (and the pressures that a government will usually have to take into account) raises complex issues. In recent years, in contrast to the older 'public interest' view of regulation, there has been much emphasis on the dangers of the 'capture' of regulatory agencies by special interests (Noll, 1989; Neven, Nuttall and Seabright, 1993; Laffont, 1993). Older studies tended to emphasize the risk of capture by the regulated enterprises themselves. But it has more recently been appreciated that capture can take many forms, including subservience to short-term political pressures or to organized lobbies other than those of the owners and managers of the enterprises themselves. The obvious remedy for capture in industry and analogous enterprises, that is to say an increased degree of political scrutiny, may be less effective against other forms of capture, and may even represent the oversight of one captured institution by another. Where the risks of political short-termism are especially severe, there are attractions in a degree of independence for regulatory agencies: not a complete insulation from the political process but rather a formal 'arms-length' relationship which ensures that political scrutiny is undertaken at intervals and according to well-defined criteria rather than continuously according to the day-to-day pressures of lobbying. (This has become increasingly popular in recent years as a prescription for central banks.) The principal advantage of a greater independence is that it increases the credibility of the agency's commitment to a consistent policy by discouraging efforts by special interests to subvert that policy.

The relationship of borrower countries to the IMF and World Bank has sometimes echoed these concerns. For instance, while many of the conditions imposed on borrowers have been perceived as genuinely irksome, conditionality has sometimes been welcomed by some elements in its government as enhancing the credibility of a reform programme that they would have wished to undertake anyway. This has, not surprisingly, been especially true of finance ministries. Even without conditionality, the fact that the World Bank has undertaken project lending that requires systematic cost-benefit analysis has imposed a kind of discipline on spending decisions that has not always been unwelcome in the borrower countries.[9] To the extent that this is true, is it systematically explicable by the kinds of consideration about regulatory capture that we have mentioned? And is there any evidence that greater accountability to borrower countries would undermine this beneficial effect?

To simplify, a degree of independence from day-to-day politics for a regulatory agency (and by extension, for a body charged with alleviating some of the failures of·a private banking system) is most likely to be desirable under one or other of two conditions: when the task required of the agency can be monitored with reasonable accuracy at periodic intervals rather than requiring continuous oversight of procedures; and when those who are in day-to-day control of the agency have interests that will lead them naturally to implement the desired policy for the agency. What do these conditions imply in the context of the international financial institutions? For the borrower countries to benefit from not having direct oversight of these institutions, the process of international balance-of-payments and development lending should be one whose overall progress can be reasonably clearly monitored according to aggregate criteria. This may be true up to a point (through the use of overall lending flows, rates of return and so forth), but has evident shortcomings. And it would be necessary for there to be at least periodic accountability to borrower countries if such monitoring were to serve any purpose. Moreover, the interests of those controlling the agency would need to be such as to ensure that the agency did its desired job. In so far as this involves significant orthodox banking functions, the fact that the institutions concerned are accountable in similar ways to ordinary banks makes evident sense. But whether that kind of accountability is adequate to ensure that they take proper account of their responsibility to perform significant non-orthodox functions is harder to say. It is true that the international institutions have in practice been very far from mimicking private sector banks (the fact that multi-lateral lending to sub-Saharan Africa increased in the 1980s when private lending dried up is a case in point). But it may still be argued (it has been conceded by the president of the World Bank itself) that these institutions have not been as responsible as they could have been to their non-traditional functions: to the distributional and other social consequences of the conditions they have imposed, for example, to their environmental effects, and to the distribution of powers within the borrowing state.

To be sure, existing arrangements must always be evaluated against realistic alternatives. The fact that the governments of many borrower countries are themselves only dubiously accountable to their citizens might mean that increasing the accountability of the international finance institutions to borrower governments does little or nothing to increase their accountability to the citizens of borrower countries (those in whose name the accountability argument has been deployed in the first place). It might also weaken the credibility of their commitment to a consistent and efficient lending policy. Nevertheless, such a reply does at least concede that there are circumstances in which these institutions should be accountable to their borrowers, even if the case is stronger in some cases than in others, and even if the benefits of such an accountability have to be set against potentially significant costs.

This leads naturally to the third issue, which is to what extent the international financial institutions do or should perform functions quite different from those of banks: channel foreign aid, for instance. (The exercise of social and political conditionality is clearly not at all a banking function.) The World Bank's soft loans affiliate, for example, the International Development Association (IDA), makes loans which contain strong implicit grant elements. It is clear that some bilateral donors (including Japan, which is now the most generous) prefer to channel some of their aid through the multi-lateral institutions in this way because they believe the money will be 'better spent' (though it is also clear that some bilateral donors – often the same ones – also like to tie their bilateral aid to spending on their own goods and services, whether or not this answers effectively to the recipient's needs).

To the extent that foreign aid is seen as a gift from one country to another, which the donor is free to spend in any way it wishes and on which it may impose any conditions it wishes, then it would be hard to argue a case for the accountability of whatever institutions were charged with dispensing such aid. To the extent that aid is seen as part of a wider contract to collective international welfare, analogous perhaps to distributive taxation rather than to private charity within states (albeit lacking an explicit mechanism of coercion), then its use as an instrument of conditionality is compromised if the decisions about it are not collectively accountable. And the arguments in favour of limiting the accountability of bodies charged with performing more or less banking functions (on the grounds that these represent relatively technical exercises whose performance can be monitored and which in any case will be most efficiently performed under the scrutiny of lenders who have investments at stake) scarcely extend to the distribution of foreign aid, the purposes of which are less technical, more contestable and more bound up with the expression of collective purpose than those even of development banking. Certainly, it may be desirable to disburse aid according to criteria that parallel those governing the disbursement of loans. It may accordingly be desirable to entrust the disbursement of such aid to bodies that already have experience in managing loans. It may even be true that democratic governments in recipient countries might want to bind the hands of possibly less democratic successors by voting to require the disbursing institutions to release aid only to democratic governments. But, at most, such arguments imply that the disbursement of aid (including the exercise of conditionality) should not be accountable to governments that are not themselves accountable. To the extent that aid and banking may be effectively performed together (there are economies of scope in their exercise, as the jargon has it), these are as much arguments for increasing the accountability of the banking function as for diminishing the accountability of aid.

Foreign aid is more than an unaccountable gift. This much is implicit in our search for a rationale for the exercise of conditionality by donors, since if aid is an unaccountable gift, its exercise as an instrument of conditionality needs no rationale. If that is true of gifts it is true *a fortiori* of investments. Donors who are not troubled by using conditionality to bring about their preferred vision of good government will have neither the need nor the time for the idea that they or their citizens have an implicit contract with the governments or citizens of recipient states. But to the extent that they do wish to ground their actions in the conception of such a contract, they will appreciate that conditionality requires some accountability to the other parties to the contract. There may indeed be arguments for separating off the exercise of the more technical banking functions of the international financial institutions (like the functions of an independent regulatory agency). But these arguments do not extend to the distribution of aid or the exercise of conditionality except in so far as this is directly linked to the exercise of the banking function. The conclusion of our argument in the first part of this paper, that conditionality is an appropriate instrument of international relations, implies either that this conditionality should be exercised by different institutions from those undertaking banking functions, or that there are grounds for increasing the accountability of these institutions.[10]

CONDITIONALITY'S CONDITIONS

This is not to say that the conditions of lending that are suggested by an international institution (or a bilateral donor) must be acceptable to the government of the borrowing state or its citizens. International institutions and states in their role as donors, we are arguing, exist to enhance the capacity of borrower governments to enhance the benefits of social cooperation. This is the implicit contract between the two. If either side has reason to believe that the other is not observing it – if the recipient believes that what the donor is demanding is not likely to enhance those benefits, or if the donor believes that what the recipient is proposing is not likely to do so – it can either withdraw or ask the other to revise its policy.

To withdraw, however, is in the interests of neither side. And it would seem that for a donor to insist that the government of a recipient state revise its policy is to threaten the sovereignty of that state: to threaten, in the common phrase, to 'interfere in its internal affairs'. The phrase is common, but exact. It makes it clear that the threat (if threat it is) is not to the state's very existence, its jurisdiction over its territory and its citizens. It is a threat to one or more of the ways in which those governing the state exercise that jurisdiction. When the principle that guides the modern conception of state sovereignty was first formulated in the negotiations in Westphalia in 1648 to end the Thirty Years War, this distinction was deliberately not drawn. 'Electors, princes and states of the Roman Empire', the agreement affirmed, 'are . . . established and confirmed in their ancient rights, prerogatives, liberties, privileges' and the 'free exercise of territorial right', and 'never can or ought to be molested herein by any whomsoever upon any manner or pretence.' European imperialism later revised that right to apply only to the civilized. In the name of nationalism and democracy, it has subsequently been restored to all. 'All peoples', the United Nations' *Declaration on the Granting of Independence to Colonial Countries and Peoples* put it in 1960, 'have a right to 'self-determination', and no 'inadequacy of political, economic, social or educational preparedness' (let alone, as Europeans once expected, a willingness to accept Christ) should henceforth be a barrier to statehood. But it is increasingly said – not least in the donor countries, which have gone some way towards discharging them for their own citizens – that statehood itself has obligations. The *de jure* right to it carries *de facto* duties.

We have preferred to specify these in a general way. In some circumstances, certain levels of economic prosperity, social security and education (even perhaps certain ways of reaching each of these ends) may be necessary to enhance the benefits of social cooperation. A certain sense of community, call it 'nationhood', and a certain kind and degree of 'democracy' may be necessary too. But as we have said, this last may also in some circumstances not be so. There are many possible views of what it might be to enhance the benefits of cooperation and of how best to do so, and these will depend on the circumstances. For this reason, it seems more sensible to formulate the first duty of the state, and for the international institutions and other donors to formulate their conditions, as means to this most general end. What the means themselves are is an inherently political question. It follows that what they might in any case be should be open to debate and negotiation between the parties concerned. The appropriate criterion in such discussions would therefore be not whether each side accepts what the other proposes, but whether each could not reasonably reject it (Scanlon, 1982). The onus would be on the international institutions (and other donors) reasonably to reject what potential recipients suggest; not, as it is at present, on the recipients to accept what the donors propose. And if these conditions of conditionality were acknowledged, the government of a recipient state would actually be able to exercise more sovereignty, not less, over its 'internal affairs'.

'Good government', in short, and thus good government for development, turns on the will and capacity to enhance what cannot reasonably be denied to be the benefits of social cooperation in the circumstances in question. There may be circumstances, domestic and international, in which such government is consistent with a competitive democracy, as it has been in Venezuela, Botswana and Malaysia. There have been and remain circumstances, those of the politics of Burma before 1962 or Indonesia before 1965, for instance, and in their different ways those of Brazil, Jamaica and Pakistan now, in which it is not. There have been and remain circumstances, those in South Korea until the 1980s, for instance, and possibly those in China and in several sub-Saharan African states now, in which it is more consistent with a regime of a different kind. This is not surprising. The ideal constitution of what would now generally be described as a 'liberal' kind, the corollary of competitive democracy, is one in which, as Montesquieu explained, the two parts of the legislative power (the two assemblies) 'will be chained to each other by their reciprocal faculty of vetoing', and in which 'the two would be bound by the executive power, which will itself be bound by the legislative power'. Its result, Montesquieu himself was pleased to conclude, would be 'rest or inaction' (1989: 162). But inaction is scarcely conducive to development. What a contractualist view allows is an alternative which, unlike a utilitarian consequentialism, does not prejudge what action would lead to, which remains open as to how, once what it should lead to is agreed, it might do so, and remains open also, in a way that some recent arguments for 'good governance' do not (World Bank, 1992: 155), to politics.

One question remains. What if a potential recipient can reasonably be said not to be governing well, and refuses to change? The donor has only two options. One is to turn away, condemning the citizens to a state of affairs that they may find it next to impossible to change. The other is to suspend its conditions and lend anyway. Each is undesirable. At present, however, there is no other. Only if we were to inhabit a world in which all agreed that states had a duty to enhance the benefits of social cooperation between their citizens, a world in which all agreed that any government which did not meet this obligation could justifiably be coerced by others, could we say that the donor should maintain its stance and intervene.[11] Such a world – which on a wholly different view of what was acceptable, the delegates in Westphalia in 1648 were determined to reject – would have its attractions. It would be a world in which it was agreed that what had been wrong with the civilizing mission of imperialism and what some have seen as its neo-imperialist successors was not the idea of a civilizing mission, but imperialism. (It would also have to be a world in which intervention might actually have an effect.) And it would have to be a world, as we have said, in which the donors were themselves accountable. The practice of development, a civilizing mission of a more civilized kind, will be incomplete so long as such accountability does not exist and the interventions it could allow are not accepted.

NOTES

1 It is true that one can formally define a version of utilitarianism that makes the maximand agent-relative (for example, parents might be required to place greater weight on the welfare of their own children). Nevertheless such a theory (as opposed to one which makes the greater duty of parents towards their own children purely a pragmatic consequence of the parents' greater knowledge of and proximity to their kin), though formally coherent, is not substantively compelling. Scanlon (1982) points out that utilitarianism, as an ethical view, is fundamentally motivated by a meta-ethical view that the only fundamental moral facts are facts about individual well-being (as opposed, say, to facts about historical or contractual relations between persons). If so, these are facts for whichever agent is contemplating them, and provide no explanation for why different agents might have fundamentally different duties and responsibilities.

2 The distinction here is the one familiar to liberals between 'the right' and 'the good'. It is of course easier to sustain conceptually than it is politically. In his more recent thinking, Rawls (1993) has characterized it as an 'overlapping consensus'. This is not a shared morality, merely an agreement on the principles of public life, in which citizens exercise power as a corporate body. This consensus, he argues, is required only among those ethical and religious views which are 'reasonable', that is to say intelligible, in the circumstances in which they are held and held seriously, and whose adherents do not try to convert others. Whatever reasons these people may have for entering public life, Rawls's expectation – or hope – is that the deliberation of 'public reason' can proceed without them. He also hopes that this deliberation will deliver principles of justice of the kind he first attempted to defend in a more principled way. The difficulty is that some views – the public ownership of productive assets, adherence to the *shari'a*, militant feminism – may be reasonable in the first sense but not the second: their proponents are almost bound to try to convert others to them, and it is difficult to see how the public deliberation of many matters can proceed independently of the reasons that socialists, Muslims or feminists have for their views. For it to do so, one can argue, such people would have to be liberals first and whatever else it is they are second. The dilemma was sharply revealed in the Algerian government's refusal in 1992 to countenance the electoral victory of the anti-democratic Islamic Front.

3 Mapel (1992) is a review of what it can be to look at international relations in a contractarian way. He emphasizes that it enables one to think about 'reciprocity' between states and, by implication, other agents in international affairs. Barry (1989: 483) disputes that there can be any reciprocity between the richest states and the poorest, and argues that if inequalities between nations are to be redressed, the rich must want to act reasonably towards the poor (see also n. 11). We here assume that the rich countries' support of international institutions to extend aid for development indicates that the desire – however weak and imperfect – exists already.

4 The first chapter of the agreement to establish the EBRD states that 'in contributing to economic progress and reconstruction, the purpose of

the Bank shall be to foster the transition towards open, market-oriented economies and to promote private and entrepreneurial initiative in central and eastern European countries committed to and applying the principles of multi-party democracy, pluralism and market economics.'

5 It is true that the United States had a crucial influence on the internal politics of these two countries, as on those of many others in the South. But it is important to remember that there were often sharp divisions in Washington between the State Department, the Pentagon, the CIA and the President, and that the policy of 'the United States' was accordingly unstable and often inconsistent. Schraeder (1994: 51–113) gives a good account of the policies towards Congo-Kinshasa/Zaïre between 1960 and 1992. On the problems presented more generally for constitutional democracy in sub-Saharan Africa, see Hawthorn (1993); on those for Korea before the change in 1987–8, see Henderson (1987); and for the subsequent manoeuvrings in Seoul under the new constitution, see Lee (1990).

6 The need for such powers is occasionally admitted. An example is an interview with William Rhodes, now a vice-chairman of Citicorp, who led the international banking community's response to the so-called 'debt crisis' of the 1980s (Rhodes, 1992). The political consequences of such powers for democracy in the 1980s are criticized by Bruno (1993) and Przeworski (1993). (But one consequence of the policies they promote is that the state will be accountable, if it is accountable at all, for less; as and when democracy extends, therefore, the citizens, or their representatives, will have more say over fewer issues.) The battle between Dia and Senghor in Senegal in 1962–3 is a particularly clear and vivid example (but only one among many) of the competing claims of development and compromise under democracy (Vaillant, 1990: 300–38). A recent essay by an assistant administrator of the US Agency for International Development is a not uncharacteristic piece of post-Cold War piety about the connection between democracy and development and the contribution that the United States can make to both (Bissell, 1992).

7 There is a qualification to this argument. To the extent that banks act as monitors of the behaviour of the parties to which they lend, a decision by an existing lender to suspend lending may have more serious adverse consequences for a borrower (by sending negative signals about the borrower's creditworthiness) than a decision by some other bank not to make an initial loan.

8 We should distinguish between projects that, because of their beneficial impact on poverty, are socially profitable according to a criterion that appropriately weights income according to the welfare of the recipient, and those that improve the distribution of income even though they are socially unprofitable even by the weighted criterion. Projects of the latter kind are usually undesirable since they are typically inferior to a simple transfer of incomes via the tax and benefit system; even if (because of the failings of that system) they are worth undertaking in any particular case, they are best thought of as part of a general policy of redistribution that is undertaken by a different agency from one that specializes in banking.

9 Little and Mirrlees (1991) are however highly critical of the World Bank's actual implementation of cost-benefit analysis.

10 Analogous criticisms have been made about the absence of provisions for the political control of fiscal policy set out in the 1991 *Treaty on European Union* (the so-called Maastricht Treaty). Many of these criticisms also, however, do not distinguish between banking and non-banking functions.
11 Barry comes to a similar conclusion. He defends a fairer share of resources between states, argues that it is reasonable that transfers should be made irrespective of the justice of the recipient's internal arrangements, but adds that there can be legitimate international interventions to improve those arrangements (1989: 492).

REFERENCES

Ascherson, N. 1992a: 1989 in Eastern Europe: Constitutional Representative Government as a 'Return to Normality'? In J. Dunn (ed.) *Democracy: The Unfinished Journey, 508 BC to AD 1993*. Oxford: Oxford University Press, 221–37.
Ascherson, N. 1992b: The Bank that Likes to Say 'Only on Condition . . .'. *The Independent on Sunday*, 12 July, 5.
Barry, B. 1989: *Democracy, Power and Justice: Essays in Political Theory*. Oxford: Clarendon Press.
Bissell, R. E. 1992: Who Killed the Third World? In B. Roberts (ed.) *U.S. Foreign Policy after the Cold War*. Cambridge, Mass.: MIT Press, 91–100.
Bruno, M. 1993: *Crisis, Stabilization and Economic Reform*. Oxford: Clarendon Press.
Dasgupta, P. 1993: *An Inquiry into Well-being and Destitution*. Oxford: Clarendon Press.
Hawthorn, G. 1993: Sub-Saharan Africa. In D. Held (ed.) *Prospects for Democracy: North, South, East, West*. Cambridge: Polity Press, 330–53.
Henderson, G. 1987: The Politics of Korea. In J. Sullivan and R. Foss (eds) *Two Koreas, One Future?* Lanham, Md.: University Press of America, 95–118.
Laffont, J. J. and Tirole, J. 1993: *A Theory of Incentives in Procurement and Regulation*. Cambridge, Mass.: MIT Press.
Lee, M. 1990: *The Odyssey of Korean Politics, 1987–1990*. New York: Praeger.
Little, I. M. D. and Mirrlees, J. 1991: Cost-benefit Analysis at the World Bank. In *World Bank Development Economics Conference*. Washington, DC: World Bank.
Mapel, D. R. 1992: The Contractarian Tradition and International ethics. In T. Nardin and D. R. Mapel (eds) *Traditions of International Ethics*. Cambridge: Cambridge University Press, 180–200.
Montesquieu 1989 (1748): *The Spirit of the Laws* ed. and trs. A. M. Cohler, B. C. Miller and H. S. Stone. Cambridge: Cambridge University Press.
Neven, D., Nuttall, R. and Seabright, P. 1993: *Merger in Daylight: The Economics and Politics of European Merger Control*. London: Centre for Economic Policy Research.
Noll, D. 1989: Economic Perspectives on the Politics of Regulation. In R. Schmalensee and R. Willig (eds) *Handbook of Industrial Organization I*. Amsterdam: Elsevier.

Przeworski, A. 1991: *Democracy and the Market: Political and Economic Reforms in Eastern Europe and Latin America*. Cambridge: Cambridge University Press.

Przeworski, A. 1993: Economic Reforms, Public Opinion, and Political Institutions: Poland in the Eastern European Perspective. In L. C. B. Pereira, J. M. Maravall and A. Przeworski *Economic Reforms in New Democracies: A Social-democratic Approach*. Cambridge: Cambridge University Press, 132–220.

Rawls, J. 1971: *A Theory of Justice* Oxford: Oxford University Press.

Rawls, J. 1993: *Political Liberalism*. New York: Columbia University Press.

Rhodes, W. 1992: Fear brings People Together. Interview. *Financial Times*, 30 July, 5.

Scanlon, T. M. 1982: Contractualism and Utilitarianism. In A. Sen and B. Williams (eds) *Utilitarianism and Beyond*. Cambridge: Cambridge University Press, 103–28.

Schraeder, P. J. 1994: *United States Foreign Policy toward Africa: Incrementalism, Crisis and Change*. Cambridge: Cambridge University Press.

Schumpeter, J. 1950 (1942): *Capitalism, Socialism and Democracy*. New York: Harper.

Seabright, P. 1993: Pluralism and the Standard of Living. In A. Sen and M. Nussbaum (eds) *The Quality of Life*. Oxford: Clarendon Press, 393–409.

Sen, A. and Williams, B. 1982: Introduction. In A. Sen and B. Williams (eds) *Utilitarianism and Beyond*. Cambridge: Cambridge University Press, 1–21.

Sunstein, C. 1991: Preferences and Politics. *Philosophy and Public Affairs*, 20, 3–34.

Vaillant, J. G. 1990: *Black, French, and African: A Life of Léopold Sédar Senghor*. Cambridge, Mass.: Harvard University Press.

World Bank 1992: *Governance and Development*. Washington: World Bank.

PART II
Case Studies

5

Development, Democracy and Civil Society in Botswana

JOHN D. HOLM

INTRODUCTION

In the 1960s and 1970s, analysts of African politics argued that development brings democracy. Very little development occurred during this time, which obviated the possibility of serious testing of this proposition. The hypothesized relation of these two variables was reversed in the mid-1980s. It is now said that democracy promotes development. Empirical analyses of the latter hypothesis have been few, and the evidence in support minimal. The problem is again one of finding worthwhile empirical tests. About the only option for studying the relationship of democracy and development in Africa is through a case study.

The best case is Botswana. This southern African state has had a developing economy and an emerging democracy for three decades. Two generalizations guide the analysis which follows: (1) lack of democratic control over the state bureaucracy has been central in Botswana's development; and (2) the local political culture shapes the impact of development on the democratization process.

The end of colonial rule in Botswana brought the establishment of a bureaucratic state and a liberal democracy. Rather than the two checking each other, top bureaucrats excluded elected politicians from most key decisions (Bachrach and Baratz, 1970). The bureaucrats' main priority was planning and executing a series of successful six-year development plans. For the last 30 years, Botswana's growth rate has been one of the highest in the world.

The resulting societal modernization has brought multiplying pressures for democratization. These pressures are most manifest in the attempts of various group leaders and their followers to influence government, that is to form a civil society. The group leaders in particular have come to realize that their impact on government departments is not guaranteed by the existence of free elections and a parliamentary system. Each organization must struggle for access to, let alone influence over, the autonomous and well-organized Botswana government. Of particular significance to this conflict is the fit of democracy with Tswana culture. Top state bureaucrats and democracy advocates sometimes seek justification for their causes in Tswana tradition. On other occasions they voice the need to redefine Tswana culture, quite often advocating foreign forms of participation.

This chapter begins with brief descriptions of Tswana political culture, the country's economic development, and the operation of the parliamentary system. Each section considers significant changes taking place relative to democratization. Then the discussion shifts to barriers to further empowerment of civil society. The final section identifies factors which have enhanced or are likely to enhance the power of civil society.

TSWANA POLITICAL CULTURE

Tswana social and political structures were authoritarian and highly stratified.[1] The chief allocated most economic resources, served as head of the judicial system, was the final authority on political questions and was perceived to possess great extra-worldly power through his powerful ancestors. Reinforcing his authority was the highly stratified character of Tswana society. At the top were the chief's relatives. While they quarrelled with the chief, they still had a vested interest in supporting the prevailing political structure. Below this royalty were those who belonged to the same Tswana ethnic group as the chief. Then came persons from other Tswana tribes followed by other sedentary Bantu groups, most prominently the Kalanga. At the bottom were hunter-gatherers who had no right of access to Tswana political structures. Within this system, women and youths had little right of political expression except through older males in their household.

There were a few controls on the chief. In court cases he was expected to listen in *kgotla* (a gathering of all adult males) to his uncles and other respected elders as to their views of the law and its application to a given case. On major political decisions the chief also went to the *kgotla* to announce his likely decision and hear the public reactions. *Kgotla* etiquette was that elders did most of the talking and their opinion was expected to prevail.

During the colonial period (1885–1965), the British made some attempts to change Tswana political and social structures in a democratic direction. They sought to give the *kgotla* more power *vis-à-vis* the chief by using it to appoint chiefs and to constrain and depose ineffective ones. In the course of the 1930s, the colonial government turned to the *kgotla* for approval of local development programmes (Mgadla and Campbell, 1989: 54–6).

The British also promoted the equalization of hunter-gatherers and insisted that other non-Tswana groups should have more opportunities to participate in the traditional political system. Change was minimal at best. It was only at the end of colonial rule that minorities were brought into politics. The British and local politicians agreed that all adults would have the right to vote for MPs and councillors. In the first parliament all but two members were Tswana. Over the intervening years the number of non-Tswana has gradually expanded, revolutionizing the composition of Botswana's ruling class. Otherwise, authoritarian political patterns have persisted, though the domination is now bureaucratic in form. It is to the economic base of this new domination that we now turn.

THE ECONOMY

Since 1965 Botswana has averaged a real growth rate of around 10 per cent per year. State planners have made the key decisions as far as the character and extent of investments. Their first focus was on balancing the budget, which was done by a very favourable renegotiation of the country's customs agreement with South Africa. In the 1970s, they concentrated state investments on a copper-nickel complex and three diamond mines. The former has operated at a loss, though it employs a large work-force (5,500). The diamond mines turned Botswana into the largest monetary producer of this gem in the world. While the multi-national De Beers Corporation manages the mines, the government's profits from diamonds cover around 60 per cent of its revenues. In the 1980s and 1990s, state planners focused on reinvesting this income in diversification of the economy, including coal and soda ash mines, an emerging manufacturing sector and a considerable expansion of transportation and communication systems (MFDP, 1991: 118–49; Harvey and Lewis, 1990).

Several aspects of this managed growth should be noted. First, bureaucratic norms are pervasive. Entry into the civil service and the position obtained is based almost completely on the level of formal education completed and performance in examinations. Civil service advancement is then governed by internal evaluations. External intervention through political influence and corruption is minimal, especially by African standards. In part, this results from a Tswana penchant for following the rules (Alverson, 1978). In addition, Africanization has proceeded at a very slow place, thus insuring that most technical management positions remain with persons inclined to resist political influence.

Second, the planning elite keeps wages and consumption at the lowest levels possible. To this end, government controls incomes[2] and frustrates the development of strong unions (Mbononi, 1989: 139–41, 154–5). As an added restraint on consumption, the central bank fixes the value of the country's currency, the pula, low, relative to major foreign currencies.

Third, the planners have committed a considerable amount of the government's diamond income to mass public services including education, health and welfare programmes. In so doing, the Botswana government has minimized some adverse consequences of modernization. For instance, a massive government low-income housing programme has reached a substantial portion of the new arrivals in the towns. As a result, 'there has been virtually no squatter problem within Africa's most rapidly growing urban population' (Lewis, 1993: 24).

Economic planners have been able to formulate and carry out their plan because they had the support of Seretse Khama, the first president, and now have the confidence of Quett Masire, the second president. The two presidents have protected the civil service from most political interference. Politicians must deal only with permanent secretaries who both presidents have insisted should give no political favours.

The top planners take advantage of their independence to propagandize for their programmes. Economists and other planning experts regularly lecture politicians, journalists and interest groups on policy changes. Both Presidents Khama and Masire insisted that their Botswana Democratic Party (BDP) use state plan objectives as the main content of election manifestos.[3] In effect, development planners set the public development agenda. Moreover, they block others from access to this agenda by rigorously enforcing a planning regulation that no development funds are allocated unless a project is in the current plan or has gone through a supplementary review process which takes over a year.

The top planners see their judgements as beyond question, and their primary duty relative to politicians is to raise 'the general level of economic literacy' (Lewis, 1993: 19). Every attempt is made to close off discussion of possible trade-offs to their policies. For instance, at the urging of the Ministry of Finance officials, Botswana maintains foreign exchange reserves one-third above any other country in the world in terms of months of import coverage (UNDP, 1993: 174, 175, 204). Policy documents circulating on this topic within the Ministry of Finance do not deal with the opportunity costs of such huge reserves; the authors simply list the risks of not doing so. The planners assume that as long as they are doing well for the Botswana economy, they are providing the service elected politicians require; for politicians to have a choice is to give them a chance to make the wrong decision.

The planners act as if they were traditional Tswana chiefs and periodically consult the public. On major programmes (for instance those concerning land privatization, conservation and low-income housing) they have commissioned public opinion surveys to find out citizen opinions of possible policy options. Not included in these surveys are questions about whether the public perceives that a problem exists or that a government solution is desired. At the village level, government officials are very concerned that projects are approved in *kgotla* or local council. If a veto is forthcoming, negotiation takes place until an acceptable alternative is found.

Top civil servants represent their consultation as consistent with Tswana tradition. The problem is that this government accountability has little leverage over the process by which policies are decided and funds are allocated. To understand Botswana's democratic vacuum in this regard we need to explore the operation of the parliamentary system.

BOTSWANA'S PARLIAMENTARY DEMOCRACY

Botswana has a parliamentary system in which the president occupies the dominant power position. A candidate is elected president if a majority of the winning MP candidates officially declare their support for this person at the time of their nomination. Once elected, the president appoints his cabinet without approval from Parliament. He also appoints four 'specially elected' MPs who vote with the 34 popularly elected members. The president cannot be removed by a vote of no confidence; rather such a vote brings dissolution of parliament and a new election.

In addition to the above powers, the first two presidents, Khama and Masire, have dominated parliament because of their strong leadership position in the ruling party and because of the large majorities the BDP regularly enjoys in parliament. Khama used his position as the heir to the chieftaincy of the largest ethnic group in Botswana to enhance further the prestige of the office of president.[4] Many rural citizens perceived that as president Khama was in fact the *kgosi* (chief) of all Botswana.

Khama and Masire have dominated their cabinets as well. Each appointed as specially elected MPs highly capable persons, most being former civil servants with a minimal mass political base. These former civil servants have served as the planners' principal advocates in the cabinet and parliament.[5] They also ensure that the President is effective in articulating and promoting the planners' various programmes.

Parliament finds itself confronted with a powerful president who supports and is supported by a well-organized and confident civil service. MPs have little option but to rubber stamp policies developed by the civil service. Few are sophisticated enough to criticize these policies, and they have no staff to brief them. Moreover, any attempt to challenge proposals backed by the president and the permanent secretaries is likely to bring extraordinary pressures on MPs from the ruling party.

Further reducing the incentive of parliament to challenge either the president or the civil service is the fact that voters, particularly in the rural areas, chose their representatives largely on the basis of ethnic loyalties. They are unconcerned by issues, government performance or even the personality of the candidates.[6] This fact has two important implications. First, interest-group leaders have little leverage over rural politicians who make up over 80 per cent of Parliament and 90 per cent of BDP MPs. The politicians know that their election does not depend on gaining the support of particular interests within a constituency. Thus, leaders of these groups avoid election politics. No interest group in Botswana endorses candidates, or, except for one case, attempts to mobilize election contributions.[7]

Second, the political parties mainly contest for who can best represent each ethnic group.[8] This means that increasingly all candidates come from the numerically dominant ethnic group in a constituency and perceive themselves speaking for this group. Minorities heretofore dominated by Tswana headmen appointed by the chief (usually a relative) now choose one of their own as representative to parliament and the local council. In the process, the Tswana ruling class is becoming more diverse. It includes many commoners, minorities (there were at least seven non-Tswana in the 1989–94 parliament), a few women (two in the 1989–94 parliament), and even an occasional hunter-gatherer (three out of ten were elected to the Ghanzi local council in the 1989 election). The ruling BDP fights elections by building up a coalition of ethnic groups. In terms of development planning, the party has one concern, namely that all ethnic groups share equally in the results of the country's economic growth. The party's thinking is that this distribution ensures that none of the country's ethnic groups has reason to complain at election time. From the planners' perspective this means some inefficient allocation of resources – for instance in placing schools, job programmes and health centres in areas with low population density.

Some political economists (Parson, 1981; Picard, 1980; Tsie, 1993) argue that a wealthy cattle-holding class dominates the Botswana state through its control of the BDP. Their main evidence is that BDP MPs and a few high civil servants have large cattle holdings. This contention is questionable. As already noted, the BDP's control of parliament has not led to domination of the civil service. There is not even much evidence to suggest that the bureaucracy has tried to buy off the BDP with subsidies to the cattle sector. Most ranking civil servants perceive the cattle sector as grossly inefficient. Thus they have formulated a number of programmes, most associated with the Tribal Grazing Land Policy (TGLP), to commercialize rural cattle production. Few cattle owners have shown much interest in TGLP. Those who have accepted state funds to commercialize have resisted changing their practices in any significant way (World Bank, 1985; Tsimako, 1991). The result has been a stand-off between the state and the cattle sector and a gradual decline in state development expenditures on agriculture. Whereas eight per cent of the 1973–8 plan was invested in agricultural projects (MFDP, n.d.: 39), the 1991–7 plan has reduced this portion to two per cent (MFDP, 1991: 114).

Equally revealing is the fact that, with one or two exceptions, politicians' cattle businesses are models of economic mismanagement. Equipment is in disrepair; the animals are poorly attended to; and offtake rates demonstrate no interest in profit maximization. At best, wealthy Tswana (including MPs) retreat to cattle posts for rest and relaxation on weekends and holidays. As businesses, most cattle posts are hardly the focus of any sort of entrepreneurial or capitalist activity, let alone the power base for a class intent on dominating government investment policies.

In summary, parliamentary democracy has produced little in terms of civil society control over the state. The idea of groups in society giving direction to government authorities has not taken hold. As in the traditional system, those in political authority formulate new policy directions. Civil society remains a series of ethnic groups struggling for their fair share. Even elite cattle owners have not succeeded in promoting policies in their interest. Instead, an educated mandarin class dominating the ministries has proceeded to develop the Botswana economy at a rapid rate with most of the profits returning to state coffers.[9]

BARRIERS TO CIVIL SOCIETY

Much analysis of democracy focuses on the presence or absence of elections and political rights (Huntington, 1991: 3–13). From this perspective Botswana looks very good, as shown in the annual Freedom House reports. However, a reality of all democracies is that citizen influence through elections is mediated by a number of cumulatively significant aspects of the social and political structures. These structures determine the influence on government of social groups, mass media and intellectuals.

Civil society expands as such structural constraints decline. In developing countries, civil society tends to be limited by substantial barriers. This is sometimes because of lack of economic development, but also because of the authoritarian character of political structures. Laws and customs provide little access or open space for civil society. The importance of elections and political rights is that they provide opportunities for the struggle necessary to educate and organize the public to participate in the policy process through civil society.[10]

Botswana illustrates some classic barriers to the organization of civil society in developing countries where political freedom and competitive elections exist. Four such barriers will be discussed: government secrecy, the weakness of opposition political parties, marginal group resources and a narrow view of politics in the traditional political culture.

Government secrecy

The Botswana government is very efficient in keeping politically significant information about its operations out of the public realm. Frank reviews of agencies and programmes are rarely made public. Government budgets provide minimal detail. In the case of the parastatals, budgets do not appear until after the financial year is completed and then only in sketchy form. The reservoir of persons capable of ferreting out critical information on ineffective government programmes is minimal. Most elected councillors have less than eight years of formal schooling. Most MPs have not gone beyond high school. A few journalists have been to college, but almost none have any extended formal training in their profession. Intellectuals, found mostly at the university, are few in number and many are fearful that criticism of government could stunt their careers. Only three interest groups, two dominated by expatriates, allocate any substantial amounts of money to research on policy issues. In sum, government is confronted with almost no social group capable of investigating and analysing its operation or policies.

Opposition parties

Compounding this information vacuum is the weakness of the political opposition. One way civil society organizes for political action is through a political opposition. This process is most notable in countries (Poland, Chile and South Africa) where potentially diverse political groups unite as a social movement to promote democratization. In Botswana, the disunity within and among opposition political parties and the legal context in which they operate immobilizes civil society.

Three opposition parties have won seats in Parliament or local councils over the last 25 years. They have had few constraints on their political freedom. In spite of this context, the three parties have posed no serious electoral threat to the BDP. They have won majorities in a few local councils and at most 23 per cent of the contested seats in Parliament. In the 1989 elections, the opposition won three seats out of 34, even though they secured over one-third of the vote.

The reasons for this poor showing are several. Without question, the success of the government's development plans and the positive impact of social and welfare programmes makes the BDP a formidable electoral challenge. However, in a number of cases the opposition loses to the BDP simply because they cannot unite behind one candidate. In the 1989 elections the opposition parties lost in five parliamentary constituencies while winning the majority of the popular vote.

The leaders of the opposition parties have attempted on numerous occasions to negotiate a united front for the next election, but to no avail. Part of the reason for this disunity is ethnic mistrust among the parties, as each has a tribal base. Part also stems from their different views of development. The Botswana National Front (BNF) is based largely in urban areas and gains support by calling for the redistribution of wealth to wage earners. On the other hand, the Botswana Peoples Party and the Botswana Independence Party are more concerned with ethnic discrimination against the Kalanga and Bayei respectively. The main opposition party, the BNF, is further hobbled by often uncontrolled internal conflicts based on ideology, generation and region. The leader of the party for the last 25 years, Kenneth Koma, has been unable to enforce any discipline or compromise. Party congresses often end up excommunicating or alienating a sizeable number of members rather than mobilizing them.

The law further weakens the opposition. Government regulations prevent state employees including teachers and those employed by parastatals from taking an active role in politics. Such a restriction is reasonable in terms of maintaining a neutral government organization. However, since government employs over half of the educated population, including the vast majority of persons informed about policy issues, it means that the pool of politically sophisticated persons available to opposition parties is very small.

Another restriction which favours the BDP is that youths under 21 cannot vote. For many older Tswana who believe that young people should not speak in *kgotla*, lowering the voting age is out of the question. On the other hand it is the young who are much more adversely affected by the various forces of development than their elders. Their exclusion hinders them from voicing their political discontent.

A final legal barrier to the opposition parties is the delimitation of constituency boundaries. According to the constitution, parliamentary boundaries may be skewed from equality in population numbers to take account of 'natural community of interest, means of communication, geographical features, density of population, and the boundaries of Tribal Territories and administrative districts' (section 66,2). This provision legitimizes maldistribution of parliamentary representation in favour of the rural areas. For the 1989 election, the average urban parliamentary constituency was 70 per cent larger than rural ones. In addition, the boundary commission has seen fit to add rural areas to several urban constituencies to give the BDP greater competitive advantage. The result is that the urban-based BNF has never been able to win a proportion of parliamentary seats anywhere near equal to its popular vote.

In sum, Botswana has elections but all contestants other than the BDP are weak. The internal conflicts of the opposition leave it myopic to the possibilities of mobilizing civil society, and the laws favouring the BDP give little reward for such mobilization. The opposition could well remain weak until the ruling party self-destructs due to internal conflict, as happened in Japan.

Interest groups

It was noted above that the ethnic character of Botswana electoral politics leaves little room for interest-group intervention. Interest groups are also weakened in their influence by their minimal resources. Most organized groups do not have the kind of resources needed to have an impact on government, that is the trained staff, money, communication with their members and regular access to politicians. At best they may have a staff of one or two full-time persons. Many have no permanent employees. Dues are nominal (about the equivalent of US$0.50) and often not paid. The main link with members is a delegate meeting once a year. Newsletters are rare. Almost all interest groups, whether they are labour unions, professional organizations or public service groups, have predominantly non-political agendas. For instance, the main teachers' organization spends most of its energies running music and athletic competitions among schools. Government encourages these non-political activities by providing generous financial support, and thus covers all the expenses of the music and athletic competitions. Since it is difficult to collect much more than minimal dues, many organizations look to government subsidies to maintain their existence. There is a cost; the leadership must be cautious about criticizing government policies.

The vast physical expanse of Botswana compounds the problem of interest groups. The country is the size of France (or Texas) yet only has a population of 1.3 million. This means that communication among members of an organization living in various parts of the country is costly in time and resources. Travel to and from a national meeting can take up to four days. It is not unusual for executive committees to meet only twice a year.

In part the development of civil society in Botswana is a matter of economic resources. As more income becomes available in various sectors of the economy, more interest-group activity can be supported. However, another part of the problem is the narrow Tswana view of politics. The next section addresses this cultural factor.

Tswana political culture

Most Tswana, even the educated, have a narrow view of 'politics'. The concept includes activities related to political parties, elections and representatives to parliament and local councils. Politics does not include the policy process of the civil service, activities of organized groups, traditional authorities or the court system. The implicit assumption is that civil society and politics are separate. From this perspective, there is no need to speak to, or influence, politicians to change government policies. Rather, a person or group desiring change petitions or consults with civil servants, traditional authorities and judges.

This view of politics is most evident at the local level where the chief and his *kgotla* play an important role in decision-making. The government has made the chief a part of the civil service and insists that he and his headmen be 'non-political'.[11] When the civil service uses the traditional *kgotla* to consult with a community, the chief's duty is to ensure that the talk is non-partisan. Since political parties were not involved historically in the *kgotla*, most older villagers see little problem with this barrier to partisanship. However, the net effect is to drive partisanship underground on local issues, thus giving the idea that civil society and politics are separate entities. For the BDP this is not a problem since the party supports most policies generated by the civil service anyway. On the other hand, the opposition is precluded from linking partisanship at the national level with concerns which have immediate meaning at the grass roots.

DEMOCRATIZING DEVELOPMENT IN BOTSWANA

The process by which civil society will develop more control over Botswana's development bureaucracy is by no means clear. From the experience of recent years, several factors appear to be critical.

One important influence toward democratization already operating is the example of South Africa. Many Tswana have been impressed by the strong role which organized groups played in bringing the white regime to the negotiating table. The most direct impact has been on trade unions. The South African unions have bargained for substantial increases in their wages, disregarding government attempts to control incomes, and have both pressured and supported the African National Congress on political and economic issues. Many Tswana union leaders have decided to imitate this example. Government itself has been forced to acknowledge in this climate that restrictive union laws must be revised.

Also stimulating the development of Botswana civil society has been the role of the South African private press in exposing the secret activities of the country's white government and its ANC rival. Botswana's three weekly private newspapers have put increasing pressure on government with respect to scandals and policy questions. For the first time, they have forced the release of reports on secret investigations into corruption. The resulting publicity from two such reports was critical in forcing the BDP to sack three ministers. The newspapers are also becoming important on policy matters. In 1991, their criticism obliged the Ministry of Mineral Resources and Water Affairs to abandon a proposed Okavango water scheme because of negative environmental effects.

A second major force for democratization in Botswana is the breakdown of BDP unity. Until the mid-1980s the party operated as a cohesive political machine. Conflict was minimized by allowing the president to appoint the national leadership. Since then this cohesion has begun to crumble as organizational conflicts have resulted in highly contested elections for party offices.

The conflict reflects a number of fissures. First, younger local leaders resent the failure of their seniors in the cabinet to force the civil service to respond to grass-roots concerns. Second, members from Bamangwato believe they have been excluded from party leadership since Khama died and the president has come from the south. Finally, the more capitalist members of the party are frustrated by the failure of the more senior, cattle-owning leaders to force the civil service bureaucracy to formulate policies which support and subsidize Tswana entrepreneurs.

All these conflicts could split the BDP under the right circumstances. A most likely occasion is when Masire steps down as president. No heir apparent exists. If a BDP split occurs, the opposition BNF is likely to have a better chance at winning a number of districts simply because the BDP will divide its vote. In addition, it is very possible that some dissident BDP members might join the opposition and take their followers with them. With the exception of a north–south split provoked by the Bamangwato, BDP conflict will almost certainly render development issues more important, meaning ultimately that parliamentary politics will supplant the planning process.

Still another force for democratization is likely to be a serious downturn in the economy. The 25-year upward trend is bound to slow down or reverse, especially when the diamond market suffers a setback. As the BDP has taken credit for the upswing, it will suffer with the first serious recession. Interest groups are likely to be inspired to mobilize their members to fight to maintain their current share of national resources. Opposition parties could exploit the resulting conflict to promote a partisan realignment which is more issue-or class-based.

Finally, contagion has played an important role in Botswana's democratization. One group does something to extend participation and others quickly imitate it. One of the most striking examples was the introduction of party primaries for choosing election candidates. After Masire assumed power in the early 1980s, the BDP leadership decided to use primaries as a means to bring new blood to their 1984 ticket. All paid-up party members were given one vote. To keep things under control the BDP stipulated that vote counts would not be made public and the National Executive Committee would make the final decision on each candidate. In 1989, the opposition parties also adopted primaries when competition existed in a constituency for a nomination. However, the opposition went one step further. They made the vote public and did not allow national leaders to override the results.

Other examples of this contagion are manifest. Thus, in the late 1980s the mine workers' union increased its dues to $4.00 per month in order to support a larger staff organization. Other unions have followed. A European-dominated chamber of commerce is stimulating an African-oriented one. The founding of an accountants' association has stimulated talk among lawyers about a similar organization for themselves. Some mine-union leaders are even proposing to endorse a party at election time. The contagion from this change could challenge the Tswana narrow view of politics.

While the barriers to Botswana's civil society are starting to crumble, the process is slow. However, the direction of change is clear. The civil service will become more accountable, at least to those organized groups in civil society.

CONCLUSION

Botswana's civil service has engineered one of the most impressive economic growth advances seen in the third world. It has done so in a country facing major problems. At independence there were scarcely any formal educational institutions above the primary level; government income could only provide for slightly more than half its recurrent budget. In recent years, the country has been surrounded by states embroiled in bloody civil wars. Now, because of its development success, the state bureaucracy stands accused of stalling the spread of democracy.

While Botswana's civil service must share some blame for the lack of democratic progress, the character of elections and party conflict have prevented serious societal influences from being brought to bear on government. The main reason is that the BDP has put together a winning coalition based on ethnicity. The result is a *de facto* one-party state in which development issues only have marginal impact on voter choice. Another factor contributing to the independence of the bureaucracy is that organized groups do not have a power base providing access to, let alone a say in, the policy-making process. Finally, Tswana political culture protects the bureaucracy from political influence by defining civil service policy-making as nonpolitical.

The leadership of the Botswana state, namely permanent secretaries and the first two presidents, have taken advantage of the state's autonomy to implement an ambitious development agenda. The state has kept wages down, channelled substantial funds to capital investment, recruited the best graduates from the educational system to the public service and associated private corporations, hired large numbers of expatriates where skill shortages existed and prevented organized groups from challenging their decisions. High growth rates have given this autonomous state considerable legitimacy.

Only in the last decade have societal pressures for democratization begun to undermine the ability of civil service mandarins to direct the economy. Economic growth has created sizeable middle and wage-earning classes demanding more income and less control from government. For these classes, the fact that the growth rate may slow as a result is of no great consequence. Some are turning to the BNF to achieve their goal, in spite of its political ineptness. Others are supporting dissent within the BDP. Whether the BNF will triumph or the BDP will challenge the state bureaucracy first is an open question. Regardless, multi-party competition will increase; wage levels will rise; imports from South Africa will expand; and the press will become more critical of government. Most important, organized groups from unions to professional associations and women will demand at least a veto over policies affecting their interests. In the process, ethnicity will not disappear as a factor in elections, but it will become part of a more complex mix of political coalition-building. To be sure, all this change will take place at a slow pace because the Tswana definition of politics must first expand to include civil society and the state bureaucracy.

The one factor which could stall the demise of Botswana's developmental state is the character of the increased multi-party competition. Existing parties may fail to expand their coalition bases. Both the BNF and the BDP have been extremely rigid as far as including new groups. As a result, the number of parties may further expand and produce unstable majorities in the National Assembly. Like the Fourth Republic in France, the political in-fighting could leave the bureaucracy in charge to make policy by default.

The Botswana case indicates two relationships which often go unconsidered in discussions about the interaction of development and democracy. First, elections and political rights need not obstruct a bureaucratic elite from dominating the development process and engineering considerable economic growth. In this regard, the thesis of Gerschenkron (1962) that countries late to development must abolish liberal democratic structures is not supported. Democratic structures, even though they meet conventional Western norms, can serve as a façade for autocratic development processes when civil society and political party competition are restricted in their impact on government policy processes.

Second, the linear relation of economic growth with democratization is mediated by a number of factors which can hinder the emergence of civil society and the accountability it requires of government. In Botswana's case, the planners' authority is preserved by a number of factors. They have modelled themselves after the Tswana *kgosi* and restricted popular influence to 'consultation'. They have used the state's growing economic wealth to redirect democratic forces to activities which dissipate group influence. And they carefully hide behind the Tswana definition of the civil service as nonpolitical. The net effect is to slow the growth of civil society in spite of massive economic growth.

There is a tendency to see Botswana as exceptional. The future may be different. If African countries are to move toward both democracy and development, they may be well advised to adopt this 'exceptional' path where a committed developmental political elite promotes development, and democracy emerges gradually as a result of the interaction of development and local traditions. The demands by many African intellectuals and Western foreign aid organizations that states on the continent democratize first in order to promote development could well put the cart before the horse. Botswana demonstrates that the primary need is to form a political coalition of elites committed to development. Until such a basis for a developmental state emerges, democracy or foreign aid may make little difference.

ACKNOWLEDGEMENTS

Rodger Govea and James Pletcher provided helpful comments on earlier drafts of this essay. Amy Poteete encouraged the author to look more closely at the role of culture in Tswana political change.

NOTES

1 See for instance the account in Fortes and Evans-Pritchard (1940) where the Tswana are characterized as representing authoritarian African traditions.
2 The government incomes policy originated in 1972. The essence of current policy is that salaries paid by government are 'regarded as a firm guideline by employers in the private sector' (Republic of Botswana, 1990: 1).

3 See Ministry of Finance and Development Planning (MFDP), *National Development Plan 1979–1985* and *National Development Plan 1985–1991* and compare them with the Botswana Democratic Party election manifestos for 1984 and 1989 respectively.

4 Khama never assumed the role of chief of the Bamangwato because the colonial government refused to allow him to do so, fearing that the newly elected Afrikaner government in South Africa would be outraged.

5 In the 1989–94 cabinet, the minister of finance is the former permanent secretary to the president, and the minister of presidential affairs (this office supervises the civil service, all information activities, the police and the military) is the former top general in the army. In the post-election cabinet the two still play dominant roles, though the latter has moved to external affairs.

6 There are some exceptions with respect to personality (Holm, 1987).

7 The one exception is the Botswana Confederation of Commerce, Industry and Manpower. An employers' federation dominated by European capital, its leaders informally raise money for the BDP.

8 Many analysts argue that ethnic conflict does not have a major influence on Botswana politics. Thus Balefi Tsie says this is the case because Botswana's 'population is composed of Tswana speaking "tribes" who share common traditions, customs, and beliefs' (1993: 30). This approach overlooks the fact that the eight Tswana tribes in the country have for several centuries contested (including by war in the nineteenth century) for 'political' power and still do so in the modern context. Moreover, it fails to recognize that over a third of the population speak Setswana but consider themselves to be non-Tswana oppressed by the eight major Tswana groups.

9 Lest it be thought that the civil service class operates only in consideration of the national interest, two aspects of their private economic behaviour should be noted. First, civil servants are allowed to invest in private enterprises so long as they do not have controlling interest and do not directly deal with the enterprise in their roles as civil servants. Top civil servants have made a number of such investments, although in some cases they lost their money. Second, most top civil servants retire early (45 to 50 years of age) and either start their own businesses or find top positions with large corporations, most of which are foreign.

10 There are countries where civil society's expansion precedes liberal democracy: examples are United States, India and South Africa (for the Africans, Coloured and Indians).

11 A chief who becomes too political can be reprimanded or dismissed. Only by resigning can a chief run for elected office.

REFERENCES

Alverson, H. 1978: *Mind in the Heart of Darkness.* New Haven, Conn.: Yale University Press.

Bachrach, P. and Baratz, M. 1970: *Power and Poverty.* New York: Oxford University Press.

Fortes, M. and Evans-Pritchard, E. E. 1940: *African Political Systems.* London: Oxford University Press.

Gerschenkron, A. 1962: *Economic Backwardness in Historical Perspective.* Cambridge, Mass.: Harvard University Press.

Harvey, C. and Lewis, S. R. 1990: *Policy Choice and Development Performance in Botswana.* London: Macmillan Press.

Holm, J. D. 1987: Elections in Botswana: Institutionalization of a New System of Legitimacy. In F. M. Hayward (ed.) *Elections in Independent Africa.* Boulder, Colo.: Westview Press, 121–47.

Huntington, S. P. 1991: *The Third Wave: Democratization in the Late Twentieth Century.* Norman, Okla.: University of Oklahoma Press.

Lewis, S. R. 1993: Policy-making and Economic Performance: Botswana in Comparative Perspective. In S. J. Stedman (ed.) *Botswana: the Political Economy of Democratic Development.* Boulder, Colo.: Lynne Rienne, 11–25.

Mbononi, I. 1989: What Should be the Role of Trade Unions? In J. Holm and P. Molutsi (eds) *Democracy in Botswana.* Athens, Ohio: Ohio University Press, 139–41.

Mgadla, P. T. and Campbell, A. C. 1989: Dikgotla, Dikgosi and the Protectorate Administration. In J. Holm and P. Molutsi (eds) *Democracy in Botswana.* Athens, Ohio: Ohio University Press, 48–56.

Ministry of Finance and Development Planning (MFDP) n.d.: *National Development Plan: 1973–1978.* Gaborone: Government Printer.

Ministry of Finance and Development Planning (MFDP) 1980: *National Development Plan: 1979–85.* Gaborone: Government Printer.

Ministry of Finance and Development Planning (MFDP) 1985: *National Development Plan: 1985–91.* Gaborone: Government Printer.

Ministry of Finance and Development Planning (MFDP) 1991: *National Development Plan 7: 1991–1997.* Gaborone: Government Printer.

Parson, J. D. 1981: Cattle, Class and the State in Rural Botswana. *Journal of Southern African Studies,* 7, 236–55.

Picard, L. A. 1980: Bureaucrats, Cattle, and Public Policy: Land Tenure Changes in Botswana. *Comparative Political Studies,* 13, 313–56.

Republic of Botswana 1990: *Report of the Presidential Commission on the Review of Incomes Policy.* Gaborone: Government Printer.

Tsie, B. 1993: The Political Context of Botswana's Development Performance. *Southern African Political Economy Magazine,* September, 35–40.

Tsimako, B. 1991: *The Tribal Grazing Land Policy (TGLP) Ranches: Performance to Date.* Gaborone: Ministry of Agriculture.

United Nations Development Programme (UNDP) 1993: *Human Development Report: 1993.* New York: Oxford University Press.

World Bank 1985: *Botswana National Land Management and Livestock Project: Staff Appraisal Report.* Washington: The World Bank.

6

Dilemmas of Democratic Development in India

SUDIPTA KAVIRAJ

INTRODUCTION

Abstractly, it is possible to relate democracy and development in four different ways. (1) They can be seen as being functionally related; that is, each process supports and helps maintain the other.[1] Or they can be sequenced in two opposite ways. (2) Democracy can be seen as precondition, in a literal sense; that is, it must occur or begin to occur before development can take place. (3) Conversely, development can be seen as a precondition for democracy; that is, the delicate political arrangements required in democratic governance can be seen to be possible only after some development has taken place. (4) Finally, in a stance of radical scepticism, it can be maintained that they have no explanatorily significant connection and that their happening at the same time is a matter of pure contingency. This picture is of course highly simplified. Each one of these positions can be inflected and refined; but it is helpful to begin with these main lines of historical possibility.

The history of development is not merely a history of a set of policy-making practices; it also includes, emphatically, a history of ideas. A fairly significant change has occurred in the last two decades in thinking about development, compared with the dominant ideas of the post-war years. It is essential to overcome the temptation to believe effortlessly that the presuppositions governing the current debate are transcendentally true, and that from the security of these correct assumptions we assess the fallible hypotheses of earlier generations. It is a much better strategy to accept the dimension of the history of ideas as crucial, and recognize that we judge their paradigms of thought from within our own, and not from a point which is free from any paradigmatic location. Our great advantage is that we can consult the complex history of development of the last 40 years, which they could not do.

One major change between the 1950s and the 1990s is the triumph of a kind of 'technical rationality' in thinking about the connection between democracy and development. Recent analysts are more inclined to see democracy *instrumentally*, as a means for the realization of economic growth, rather than an independent value in itself. This was not common in the years after the Second World War. In order to understand and judge the perspectives about democracy and development which underlay the politics of the post-war world, it is essential that we correctly read their sense of historical possibilities.

THE INTELLECTUAL BACKGROUND TO INDIAN DEVELOPMENT

Development thinking in India, as indeed everywhere in the 1950s, was determined by what were supposed to be the 'lessons' of the history of the West. But the history of 'Western development' was an ambiguous idea, because growth trajectories varied a great deal from one Western country to another. Secondly, the infinity of facts which made up economic history did not 'offer lessons' in themselves, only theoretical interpretations, which reduced this evidence into various narratives or readings. And the lesson of Western economic development could appear significantly different according to varying readings of its great archives. Throughout the first part of the century, political thought in the West debated the relation between economic growth and political forms through ideological disputation between liberal and socialist doctrines. It was usually believed that the historical evidence of economic modernity showed a secular trend towards acceleration of economic growth, and most interpreters found a Marxisand language the most apt to describe this lesson of history. Capitalist development took longer to mature in the West European societies, especially in the 'classical' cases of Britain and France. As capitalism moved towards the East, it followed what Marx had termed the logic of the 'second way' of capitalist transformation.[2] Economic processes constitutive of capitalist modernity, the size of factories, the concentration of capital and labour, improved communication and management went faster in countries which started late. The sequence of industrialization was altered. While classical transformations had been led by consumer goods industries which produced a demand for capital goods industries afterwards, in late capitalist countries, heavy industries, especially steel and metals, grew at the same time and sometimes led the process of industrialization. This bore a particularly strong connection with political forms, because often in late capitalist societies the demand for capital goods and metals industries was supported by deliberate state policies. Significantly, however, in the classical Marxist schema, faster economic growth towards capitalist modernity was purchased at the cost of a distinct retardation of the process of political democracy. In states like Germany and Russia where capitalist development began late and went faster, the processes of democratic political transformation went slower than in France and England, and were eventually unsuccessful, resulting generally in the creation of a Bismarckian state of paternalistic authoritarianism (Marx, 1848). Implicit in the orthodox Marxist reading of European economic history, therefore, was a highly complex hypothesis about the relation between the processes of development and democracy. The logic of capitalist economic change and the process of democratization were seen to be asymmetric. Fast capitalist development could be achieved at the cost of a slower or unsuccessful democratic transformation.

Indian nationalism produced a rich literature interpreting modernity as a historical condition, but it was generally negligent about questions of economic growth and the institutional forms conducive to it. Nationalists relied on the comfortable assumption that since economic backwardness was related significantly to colonial domination, its removal was bound to improve economic conditions. Two political groups, however, did devote more attention to the problems of economic distribution and the arrangements of production after independence. Left-wing groups inside the Congress began to press for redistributive commitments from the 1920s, and extracted an expression of mildly reformist intentions in 1932 from a largely reluctant conservative party (Gopal, 1975). Industrialists who supported the Congress campaign for independence produced a more practical outline for economic policy in 1944, called the Bombay Plan, urging the future national state to provide an industrial infrastructure and protection for indigenous industry against foreign competition (Kidron, 1965; Bagchi, 1971; Markowitz, 1985). But despite these moves, Congress was not expressly committed to any clear economic strategy at the time of independence.

Eventually, through a number of fortuitous circumstances, the government after independence came to be dominated by Jawaharlal Nehru; but he exercised a curious type of dominance in the Congress party. By the deaths of Gandhi and Sardar Patel, his only credible competitor, Nehru became the uncontested leader of the Congress. Yet its socialist segment, which could support his reformist initiatives on development, left the Congress soon after independence to join the opposition. Nehru occupied a strange position of glory inside the Congress, as a supreme leader with a fatally weakened following.

Since he did not enjoy much support inside his party he was forced to shift the focus of effective control over economic policy-making away from the party to a bureaucratic Planning Commission. The course of Indian planning was to be significantly determined by Nehru's dominance and vulnerability.

Undoubtedly, Nehru's thinking about the historical logic of development was deeply influenced by his admiration for Marxist theory in his younger years; and, like most of his intellectual contemporaries, Nehru had no doubt that the history of Europe showed countries like India 'the image of their future' (Gopal, 1975; Chatterjee, 1986). By the time he was preparing to take over as India's prime minister, his thinking on political economy had undergone considerable change from his early 'scientific socialist' years. By the late 1940s, he had abandoned the orthodox Marxist position on the starkness of the choice between communism and capitalism, and was inclined towards a social democratic view similar to that on the left wing of the British Labour Party. On one fundamental point, however, he was closer to Marxists than social democrats: his understanding of the structure of the world economy remained strongly influenced by the Marxist thesis about economic imperialism. Thus Nehru's economic thinking was an interesting, and surprisingly consistent, amalgam of three different elements. A large theory of the world economy taken from Marx and Lenin framed an intermediate-level theory of state intervention in the economy in the interest of employment and welfare which was distinctly Keynesian. But Nehru's design had to contain answers to specifically Indian problems for which neither Marxism not Keynesianism provided any clear instruction or precedent, and these were tackled by intelligent improvisation (Nehru, 1958). At the time, the main alternatives in development seemed to be between three models of political economy: an unrestrained free-market capitalism, a modified welfare-state capitalism and a more radical communist model which involved a complete sacrifice of democratic liberties. For someone with Nehru's intellectual sympathies, the effective choice was reduced to one between welfare capitalism and a communist state. Both social democracy and communism gave priority to the norm of equity in economic distribution, but they differed sharply on the trade-off between economic and political objectives. Communism appeared to Nehru to sacrifice entirely the value of political democracy in a more single-minded, or ruthless, pursuit of economic growth accompanied by distributive equality, although with hindsight it seems that this view of communism's growth capacity was too optimistic. Social democracy, by refusing to abandon democratic forms, was obliged to achieve somewhat slower growth, and less effective distributive equity. At the heart of this model of political economy were considerations about two sets of trade-offs. First, there was a trade-off, within economic objectives themselves, between the rapidity of growth and the pace of redistribution. Secondly, there was a more complex trade-off between these two economic goals on the one side and political democracy on the other. Nehru seemed to concede, entirely unproblematically, that communist regimes were able to attain *both* higher rates of growth and more equitable distribution in a shorter span of time, but at the cost of total sacrifice of political liberty, a price too high for his liking (Nehru, 1958). His writings often conceded that the attainment of both growth and equitable distribution would take much longer through a democratic path. Still, it was worthwhile because of the intrinsic value of democracy itself. In Nehruvian political economy, unlike in some more disabused modern debates, the relation between democracy and development raised a more difficult problem. It was not a decision about the instrumental effectiveness of democracy in achieving economic growth, but the differently constituted problem of finding a balance, both in principle and in terms of historical feasibility, between two equally indispensable and incommensurable values.[3]

DEVELOPMENT AND POST-COLONIAL SOVEREIGNTY

There is an ironical anachronism in the generally cited retrospective assessments of the Nehruvian planning model. The East Asian economies, in comparison with which Nehruvian performance is now considered ludicrously inadequate, appeared, from his point of view, singularly unattractive. For the first generation of post-colonial leaders, the overriding concern was the preservation of sovereignty. Also, at that early stage of decolonization, the ease with which independent states could slide from an unconvincing imitation of Western democracy to indigenous authoritarianism was not so apparent. Unlike third world politicians of today, they did not stand amidst the rubble of broken constitutions. Not surprisingly, their sensitivity and interest were both turned towards those dangers which could reduce the sovereignty gained after such effort. One of Nehru's lasting intellectual achievements was devising the idea of nonalignment. It may seem to be a tired commonplace in 30 years' retrospect but, at the time when it was first adumbrated, it was a radically new idea, and very unpopular with the superpowers which dominated the world. There was a surprising underlying agreement between the Americans and Soviets about the inescapable bipolarity of the post-war world, and in that sense working that bipolar system was a kind of cooperative game between the two superpowers. It required considerable political imagination to conceive of large spaces of possible practical action between the two great and increasingly menacing military systems; and it was no mean feat of political persuasion to convince several third world states to see the world through this internationally disobedient perspective.

To the generation which created independent nation-states after

long struggles with colonial powers, therefore, the major consideration in thinking about development was less the relation between
democracy and development than that between development and
political sovereignty. Nehru, in a sense, extended the line of thinking
originally developed by the first generation of economic nationalists
like Naoroji and R. C. Dutt (Chandra, 1973). Influenced by Western
political economy, but using it to interpret India's economic decline
under 'un-British' rule, the economic nationalists had argued that
British colonial dominion over India led to a drain of wealth back
to the metropolis (Naoroji, 1901). It was not difficult for imaginative readers of Marxist political economy to find in the theory of
imperialism an appropriately radical extension of nationalist 'drain
theory'. Schematically, they accepted the fundamental thesis of the
theory of imperialism that the difference in political and military
effectiveness between the modern West and its colonial territories
lay in the latters' failure to generate independent industrialization.[4]
Since industrialization translated so directly into military and political control, it followed that mere political independence from the
imperial power might not be enough for the effective preservation of
sovereignty. Actual control over the fate of modern societies was lost
and regained by economic means. Consequently, political independence could degenerate rapidly into a hollow ritual if the economy
was not able to achieve growth. For Nehruvian political economy,
achieving growth itself was insufficient politically. Two other objectives were inextricably connected to growth in the broad sense.
Growth in GNP or consumer goods industries alone would not fulfil
the political objective of the nation. Heavy industries provided the
base for a mature industrial society. Besides, dependence on others
in heavy industries like steel, metals, petrochemicals and power might
lead to a fatal attenuation of economic independence in spite of
formal political freedom. Serious growth therefore meant industrialization in the heavy industries sector.

But development also had an internal dimension, not just the
protection of sovereignty from external threats. It had to be preserved from the justified dissatisfaction of its own citizens. This
pointed towards a second political consideration which connected
concerns for development to the question of distributive justice.
To those well versed in the history of popular disturbances in the
nineteenth-century West, insufficiency of food or serious inequality
in distribution could eventually imperil a state, particularly because
a democratic government could not have recourse to repression on
a scale used by autocratic European states against their rebellious
poor.

An outline of economic modernization which would fulfil all these
political objectives was gradually devised through the process of economic planning.[5] It was based on a plan of industrialization favouring fast growth of heavy industries in the state sector, with other
sectors left free for the energies of private enterprise. Economists

who framed the ideologically crucial Second Five-Year Plan foresaw difficulties in the rural sector if employment was not generated, as the plan for heavy industrialization was calculated to create jobs slowly and required long gestation periods. A crucial requirement for successful industrialization, therefore, was land reform, and eventual reduction of social and income inequality in the rural sector of the economy. The planning process in India, if we take the ideas developed in the first three plans together rather than any single document, showed a development design which theoretically reconciled these objectives, and produced a fairly internally consistent structure of economic reasoning (Chakrararty, 1987; Bagchi, 1991; Bhagwati, 1993). In Indian nationalist thinking in the early years after independence considerable thought was given to the connection between political and economic objectives of the nation and its state. There was much detailed deliberation on the possible relations and trade-offs between democratic institutions and the structure and direction of development, both in productive and distributive terms. But what 'democracy and development' meant to them was considerably and interestingly different from what they have come to mean in today's debates. The communist system was considered a great success due to its two enormous achievements: its ability to industrialize much faster than first world countries had, and its ability to withstand, practically without external assistance, the military-industrial might of Fascist Germany using the industrial power of the entire European continent. It was a triumph of autarky. In that context, imitating the political-economic model of a state like South Korea, such a beacon of successful growth in today's literature, was inconceivable; its economic potential in the 1950s did not appear sufficiently strong to be attractive, and its evident political subservience to the United States made that even more unappetizing. And despite American effort at persuading the world that South Korea constituted an indispensable part of the free world, its political system under Syngman Rhee appeared suspiciously close to authoritarianism. Even Pakistan, the more relevant counter-example, which was aligned, pro-West and military-ruled – and attracted great quantities of economic and military assistance from the United States as a direct consequence of these qualities – appeared singularly unattractive. But in terms of the central ideas, and the way the question was set, the fundamental difference was perhaps the treatment of democracy as an independent value, rather than a purely instrumental subsidiary means for the achievement of growth. In that sense the political element has declined remarkably in the discourse of modern political economy. In the general celebration of the economic growth of the East Asian countries, there are few audible murmurs of anxiety about their indifferent democratic record. These states have benefited systematically from the political forgetfulness of institutions and opinions which display an admirable vigilance about the rights record of the entire third world but become curiously absent-minded in their political accounting when they turn to East Asia. It is of course possible to devise a plausible historical theory which can circumscribe those anxieties by asserting that successful development would later generate internal pressure for democracy, as they well might in the long run, and as, indeed, they did in South Korea. In case these societies successfully democratize in future, it could be possible to say that authoritarian politics was a price paid historically for generating the initial lift into take-off.

THE HISTORICAL EXPERIENCE OF THE NEHRUVIAN DESIGN

The historical trajectory of the Nehruvian system was marked by paradox. Nehru's own reading of history, in his eloquent letters to his daughter, displayed a romanticism common to European radical thought in the 1930s. It saw history as a humanist narrative, regarding 'the people' romantically as the source of all political and intellectual creativity. This view of history fitted the requirements of nationalist rhetoric beautifully, though a small problem of internal consistency was created by the preponderance of peasants in the Indian historical landscape. European radical thought, under the influence of Marx's ineradicable prejudice, was less than optimistic about the peasant's cognitive or intellectual powers. The peasantry was seen to consist of unreconstructed traditional groups whose poverty was unrelieved by the cognitive privilege of the working class, despite an occasional concession made derisively to the cunning of the *muzhik*. But usually this was a slyness that did not extend beyond small situations in which the devious peasant could get the better of his superiors in insignificant contests. But, as a rule, the peasants were not granted either the cognitive mastery of the processes of modernity, like the proletariat in Marxist theory, or an independent political imagination. As the majority of the Indian masses who were given the gift of electoral rights were illiterate peasants, a certain apprehension about how they would use these powerful instruments of policy control remained in the minds of the Nehruvian leadership.

Secondly, the leadership also appreciated indirectly that the making of longer-term economic policy must be done in relative political calm, away from the immediate pressures of parliamentary re-election. Proper decisions about development matters required specialized technical knowledge of the economy, which 'the people' and their legislative representatives lacked, and they must be protected from the consequences of their own literal sovereignty. Even statesmanly politicians, gifted with historical foresight, might make economic decisions better if they were not made conditional on moves of everyday political survival. This idea of relative autonomy of long-term economic decisions was given an institutional form by making the Planning Commission independent of the constitutional representative structure to ensure greater insulation and flexibility in decision-making. During the period under Nehru, this institutional mechanism functioned well, and gave the Commission both authority and autonomy. Subsequently, this went against the Planning Commission's interests, as leaders less appreciative of the virtues of planning could marginalize it with few consequences.

A common argument in the debate about democracy and development is that democracy brings economic and political life too close together for sober, longer-term calculation in development decisions. Pressure for populist measures aimed as short-term gains forces governments to disperse resources in immediate handouts to some political groups,[6] either because they are more discontented or simply better organized, taking them away from potentially more purposeful long-term use. The actual political situation in the Nehru period approximated to an ideal equipoise (Rudolph and Rudolph, 1985). The government received its legitimacy from periodic multi-party elections, but did not have to bribe voters by wasteful pre-electoral inducements. Its decision-making therefore had both the requisite political legitimacy from democratic procedures and the required distance and insulation from daily politics necessary for detached technical evaluation of projects. It was this necessary distancing of daily politics which conferred remarkable power in the hands of intellectual planners like P. C. Mahalanobis who prepared the design for the Second Five-Year Plan. But this obviously depended entirely on the comfortable incumbency of Nehru himself and the Congress leadership.

Despite this, the actual course of events in the Nehru period diverged significantly from the rational and consistent causal lines envisaged by the planning documents. This divergence was not in terms of an abandonment of the planning targets or the arguments behind them, but in the political translation of the development objectives. It has been argued, plausibly, by Marxist writers, that if we consider the highly unequal distribution of benefits and assets after independence, it is clear that Indian society was dominated by a ruling coalition of three different social groups: business interests, large landholders and the managerial-bureaucratic elite (Bardhan, 1985). The coalition was a necessity for their domination: none of these social groups had sufficient power, authority or influence in Indian society to impose its dominance on society at large. It was only as a coalition that they could ensure their dominance over other groups (Kaviraj, 1988). It could be argued that this coalition was inherited rather than created by the Nehruvian system. The capacity of these groups to exercise disproportional authority in society and their consequent ability to turn distributive inequalities their way was an established fact of economic life before independence. Only the reliance on planning and the creation of a large state sector expanded the size of the state bureaucracy and altered its nature. But translating the plan targets into practice had to be done through political instrumentalities available to the new elite, like state Congress parties, and state legislative assemblies. Due to their social composition, some of these were hardly suitable instruments for even mild social redistribution.

The first objective of Nehruvian planning, protection of political and economic sovereignty, especially its policy of protectionism towards the indigenous bourgeoisie, naturally drew support from industrial interests. But its other objective, social and redistributive reform, however moderate, was unlikely to attract support from that quarter. Social inequality had two great arenas in post-independence India: the poverty of the destitute marginal work-force concentrated in cities, and the poverty and destitution of the poor peasantry in the villages. Any redistributive move by the government would have gone seriously against the interests of the two major constituents of the ruling coalition in India, the capitalist employers and rural landed magnates. At the time, the government showed some urgency about rural inequality, since increase in agricultural productivity was an immediate necessity, and economic thinking inside government favoured the view that if land was redistributed to the poorer peasants, this would provide the critical incentive for higher productivity (Chakravarty, 1987). The central government under Nehru, prompted by the planners, pressed land reform legislation on state governments, which had constitutional jurisdiction over agriculture. State Congress leaders often came from the class they were now exhorted to dispossess, and it was not surprising if they seemed less than enthusiastic towards such high-minded self-destruction (Frankel, 1978). But more critically, electoral mobilization in the years after independence often depended crucially on support of the local landed elite which held poorer peasants and artisans under their control through a variable mixture of social authority and usurious compulsion.

The Congress party was thus led into a life of utter contradiction. It wished to appear to the poor as a party intending eventual social reform, and to the propertied as the one which defended them from expropriation. Apparently, such divergent objectives could be followed if they were temporally disjointed; and the Congress under Nehru largely opted for serving the interests of the propertied in the present and of the poor in a sufficiently distant future. But as it became clear that its support for property was immediate and for reform eventual, it came to be regarded as a party of the social *status quo*. This practical strategy served to return the party to power in the first three general elections with comfortable majorities; but it meant a life of contradiction for development policies and political economy. The theoretical thinking of the central government, especially the planners, required some redistributive effort, which was translated into legislative programmes. At the legislative stage, the Congress state governments showed their reluctance; more practically, they ensured that the legislative injunctions failed abjectly in implementation.

By the time Nehru died, the Congress party was already facing serious electoral problems. The Communists won a symbolic, though slender, victory in the elections in the state of Kerala in 1957, and had to be forced out of office through a political ruse rather than by straightforward democratic means. Most significantly, Nehru's government could not overcome the constant pressure arising from chronic food shortages, and consequent dependence on American food aid. In the late 1950s food riots took place in many parts of India, and indicated a serious erosion of Congress legitimacy. The prospects for Congress did not look promising even with the reassurance of Nehru's leadership. After his death, and that of Lal Bahadur Shastri soon after, with Indira Gandhi insecurely in power and besieged by economic crisis and political dissensions inside the party, things looked very grim. When it went into the fourth general election in 1967, Congress was defeated in most North Indian states, though it held onto the central government by an insecure majority.

A final paradox needs to be recorded in the story of Indian politics. The political elite during Nehru's time had sought to link poverty to democracy through a programme for community development and *panchayati raj*.[7] Introduction of self-government in the villages was seen as an opportunity for the rural poor to use the weight of their numbers to overbalance the traditional dominance that small coteries of the economically powerful enjoyed over them through economic means. This was a direct attempt, from the top down, to link democracy with development and to induce ordinary people to link the power of the poor to the instruments of democracy. Unfortunately, the results were surprisingly negative. In most cases, the landed elite used their usurious control over the poorer peasantry to bring them into line and make them cede the formal powers of local self-government to the dominant landed groups. Eventually, the consequence of the local self-government reforms came to be largely the opposite of what Nehruvian reformers had expected. Instead of undermining the economic power of a small rural elite and empowering the poor, it gave to the dominance of that elite itself the dubious seal of electoral approval, adding to economic effectiveness a new form of political legitimacy. It was only later, when politicians in the 1970s sought to mobilize ordinary people in desperate moves to win elections, that the questions of disadvantage and democracy were somewhat more successfully linked.[8]

DEMOCRACY AND DISCONTENT AFTER NEHRU

Political instability after Nehru's death was not entirely unexpected. The legitimacy acquired through leading the nationalist movement was qualitatively different from the more perishable variant gained through electoral success. Obviously, the next generation of political leaders could not expect to enjoy the generosity of consideration that a loyal nation gave to its national leaders. Legitimacy was bound to be a more mundane and short-lived affair. Lal Bahadur Shastri, Nehru's successor, enjoyed both types of reputation and legitimacy. But Shastri died suddenly, leaving the Congress entirely unprepared for a leadership contest. Indira Gandhi, who led the Congress during the disastrous elections that followed, had gained the premiership not by her strength, but because of her appearance of weakness (Kaviraj, 1986). Her vulnerability in the first few years of office was reflected in all spheres of India's public life. Persistent difficulties with the balance of payments forced the new government to accept suggestions from international financial institutions to devalue the rupee (Frankel, 1978). This was the worst possible move in the situation, costly in both economic and political terms, since it undermined her political authority without giving dramatic economic results. The Congress party under Indira Gandhi's leadership seemed besieged on all sides – in economics and politics, both internally and externally. Indira Gandhi devised an effective political strategy to break out of this encirclement through a new kind of populism, using unconventional measures which broke the mould of traditional Congress politics of quiet appeasement and coalition-building of all social groups, or at least those which had power or volubility. Her political moves towards populism annoyed and alienated the traditional leadership of the Congress, and brought support from the left wing inside the party, heightening internal dissension. Eventually, Indira Gandhi's faction broke the Congress party on ostensibly ideological lines, brought in measures to nationalize the largest banks and abolished the privy purses that had been granted to the former rulers of the princely states under the Nehruvian dispensation at the time of the transfer of power.[9] The significance of these moves was rhetorical, rather than practical. They invited the electorate to see the world and imagine political possibilities in a certain way, rather than alter the structure of that world in a fundamentally radical fashion. Yet rhetoric is part of the substance of politics, and the symbolic move of dispossession of the princes, who were in any case historically superseded, tied in perfectly with her slogan during the crucial elections of 1971 for the 'removal of poverty'. Nationalization of banks did not immediately help redistributive measures, but only increased the government's powers of financial control over parts of the private capitalist economy. But they served to create an effective radical illusion, which persuaded the electorate to give Mrs Gandhi an unprecedented margin of victory.

DEMOCRACY AND POPULISM

Indira Gandhi won an unprecedented majority in her second national elections, much larger than any Nehru ever had. Ironically, the declared objectives on which she won that election were too radical to be realized. The structural reasons for which much more moderate reform measures came to nothing earlier were bound to impede the dramatic new undertaking of the removal of poverty. The structure of social privilege had not changed, nor had the resolve of the government, nor its dependence on the propertied elite. But the importance of her populist move lay elsewhere. It was not meant to alter social structure. It was to alter the map of political imagination, which it did with great success. I have analysed elsewhere how this election altered the framework of democratic politics in India, turning elections into referendums, dislocating the normal process of translation of everyday grievances into votes (Kaviraj, 1986). Eventually, Indira Gandhi's political moves changed the entire structure of politics in India since, as a result of her success, other parties began to imitate her slogans and invent still more radical, and impracticable, ones.[10]

Slowly, Indian politics underwent a fundamental change towards a newer and deeper form of activation of the common people.[11] The radical rhetoric did not alleviate poverty, but it quickened the process which Tocqueville depicted with incomparable acuity, establishing the principle of political equality and dignity indelibly in the political world.[12] A certain decline of the etiquette of democratic politics which the middle- and upper-class politicians of the Nehruvian era generally observed occurred through the entry of the emergent farmer politicians who spoke in the vernacular and were far less respectful towards norms of parliamentary decorum, which they considered Western and alien. Etiquettes of restraint, vestiges of Victorian political manners which survived longer in India than in Britain, were abandoned for a more direct, earthy, vernacular style which increased in stridency as the new politicians began to compete in populist postures and a more ruthless canvassing for votes. By the 1970s, elections had become much more important for both the electors and the representatives. Voters appreciated that though they were consulted only once in five years about who should rule over them, this was a useful opportunity to extract serious concessions. Moreover, due to ministerial instability, such occasions came at shorter intervals than five years, a fact which the voter did not regret. Also by the 1970s, the economic powers of the state and its asset-controlling reach had grown so formidably that elected politicians, at every level, controlled considerable resources for disbursement and use. Since the only route of entry to that fund of state resource was through elections, for small politicians elections came to mean a great deal more than they did to 'unprofessional' politicians of Nehru's time.[13] Elections also came to be associated much more directly with the prising of concessions from the government by the use of bloc votes of various kinds. By introducing the new populist politics, Indira Gandhi also brought in much greater mortality of governments, as their entry depended on the promises they made. Since the promises which could bring them to power were mostly impossible to keep, governments were turned out in the following election or given a substantially reduced majority, bringing in not exactly a bi-party system in the conventional sense, but a system in which governments, at the state level at least, have been regularly replaced.

Essentially, the years after Nehru saw two processes occurring at the same time. Only after practising electoral democracy somewhat unbelievingly for 30 years did the poorer sections of the Indian electorate appreciate the great power of these formal instruments and comprehend that these were not only festive occasions on which they could vote one segment of the elite into ministerial power against another. These were also instruments which could lead to decisions that affected the everyday and long-term distribution of powers and opportunities. In the longer run, therefore, political democracy has had an effect going in the same direction as in the European case. In the West, political enfranchisement made earlier levels of economic inequality under capitalism insupportable and broke the mould of earlier social stratification for the more moderate inequalities of the welfare state. In India, too, the appreciation of the right to vote has led in the direction of a sharpened sense of iniquity and an attempt to use electoral politics to rectify it. Above all, democracy in the post-Nehru era has gradually conveyed to the Indian electorate the pervading, elusive but crucial modern idea of the plasticity of the social world, and democracy and development both as frameworks of collective intentions to shape it in preferred forms.

But it will be wrong to expect a simple re-enactment of the episodes of European history. First of all, the sequence in which significant social processes occur is bound to be different between European development and India. In the West three major historical processes had been substantially complete before transformations towards modern democracy began. The capitalist disciplining of a peasant work-force through brutal production regimes, establishment of a secular state to avoid endless civil wars between religious groups vying for political control of the state and the birth of a modern 'civil society' of individuation – all preceded the start of the democratic process.

In Europe, capitalist development from the seventeenth century had dissolved traditional identities to a substantial extent and replaced communitarian images of human living with the idea of a 'civil society' made up of atomized individuals. The European democratic process happened in the context of a civil society which used as the normal discourse of modernity a language of rights and saw individuals as their bearers or subjects. Consequences of democracy are likely to be different in India precisely because of the insufficient spread of the social logic of *gesellschaft*. In one respect in particular the connection between democracy and disadvantage has gone in a somewhat unexpected direction. Much of modern democratic theory presupposes in its arguments a certain way of conceptualizing the social world, based on individual selves as the fundamental units for the calculation of welfare. Collaterally, democratic theory thinks of groups as condensations of these individuals around common interests, which are intense but impermanent, as the major form of *collective* identity.

In Indian society, despite the inroads modernity has made into traditional forms of communitarian bonding of people, the process of individuation has not remade the entire logic of the social world. Perception of disadvantage often tends to be more collective than individual, but collectivity itself is seen in a non-modern manner, as solidarities that are not interest-based. Disadvantage is seen more as unjust treatment of whole communities, like lower castes, minority religious groups and tribal communities, which are thus seen as potential political actors for social equality. If poverty is defined as a socially unindexed deprivation/inequality, the resentments expressed through democratic means in recent Indian politics are not against poverty. Poverty is a universalistic term, and would apply to any individual meeting its economic criteria, irrespective of his or her social identification. To see in modern Indian politics a democratic struggle against poverty is conceptually absent-minded. Certainly, people who are part of democratic mobilizations are predominantly poor, but the principle of their self-identifying action is not poverty but *discrimination*. And the relevant unit of social analysis is not the individual, but the *community* (Chatterjee, 1994). This makes it possible for them to be acutely conscious of state indifference towards their demands, but completely indifferent towards parallel demands of others. It is also essential to remember that mobilization against poverty and against discrimination can yield quite different lines of actual political mobilization, and therefore very different historical consequences.

One of the reasons why the trajectory of enfranchisement has produced unfamiliar results is that the collective actors that have emerged powerfully into the arena of democratic politics, dominating its conflicts and transactions, are not *interests*, but *identities*.[14] The idea of self-determination has thus taken the popular form, not of Kantian moral autonomy of self-defining individuals, but of assertive identity groups speaking the language of autonomy with very different effects. The relation between the autonomy of individuals and of these identity groups is not symmetrical. Most of these movements would not allow their individual members the choice of defining themselves but forcibly subsume their aspirations in collective demands to the state and other groups.[15] Democratic participation has thus created a new stage in which there is a distributive game going on in which the primary actors are not individuals, or their interest-based combinations, like trade unions, chambers of commerce, or more evanescent issue-based pressure groups. Social groups based on identity, either in terms of the caste system, or regions,[16] and not impermanent interest coalitions, are the primary actors; the individuals belonging to those groups are incidental beneficiaries of successful political actions.

But this seems to bring in at least a potential contradiction between the social presuppositions of democracy and the operation of its overt political rules. It is generally acknowledged that the conventional rules of democracy simply assume the historical presence of a certain type of society which was nearly universal in the West by the nineteenth century, but not elsewhere outside Western civilization. This picture consisted of a distinction between a civil society (which was a description of the social whole without its political institutions and which was made up of the constant fission and fusion of interest groups) and the state. Impermanence of the interest groups rested in turn on a vision of individuals as selves who could revise their identity, and who benefited differentially in the constant fluctuations of the market (Khilnani, 1994). It was therefore a picture of a social world in which identities, affiliations, aspirations, even selves, were constantly remade, and interests incessantly renegotiated. Historically contingent and transient majorities held power in democracies, with the corollary that in democratic systems, no group ever permanently lost. In fact, and in spite of this picture of a civil society in constant flux, democratic theorists spent considerable time debating how potentially permanent majorities, of the poor, or the uncultured, or the uncouth, could be kept from imposing a 'tyranny of the majority' through its elective institutions.[17] This individualist picture of society, which is an assumption of political sociology behind much of modern Western democratic theory, is unavailable in India, except perhaps in a few big cities. Even in these, it may be found only in the social behaviour of a small highly Westernized middle class. Otherwise, the democratic game and its outcomes has become fundamentally different because it is being played by a different species of players.

There are several distinct justifications of democratic government. It is sometimes justified by the moral preferability of its operative elective rules, and defended primarily because it is a government by choice. It is often justified by the alleged rationality of its decisions because all types of calculations and scenarios are consulted, albeit differentially, in the process of democratic decision-making. But it is not the least of democracy's attractions that it is a government which makes dominance strictly impermanent (Przeworski, 1991) and generally random.[18] Because of the great diversification of interests in modern societies, it is unlikely that large modern societies would be dominated by a permanent majority. Permanent majorities are inherently threatening for the moderation of democratic government, because that would equally mean permanent exclusion of some groups. The volatility that Indira Gandhi's populism has brought into modern Indian politics has released political forces which have engaged in a search for permanent and invincible majorities. Political strategies of three very different groups represent these majoritarian urges in Indian political life today: the Hindu majority of the Bharatiya Janata Party (BJP), the lower-caste majority of the backward-caste politicians and the aspiration of the Hindi linguistic chauvinists to establish exclusive control of the polity. Till now the edges of these majorities have cut against one another. In particular, the majority of lower-caste groups have gone against the consolidation of a Hindu religious majority, but it is impossible to rule out a sudden sense of affinity among them, or different constituent blocs. It is doubtful if Indian democracy could survive if any of these actually come to power, either singly or in some combination.

Democracy has, thus, raised the question of both political equality and majoritarian dominance. Its language has been read, irreversibly, to support both the demand of lower-order groups for equality of treatment, and the claim that systematic inequality against some groups, if sanctioned by a large majority, is permissible. The language of democracy has thus exacerbated the sense of disprivilege and discrimination, however disingenuous it is in some cases.[19] During the Nehru years most political parties were confident that if disadvantage and democracy were to be linked, the major form of social conflict in India would centre around the problem of poverty and class conflicts between the rich and the poor. Ironically, when this connection has eventually been made, it has not favoured class politics in the normal sense at all. Assertions through democratic means have led to an inexplicable decline in class politics, reflected in the confinement of communist influence to its traditional bases in West Bengal and Kerala. Class politics seeks to bring the weight of the overwhelming numbers of the poor into play by organizing them into self-recognizing political groups. However, when disadvantaged groups organize on the basis of caste, or resentment against regional deprivation, they have behind them not merely the numbers of vast groups of genuinely dispossessed people, but also the resources of those among them who enjoy at least *partially* the advantages of elites. It is the combination of the vast *numbers* of the dispossessed and the *resources* of a section of the elite which makes these mixed coalitions much more effective in short-run electoral competitions. As a consequence, these groups press for a peculiar brand of social equality which calls for equal treatment of whole groups in a field of communities, and not of individuals in the field of 'civil society'.

Another way of putting it could be to say that their politics is more concerned with *external* rather than *internal* equity: that is, equality between groups rather than equality amongst group members. This certainly intensifies lines of social division, but these divisions are between vertically integrated communities, like one caste against another, or the peasants against the city-dwellers, rather than the differentiation amongst them on class lines expected by both classical Marxist and liberal thought. The net effect of this kind of politics which energizes relatively disprivileged groups to make immediate demands on the state is in a sense to *increase* the centrality of the state to all social processes. At the moment, this brings them into direct conflict with business and middle-class opinion which supports liberalization measures aimed at reducing the activity of the state in the economic sphere. It has also altered the politicians' relation to the state as an economic institution. Politicians during the Nehru era were mostly successful professionals who did not come into politics for pecuniary advancement. In the years after Nehru, a new brand of politicians has gradually moved into state and central level politics. They have turned their political position into an instrument of economic gain. The obstructive power of the byzantine bureaucracy enhances the ability of politicians to block commercial or industrial projects unless they get some illegal gratification; and the insecurity of their tenure because of the great volatility of the negative votes has made their demands on the resources of the state even larger. The state, as a consequence, is seen as an economic institution from a very different point of view, as the provider of a stock of funds over which politicians would have unaccountable control; and this unaccountability is legitimized by using part of the surplus at the state's control for distribution among their immediate supporters and social constituency. It is not surprising, therefore, that the state sector of the economy, once established with the explicit purpose of modifying the effects of capitalist enterprise, is gradually turned into a more retrograde developmental institution representing endemic corruption, inefficiency and unaccountable control over resources by corrupt politicians.[20]

The Indian state today can thus be plausibly accused of frittering away in two ways the scarce resources raised primarily by indirect taxation on poor citizens. Its everyday functioning involves distribution of patronage by politicians rather than meeting any objectives of providing support for commonly required infrastructure, or subsidizing capital stock. Besides, use of monetary incentives to groups to vote for parties fuels the classical misgiving about democracy, that it encourages short-term political spending rather than wiser outlays on long-term economic priorities. Additionally, such concession to groups must be utterly contingent, depending on their transient bargaining power. This contingency makes it impossible to follow any long-term development planning which requires periodic monitoring of results or targeting of resources with a long time horizon. The effect of electoral democracy on governments without a deep-level legitimacy has certainly confirmed this hypothesis. As governments in the period after Nehru have not remained in power for long, they have usually not been there to be blamed by the time the damages caused by their policies become apparent. Shorter life expectancy in governments encourages economic irresponsibility.

The Nehruvian system has thus drawn a great deal of unjustified criticism in recent debates because of its lack of dramatic success in economic development; but there are important extenuating circumstances. First, the terms in which it is condemned are not identical to those in terms of which it would have measured its own success. It is because democracy has dropped to the level of a purely instrumental role that its achievement appears negligible. If the successful practice of democracy, in a historical context marked by a general failure of democratic governments in the third world, is seen as a value, its achievements have been considerable. Besides, it seems more apt to say that its successes were transcended by historical developments within India and in the world political economy; in its own terms, it was successful, even economically. By the late 1960s fundamental changes had occurred in the political and economic structures of the Congress system in India, so that under the misleading appearance of continuity, what operated in practice was a substantially new system of distribution of power and management of development. So the failure of the later leadership to preserve the Nehruvian model gave rise to a new model of political economy, unmarked by a name, which in fact was the model which failed, not the one he set up. Finally, the Nehruvian development model was surely based on import-substituting industrialization leading to self-reliance – a policy entirely appropriate to the structure of the international economy after the Second World War. But after the 1970s there was a fundamental restructuring of world capitalism through the reorganization of trade flows, access to developed markets and development of new products which superseded the earlier structure of world production. The opportunities created by this new structure passed India by, because its economic policies were never developed for export-led growth. Indian planning did not adapt to the reinvented capitalism of the 1980s sufficiently early, remaining locked into its previous designs. It is hard to say that the Nehruvian design failed; rather its successes, significant but limited, were overtaken by history.

CONCLUSIONS

The historical process of democratization in India was quite different from Europe. The first difference consisted in the temporal sequence of the relation between democracy and other essential processes of European modernity. These included secularization of the polity, creation of an individuated 'civil society', and the formation of a modern capitalist economy through the displacement of large segments of the peasantry from the land with the imposition of modern work discipline on them, since the productivity of capitalism is intimately connected to the disciplinary aspects of the factory regime. In the history of the West, all these processes of the creation of modernity happened, and stabilized themselves, *before* the serious pressures for democracy and the extension of suffrage began. In India, by contrast, these processes are going on at the same time, and are showing that the logic of one could seriously affect, hinder or alter the logic of others. In two ways the trajectory of democracy in India already appears significantly different. Contrary to modernist theories, democracy has not simply undermined and eradicated traditional identities, like caste and religion, but altered them. As a consequence, it becomes difficult to describe what is happening within the resources of the conventional dichotomy of tradition and modernity. Caste groups recognized the opportunities provided by parliamentary politics and utilized them in most innovative ways, forcing parliamentary democracy to acknowledge surreptitiously their existence. So caste has not disappeared; but nor are caste groups unchanged. Under the pressure of parliamentary democratic politics, people have moved away from traditional self-descriptions like Brahmins or Shudras into utterly untraditional ones, like Scheduled Castes, a category created by the constitution, or the currently turbulent 'intermediate castes', a group invented by older groups to take advantage of the logic of the electoral system. It is hardly surprising that illiterate peasants would in their everyday discourse use English terms to indicate these formations, since there are no traditional concepts for them in the vernaculars. As democratic forms become better entrenched, and opportunities better appreciated by common people, traditional forms of identity have not disappeared but have adapted to modern structures. Are these castes traditional or modern?

A similar transformation can be seen in the case of religious identity. Traditionally, both Hindu and other religions were deeply segmented, such that the practical religion of people was sects rather than large doctrines like Hinduism or Islam. Pressures of electoral politics have had a similar influence on religious identities as well, producing leaders who appreciate the enormous electoral advantages of the support of an unfractured Hindu or Muslim community. This exacerbates conflicts between communities, but on modernist political grounds, not strictly religious ones. This also leads to the paradoxical situation where religious identities create unprecedented trouble in the public sphere, while there is incontrovertible evidence of a constant depletion of the sacred in the private lives of people. Thus political assertion of religion is being organized by communities whose members are less deeply religious in their beliefs. One of the remarkable things about Indian democracy however is that despite considerable dissatisfaction about such issues as the state, economic growth and social conflicts, no social or political group has expressed dissatisfaction with democracy. This seems to confirm Tocqueville's notion that democracy is not merely arguably the best form of government but, once established in a society, it is historically irreversible.

In the more restricted field of the relation between development processes and political regimes, the historical experience of India is no less paradoxical. Economic development, whether driven by unrestricted capitalist enterprise or supervised and planned by the state, requires fundamental political order. If democracy operates well within the context of an established political order, it does not conflict with the logic of economic growth. But in the third world, where states themselves are often not sufficiently entrenched, democratic politics can accelerate and multiply demands to an extent that political order itself is undermined. In the Indian context, the two stages of Indian democracy, in the Nehru years and after, show rather contrary things about the relation between democracy and development. The second phase clearly shows that populist 'democracy' might impede longer-term planning for development, if the connection between electoral cycles and distribution of state resources comes too close. But the earlier Nehruvian experience shows that this need not be so. The Indian political system may gradually evolve into a democracy of identities rather than of interests, which promotes greater equality among collectives (not among individuals) at the cost of slowing down overall growth. As the state's inability to take decisions free from such pressures becomes apparent, social groups interested in faster growth press for liberalization and the removal of sectors of the economy from the state's directive sphere. The attempt in the early 1990s to concentrate important decisions in the Finance Ministry headed by a political outsider is, in a strange way, an attempt to restore the autonomy of the economic decision-making process from pressures of electoral politics, though its effects would be in the direction of liberalization rather than state control.[21] It appears that successful economic development, either through a state-led strategy or a market-led one, requires equally a certain distanciation of economic policy-making from pressures of political survival, and an assurance that a policy would be pursued long enough to reveal both its advantages and potential faults. It seems that in the shorter run, at least, Indian political economy is moving towards an arrangement of a typical capitalist democracy, in which productive decisions are taken by a bourgeoisie relatively free of the state's control and driven primarily by market forces. However, the pressures of democratic politics use the state to establish secondary distributive mechanisms to counteract the worst inegalitarian consequences of market forces. The considerable resources the state requires to perform this function of dampening bourgeois inequality came, in the case of the West, from taxation. But, in the Indian case, it came from state control over productive enterprises. If liberalization reduces that control over productive state enterprises, the distributive responsibilities of the state would face a deep crisis, as its chances of appreciably raising revenue through dramatically increased taxation do not appear very good.

Democracy would thus appear to mean very different things to different classes in Indian society. To the more privileged sections of society, it would mean the freedom of enterprise, and the consequent benefits of inequality; to the lower orders, it would mean equality, at least between communities. Between these two contradictory but, in their own ways, equally plausible readings of what democratic institutions offer, Indian democracy will continue on its paradoxical and surprising history.

NOTES

1 As with most functional statements, this tends to evade the problem of origins. However, it is possible to argue a position consistent with this functional view. It can be asserted, for example, that the occurrence of either process would create pressure for the occurrence of the other.

2 Marx dwelt on these themes at several stages in his work. The 'two ways' thesis occurs in *Capital III* (1894); but the main ideas of the thesis were advanced in Engels's *Revolution and Counter-revolution in Germany* (1852) and Marx's article 'The Bourgeoisie and the Counter-revolution' (1848).

3 Thus the use of the expression 'trade-off' is a bit inappropriate: there is a trade-off between democracy and development in the sense that more of one means less of the other; at the same time, trade-offs are easier between two things of a similar type; here it was between incommensurable values.

4 There has been some interesting development in historical research on this question recently. Several historians now claim that this picture was untrue, and India was on the brink of an indigenous capitalist growth in the eighteenth century. See Bayly (1990) and Washbrook (1988).

5 It is important not to confuse planning in India with Soviet-type state planning. Without doubt, Indian planning was inspired by the example of what was taken then as the unqualified successes of Soviet growth management. Like the Soviet system, planning was done and to some extent controlled by the state; but there the similarities ended. The state direction of the economy had to be very different because India had a capitalist economy, and not a state-controlled one, and its political system was democratic, not totalitarian. Both the ambition and the ability of the Indian state in economic matters were altogether more modest than that of the Soviet Union.

6 Three types of groups in India have been targets of such handouts before elections: first, the really poor or dispossessed because of their numbers; second, disgruntled groups if they had some contingent powers of blackmailing the government on an issue; and third, organized groups which simply used their strategic position in the economy's financial or communication system and cashed in their powers of disruption. Airline pilots and bank employees, not exactly among the sorely deprived, have used their leverage to great effect, for instance.

7 *Panchayati raj* was a model of local self-government, especially in the villages, strongly supported by Gandhi. It was not given much attention in the initial stages of constitution-making and was dropped into the Directive Principles of State Policy, the constitution's basket of ineffectual good intentions. Later it was revived by Nehru's government to engineer changes in the rural power structure.

8 However, I shall argue below that even this development has to be carefully analysed. What has found expression through democratic channels is resentment against discrimination, not strictly against poverty.

9 At the time of independence, the new state forced the accession of earlier 'princely states', but the former princes were given an assured

payment from the government of India. It was more a relic of the past than an effective institution.

10 After Indira Gandhi's success with the slogans of *Garibi Hatao* (remove poverty), another attempt at a similar populist move was the initiative to introduce a right to work into the Indian constitution as a display of political belief rather than serious policy during the premiership of V. P. Singh.

11 I hesitate to use the term participation because of the common associations of the word, particularly the idea that by political activism people share in some sense in the making of eventual decisions by the government. The case in India seems to be somewhat more complex and untidy. It is doubtful if the greater assertion of ordinary people actually affects the government's decisions, but these certainly have an effect on the political world in which the government has to function.

12 In his *Recollections*, Tocqueville reports a remark by a fellow legislator about the introduction of democracy in France: ' "Has the world ever before seen anything like what is happening today? What country has gone so far as to give votes to servants, the poor and soldiers? Admit that no one had even imagined that until now." And he added, rubbing his hands: "It will be very curious to see what all this produces." He talked about it as if it were a chemistry experiment' (Tocqueville, 1971: 228). This fits the Indian situation perfectly.

13 In common political discourse in India, the term 'professional politician' has come to mean a person who has no other career except through electoral politics. By contrast, politicians in the Nehru era were often distinguished professionals, lawyers, doctors, teachers and others, who could and did go back to their professional roles after their political careers.

14 Even in democratic polities, there is usually a penumbra of violent conflicts surrounding the more orderly space of constitutional exchanges. In a country of India's size and diversity, sometimes conflicts which originated inside democratic political spheres have festered for long and spilled over into unconstitutional forms of contests with the state, though remarkably some of these insurgencies have also crossed that boundary back again into a kind of electoral normality. In both these spheres, of strictly constitutional and extraconstitutional politics, the main actors have begun to be identities. In all of the major political problems in India – Punjab, Assam, Kashmir, Jharkhand – the central demand is not for the removal of poverty but of discrimination.

15 But it must be observed that such conflicts between individual and group autonomy have not commonly arisen. And, interestingly, intellectuals who, according to the legends of Western modernity, are the most likely to assert individuality, have rarely spoken against these demands and asserted their right to be Kantian individuals.

16 Movements of *dalits* constitute examples of the first type. Regional movements like Punjab, Assam, Kashmir, Jharkhand constitute the second group. Kashmir is an interesting case, where there is an internal conflict between two strands of identity. Kashmiri dissidents are united in their opposition to the Indian state, but they differ in their interpretation of their own identity. One group sees their movement as a purely regional movement of all Kashmiris; others see it as a convex identity of Kashmiri and Muslim at the same time, which tends to exclude non-Muslim Kashmiri groups from their sense of their collective self.

17 Although Mill is the author of the classical text on this point in the chapter on the tyranny of the majority in his essay *On Liberty* (1859), this theme runs through a long tradition of political thought from Madison through Tocqueville to Mill and beyond.

18 It requires great ingenuousness to believe that democracy can put any social group or coalition in dominance wholly at random, as some strands of romantic liberalism claimed in the past; but it does include a rule of randomness in the sense that the interest coalitions are about sets of issues, and individuals belong randomly to the groups which enjoy majorities on these questions.

19 An instance is the BJP claim that Hindus are discriminated against in a country in which they are a majority by an alien, secular state ideology intent on giving concessions to Muslims and other religious minorities. But what is interesting in studying political rhetoric is the fact that the aspiration of the majority to place its adversaries in permanent disadvantage has to speak in a language of injustice and 'discrimination' against itself.

20 Some economists believe that in strictly productive terms the performance of the state-sector industries is not seriously inferior to the private industries. But rents imposed by politicians and unproductive expenditure by the managerial stratum impose a surplus cost which makes them non-competitive.

21 In that sense the present government is doing exactly what Nehru did, though in support of an opposite kind of economic policy. It has given enormous powers of relatively autonomous decision-making to the finance minister who can use this effectively, partly because he is protected by prime ministerial authority and partly because he is not a professional politician and hence not dependent on electoral return. While under Nehru this autonomy was required to protect planners from pressures of vested interests, in recent times the government has created a similar autonomy for the finance minister to drive through liberalizing reforms against 'vested interests' calling for preservation of state control.

REFERENCES

Bagchi, A. 1971: *Private Investment in India 1900–1939*. Cambridge: Cambridge University Press.

Bagchi, A. 1991: From a Fractured Compromise to a Democratic Consensus: Planning and Political Economy in Postcolonial India. *Economic and Political Weekly*, XXVI, 611–28.

Bardhan, P. 1985: *Political Economy of Development in India*. Delhi: Oxford University Press.

Bayly, C. 1990: *Indian Society and the Making of the British Empire*. Cambridge: Cambridge University Press.

Bhagwati, J. 1993: *India in Transition*. Oxford: Clarendon Press.

Chakravarty, S. 1987: *Development Planning: The Indian Experience*. Oxford: Clarendon Press.

Chandra, B. 1973: *Rise and Growth of Economic Nationalism in India*. Delhi: People's Publishing House.

Chatterjee, P. 1986: *Nationalist Thought and the Colonial World: A Derivative Discourse?* Delhi: Oxford University Press.

Chatterjee, P. 1994: *The Nation and Its Fragments*. Princeton, NJ: Princeton University Press.

Engels, F. 1852: *Revolution and Counter-revolution in Germany*. Peking: Foreign Language Press, 1977.

Frankel, F. 1978: *India's Political Economy*. Princeton, NJ: Princeton University Press.

Gopal, S. 1975: *Jawaharlal Nehru: A Biography*, vol. I. London: Jonathan Cape.

Kaviraj, S. 1986: Indira Gandhi and Indian Politics. *Economic and Political Weekly*, XXI, 1697–708.

Kaviraj, S. 1988: Critique of the Passive Revolution. *Economic and Political Weekly*, XXIII, 2429–44.

Khilnani, S. 1995: Development of Civil Society. In E. Rothschild and G. Steadman Jones (eds) *History and Development*. Oxford: Oxford University Press.

Kidron, M. 1965: *Foreign Investment in India*. London: Oxford University Press.

Markowitz, C. 1985: *Indian Business and Nationalist Politics*. Cambridge: Cambridge University Press.

Marx, K. 1848: The Bourgeoisie and the Counter-revolution. In K. Marx and F. Engels 1972 *Articles from the Neue Rheinische Zeitung 1848–49*. Moscow: Progress Publishers.

Marx, K. 1973 (1894): *Capital III*. Moscow: Progress Publishers.

Marx, K. and Engels, F. 1972: *Articles from the Neue Rheinische Zeitung 1848–49*. Moscow: Progress Publishers.

Mill, J. S. 1982 (1859): *On Liberty*. Harmondsworth: Penguin.

Naoroji, D. 1901: *Poverty and Un-British Rule in India*. London: Sonnenschein and Co.

Nehru, J. 1958: *The Basic Approach*. New Delhi: AICC Publications.

Przeworski, A. 1991: *Democracy and Markets*. Cambridge: Cambridge University Press.

Rothschild, E. and Steadman Jones, G. (eds) 1995: *History and Development*. Oxford: Oxford University Press.

Rudolph, L. and Rudolph, S. 1985: *In Pursuit of Lakshmi*. Chicago: University of Chicago Press.

Tocqueville, A. de 1971: *Recollections*, trans. George Lawrence, ed. J. P. Meyer and A. P. Kerr. Garden City, NY: Doubleday and Co.

Washbrook, D. 1988: Progress and Problems: South Asian Economic and Social History c.1720–1860. *Modern South Asian Studies*, 22, 57–96.

7

A Circle of Paradox: Development, Politics and Democracy in South Korea

CHUNG-IN MOON AND YONG-CHEOL KIM

INTRODUCTION

Despite the haunting legacies of Japanese colonial rule, the Korean War and sporadic political and social ruptures, South Korea has transformed itself from one of the world's poorest economies into a forerunner of the Newly Industrializing Countries (NICs). Its per capita income rose from $103 in 1963 to $7,435 in 1993, and growth rates, which averaged 3.4 per cent per annum during 1954–62, have exceeded over ten per cent per annum since 1965. The expansion of exports has also been phenomenal. Total exports increased from $40.9 million in 1962 to $76 billion in 1993, making South Korea one of the most competitive export economies in the world. In contrast with many other developing countries, rapid growth has not seriously distorted either equality or quality of life. Economic concentration has emerged as a major social concern since the mid-1970s, but the distributional effects of economic performance have remained relatively favourable. South Korea has also shown a remarkable improvement in the quality of life of its people. Average life expectance increased from 53 years in 1961 to 71 years in 1992. The literacy rate and other social and economic indicators reveal that South Korea has almost reached the level of the advanced industrial countries (Song, 1990; Sakong, 1993; Economic Planning Board, 1994).

Such impressive performance has attracted worldwide scholarly and policy attention. While some have presented South Korea as a stellar case of a successful export-led growth strategy (Belassa, 1981; Krueger, 1983; Corbo, Krueger and Ossa, 1985), others have cited it as a role model for economic growth with equity (Bergsman, 1979; Leipziger et al., 1992). More recently, the effective management of economic crisis in the early 1980s has made South Korea a textbook example for neo-conservative reforms involving macroeconomic stabilization and structural adjustment in the third world (Corbo and Suh, 1992).[1] South Korea has offered ideal empirical raw materials for those who would refute the *dependencia* thesis as well as those claiming victory for the invisible hand of the market or the visible hands of state managers. Learning from South Korea has become a new fad in the study of third world development.

South Korea's glowing developmental experiences have not been without drawbacks, however. Chronic trade-offs between development and democracy have severely tarnished the image of its success. The impressive economic growth during the 1970s was marked by the advent of the repressive Yushin regime, and the success of stabilization and structural adjustment in the first half of the 1980s was often attributed to the iron fist of Chun Doo Hwan's quasi-military rule. Since 1987, however, South Korea has experienced a remarkable democratic opening. After a precarious five-year period of democratic transition under Roh Tae Woo (1988–92), South Koreans elected Kim Young Sam as the first civilian president since 1960, in a fair and free electoral competition in 1992. Since his inauguration in February 1993, Kim has been fostering the process of democratic consolidation through a series of assertive reform policies.

Despite the uncertain future of democratic persistence and consolidation, the progress of development and democracy in South Korea deserves accolades. The Korean odyssey, which has sailed through underdevelopment and authoritarianism, raises three interrelated theoretical and empirical questions. The first question centres round links between regime type and developmental performance. Is an authoritarian mode of governance a prerequisite for development? Can developmental dictatorship be justified in the light of the South Korean experiences? The second is related to the interlocking nexus of economic and democratic development. How, and to what extent, does development facilitate or inhibit democratic opening? Is the transition to democracy independent of developmental processes? What are the transitional costs of democratic opening? Finally, what are the democratic prospects in South Korea? How viable is democracy in South Korea? What institutional design will minimize the trade-off between growth performance and democratic stability?[2] This chapter is designed to explore these questions through an examination of South Korea's experience of development and democracy.

AUTHORITARIAN GOVERNANCE AND THE DEVELOPMENTAL STATE

The Park regime

Several contending approaches have been advanced in explaining South Korea's developmental experience. While neo-classical economists attribute the Korean economic success to an outward-looking development strategy, market-conforming state intervention, and human capital investment (Krueger, 1983; World Development, 1988), historical structuralists identify macro-historical forces and their conjunctural dynamics (for example, colonial legacies, state and social formation and geo-politics) as prerequisites for capitalist development in South Korea (Cumings, 1984; Woo, 1990; Gereffi and Wyman, 1990). Some have ascribed the Korean miracle to its Confucian culture, authority structure and social networks (Pye, 1985; I. G. Kim, 1987; C. H. Lee, 1990). More recently, however, the developmental state paradigm has emerged as a powerful alternative. According to this view, South Korea's impressive economic performance is not simply a product of market forces or cultural and historical legacies, but an outcome of conscious efforts by the state. The South Korean state has placed top priority on economic development, operationalized in terms of growth and exports. In order to achieve these goals, the state has actively intervened in the market to guide, coordinate and discipline the private sector through strategic allocation of resources and the use of diverse policy instruments. Effective strategic intervention has been ensured by rational, competent and meritocratic bureaucrats who are insulated from political and social pressures (Jones and Sakong, 1980; Haggard and Moon, 1983; Johnson, 1987; Amsden, 1989; Wade, 1990; Haggard, 1990; Kang et al., 1991).

Central to the developmental state are its strength, autonomy and strategic intervention for capitalist development, which not only restrain state predation, but also minimize social rent-seeking (Evans, 1992). Where have these attributes originated from? While Japanese colonial rule shaped an overdeveloped state structure, national division and the rise of anti-communism cultivated a hegemonic ideology legitimizing the capitalist developmental trajectory (Choi, 1989; Lim and Paik, 1986). But most important is the advent and deepening of an authoritarian mode of governance. Johnson (1987: 143–6) attributes the autonomy and strength of the South Korean state to the authoritarian governance in which a military-dominated single party regime was instrumental in mobilizing and allocating financial resources, disciplining civil society and suppressing political opposition. In a similar vein, Cumings (1984) coins a new term, the 'bureaucratic-authoritarian industrializing regime (BAIR)', to describe the political foundation for capitalist development in South Korea. S.-J. Han (1988) argues that rapid economic growth and industrial deepening have been facilitated by a bureaucratic-authoritarian regime.[3] Haggard further corroborates the link between an authoritarian regime and developmental performance by stating: 'since authoritarian political arrangements give political elites autonomy from distributional pressure, they increase the government's ability to extract resources, provide public goods and impose the short-term costs associated with efficient economic adjustments' (1990: 262).

Developmental dictatorship, which pits economic growth against democracy, has been one of the central themes of the political economy of development in South Korea. Developmental experiences under Park Chung Hee (1961–79) and Chun Doo Hwan (1980–7) seem to generate some empirical support for the 'elective affinity' between regime type and economic performance.

Park seized political power through a military coup in 1961, but instantly faced an acute economic crisis. Protracted poverty, inflation and unemployment plagued Korean society. Park overcame these economic difficulties through a sequential pursuit of macroeconomic stabilization (1963), liberalization (1964) and the transition to export-led growth strategy (1965). In order to facilitate the structural transformation of the Korean economy, Park undertook a series of institutional and policy reforms involving interest rates, foreign exchange rates, tax, credit and other administrative measures. A pool of incentives for the export sector, coupled with government mobilization and strategic allocation of financial resources, boosted economic performance. The growth rate rose from 2.2 per cent in 1962 to 12.7 per cent in 1966, and exports reached $250 million in the same year, a six-fold increase from 1962. In the mid-1970s, shifting comparative advantage and national security considerations propelled Park to transform the Korean economy from its emphasis on labour-intensive light industry to heavy and chemical industries. The Korean government prioritized six strategic sectors (shipbuilding, steel, heavy machinery, automobiles, electronics and petrochemicals), and allocated more than two-thirds of investment funds to these sectors in the second half of the 1970s. The big push produced immense inflationary consequences, resulting in a major economic collapse in 1980 (Haggard and Moon, 1983, 1993; Song, 1990).

Judged solely from the short-term disaster of the heavy and chemical industrial drive, Park's economic performance can be seen as a failure. However, net assessments indicate that the Park regime's economic performance was extraordinary. During Park's 17-year rule, the South Korean economy underwent profound transformation. Per capita income rose from $82 in 1961 to $1,546 in 1979, and exports increased from $40.9 million in 1961 to $15 billion in 1979.

It was during Park's rule that South Korea experienced its first balance of payments surplus ($12 million) in 1977. The unemployment rate decreased from 8.1 per cent in 1962 to 3.8 per cent in 1979. The Park regime was also instrumental in turning the subsistence agricultural economy into an economy based on manufactured exports. Extensive investments in social infrastructure and human capital, transformation of national ethos from chronic nihilism into a 'can-do' spirit (*hamyon doinda*), and social rewards for risk-taking entrepreneurship had all laid the foundation for unprecedented development performance. More importantly, short-term failure of the heavy and chemical industry push turned out to be a major asset for enhancing international competitiveness in the 1980s (Haggard and Moon, 1983, 1993; Song, 1990; Amsden, 1989; World Bank, 1993).

Several factors account for the developmental performance during the Park period. First is the efficient, consistent and coherent policy choices adopted by the regime, as well as their effective implementation, all of which ensured policy credibility. Second, the primacy of technocratic rationality, bureaucratic unity and insulation of economic policy-making from social and political pressures have served as the institutional basis for effective economic policy management. Third, bureaucratic unity and depoliticization of economic policies were achieved through executive dominance resembling an 'imperial presidency', an institutional configuration rather unique to the Park reign. Finally, leadership commitment to capitalist development played an important role (Cheng and Krause, 1991; World Bank, 1993).

The 'imperial presidency', the cornerstone of Korea's developmental state, was facilitated through the consolidation of an authoritarian mode of governance. After three years of harsh military rule, Park made a transition to civilian rule in 1963 and allowed limited political competition throughout the 1960s. A major change came in 1969, however. Despite extensive civil protests, Park amended the constitution to allow him to run for the presidency for a third term. The move, coupled with a sharp economic downturn, brought about negative political repercussions, undermining his popularity. In the April 1971 presidential election, Park was nearly defeated by Kim Dae Jung, a prominent opposition leader. The May 1971 general election dealt another blow to the Park regime. Despite election rigging, the opposition party performed well and posed a major challenge to the majority of the ruling Democratic Republican Party in the national assembly. An acute sense of regime crisis amidst an eroding national security situation, combined with weak economic performance, compelled Park to take drastic measures. In 1972, Park dissolved the national assembly and declared the new Yushin constitution.[4]

The Yushin regime provided Park with unprecedented executive power. Presidential tenure was extended from four years to six years, with no term-limit. Electoral competition was virtually banned. The president was elected through an electoral college in which one-third of the members were appointed by himself. Under the Yushin regime, the president enjoyed unlimited executive power through which he could dissolve the national assembly and take emergency measures whenever it was deemed necessary for public safety and national security. More important, the Yushin constitution virtually guaranteed executive control of the national assembly by allowing the president to appoint one-third of its members, while the remaining two-thirds were directly elected by the people (Henderson, 1988; Sohn, 1989; Yoon, 1990).

With this institutional design, the Korean state under Park prevailed over political and civil society. During the Yushin period, political opposition was systematically repressed, and the popular sector was excluded from the political process. In controlling civil society, the Park regime relied on several instruments. Among these were legal instruments such as the National Security Law, the Anti-communist Law, the Social Safety Law, the Law concerning Collective Demonstration and various other forms of presidential emergency decrees (Sohn, 1989; Yoon, 1990). During the period 1970–9, a total of 5,238 persons were arrested under these politically motivated legal instruments (H. J. Kim, 1992: 615). Corporatist control of societal actors and groups through cooptation and intimidation was extensively used in enforcing order. The Korean state virtually organized, subsidized and controlled both peak and grass-roots organizations (Y. L. Kim, 1990; J. J. Choi, 1989; Y. C. Kim, 1994). Finally, the security and intelligence apparatus were extensively used to control political and social opposition. The Korean Central Intelligence Agency (the KCIA), the National Defense Security Command and the police were all actively engaged in controlling and intimidating opposition elements (H. J. Kim, 1992).

In view of the above, state strength and autonomy under Park were not achieved through consensual social pacts, but by harsh authoritarian rule of coercion, intimidation and threats. It is, however, misleading to assert that the Park regime was based solely on naked authoritarian rule. Although Park's strategy for economic growth, heavy industrialization and export expansion excluded and repressed the popular sector, especially labour, Park crafted a subtle 'developmentalist' coalition with big business and the rural sector. While he cultivated and coopted big business by extending financial, tax and administrative incentives, the rural sector was coopted, organized and mobilized through the New Village Movement. The pattern of political alignment involving Yeochon Yado (rural support for the ruling party, and urban support for the opposition party) was not accidental, but an outcome of Park's carefully orchestrated coalition strategy. While big business provided Park with the economic foundation for political legitimacy by serving as the agency for growth and exports, the farm sector enriched the flavour of popular support for the Park regime (Moon, 1988).

Developmental performance under Park can then be seen as a product partly of state strength, autonomy and subsequent policy credibility, which was secured through hard authoritarian rule based on the selective cooptation and exclusion of civil society. Ironically, its very strength and autonomy accelerated the demise of the Park regime by deepening structural rigidities in political and policy management. Political accountability was severely damaged and policy feedback began to falter. Despite explicit risks of inflationary consequences, as well as internal and external warnings, Park blindly pursued his big push for industrial deepening and expansionary policies, thereby sowing the seeds of economic crisis. Unending harsh authoritarian rule also offered the pretext for strengthening the popular sector in opposing the Park regime. Worsening distributional consequences of the big push fuelled popular discontent, which became increasingly violent and pervasive. The ruling circle was divided over the issue of how to manage emerging socioeconomic and political crises, and this division, along with personal feuds among key presidential aides, led to Park's assassination by his trusted lieutenant, Kim Jae-Kyu, who was then director of the Korean Central Intelligence Agency. This episode of developmental performance under Park reveals a quintessential paradox of developmental dictatorship. While authoritarian rule was instrumental for regime survival and economic performance, the very process of development hastened the collapse of the Park regime.

The Chun regime

Economic performance under Chun Doo-hwan, who seized political power first by undertaking a mutiny within the military in 1979, and then through a quasi-military coup in 1980, also illustrates an interesting empirical case on the correlates of regime type and development. When Chun came to power through military intervention, he inherited a mounting economic crisis from the previous regime. The growth rate plunged to negative 5.5 per cent, current account deficits recorded $5.5 billion, foreign debts reached $34 billion and inflation was well over 30 per cent. Stabilizing the economy was an urgent political imperative. Chun's response took the form of neoconservative reforms involving structuralism using orthodox instruments (Foxley, 1983: 17). It aimed not only at short-term adjustment through macroeconomic stabilization, but also at a radical transformation of the economy through restructuring industry, liberalizing the financial sector, opening up the economy to free trade and redefining the role of the state *vis-à-vis* the market.

Pursuing short-term adjustment and transforming the national economy had inflicted substantial social costs and elicited intense political opposition from the affected sectors of society. As part of macroeconomic stabilization, the Chun regime pursued an austere fiscal policy by cutting farm subsidies (for example, the grain management fund and the fertilizer account), downsizing defence spending and streamlining state enterprises. Tight monetary policy was also simultaneously undertaken by reducing the size of private credit allocation, eliminating policy loans and implementing quarterly money supply targets. Along with this, wages in the public and private sector were frozen. Structural adjustment was also drastic and sweeping. Industrial structure was realigned in such a way to enhance international competitiveness, and extensive efforts were made to diffuse industrial concentration through the enactment of the Fair Trade and Anti-monopoly Act. Policy preference was redirected to small and medium-sized firms over the big firms (*chaebol*). The banking and financial sector was also subject to rationalization and liberalization. The Chun regime pushed for the opening of trade and foreign investment regimes. Along with this, direct and discretionary state intervention in the economy was replaced by market logic and indicative planning (Moon, 1988; Haggard and Moon, 1990; Corbo and Suh, 1992).

The neo-conservative reforms under Chun were remarkably successful. The long-term consequences of the structural adjustment measures still remain to be seen, but the short-term results of stabilization were very successful. During the reform period (1981–5), austerity measures curbed inflation from 28.7 per cent in 1980 to 2.3 per cent in 1984, while sustaining high growth rates (9.5 per cent in 1983, 7.5 per cent in 1984, 7.0 per cent in 1985 and 12.9 per cent in 1986). Balance of payments deficits were greatly reduced from $4.4 billion in 1981 to $1.37 billion in 1984, resulting in a record surplus of $9.9 billion in 1987. Unemployment declined from 4.5 per cent in 1981 to 3.9 per cent in 1986 (Economic Planning Board, 1988). By all accounts, the South Korean economy overcame the lingering legacy of the Park regime, and returned to revitalization.

Given a myriad of failed episodes of stabilization and structural adjustment in the third world, the South Korean case was quite extraordinary (Haggard and Kaufman, 1992; Nelson 1990). Several institutional factors explain the success: a quasi-revolutionary military leadership and its commitment to the reforms, executive dominance, the ascent of a new technocratic group defying the logic of Keynsian expansionism under Park and the insulation of economic decision-making from popular pressures (Moon, 1988; Haggard and Moon, 1990; Corbo and Suh, 1992). As with the Park regime, this institutional set-up was predicated on authoritarian governance.

Institutionally speaking, the Chun regime was milder by comparison with the Yushin system. Presidential tenure was limited to one seven-year term, and presidential power was substantially curtailed. Although a new constitution did not allow executive control over the legislature, opposition political parties were organized and controlled by the government. Freedom of expression and association was seriously limited. Labour, mass media and schools were under tight government control and censorship. The primary tools of governance were legal and administrative systems and the security and intelligence apparatus. Chun retained and utilized old legal systems of the National Security Law, the Anti-communist Law and the Law on Collective Demonstration, while introducing new laws such as the Law on the Purification of Political Activities and the Social Protection Law. During the Chun regime, a total of 12,039 people, far more than under Park, were arrested under these politically charged legal instruments (H. J. Kim, 1992: 616). The National Security Planning Agency (formerly the KCIA) and the National Defense Security Command became more active in political surveillance and control than under Park. Armed with these legal and institutional instruments, the Chun regime excluded the popular sector, neutralized political opposition and repressed popular protests. An interesting development is that the Chun regime even subjected big business to tight control and intimidation, as evidenced by the bankruptcy of the Kukje group, then the seventh largest *chaebol* in South Korea.[5] It was through this repressive authoritarian rule that the Chun regime could insulate the economic realm from intense politicization, impose uneven costs of adjustment across social sectors and implement neo-conservative reforms without interruption.

The Korean case clearly shows an affinity, if not necessity, between an authoritarian regime and developmental performance. Authoritarian rule assisted the Korean state to overcome the collective action dilemma by shielding the economic arena from the pressures of social and political groups. However, the authoritarian mode of governance is at best a necessary, but insufficient, condition for developmental performance. From Albania to Zaïre, the world is littered with examples of authoritarianism undermining economic development. It is through a historically specific blending of authoritarian politics with many other factors such as microeconomic institutions, leadership quality, ideology and commitment, social networks and bureaucratic competence that the South Korean state has been developmental rather than predatory (Evans, 1992; Gourevitch, 1993; Bardhan, 1993; Przeworski and Limongi, 1993). Furthermore, while the developmental state might be instrumental for efficient and coherent policy choice and effective implementation, it may not necessarily guarantee good developmental performance. Several intervening variables such as the boom and bust cycle in the national and international economy have influenced economic performance. Thus, linking the developmental state to economic performance via an authoritarian regime is tantamount to committing the fallacy of second-order causation (Moon, 1990; Moon and Prasad, 1994).

FROM AUTHORITARIANISM TO DEMOCRATIC OPENING: STRUCTURE, CULTURE AND LEADERSHIP CHOICE

One of the great ironies in the political economy of development in South Korea is the weak link between developmental performance and leadership popularity. As with Park, Chun vigorously pursued neo-conservative reforms in order to enhance his popular support and to ensure regime survival through economic growth and stability. However, the success of the reforms was not translated into political dividends. Despite explicit signs of economic revival, Chun was not able to win popular support. The ruling Democratic Justice Party suffered a near defeat in the general election of February 1985. Popular protests led by college students continued thereafter, while the general populace expressed growing cynicism toward the regime. Political opposition centred round the issue of constitutional amendments which would allow a direct presidential election. In April 1987, Chun revoked his initial pledge to amend the constitution to allow a direct presidential election. The move caused the opposition party and the popular sector to forge a united front, resulting in more organized and intensified popular protests. A critical conjuncture took place in June 1987. The death of a college student by police torture ignited fierce student demonstrations. Ordinary citizens, formerly indifferent, began to endorse and even participate in street demonstrations. Faced with a severe political crisis, Chun let Roh Tae Woo, his classmate from the military academy as well as his heir apparent as head of the ruling Democratic Justice Party, announce the June 29 Declaration.[6] Roh's move paved the way for a democratic opening by pledging a series of political reforms including constitutional amendments (M. Lee, 1990; Cotton, 1993; H. J. Kim, 1992). The crisis of the Chun regime can be largely attributed to its overall ontogenetic legitimacy problems: illegal seizure of political power, military intervention, repression of human rights and dictatorial rule (Moon, 1988). Nevertheless, the ruling regime anticipated that successful economic reform would mitigate these negative legacies and eventually bring political pay-offs. Contrary to expectations, it delegitimized the Chun regime and precipitated the process of democratic opening.

Why this paradoxical outcome? What facilitated this transition from authoritarianism to democratic opening? Three factors are responsible for the transition: structure, culture and leadership choice.[7] First, the process of development has profoundly realigned the structural foundation of Korean society by altering the distribution of power between the state and social forces. Politics and economic outcomes have a recursive relationship. Politics shapes economic outcomes, while economic transformation often shifts the terrain of political life and the conditions of regime consolidation (S. J. Lee, 1991; Choi, 1993a; Seong, 1993). Second, three decades of modernization and economic development have also shifted the political culture of the Korean people. Conservative authoritarian values were increasingly resisted, while democratic values were gradually being appreciated. The culture shift altered the political behaviour of social forces, playing a critical role in inducing political liberalization (A. Lee, 1993). Finally, structure and culture do not unilaterally determine the nature and direction of political change. Democratic transition involves complex and uncertain processes of interactions between the regime in power and social forces. Depending on the relative distribution of power and strategic actions, trajectories of political change can vary. In this context, leadership choice becomes an important variable (Im, 1990).

The origin of the democratic transition in 1987 can be traced back partly to Chun's pursuit of neo-conservative reforms, the resulting realignment of social forces and a growing disjuncture between political power and social support. As noted, Park orchestrated export-led industrialization by forming a 'developmentalist' coalition through the cooptation of big business, side-payments to farmers and political control of labour. While the 'hegemonic pact' of the state and business was crucial for economic performance and regime survival, farmers provided the regime with the flavour of popular support, though limited and manipulated. Chun's neo-conservative reforms accelerated the dissolution of this coalition, however. The reform campaign consciously chose big business as the prime target by blaming the close connection between big business and political power (*chungkyung yuchak*) under the Yushin constitution for corruption and economic crisis. The Chun regime squeezed the *chaebol* from all sides: tight credit control, forced mergers and consolidation of the heavy and chemical industries through industrial rationalization and the enforcement of tight monopoly regulation law. In reaction, the Federation of Korean Industries, the peak organization of big business, openly criticized the government. As government–business relations became strained, the support of big business for the regime also waned. The Chun regime also undermined the conservative coalition by victimizing farmers. In the name of fiscal austerity, the government cut the grain management fund (the rice price subsidy) and eliminated the fertilizer account (the fertilizer subsidy). American pressure and structural adjustment efforts also forced the government to liberalize import markets for farm products. Subsidy cuts and import liberalization, coupled with mounting farm debts, turned farmers against the Chun regime. The exclusion of big business and farmers posed a major political dilemma, as these were the only social forces compatible with the conservative ideological tenor of the Chun regime (Moon, 1988; Moon, 1994).

The dissolution of the developmentalist coalition coincided with the rise of the popular sector's horizontal coalition and mobilization (S. J. Lee, 1991). As under the Park regime, the Chun regime continued to exclude the popular sector, especially labour. During the reform period, real wages lagged behind labour productivity, and the labour movement was forced to undergo a restructuring that significantly weakened its political clout. This repression and restructuring, however, gave birth to militant, independent labour movements (J. T. Lee, 1988; Y. C. Kim, 1994). The urban poor and dissatisfied farmers also became politically organized and proactive.

Under Chun, the popular sector was no longer pacified. A new generation of intermediaries such as college students, dissident intellectuals and militant church groups effectively tapped the volatile popular sector by forming the Movement Circle (*Undonggwon*).[8] Of these, college students emerged as a key agent in forming dense and extensive networks within the popular sector through careful penetration of marginalized social forces such as labour, farmers and the urban poor. They also took initiatives in staging formidable anti-regime campaigns through intensive street demonstrations. The power and visibility of the student movement served as the critical catalyst in precipitating regime transition in South Korea (Kang, 1988; S. J. Lee, 1991; Dong, 1987). It is ironic to note that Chun's harsh authoritarian rule reinforced ideological unity, organizational strength and the mobilizational capability of the popular sector, resulting in the formation of a powerful opposition bloc to the ruling regime.

No ruler can rule without a foundation of social support. Chun was no exception. In the process of neo-conservative reforms, he alienated virtually all the organized forces, both weak and strong. But being aware of the risk of naked political power without an undergirding social coalition, Chun sought to win support from the 'silent' majority of consumers, savers and, especially, from the middle class which occupies a strategic position in Korean society, at the expense of organized social forces. The middle class (that is, owners of small and medium-sized firms, professional, managerial and technical workers), which had rapidly expanded throughout the 1960s and 1970s, became a natural target of popular appeal for the ruling regime.[9] Macroeconomic stabilization and structural adjustment succeeded in reducing broad-based social costs (for instance, inflation) and in re-establishing growth which allowed all to benefit. However, the middle class, the principal beneficiary of the reform, did not show political support for the regime. On the contrary, it proved to be a free-rider, and even a spoiler, by endorsing and supporting student protests at the critical juncture. Had it not been for the middle-class revolt of June 1987, Chun's acquiescence to constitutional changes would, in all likelihood, not have occurred. Given the regime's ontogenetic unpopularity, political support would have been more effectively consolidated through sectorally specific patronages. The reforms did not produce such rewards but rather undercut them through the reduction of rents to favoured groups. Macroeconomic success was not translated into political support due to the dilemma of collective goods (Moon, 1988). 'Betrayal' of the middle class pitted the entire civil society against the state and regime. Naked, coercive power alone could not sustain its survival.

Structural realignment of the coalition base shaped by the neo-conservative reform was not the sole determinant of the democratic opening. Equally important was the shifting pattern of political culture. While structure shapes political space and the terms of political engagement, culture cultivates a system of beliefs and values in which political action is embedded (Karl, 1990). Despite some reservations on positive correlation between political culture and democratic development in South Korea (Shin, Choy and Cho, 1994; C. L. Kim, 1988), several puzzles warrant the cultural explanation. Why did the middle class explicitly support popular protests, departing from its previously conservative stance? How could the popular sector be more organized and militant under Chun than under Park? Why did such intermediaries as students, dissident intellectuals and church leaders become more politically active under the Chun regime? Their structural position and the logic of political calculus alone cannot answer these questions. Rapid modernization and development have nurtured a pro-democratic consensus and values, affecting the pattern of middle-class political behaviour and facilitating the transition to the democratic opening.

Development has influenced the formation of political culture in two important ways. One is the evolutionary process of 'culture shift' which impacts on political behaviour (Inglehart, 1984, 1990; A. Lee, 1993); the other is the strategic inducement of cultural change by social intermediaries for political purposes. While the former was instrumental in eroding middle-class conservatism, the latter brought about militant political activism by the popular sector. Both Park and Chun justified their authoritarian rule in the name of development and modernization. Underlying the justification was the inescapable trade-off between survival needs (national security and economic growth) and political freedom. By the mid-1980s, however, poverty, hunger and underdevelopment no longer haunted the Korean people as their physiological needs were being met. Furthermore, the spread of education and mass communication, as well as growing exposure to the outside world, began to reshape the entire *gestalt* of the Korean people in which national security and economic growth could no longer be tolerated as a *deus ex machina*. The old political logic involving a substitution between ballot and bread began to lose its popular appeal. Needs for self-actualization such as political freedom, human rights and human dignity became more valued (Shin et al., 1989: 63; H. J. Kim, 1992: 530–2). According to a survey conducted in 1988, 79 per cent of 2,003 respondents believed that dictatorship should not be tolerated under any circumstances. Only 10.6 per cent believed that dictatorship should be tolerated if necessary. A great majority also responded that economic growth and national security should not victimize political freedom and social justice (K. W. Kim, 1988). The proliferation of pro-democratic values and growing intolerance with protracted authoritarian rule created 'tunnel effects' (Hirschman, 1979), pulling the middle class out of the conservative closet, and motivating it to render both tacit and explicit endorsement of anti-regime protests.

Radical mobilization of the popular sector has been closely related to the strategic inducement of cultural changes. Traditionally, workers, farmers and the urban poor were considered to be unorganized masses without a clear ideological stance. During the Chun period, however, they became better organized, ideologically vigilant and politically active. The change resulted partly from political and ideological education by radical students and church activists. Under the Yushin regime, college students and church activists were detached from the popular sector, and their political activism was confined to issue-specific protests without encompassing ideologies, strategies and organizations. In the 1980s, however, these intermediaries were well armed with radical ideologies, such as Marxism and liberation theology, and began to spread these new ideologies to the popular sector through systematic penetration and organized education and indoctrination. Such efforts awakened the political consciousness of marginal forces, and sharpened their strategic behaviour in opposing the authoritarian Chun regime as well as the capitalist system as a whole. *Minjung* (popular) democracy has emerged as their political goal, and their strategies and tactics have become much more refined. The success of student demonstrations, vital to the democratic opening of 1987, cannot be separated from the advent and diffusion of these new ideas and values among wide segments of the popular sector (Kang, 1988).

Although structure and culture shaped the distribution of political power and the mobilization pattern of the popular sector, they did not dictate the mode of democratic transition. Structural realignment, cultural shift and resulting social pressures served merely as input variables, which created contingency and uncertainty. Political changes are ultimately shaped by two-way interactions between social pressure and leadership response (Rustow, 1970; Karl, 1990; O'Donnell and Schmitter, 1986; Huntington, 1991). Extensive popular protests in May and June 1987 produced a division within the ruling circle. While the National Security Planning Agency and the police advocated a hardline stance, moderate elements in the ruling party favoured accommodation. Given his organic ties with the military, Chun could have crushed popular protests by resorting to coercive measures.[10] But he avoided the violent path, and chose a compromise option despite the hardliners' intense opposition. The compromise, embodied in Roh Tae Woo's June 29 Declaration, prevented bloodshed and enabled democratic reform. In this sense, the democratic opening of South Korea was neither a unilateral victory of civil society over the ruling regime, nor a controlled reform from above. It was a tacitly negotiated outcome between the hegemonic pact and the ascending popular sector (Karl, 1990: 38) in which leadership choice offered the critical turning point for political liberalization. Obviously, Chun's choice was constrained by structural realignment and culture shift precipitated by developmental processes. In Huntingtonian terms, thus, democratization in South Korea resembles 'transplacement or ruptforma', which is a joint product of action by the ruling regime and opposition groups (Huntington, 1991–2: 582).

DEMOCRATIZATION AND DEVELOPMENTAL PERFORMANCE:
ASSESSING TRANSITIONAL IMPACTS

The democratic opening of 1987 has produced sweeping changes. The most important changes involved institutional restructuring. A constitutional amendment in October 1987 replaced the indirect presidential election with a direct one, which was held in December that year. In a four-way race, Roh Tae Woo barely won the election with 36 per cent of the vote. In the general election held in April 1988, the ruling Democratic Justice Party failed to secure a majority in the national assembly. Indecisive outcomes indicated that relatively fair electoral competition had been restored. Additionally, self-autonomy for local governments was implemented as promised by the June 29 Declaration. Local (town and city) councils and provincial assemblies were set up, and nation-wide elections were held. Freedom of association and expression were institutionally ensured with the abolition of the Basic Press Law, which had served as a legal instrument for controlling the mass media. Political prisoners were released, and other malignant statutes were amended or removed, including the labour law, laws governing collective protest and the social purification law (Cotton, 1993).

These institutional changes fuelled an unprecedented expansion of civil society (Institute for Far Eastern Studies, 1993). Democratization forced the state to relax tight corporatist control over society, significantly expanding political space for social groups. Interest groups proliferated. Most remarkable was the explosion of local labour unions. In 1985, there were 2,534 unit labour unions. Since the democratic opening in 1987, their number increased to 6,142 in 1988 and to 7,527 in 1992. In January 1990, over 200,000 workers from 770 independent unit unions organized *Chunnohyup* (National Association of Labour Unions) as a countervailing force against *Nochong* (Federation of Korean Trade Unions), the peak organization recognized by the government (Chung, 1990: 191). In a calculated reaction to existing social organizations allied with the ruling regime, the popular sector actively reconsolidated its previously underground organizations. Teachers, farmers, urban poor, intellectuals, workers and journalists have all formed new public interest groups as balancing forces against the existing government-controlled representational organizations. While 150 farmers' organizations created *Chunnongryon* (National Federation of Farmers) in March 1989 in defiance of the government-controlled *Nonghyup* (Association of Agricultural Cooperatives), 20,000 dissenting teachers ventured in forming *Chungyojo* (National Association of Teachers' Unions) in the same month posing a direct challenge to the existing peak organization, *Kyoryun* (Federation of Korean School Teachers). Urban pedlars, journalists and artists have also formed new organizations (Chun, 1989). In addition, several issue-specific organizations such

Table 7.1 Trends of labour disputes: frequency, participant and working days lost, 1984–1992

	No. of labour disputes	No. of workers involved	No. of working days lost	Strike volume*
1984	113	16,400	19,900	3.3
1985	265	28,700	64,300	10.1
1986	276	46,914	72,025	10.8
1987	3,749	1,262,285	6,946,935	755.9
1988	1,873	293,455	5,400,837	562.0
1989	1,616	409,134	6,351,433	613.4
1990	322	133,916	4,487,151	413.0
1991	234	175,089	3,257,621	288.6
1992	235	104,489	1,520,364	132.1

*In calculating strike volume, total employees are counted. (Strike volume is defined as man-days lost per 1,000 wage and salary workers.)

Source: The data for 1992 are cited from the Korean Labor Institute's *Labor Statistics* (1993a: 179) and its *Quarterly Labor Review* (1993b: 140); and the rest of them come from the *Korean Statistical Yearbook* (Korean Statistical Association 1992: 93).

as *Kyungsilryun* (Council for the Realization of Economic Justice) and *Gongchuryun* (Association for Expelling Pollution) have emerged as powerful public interest groups. These developments reveal that during the democratic transition, civil society has not only expanded, but has also polarized into two camps, conservative and progressive.

Proliferation of interest groups entailed hyper-political activism. Sound and fury echoed in the streets. Civil protests have increased exponentially. Workers' strikes rose from 276 incidents in 1986 to 3,749 in 1987, to 1,873 in 1988, and 1,616 in 1989 (see table 7.1).

Along with their increased frequency, workers' strikes became more violent. Democratization did not stop student demonstrations, either. After temporary restraints during the 1988 Olympics in Seoul, students moved into streets promoting various causes ranging from the fuller restoration of democracy, national unity, the withdrawal of US forces and campus purification. Reminiscent of political openings in 1960 and 1980, Korean society was hyperbolic and unruly. The Korean state was no longer insulated from societal pressures so that executive dominance was weakened and bureaucratic unity was diluted. Democratization and the expansion and politicization of civil society fundamentally altered South Korea's political topology.

Democratic transition was also negatively correlated with economic performance. Chun's remarkable economic recovery was significantly jeopardized through the period of democratic transition. As table 7.2 shows, the rate of economic growth plummeted from 12.9 per cent in 1986 to 4.7 per cent in 1992. A record high current account surplus ($9.9 billion) in 1987 turned into net deficits from 1990, culminating in a deficit of $8.7 billion in 1991. Inflation also soared from 2.7 per cent in 1986 to 9.3 per cent in 1991 and 6.2 per cent in 1992. Despite slight improvements in gross savings, gross domestic investment and unemployment, the South Korean economy has not been able to regain its full vitality. Since the early 1970s, the South Korean economy has undergone four major business cycles. An average interval of the cycles is eighteen months (February 1974–June 1975; February 1979–September 1980; February 1984–September 1985). But the current economic downturn, which started in 1988, has lasted more than sixty-two months, the longest recessionary period in South Korea's economic history (*Hankuk Ilbo*, 11 March 1993).

The downturn was a product of several economic factors: global recession and increasing protectionism in advanced industrialized countries; fierce competition from other NICs, second-generation NICs and China; limits to technological breakthroughs and over-consumption. However, democratization was also a crucial contributing factor. The new political environment made the Roh regime's macroeconomic management increasingly erratic, severely reducing policy credibility. Upon his inauguration, Roh pledged to undertake extensive economic reforms such as the reduction of business concentration and the adoption of progressive labour and land-related laws. As the reforms, combined with contractionary macroeconomic policy, produced a recessionary trend, Roh radically swung back to expansionary, pro-business policies, overheating the economy with rampant real-estate and stock-market speculations. Inflationary pressure was rising, and the distributional consequences became grave. The Roh regime again turned back to a contractionary stance. Wide policy swings ranging between radical reforms, expansionary and contractionary policies in a relatively short time span raised the question of policy credibility, placing the private sector in disarray. Political sensitivity to economic issues, an essential feature of any democratic polity, weakened the coherence and consistency of macroeconomic policy, which in turn impeded overall economic performance (*Hankuk Ilbo*, 17 February 1993; Moon, 1994).

The political activism of labour emerged as another destabilizing factor. As table 7.1 indicates, the democratic opening coincided with an explosion of labour disputes. Under Chun's authoritarian regime, the number of labour disputes was far fewer than 300 cases per year, and the strike volume was minimal. In 1987, however, the frequency of labour disputes increased to 3,749 cases, with over one million workers involved in such disputes, costing almost seven million working days. The strike volume increased to 755.9 (see table 7.1). Since 1988, the frequency and intensity of labour disputes has declined, but their economic costs have been enormous. Lost production in

Table 7.2 Leading Korean economic indicators (1986–1993)

	1986	1987	1988	1989	1990	1991	1992	1993es
Growth rate of GNP (annual change at 1990 constant prices)	12.9	13	12.4	6.8	9.3	8.4	4.7	4.9
GNP (US $billion)	102.8	128.9	172.8	211.2	242.2	281.7	294.5	308.9
GNP per capita	2505	3110	4127	4994	5659	6518	6749	7435
Current account (US $billion, BOP basis)	4.6	9.9	14.2	5.1	-2.2	-8.7	-4.5	0
Consumer prices (annual change at 1990 constant prices)	2.7	3	7.1	5.7	8.6	9.3	6.2	5.5
Unemployment rate	3.8	3.1	2.5	2.6	2.4	2.3	2.4	2.8
Gross savings (share of GNP)	34.1	36.8	38.6	35.4	36.1	36.4	35	34.5
Gross domestic investment (share of GNP)	30	30.1	31.06	33.6	37.2	39.6	36.1	33.9
Exchange rate (vs. US $)	861.4	792.3	684.1	679.6	716.4	760.08	788.4	802.6

Source: Korean Economic Institute of America (1994)

1987 reached 277 billion won, soaring to 419 billion won in 1989. Export losses were also substantial, reaching $1.3 billion in 1989. Sharp wage increases complicated the economic picture. In the period 1987–92, nominal wages increased by 19.5 per cent on average, while labour productivity growth remained at about 10.2 per cent. Unit labour costs increased by 8.5 per cent. Compared with South Korea's principal competitors (such as Japan and Taiwan), such wage hikes profoundly undercut international competitiveness, precipitating the exodus of domestic and foreign firms. Since 1988, some 2,600 South Korean firms have relocated production facilities abroad. Over 200 foreign firms, which had invested in South Korea for cheap but skilled labour, closed their production facilities and left the country. Both domestic and foreign firms cited increased wages as the primary cause of their industrial relocation (*Hankuk Ilbo*, 22 February 1994).

Finally, the democratic transition has held governability at bay, with direct and indirect implications for economic policy management. During authoritarian rule, civil society was tamed and disciplined by tight corporatist control, cooptation and intimidation by the state. The margin for unruly behaviour by social groups was slim. However, democratization was tantamount to opening Pandora's box. Individuals and groups have turned into maximizers of their particularistic interests. The logic of collective egoism has emerged as a pronounced norm of political behaviour and discourse. Following the lead of the labour sector, farmers, herb doctors, pharmacists, students and virtually the entire society have all engaged in collective actions to advance their interests. Decentralization of political power through local autonomy has also begun to cripple centre–local coordination. The democratic opening has radically reshaped the business climate too. Popular concerns with, and political actions for, environmental integrity and occupational safety pushed the private sector to internalize previously neglected social costs.[11] South Korea under the democratic template has increasingly approximated to a nasty portrait of Hobbesian chaos. Its appeal to organic holism (that is, nationalism), which often used to serve as a unifying force for the state and society, has been defied, and cracks in the foundation of the general will have become more visible (Lim, 1993). Indeed, pressures of distributive politics have posed a major dilemma of governability in reconciling an open, accountable, and decentralized democratic policy with effective policy management (Bardhan, 1993: 47).

It is risky to infer economic performance from institutional arrangements (Moon, 1990; Moon and Prasad, 1994; Weaver and Rockam, 1993; Gourvetich, 1993). In view of the above, however, the democratic transition seems to have entailed a negative impact on developmental performance. This might be an inevitable process of adjustment after a long period of authoritarian repression. Yet, drawing a conclusion about the trade-off between democracy and development from the South Korean case appears premature. As Cheng and Krause (1991) point out, the decline in developmental performance can be construed as merely the transitional cost of regime change, not as a permanent one. The margin of erratic policy behaviour might be narrowed over time through learning processes of trial and error, and unruly social actors may be tamed as they become more accustomed to new institutions.[12] Despite this guarded optimism, however, learning democratic practices is not easy, and the discipline of citizenship is harder than that of industrial labour. More importantly, an open, accountable and decentralized polity is bound to be accompanied by new hurdles impeding democratic governability. It is not easy for South Korea to escape from the failings of mature democracies, such as electoral cycles, pork barrel politics and the pressures of distributional coalitions (Olson, 1965, 1982). South Korea's developmental performance under democracy might show trajectories quite different to those under authoritarian rule.

CONCLUSION: DEMOCRATIC PROSPECTS AND INSTITUTIONAL DESIGN

The South Korean case presents an interesting sequence of authoritarianism, development and democracy. The sequence seems quite paradoxical. The authoritarian mode of governance was conducive to facilitating developmental processes. However, development produced a new configuration of Korean society and political culture, forcing an authoritarian ruler to choose the compromise of a democratic opening. An irony of South Korea's political economy is that the authoritarian ruler, who sought rapid development in order to enhance legitimacy, consolidate power and sustain regime survival, has actually hastened his own demise.

Democratic opening is not the end of history, however. It is just the beginning of an uncertain, long journey to consolidation, persistence and eventual deconsolidation (O'Donnell and Schmitter, 1986; Karl, 1990: 5–6). As the transitional dynamics of democratic change reveal, the democratic opening encounters a plethora of new challenges and hurdles. Can South Korea turn the transition into a stable democracy? Is democratic consolidation viable in South Korea? Pessimistic projections abound. Comparing the South Korean democratic opening to the abortive *abertura* of Brazil under the Figuiredo regime, Cumings (1989: 32) concludes that 'the Korean democratization owes more to a controlled process of opening channels and valves for the voicing of excluded interest, than to a consolidation of stable pluralist representation'. For him, South Korea belongs to 'the Third World amalgam, not to the First World'. Choi Jangjip (1993a, 1993b) echoes a similar sentiment by maintaining that South Korean democratization is incomplete in its substance, if not in procedure, and that the popular democratic forces were given only limited gains within the existing power structure. Several others have raised reservations about the prospects for democratic consolidation in South Korea because of the inconsistent, intolerant and conformist political culture and immature institution-building (C. L. Kim, 1988: 67–70; M. Lee, 1990: 143).

The inauguration of the Kim Young Sam government and his aggressive pursuit of reform politics, however, appears to defy these pessimistic projections. Kim has been effectively consolidating democratic institutions. His extensive anti-corruption campaign and the implementation of the long-delayed real-name deposit system restored accountability and public confidence in the government. By methodically purging the *Hanahoi*, the dominant military faction, he has drastically reduced the chances of military intervention in civilian politics (Moon and Kang, 1994). Equally important is that Kim has been successful in including the leadership of radical democratic forces in the political establishment. By embracing both conservative and radical elements under his political umbrella, he has been able to craft a new political reality of reconciliation and compromise. Along with this, unfinished tasks of institutional reform, such as amending the law concerning political campaign funds and the election of heads of provincial governments, are being incrementally put into place. The increased vigilance of civil society is also another valuable asset for democratic stability. Civil society has grown too strong and well organized to be easily subjugated by the state and the ruling regime. Democratization has become irreversible. Democratic consolidation is inevitably an uneven process; thus periodic setbacks do not necessarily herald its demise.

One critical variable which might affect the democratic path is inter-Korean relations and modes of national unification.[13] The Vietnamization of the Korean peninsula could mean the end of the democratic process, although this scenario is highly unlikely. Despite recent civilianizing efforts, the prolongation of heightened military tension with the North could leave the South Korean military as a potentially destabilizing factor. Thus, managing inter-Korean relations is directly linked to democratic prospects in South Korea. Equally important is the deepening of regional polarization and confrontation between the two provinces, Cholla and Kyungsang. For the past two decades, regionalism has become the most reliable predictor of electoral outcomes, superseding other social and political cleavages. Continuing regional fragmentation of voting behaviour could pose a major threat to democratic consolidation and stability in South Korea (Bae and Cotton, 1993). However, even more critical is the revival of the classical third world path to democratic instability resulting from a sequence of economic crisis, social disorder and polarization, and military intervention (Haggard and Kaufman, 1992). The story of the third world is littered with tales of the military overthrowing nascent democratic regimes because of its impatience with the problems of corruption, indiscipline and socioeconomic chaos associated with immature democracy. Two aborted *aberturas* in 1960 and 1980, as well as the precarious opening under Roh, all of which invoked a cynical nostalgia for authoritarian conservatism, are lively testimonials to this risk. Thus the most important factor in institutionalizing democracy is the capacity to avoid debilitating socioeconomic crises whilst permitting time for the learning and socialization process that constitutes democratization. It must be remembered that democracy is a framework for ordering society, not a script. It can sustain varied institutional configurations. It would be wise to develop institutions that do not heighten the conflictual potentials of democracy, as described by Kohli (1990) in the case of India.

What then are the ideal institutional alternatives for reconciling democratic consolidation with sustaining economic performance, as well as ensuring effective inter-Korean management and regional harmony? There are three possible paths: *status quo*, competitive and corporatist. The *status quo* model assumes the continuation of incomplete democracy in which institutional deformity, lingering legacies of the authoritarian past and a failure to include broad segments of civil society still prevail. This alternative does not seem desirable since it is likely to revive old wounds of political legitimacy and to sustain a high tension of regional and structural polarization, undermining policy performance. The competitive/pluralist alternative is of limited appropriateness as it is rather arcane to the Korean political climate. Extreme pluralism without corresponding institutional mechanisms could turn Korean society into an anarchic or entropic entity. An opinion survey conducted immediately after the democratic opening reveals that pluralist democracy was least favoured by Koreans (Shin, Kim and Moon, 1989, ch. 3).[14]

A solution can be sought in the corporatist formula which implies sustaining the developmental state, but without authoritarian contents. The new corporatist developmental state not only replaces insulation with organic networks and consultation, command with consensus, concentration of executive power with power sharing within the state and between the state and society, but also socializes voluntary collective sharing of social and economic burdens, not their unilateral and uneven imposition on the marginal sectors of society. This alternative may have two forms: one is centre-left, and the other centre-right (Haggard and Kaufman, 1992: 345–8). The centre-left design is predicated on the formation of a new social pact between the state, labour and business, by demolishing the old hegemonic pact, while progressively including labour in the political arena (Katzenstein, 1984; Im, 1992). On the other hand, the centre-right form resembles the Japanese model of corporatism which is based on a tight conservative coalition between the state and business, labour being partially excluded (Pempel and Tsunekawa, 1979). Given the overall social ethos, the former is more desirable but less feasible in Korea because of inherent difficulties in forming a new social pact transcending existing social and political cleavages. The future course is likely to fall between the *status quo* and the centre-right alternatives, thus implying a limited democratic prospect.[15]

NOTES

1 Neo-liberal and neo-conservative reforms are often interchangeably used. Here I adopt the term 'neo-conservative', following Foxley (1983).

2 Some of these issues have been well addressed by Johnson (1993) and Cheng and Krause (1991).

3 The bureaucratic-authoritarian paradigm (O'Donnell, 1974; Collier, 1979) has provoked extensive intellectual debate in South Korea. Im (1987) and Choi (1989: 72–80) argue that South Korea's B-A regime shares behavioural and structural characteristics similar to Latin American ones, but radically differs in its causation. While a B-A regime was a consequence of industrial deepening in Latin America, it was a cause of industrial deepening in South Korea.

4 The national security crisis, which resulted from the combination of increasing North Korea's military provocation, the Nixon Doctrine and reduction of US forces in South Korea, and the North's military superiority, is often cited as the most pronounced cause of the rise of the Yushin regime (Haggard and Moon, 1993).

5 The Kukje case has invited an interesting controversy as Kukje filed a lawsuit for regaining its assets after the democratic opening. The Kukje side argued that its collapse was a result of a political vendetta by Chun who was not happy with the Kukje's refusal to make a political contribution during his reign. However, the South Korean government has claimed that corporate mismanagement caused its bankruptcy.

6 The June 29 Declaration contained eight major items for democratic reforms. They were: the constitutional amendment to adopt a direct presidential election; electoral reforms to ensure free and fair elections; amnesty of political prisoners and restoration of their civil rights, including opposition leader Kim Dae Jung; respect for human rights and human dignity; freedom of the press; promotion of local autonomy; the creation of a new political climate for dialogue and compromise; social reforms.

7 These three variables have each constituted a distinct paradigm of its own: structuralist (Moore, 1966), political culture (Lipset, 1980) and strategic choice perspectives (Rustow, 1970; O'Donnell and Schmitter, 1986; Przeworski, 1990). They are often considered epistemologically incompatible in explaining democratic changes (Karl, 1990; Huber, Reuschemeyer and Stephens, 1993). Reflecting this trend, the structuralist camp (Moore, 1966; Seong, 1993) and the strategic choice camp (Rustow, 1970; O'Donnell and Schmitter, 1986; Im, 1990; J. J. Choi, 1993a) have emerged as the two major contending paradigms in South Korea. Risking the virtue of analytical parsimony, however, we argue that democratic changes in South Korea can be best explained by combining all three variables.

8 *Undonggwon* refers to a loose coalition of radical college students, church leaders, dissident intellectuals, workers, farmers and the urban

poor. However, S. J. Lee (1991) downplays the importance of the popular sector, especially labour, in the democratic opening of 1987. Indeed, workers, farmers and the urban poor did not participate in street demonstrations, but their increasing political activism, especially labour, offered an effective deterrent to coercive responses by the state, thus paving the way for the leadership compromise and democratic transition.

9 The middle class is another controversial concept in South Korea. See Hong (1992); Suh (1984); Dong (1993).

10 A major deterrent to Chun's use of coercive measures was his ambivalent perception of the military. Chun enjoyed strong military support, but was well aware that the political use of the military could create a pretext for military intervention. In addition, the military, especially the National Defense Security Command, opposed the idea of deploying soldiers to stabilize civil unrest for fear of a negative boomerang effect on the military itself (Moon and Kang, 1995).

11 Ample evidence is available. The central government's efforts to create a nuclear waste site on the island of Anmyondo was cancelled as a result of violent protests by local residents. The government's original plan to promote tourist development on the Cheju island through the enactment of a special law also suffered a major setback due to local opposition. Citizen protests over, and media attention to, environmental pollution, have led to tightened government regulations, increasing the burden on the private sector. Legal injunctions by the courts have also emerged as another factor in reshaping state–society relations.

12 An interesting trend is that as economic conditions worsened after 1991, labour began to show an unusual restraint. Other sectors of society have also shown self-restraint in their political activism. Hard times tend to bring Koreans together even without tight corporatist control and intimidation.

13 There are four modes of national unification: the German model (unification by the South's absorption of the North); the Vietnam model (liberation of the South by the North through military invasion, communist revolution in the South, or both); the Commonwealth model (an incremental, functionalist approach favoured by the South); and the Confederal model (a holistic approach advocated by the North). See Moon (1993).

14 The survey presented three types of democracy: liberal, popular (*Minjung*), and corporatist versions. Responses varied by age, income, and level of education, but popular democracy was most favoured on average.

15 The formation of the Democratic Liberal Party in 1990, which merged the then ruling Democratic Justice Party with two opposition parties, the Party for Unification and Democracy and the New Democratic Republican Party, is a historical testimonial to this trend. Facing acute social, economic and political crises, these parties forged a grand conservative coalition modelled on the Japanese Liberal Democratic Party. There are three major structural hurdles impeding the transition to a centre-left coalition: inter-Korean relations and national security issues, the power and influence of conservative social forces united under capitalist ideology and status-oriented traditional political culture. The resurgence of conservative political outlook is likely to narrow the scope of political inclusion, casting a limited democratic prospect. In

addition to the realignment of the party system, electoral rules, executive-legislative linkages and empowerment of the court system are equally important in charting out the future for Korean democracy.

REFERENCES

Amsden, A. H. 1989: *Asia's Next Giant: South Korea and Late Industrialization*. New York: Oxford University Press.
Bae, S. K. and Cotton, J. 1993: Regionalism in Electoral Politics. In J. Cotton (ed.) *Korea under Roh Tae Woo*. Sydney: Allen & Unwin, 170–86.
Balassa, B. (ed.) 1981: *Development Strategies in Semi-Industrial Countries*. Baltimore: Johns Hopkins University Press.
Bardhan, P. 1993: Symposium on Management of Local Commons. *Journal of Economic Perspectives*, 7(4), 87–92.
Bergsman, J. 1979: *Growth and Equity in Semi-Industrial Countries*. Washington, World Bank (Staff Working Paper no. 351).
Cheng, T. J. and Krause, L. 1991: Democracy and Development: With Special Attention to Korea. *Journal of Northeast Asian Studies*, 10, 3–25.
Cho, H. Y. (ed.) 1990: *Hankuk Sahoi Undongsa (History of Korean Social Movement)*. Seoul: Juksan.
Choi, J. J. 1989: *Hankuk Hyundaijungchiui Kuzo wa Byunwha (Structure and Changes of Contemporary Korean Politics)*. Seoul: Kkachi.
Choi, J. J. 1993a: Political Cleavages in South Korea. In K. Hagen (ed.) *State and Society in Contemporary Korea*. Ithaca, NY: Cornell University Press, 13–50.
Choi, J. J. 1993b: *Hankuk Minjujuui Iron (Theory of Korean Democracy)*. Seoul: Hangilsa.
Chun, J. W. 1989: Pokpal Jikjun! Nodongja, Nongmin, Kyosadului Minjuwha Yokgu (Time Bomb: Democratic Demands of Workers, Farmers, and Teachers). *Shindonga*, January, 388–403.
Chung, Y. T. 1990: Nodong Undongui Daeduwa Hankuk Jungchiui Gwaje (The Rise of the Labour Movement and the Task for Korean Politics). In Korean Political Science Association (ed.) *Sanupsahoi wa Hankuk Jungchiui Gwaje (Industrial Society and the Task for Korean Politics)*. Seoul: Korean Political Science Association.
Collier, D. (ed.) 1979: *The New Authoritarianism in Latin America*. Princeton, NJ: Princeton University Press.
Corbo, V., Krueger, A. and Ossa, F. 1985: *Export-Oriented Development Strategies: The Success of Five NICs*. Boulder, Colo.: Westview Press.
Corbo, V. and Sang M. Suh (eds) 1992: *Structural Adjustment in a Newly Industrializing Country: The Korean Experience*. Baltimore, Md.: John Hopkins University Press.
Cotton, J. (ed.) 1993: *Korea under Roh Tae Woo*. Sydney: Allen & Unwin.
Cotton, J. (ed.) 1994: *From Roh Tae Woo to Kim Young Sam: Politics and Policy in the New Korean State*. Melbourne: Longman.
Cumings, B. 1984: The Northeast Political Economy. *International Organization*, 38, 1–40.
Cumings, B. 1989: The Abortive Abertura: South Korea in the Light of Latin American Experience. *New Left Review*, 173, 5–32.

Deyo, F. C. (ed.) 1987: *The Political Economy of the New Asian Indus-trialism*. Ithaca, NY: Cornell University Press.

Dong, W. 1987: University Students in South Korean Politics: Patterns of Radicalization in the 1980s. *Journal of International Affairs*, 40, 233–55.

Dong, W. 1993: Democratization of South Korea – What Role Does the Middle Class Play? In J. Cotton (ed.) *Korea under Roh Tae Woo*. Sydney: Allen & Unwin, 73–91.

Economic Planning Board 1988, 1993, 1994: *Korea's Social and Economic Indicators*. Seoul: Economic Planning Board.

Evans, P. 1992: The State as Problem and Solution: Predation, Embedded Autonomy and Structural Change. In S. Haggard and R. Kaufman (eds) *The Politics of Economic Adjustment*, Princeton, NJ: Princeton University Press, 139–81.

Foxley, A. 1983: *Latin American Experiments in Neo-Conservative Economics*. Berkeley: University of California Press.

Gereffi, G. and Wyman, D. (eds) 1990: *Manufacturing Miracles: Paths of Industrialization in Latin America and East Asia*. Princeton, NJ: Princeton University Press.

Gourvetich, Peter 1993: Democracy and Economic Policy: Elective Affinities and Circumstantial Conjunctures. *World Development*, 21, 1271–80.

Haggard, S. 1990: *Pathways from the Periphery: The Politics of Growth in the Newly Industrializing Countries*. Ithaca, NY: Cornell University Press.

Haggard, S. and Kaufman, R. 1992: Economic Adjustment and the Prospects for Democracy. In S. Haggard and R. Kaufman (eds) *The Politics of Economic Adjustment*, Princeton, NJ: Princeton University Press, 319–50.

Haggard, S. and Moon, C. I. 1983: The South Korean State in the International Economy: Liberal, Dependent, or Mercantile? In J. Ruggie (ed.) *Antinomies of Interdependence*, New York: Columbia University Press, 131–89.

Haggard, S. and Moon, C. I. 1990: Institutions and Economic Policy: Theory and a Korean Case Study. *World Politics*, 42(2) 210–37.

Haggard, S. and Moon, C. I. 1993: The State, Politics, and Economic Development in Postwar South Korea. In H. Koo (ed.) *State and Society in Contemporary Korea*, Ithaca, NY: Cornell University Press, 51–94.

Han, S. J. 1988: *Hankuk Sahoi wa Kwanryojuk Kwonuijuui (Korean Society and Bureaucratic Authoritarianism)*. Seoul: Munhak gwa Jisung.

Henderson, G. 1988: Constitutional Changes from the First to the Sixth Republics: 1948–1987. In I. Kim and Y. Kihl (eds) *Political Change in South Korea*. New York: Paragon, 22–43.

Hirschman, A. 1979: The Turn to Authoritarianism and the Search for Economic Determinants. In D. Collier (ed.) *The New Authoritarianism in Latin America*. Princeton, NJ: Princeton University Press, 61–98.

Hong, D. S. 1992: Jungsancheungui Sungjanggwa Sahoibyundong (Growth of the Middle Class and Social Changes). Hanknkui Kukgawa Siminsahoi (The Korean State and Civil Society). Seonl: Hannl, 255–76.

Huber, E., Rueschemeyer, D. and Stephens, J. 1993: The Impact of Economic Development on Democracy. *Journal of Economic Perspectives*, 7, 71–85.

Huntington, S. P. 1991: How Countries Democratize. *Political Science Quarterly*, 106(4), 579–616.

Im, H. B. 1987: The Rise of Bureaucratic Authoritarianism in South Korea. *World Politics*, 39, 231–57.

Im, H. B. 1992: The State, Labor and Capital in the Consolidation Democracy: A Search for Post-Authoritarian Industrial Relations in South Korea. *Korean Social Science Journal*, 18, 7–25.

Inglehart, R. 1984: *Silent Revolution*. Ann Arbor: University of Michigan Press.

Inglehart, R. 1990: *Culture Shift*. Princeton, NJ: Princeton University Press.

Institute for Far Eastern Studies 1993: *Hankuk Jungchi Sahoeui Sae Hurum (New Trends in Korean Politics and Society)*. Seoul: Nanam.

Johnson, C. 1987: Political Institutions and Economic Development: The Business–Government Relationship in Japan, South Korea and Taiwan. In F. C. Deyo (ed.) *The Political Economy of the New Asian Industrialism*. Ithaca, NY: Cornell University Press, 136–64.

Johnson, C. 1993: South Korean Democratization: The Role of Economic Development. In J. Cotton (ed.) *Korea under Roh Tae Woo*. Sydney: Allen & Unwin, 92–107.

Jones, L. and Sakong, I. 1980: *Government, Business, and Entrepreneurship in Economic Development: The Korean Case*. Cambridge: Harvard University Press.

Kang, M. et al., 1991: *Kukga wa Gonggong Jungchaek (The State and Public Policy)*. Seoul: Bubmunsa.

Kang, S. et al., 1988: *80nyundae Haksaengundongsa (History of the Student Movement in the 1980s)*. Seoul: Hyungsungsa.

Karl, T. L. 1990: Dilemmas of Democratization in Latin America. *Comparative Politics*, 23, 1–21.

Katzenstein, P. 1984: *Corporatism and Change: Austria, Switzerland and the Politics of Change*. Ithaca, NY: Cornell University Press.

Kim, C. L. 1988: Potential for Democratic Change. In I. Kim and Y. Kihl (eds) *Political Change in South Korea*. New York: Paragon, 44–74.

Kim, H. J. 1992: *Hankuk Jungchi Chejeron (Thesis on Korean Political System)* 2nd edn. Seoul: Bakyoungsa.

Kim, I. and Kihl, Y. 1988: *Political Change in South Korea*. New York: Paragon.

Kim, I. G. 1987: *Hankuk, Munwha wa Kyungje Whalryuk (Korea, Culture and Economic Vitality)*. Seoul: Hankuk Economic Daily.

Kim, K. W. 1988: Hankukinui Minjujungchi Uisikgwa Kukga Inyum (Koreans' Perception of Democratic Politics and State Ideology). Seoul: Social Science Research Institute, Seoul National University (monograph).

Kim, Y. C. 1994: The State and Labor in South Korea: A Coalition Analysis. Columbus, Ohio: Ohio State University (unpublished PhD dissertation).

Kim, Y. L. 1990: *Hankuk Iikjibdan gwa Minjujungchi Baljun (Interest Groups and Democratic Development in South Korea)*. Seoul: Daewangsa.

Kohli, A. 1990: *Democracy and Discontent: India's Growing Crisis of Governability*. Cambridge: Cambridge University Press.

Korean Economic Institute of America 1994: *Korea's Economy 1994*. Washington: Korean Economic Institute of America.

Korean Labor Institute (KLI) 1993a: *KLI Labor Statistics*. Seoul: Korean Labor Institute.

Korean Labor Institute (KLI) 1993b: *Quarterly Labor Review*. Seoul: Korean Labor Institute.

Korean Statistical Association 1992: *Korean Statistical Yearbook*. Seoul: Korean Statistical Association.

Koo, H. (ed.) 1993: *State and Society in Contemporary Korea*. Ithaca, NY: Cornell University Press.

Krueger, A. 1983: The Effects of Trade Strategies on Growth. *Finance and Development*, 20, 5–9.

Lee, A. 1993: Culture Shift and Popular Protests in South Korea. *Comparative Political Studies*, 26, 63–80.

Lee, C. H. 1990: Culture and Institutions in Economic Development of Korea. *Korea Studies*, 14, 68–77.

Lee, J. T. 1988: Dynamics of Labor Control and Labor Protests in the Process of Export-Oriented Industrialization in South Korea. *Asian Perspectives*, 12, 152–71.

Lee, M. 1990: *The Odyssey of Korean Democracy*. New York: Praeger.

Lee, S. J. 1991: Political Liberalization and Economic Development in South Korea. *Korean Journal of Population and Development*, 20, 77–100.

Leipziger, D. M. et al., 1992: *The Distribution of Income and Wealth in Korea*. Washington, DC: World Bank.

Lim, H. and Paik, U. 1986: Hankukui Kukga Jayulsung: Dogujok Ganungsung gwa Kuzojok Jaeyak (State Autonomy in South Korea: Instrumental Possibility and Structural Limitation). In S. Y. Choi (ed.) *Hyundai Hankuk Jungchiwa Kukga (Contemporary Korean Politics and the State)*. Seoul: Bubmunsa, 225–46.

Lim, H. 1993: Group Interests Get in the Way. *Korea Focus*, 1, 10–16.

Lipset, S. M. 1980: *Political Man: The Social Bases of Politics*, 2nd edn. Baltimore, Md: Johns Hopkins University Press.

MacIntyre, A. (ed.) 1994: *Business and Government in Industrializing Asia*. Ithaca and Sydney: Cornell University Press and Allen & Unwin.

Moon, C. I. 1988: The Demise of a Developmentalist State? The Politics of Stabilization and Structural Adjustment. *Journal of Developing Societies*, 4, 67–84.

Moon, C. I. 1990: Beyond Statism: The Political Economy of Growth in South Korea. *International Studies Notes*, 15, 24–7.

Moon, C. I. 1993: Calculus of National Unification: Payoff Structure, Divergent Interests, and Political Barriers. In G. Lim and J. Williams (eds) *Korea and Its Political and Economic Future*. East Lansing: Asian Studies Center, Michigan State University, 75–88.

Moon, C. I. 1994: Changing State–Business Relations in South Korea since 1980. In MacIntyre, A. (ed.) *Business and Government in Industrializing Asia*. Ithaca and Sydney: Cornell University Press and Allen & Unwin, 142–66.

Moon, C. I. and Kang, M. 1995: Democratization and Military Intervention in South Korea: A Comparative Assessment. In J. Cotton (ed.) *From Roh Tae Woo to Kim Young Sam: Politics and Policy in the New Korean State*. Melbourne: Longman.

Moon, C. I. and Prasad, R. 1994: Beyond the Developmental State: Networks, Politics, and Institutions. *Governance: An International Journal of Policy and Administration*, 7.

Moore, B. 1966: *Social Origins of Dictatorship and Democracy*. Boston, Mass.: Beacon Press.

Nelson, J. (ed.) 1990: *Economic Crisis and Policy Choice: The Politics of Adjustment in the Third World*. Princeton, NJ: Princeton University Press.

O'Donnell, G. 1974: *Bureaucratic Authoritarianism: Argentina, 1966–1973, in Comparative Perspective*. Berkeley: Institute of International Studies, University of California.

O'Donnell, G. and Schmitter, P. 1986: *Transitions from Authoritarian Rule:*

Tentative Conclusions about Uncertain Democracies. Baltimore, Md: Johns Hopkins Press.

Olson, M. 1965: *The Logic of Collective Action.* Cambridge, Mass.: Harvard University Press.

Olson, M. 1982: *The Rise and Decline of Nations.* New Haven, Conn.: Yale University Press.

Pempel, T. J . and Tsunekawa, K. 1979: Corporatism without Labor? The Japanese Anomaly. In P. Schmitter and G. Lehmbruch (eds) *Trends Toward Corporatist Intermediation.* Beverly Hills Cal.: Sage, 231–69.

Przeworski, A. 1990: *Democracy and the Market.* Cambridge: Cambridge University Press.

Przeworski, A. and Limongi, F. 1993: Political Regimes and Economic Growth. *Journal of Economic Perspectives,* 7, 51–69.

Pye, L. 1985: *Asian Power and Politics: The Cultural Dimensions of Authority.* Cambridge: Belknap Press.

Rustow, D. 1970: Transition to Democracy: Toward a Dynamic Model. *Comparative Politics,* 2, 337–63.

Sakong, I. 1993: *Korea in the World Economy.* Washington, DC: Institute for International Economics.

Seong, Kyungryung 1993: Hankuk Jungchi Minjuwhaui Sahoejok Kiwon: Sahoe Undongjok Jupkeun (Social Origins of Political Democratization in South Korea: A Social Movement Approach). In Institute for Far Eastern Studies (ed.) *Hankuk Jungchi Sahoeui Sae Hurum (New Trends in Korean Politics and Society).* Seoul: Nanam, 85–132.

Shin, D., Choy, M. and Cho, M. 1994: *Korea in the Global Wave of Democratization.* Seoul: Seoul National Press.

Shin, D. and Kim, K. 1989: Psychological Bases of Democratic Reform in Korea: An Empirical Testing of Huntington's IvI Gap Theory. *Pacific Focus,* 4, 65–90.

Shin, J., Kim, D. and Moon, C. I. 1989: *Hankuk Minjokjuui Yonku (A Study of Korean Nationalism).* Seoul: International Peach Research Institute, Kyunghee University.

Sohn, H. K. 1989: *Authoritarianism and Opposition in South Korea.* London: Routledge.

Song, B. N. 1990: *The Rise of the Korean Economy.* Hong Kong: Oxford University Press.

Suh, K. M. 1984: *Hyundai Hankuksahoiui Gyekeub-kusunggwa Gyekeub-bunwha: Petit Bonrgeoisieui Chuserul Jungsigmuro (Class Composition and Class Differentiation in Contemporary Korean Society).* Seoul: Korean Sociological Association.

Wade, R. 1990: *Governing the Market: Economic Theory and the Role of Government in East Asian Industrialization.* Princeton, NJ: Princeton University Press.

Weaver, R. K. and Rockam, B. A. 1993: *Do Institutions Matter?* Washington, DC: The Brookings Institution.

Woo, J. E. 1990: *Race to Swift.* New York: Columbia University Press.

World Bank 1993: *The East Asian Miracle: Economic Growth and Public Policy.* New York: Oxford University Press.

World Development 1988: Special Issue on South Korea, 16(1).

Yoon, D. 1990: *Law and Political Authority in South Korea.* Boulder, Colo.: Westview Press.

8

Chile: Democracy and Development in a Divided Society

JENNY PEARCE

INTRODUCTION

Chile is widely regarded as the most successful example of both economic liberalization and democratic political transition in Latin America in the 1990s. The impressive growth record of the decade 1983–93 straddles the rule of both the authoritarian military government of General Pinochet and the democratically elected centre-left government of Patricio Aylwin which succeeded it in 1990.[1] But far more significant than a decade of growth sustained under both dictatorship and democracy are the social and political transformations which were mostly introduced by the military dictatorship and which appear to have paved the way for the remarkable improvement in the country's economic performance. This chapter explores how and why a dynamic entrepreneurial capitalism emerged under conditions of political exclusion and repression and failed to develop during the country's long history of competitive party politics and intensely contested elections.

At the core of the changes brought about under the dictatorship, is the role of the state. Angelo Codevilla believes that the Chilean experience does not, however, prove a link between dictatorship and development. Rather, he argues, it is the policies pursued that matter.

The difference between Chile's success and the lack of it in former Communist lands lies not in any superiority of dictatorship over democracy but rather in the content of policy . . . the Chilean reforms succeeded politically and economically for one reason: they shrank the state. (Codevilla, 1993: 139)

Codevilla's stress on the shrinking of the state is, however, a rather narrow interpretation of the transformations brought about by the Pinochet regime. I prefer to stress the redefinition of the role of the state and the establishment of clearer boundaries between the state and society, in particular the private sector. It is a process reminiscent of the separation of the 'public' and the 'private' in eighteenth-century Britain, through which the latter was established as the arena of economic agency in the transition to capitalism, rather than the state. This analogy cannot, of course, be taken too literally. But in the Chilean case, a palpable change in entrepreneurial culture seems to have been generated under Pinochet and has survived into the era of democracy. One author has claimed that 'the Chilean case of the 1970s and 1980s is a Latin American attempt to shift from a populist capitalism to a liberal capitalism' (Muñoz, 1988: 7).

In eighteenth-century Britain, the idea of the 'limited state' and boundaries between state and 'civil society', was 'pushed' from below by a rising class of individual entrepreneurs and their associations. But in Chile it was the state itself which took up the task during the 1970s. The guiding assumption of the Pinochet regime's neo-liberal economic policy – that the economy should rest on market forces not state direction – stood in stark contrast to the previous pattern of Chilean development, particularly since the 1930s. The state already accounted for 38 per cent of GDP by the 1950s and this figure had risen to 53 per cent by the early 1970s (Angell, 1993: 134).

Codevilla correctly stresses that it is the content of the policy pursued under the Pinochet regime which accounts for Chile's present economic success. The mere fact of dictatorship would not have been sufficient. But the dictatorial character of the Pinochet period is scarcely an irrelevant detail. Pinochet used the coercive powers of the state in ways which were crucial to the implementation of his policies, pushing through major transformations with profound – if highly uneven – implications for capital as well as labour. The dictatorship began by eliminating the organized political expression of entrenched and antagonistic class interests which had rent society apart in the course of the previous decade. It then shifted the locus of contestation away from the struggle for state power and towards survival in the market-place, eventually unleashing entrepreneurial energies in a way which has proved conducive to rapid and sustained levels of economic growth, while those unable to compete faced bankruptcy or impoverishment.

Chile is not however a country where dictatorship has been the norm. On the contrary, it is a country where competitive party politics and civilian, constitutional rule have predominated for most of this century. But Chile's economic performance during those years of democratic politics was low to mediocre, characterized by persistent inflation, external vulnerability, fiscal disorder, low levels of capital formation and growing foreign indebtedness. High levels of social and economic inequality increasingly polarized society. The election of a Marxist, Salvador Allende, as president in 1970 brought all the underlying conflicts in the society to the fore and generated a powerful right-wing backlash culminating in the military coup of 1973.

It would be very crude to conclude from this that there was a negative correlation between democracy and capitalist development prior to the Pinochet dictatorship and a positive one between dictatorship and development. The general categories of 'democracy' and 'dictatorship' do not in fact help us very much here. The hypothesis of this chapter is that twentieth-century capitalist development in Chile centred on a *particular* relationship between state, economic elites and the incorporated middle and urban working class, which contained elements of both political competition and 'accommodationism'.[2] The latter was reflected in the survival of traditional structures of economic power, such as the *latifundia-minifundia* system in the rural areas, and in the acceptance by all political actors of the state as both a major economic agent and a source of patronage and support.

This relationship failed to generate a dynamic form of entrepreneurial capitalism or an effective state. It preserved a traditional socioeconomic structure while the state took on the tasks of industrialization and modernization. But it was a state locked into the protection and promotion of partisan interests. Despite its extremely favourable natural resource endowments and the availability of relatively high foreign exchange earnings, foreign aid and investment, the Chilean economy failed to 'take off', living standards remained low and growth in any one sector was either short-lived or failed to generate a response in any other sector (De Vylder, 1976: 10). As the economy stagnated, the political order was rocked by two crucial developments. First, by the mass migration of the rural poor to the cities and the courting of their political support during the 1960s. This generated new demands and changed the balance of interests the political order had to accommodate. Second, the Popular Unity government of Salvador Allende (1970–3), initiated a project to dynamize Chilean national development through further state intervention and a redistribution of political and economic power away from the traditional elites and towards the excluded masses. The pressure on the system from the intense class conflict generated by this project proved too great, and democracy collapsed.

The Pinochet regime then accomplished a critical function for the development of Chilean capitalism: the acceptance by a significant sector of the business elite that the tasks of developing a competitive, efficient and dynamic economy rested on its shoulders, not those of the state. This is not all that the regime accomplished. The process of economic transformation under Pinochet should not be divorced from the dictatorship's role in providing a climate of confidence and security to the private sector in a society fractured by social divisions and antagonisms. The suppression of the labour movement and its political allies through imprisonment, torture, killings and 'disappearances' demonstrated the unequivocal identification of the regime with the interests of capital in contrast to its predecessor. The state may have 'shrunk' in the social and economic spheres, but for many people it remained a very powerful and greatly feared presence in other aspects of their lives.

It should also be pointed out that dictatorship was by no means solely responsible for changing perceptions of the state. This was a world-wide phenomenon of the 1980s, at least, and one which had a profound effect on thinking on the left as well as the right. The story is, as always, a complex one, in which isolating the critical variables is precarious and contentious. But one very evident factor in the ultimate success of Pinochet's neo-liberal experiment has been the shift in thinking amongst the Chilean left as much as the right. Ultimately, both the left (with some exceptions, such as the Communist party) and the right have given their support to the economic transformations brought about by the dictatorship. This undoubtedly facilitated the smooth transition to a centre-left civilian government in 1990.

This chapter will survey the key elements in the evolution of Chile's political economy in order to point to some of the particular constraints on capitalist development and to suggest the ways in which the Pinochet dictatorship helped eliminate them. Social science does not allow us to conduct experiments on what might have happened if the 1973 military coup had not taken place. Nor can this chapter enter into the extremely important and relevant debate on the social and human costs of the subsequent dictatorship, or the issues of equity and social justice which still cast their shadow over Chilean development. Chile's wealthiest quintile increased its participation in consumption by over 10 points (23 per cent) between 1973 and 1993 at the expense of the rest of the population (Ffrench-Davis, 1993: 17).

The primary aim of the chapter is to *describe* one way in which policies pursued under conditions of dictatorship seem to have contributed to the emergence of an efficient and effective capitalism. It will argue that it was not democracy as such that failed to establish the conditions for such growth in the past; it was the particular form of accommodationism between traditional elites and the new social forces which emerged with socioeconomic change. This accommodationism created a state strong enough to intervene to an ever greater extent in economic life but too weak to rise above the partisan interests which laid claim to it. Ultimately, accommodationism itself broke apart. The failure of the economy to improve living standards exacerbated the deep divisions within society and irrevocably polarized the political options for resolving the crisis of Chilean capitalism.

OLIGARCHY AND STATE: THE ROOTS OF CHILEAN 'EXCEPTIONALISM'

Chile is widely regarded as exceptional in Latin America for its relative governmental stability and electoral traditions. The country attracted a great deal of academic attention in the early 1960s, particularly from American political scientists. This was a period, like today, of intense scholarly interest in the relationship between development and democracy. American political scientists were particularly interested in Latin America, and the region figured prominently in efforts during the 1950s and 1960s to establish a positive correlation between political development (usually understood as liberal democracy) and economic development.

Chile emerged at or near the top in many of the rankings. But a great deal of this literature, which did much to establish the 'exceptional' character of the country, emphasized the more formal aspects of the political system, and some of the distinctive cultural dimensions, such as the relatively homogenous population of mostly European descent, which contributed to its social stability and sense of national unity and integration. This was a noted point of distinction for Chile from the first days of independence. As one scholar of the period has remarked: 'By the standards of Argentina or Mexico, or Peru or New Grenada, this was a very compact territory inhabited by a compact population' (Collier, 1993: 2).

The value of the 'formal' features of Chilean political life is not to be underestimated. They proved, on the whole, resilient enough to survive the years of military dictatorship and then to re-emerge and contribute to the notably smooth transition to civilian rule in the 1990s. Amongst these key features and traditions identified by many observers during the 1950s and 1960s were: respect for legality and absence of electoral fraud, attachment to legal and civilian traditions of change, a strong political party system, a highly professional and efficient administrative system and a high level of honesty and morality amongst political leaders (Gil, 1966: 312). Nevertheless, not all of Gil's features have survived intact, such as genuine democratic representation in congress and a judiciary not subject to undue pressure. Both were curtailed by the attempts of the military government to protect their legacy. Nine senators, for instance, are appointees of the Pinochet government and the judiciary has not recovered its independence or public respect after years of subservience to the military during the dictatorship. But the efficiency and relative honesty of administration, in particular, has given Chile a clear advantage over other Latin American countries where endemic corruption has hindered many efforts at political democratization and economic development.

Social and cultural factors, such as the lack of ethnic, linguistic or religious fragmentation, are also important in providing an element of continuity between the pre- and post-Pinochet epochs. These have also proved a significant factor in the re-establishment of democratic politics. However, while undeniably important, these features only point to some of the positive variables that have contributed to Chile's particular pattern of development, not to the elements which have constrained that development, though they do free us, it should be noted, to look elsewhere for those constraints. Culturally, at least, Chile possesses the sense of 'national unity and shared values' (Rustow, 1970) which may be considered necessary, if not sufficient, for both liberal democracy and capitalist development.

But the emphasis on these features of continuity and stability in Chile's past do not explain the periods of change and discontinuity (in particular the Pinochet dictatorship itself), nor the stagnation and crisis which characterized the country's economic development for much of this century. And by emphasizing the uniqueness of Chile in the Latin American context, it ignores the many features that Chile has shared with other Latin American countries, such as its external dependency, its overdeveloped state, its social inequality and political polarization.

What are the significant factors, therefore, in helping us understand how capitalist development and political system informed each other prior to the Pinochet dictatorship? In their analysis of the relationship between democracy and capitalist development, Rueschemeyer et al. (1992) have focused on three clusters of power and their interaction: class power, state power and transnational structures of power. Their approach requires complex and difficult analysis of multi-factorial interrelations which must also take account of temporality and the dynamic nature of the interactions involved. But the strength of their approach lies in its analytical power, while encompassing historical and political contingency, for example the 'timing of critical events, such as the consolidation of state power, or the expansion of industrialisation' (Rueschemeyer et al., 1992: 225).

This is a helpful rectification of much of the literature on Chile, which assumes rather than analyses the democratic nature of its political system. In their comparative analysis of development and democracy in Latin America, Rueschemeyer et al. begin with the process of the consolidation of state power following independence, arguing that where this was delayed for a long period, countries were faced with the simultaneous pressure of institutionalization of intra-elite contestation and of the political inclusion of subordinated classes, whose demands grew in the course of economic development.

The Chilean case does indeed illustrate the early emergence of a coherent and consolidated state (in the first part of the nineteenth century) and the establishment of intra-elite contestation before the pressure from below to democratize. The social and economic roots of this state lay in the relative ease with which a post-colonial economy was established and the lack of armed conflict for power between competing elites unable to assert a clear economic and political hegemony over each other. Economic hegemony lay clearly in the hands of the landowners of the Central Valley and the merchants who marketed their produce and supplied them with imported manufactured goods. Gradually other economic groups, such as the northern mine-owners, were incorporated into what became a fairly homogenous oligarchy, a factor which facilitated 'institutionalized contestation' (Rueschemeyer et al., 1992: 163).

In the absence of regionally based conflict amongst those who formed this oligarchy, the federalist, anti-authoritarian liberal reform project failed to gather momentum. A conservative, centralized and authoritarian state and a strongly presidentialist system of government were in place by the early 1830s. Nevertheless, the formal and sometimes real constitutionalism of the epoch left a lasting legacy on the country's political culture.

Rueschemeyer et al. analyse the path to initial democratization, after the consolidation of state power in Latin America. They stress such factors as the type of export economy, the level of prosperity it generated and the timing of industrialization (Rueschemeyer et al., 1992: 164). Early capitalist development in late nineteenth-century Chile was based on a prosperous mineral export economy. Taxes on nitrate exports strengthened the fiscal power of the state and provided funds for infrastructural investments and the growth of the bureaucracy. The oligarchy had sought to limit the prospects for greater state autonomy which such resources made possible, when they rebelled against the strong executive power of President Balmaceda and established parliamentary government in 1891. Now they could exercise control from their stronghold in congress '. . . not of course in any democratising spirit, but much as the English landowning oligarchy ran things in the eighteenth century' (Kiernan, 1992: 82).

Chile thus entered the twentieth century with a strong and unified central authority, but not one that had risen above the particular interests of the oligarchy. As a result, political instability was rife during the parliamentary period as different party political factions of the oligarchy strove to promote their partisan interests over others. In this context, the state failed to develop any solution (other than repression and even massacre) to the 'social question' which now erupted in Chile. A 1908 government commission found a long list of abuses in working conditions in the nitrate mines; in the towns, workers were working 14 to 16 hours a day, and the conditions of the rural workers was probably even worse (Young, 1953: 65). In 1890, 2,000 striking nitrate workers had been killed by government forces in Iquique, and labour protests, strikes and organization grew apace in the following years.

The forging of a political solution to the 'social question' and the incorporation of the urban labour force as well as the middle class into the political system required a loss of oligarchic power, though ultimately a compromise was worked out in Chile. The significant issue for this chapter is the way the shift in the 1920s from 'the politics of notables' to the politics of 'restricted democracy', via a period of authoritarian rule, was accompanied by a shift in economic policy from *laissez faire* to active state intervention and by the development of social welfare policy and programmes.

The political transition from oligarchic rule was consolidated under the authoritarian government of Carlos Ibañez (1927–31). It was accompanied by the incorporation of state-organized labour (Collier and Collier, 1991) and a notable increase in state intervention in the economic life of the country. This included the establishment of credit institutions to promote agriculture and industry, an increase in the state bureaucracy, educational reform and more (Blakemore, 1993). These developments in turn stimulated the rise of a middle class directly associated with the expanded role of the state in economic life, described by one historian as 'an expanding stratum of tecnico-political specialists' (Cavarozzi, 1976: 55).

Even before the Great Depression, which nearly everywhere in Latin America brought about increased state intervention, the Chilean oligarchy had had to come to terms with the state as an agent in development. When the authoritarian government of Ibañez itself collapsed in the wake of the Great Depression (which hit Chile with particular severity), there was no turning back to the past, either politically or in the sphere of economic policy. The Depression highlighted the extreme external vulnerability of the Chilean economy through its dependence on nitrate and copper exports, foreign loans and investments, and paved the way for a conscious strategy of national industrialization.

'ACCOMMODATIONISM' AND THE STATE: 1930–1964

The process of capitalist development in Chile between 1930 and 1973 took place within a political context of intense party political competition. Underpinning the multi-party system were two basic class alignments, 'alliances' or 'political cleavages', as the Colliers describe them, with sectors of the middle class playing the pivotal role in each, and often oscillating between the two (Collier and Collier, 1991: 362).

The predominant 'alliance' for much of the period was the political compromise, or 'accommodationist alliance', between a large sector of the rising middle class and the interlocking upper class which 'owned the great estates, factories, mines and banks (and) probably accounted for less than 10 per cent of the population'

(Drake, 1992: 89). This political 'alliance' permitted the economic elite to hang onto its powerful economic interests and electoral base. In the case of the large landowners, the latter was guaranteed by their control of the vote of the rural poor on their estates. The middle-class technocrats, professionals and politicians in the government and state apparatus, on the other hand, were able to embark on a state-managed national path of development based on import-substitution industrialization, financed from export revenues (Grant, 1983). Their interests were articulated mostly by the Radical party. The 'alliance' was united in a concern to keep control over any mobilization from 'below'.

A second 'alliance' was formed between radicalized sectors of the middle class and the urban working class, a populist alliance which, following a period of coalition with the Radical party in the late 1930s and 1940s, increasingly differentiated itself from the accommodationism that party represented, and pushed for a more nationalist, protectionist and ultimately anti-monopolist and redistributionist model of development. This eventually shaped the Popular Unity project which emerged in 1970. The Christian Democrat government of 1964–70, which included representatives of both 'alliances', sought but failed to reconcile the growing polarization between the two, with a moderate, US-backed programme of reform which courted the political support of the rural migrants flooding into the towns, particularly to Santiago. The population of that city doubled between 1952 and 1970 as state promotion of industrial development in the Santiago–Valparaiso area attracted peasants from an increasingly stagnant agricultural sector.

Common to all the political projects of the period was the central role accorded the state in the development process. A complex and fragmented administrative system developed, with a proliferation of decentralized agencies, each of which operated with considerable autonomy, but with 'close links with the sector it was supposed to oversee to the detriment of overall planning' (Angell, 1993: 139). Business elites became increasingly dependent on the economic agencies of the state, but were able also to exert their influence within them. The main instrument of state economic intervention was the State Development Corporation (CORFO) established in 1939. CORFO was a semi-autonomous agency which channelled credit, mainly to industry and the construction sector. Major business associations were given voting representation on the governing council of CORFO and other state agencies which emerged during the 1940s (Cusack, 1970: 108). Thus any initial suspicion they had towards state intervention was allayed by the benefits which accrued to the private sector from state support. Indeed, an interesting study of the attitudes of Latin American enterprise managers towards the role of government in the development process, which included a detailed study of managerial attitudes in Chile 1959–60, concluded in the following way:

[the state] was mostly thought of as an institution to get things from, rather than one to which everyone should contribute . . . Aid or subsidies, for that matter, were seldom considered to be bureaucratic government intervention . . . real negativism towards the state or uncompromising laissez-faire thinking seemed confined to a group of *neoliberales* in Venezuela. (Lauterbach, 1965: 219).

State *investment* was concentrated in areas which underpinned the growth of consumer industry, for example in public utilities, petroleum, pharmaceuticals; state *aid* went to major Chilean capitalists in the light manufacturing sectors. Import restrictions and exchange-rate subsidies were also introduced to limit foreign competition (Grant, 1983: 155). Chilean industry was characterized by a high degree of concentration and enjoyed a fruitful combination of 'protection and monopoly profits' (Angell, 1993: 146). By the early 1950s, CORFO accounted for 'nearly one-third of total investment in capital equipment and nearly one-fourth of total domestic investment' (Drake, 1993: 109). One-third of CORFO's investment funds came from foreign sources, particularly the US Export-Import Bank. The pattern of industrialization brought Chile into even greater dependence on the United States, a dependence already significant in terms of foreign trade and sources of investment. This would later fuel the nationalist content of the development alternatives of the 1960s and early 1970s.

The populists could support these policies for a while as organized urban labour was privileged with welfare and union benefits, although social inequalities remained acute in society as a whole. Kalman Silvert, a renowned American scholar of Chilean politics, made the following observation in 1964:

Probably about a fifth to a quarter of all Chileans live in what we think of as modern society: they can aspire to higher positions for their children without being unrealistic; they can talk and gather and write and read freely; they can make a fairly wide occupational choice; they have access to government and can be assured of equality before the laws; they can enjoy a wide array of material fruits of industrial life; they can belong to unions and political parties and pressure groups and professional societies, and they can assume that their vote has some significance. (quoted in Fagen and Cornelius, 1970: 8)

However, the dynamic period of industrial production based on import substitution was showing signs of stagnation by the 1950s, and inflationary pressures were mounting. On average, inflation exceeded 25 per cent a year between 1920 and 1970 (De Vylder, 1976: 10). And despite the massive state subsidies to domestic industry, per capita income had grown by only 1.4 per cent between 1940 and 1960 (Drake, 1993: 125).

POLARIZATION AND THE STATE: 1964–1973

It was in this period that the two 'alliances' began to move further and further apart in their analysis of how to deal with 'sectoral stagnation' or 'stagflation' as it was called (De Vylder, 1976: 9), while the Christian Democrats tried to steer a 'third way' between 'capitalism' and 'Marxism', as the polarized alternatives had come to be labelled. Essentially, while some (monetarists) argued that inflation was due to financial mismanagement, others (structuralists) traced Chile's problems to its 'foreign trade dependency, archaic modes of production (especially in agriculture) and political struggles over government largesse amongst entrenched vested interests' (Drake, 1993: 125). Variants of the latter interpretation dominated attempts by the Chilean state to redefine the axis of development between 1964 and 1973, amidst growing pressures from increasingly politicized and previously excluded social groups.

The Christian Democrat government of Eduardo Frei offered a programme of economic modernization, reform and 'social promotion' amongst the urban and rural poor. Its programme of agrarian reform and rural unionization aimed at replacing the old *latifundia* with communally run farms. The 'Chileanization' of the copper mines proposed a partnership with US capital. Its proposals for industry involved taking the sector onto a new phase of import substitution. Public investment grew at an annual rate of 10 per cent between 1964 and 1970, 'giving the government direct or indirect control of about three-quarters of all investment decisions by the end of the period' (De Vylder, 1976: 20). Despite these efforts, the government 'proved unable to change the fundamental behaviour of the economy' (ibid.: 22), and inflation and stagnation had returned with a vengeance by the late 1960s.

The Allende government which followed went much further. Its programme aimed not to reform or curtail but to abolish the power of foreign and national monopolistic capital and *latifundismo*, while seeking an alliance with small and medium capital as well as the workers and peasants to whom it made a direct appeal. The government nationalized the copper mines. It expropriated more *latifundia* in its first 14 months than during the whole of the previous administration and took over virtually the entire financial sector. By 1973, manufacturing enterprises in the state sector of the economy accounted for more than 40 per cent of total industrial production and employed 30 per cent of the industrial labour force (Angell, 1993: 165). Popular power and participation were important elements of the government programme, though many rural and urban workers sought to push the meaning of this beyond the intentions of the government.

The Chilean private sector viewed these two governments, in particular that of Allende, with mounting fear. The middle classes and small and medium entrepreneurs saw Allende's government as an assault on the very notion of private property. Others have interpreted the actions of these governments as efforts to modernize the Chilean economy and to align it with a new conception of 'national' development involving two major features. The first was a strategy of development which was opposed to dependence on the international economy and foreign investors (a much stronger aspect of the Allende government). The second feature sought to increase the economic and political participation of the urban and rural poor within the society. David Cusack has shown how even the more moderate initiatives of the Christian Democrat government (1964–70) were viewed with deep alarm by Chilean private enterprise (Cusack, 1970). Hitherto, it had backed state intervention because its influence in the state had remained strong and state initiatives either left its interests intact or promoted them. Under the Christian Democrats, problems and threats to the business community increased while its ability to influence the state diminished (Cusack, 1970: 27). Under the Popular Unity government (1970–3), any remnants of accommodationism disappeared. The populist alliance in power now sought the collaboration of the 'nationalist' sectors of Chilean industry around a project of structural reform and national development. But the quid pro quo was for them to accept a permanent redistribution of political and economic power towards the urban working class. The cost was too high, and with the backing of the United States, whose interests were also threatened by the explosive nationalism released, the private sector as a whole and a large section of the middle class, including the accommodationist wing of the Christian Democrat party, united behind the military coup which overthrew the Allende government in September 1973.

PINOCHET'S 'SILENT REVOLUTION'

Seen against the background of Chile's pattern of development since the 1930s, the Pinochet coup can be understood as much more than a virulent right-wing response to a loss of class power. It was that, too, of course. But it also turned out to be the expression of a project to modernize and reorganize Chilean capitalist development. For the purposes of this chapter, that is its central significance.

The early years of the regime consisted of economic recovery from what the armed forces considered the excessive political interference and inefficiency of the Allende government. Greatly influenced by the monetarist interpretation of Chile's ills, the military gathered an economic team whose credentials lay in their perceived technical skills and non-political approach to economics (Foxley, 1983: 95). Reducing inflation was the priority task of the administration. Inflation was understood to be due to the rapid expansion of the money supply to meet an ever-growing fiscal deficit. The origins of the deficit lay in the over-blown public sector. Thus the reduction of public employment and the privatization of public enterprises became both the recipe for dealing with immediate inflationary pressures, and the origins of a longer-term policy of structural change towards a model of development based on a significant private sector, not the state (Foxley, ibid.).

The state soon withdrew from many areas where it had played a key role in the past. By 1978, government investment had fallen to almost half its 1970 level and there were significant reductions in social expenditure in housing, education, health and social security (Angell, 1993: 184). Public sector employment was reduced by 21 per cent between 1974 and 1978. State enterprises were sold on extremely advantageous terms to the buyers, and 'by the end of six years, the Chilean economy was well on its way to becoming an open economy with few barriers to international trade' (Foxley, 1983: 72).

Organized labour found itself completely excluded from any influence in the emerging new Chilean economy. No collective bargaining was allowed, strikes were forbidden and by 1989 average wages were 8 per cent lower than in 1970 (Ffrench-Davis, 1993: 13). In September 1979, Pinochet announced the measures, known as the seven modernizations, which would pave the way for longer-term structural changes in the Chilean economy. These included radical shifts in labour policy, social security, education, health, agriculture, justice and regional decentralization.

But what of the participation of the private sector in the conceptualization of the 'silent revolution'? Through various associations, or *gremios*, the private sector had played an important role in the mobilizations against Allende and in support of the coup. In 1973 it was in a position to offer an alternative model of its own. But as Cecilia Montero has shown in an important study of entrepreneurs in the transition to democracy, ideological heterogeneity rather than a coherent programme, characterized the economic elite at the time of the coup. The dominant philosophical and political currents within the elite at the time were the corporatist thinking of the *movimiento gremialista* and conservative nationalism, both of which demanded a strong, interventionist state (Montero, 1993: 50). The influential ideas on the dictatorship came not from these schools of thought, but from economists trained in the University of Chicago, and the package of neo-liberal ideas they brought with them, which included an emphasis on technocratic rather than 'political' decision-making, individualism, anti-statism and, of course, total faith in the market as the more efficient allocator of resources.

The private sector itself was thus kept rather apart from the elaboration of Chile's new model of development, and Montero makes the important point that 'the Pinochet government, whilst it did favour the private sector, ... also regularised its behaviour in the sense of imposing a discipline upon it that it was not accustomed to' (Montero,

1993: 45). Indeed, it is a major argument of this chapter, that the significance of the Pinochet dictatorship lay in enabling the state to do just that, to discipline capital as well as labour, in a way that was ultimately favourable to the former and to capitalist development in Chile, a process that still remains unique in Latin America.

The ideological initiative of the 'Chicago Boys' gradually and unevenly began to penetrate the thinking of significant groups in the private sector in the 1970s and 1980s. As the neo-liberal policies began to impact after 1975, Chile's many small and medium-sized enterprises found themselves very adversely affected by policies which favoured orientation towards international, not national, markets. Guillermo Campero has shown how frequent clashes took place between entrepreneurial sectors and the government, though these were rarely open and public, partly due to the persistent political support for the military government amongst the entrepreneurs (Campero, 1991: 132–3).

The groups which were most critical of government economic policy were truck owners, merchants, small and medium-sized landowners and some industrialists, especially those who had benefited most from state protection in the past and had been amongst the most militant in defending their interests against Allende. Larger enterprises, smaller in number but much more powerful, were better able to compete as the rules of the economic game shifted, and a process of further concentration of economic power began to take place in agriculture, industry and, in particular, in banking and finance. However, a great deal of economic activity was speculative. It was fuelled by the country's easy access to foreign credit rather than being a consequence of the demand for productive investment. The reduction of protective tariffs, high real interest rates and the collapse of internal demand had all weakened the competitive capacity of the productive sectors of agriculture and industry and forced them into debt in order to survive. This became apparent as the international recession of the early 1980s hit Chile with particular severity and provoked a wave of bankruptcies. Even the larger entrepreneurs, organized in the Confederation of Production and Commerce (CPC) and who had benefited most from the military government's politics, now grew anxious and sought state intervention.

Campero's account of the entrepreneurial response to this crisis is interesting. He shows that entrepreneurs had so lost their direct influence over the government that they were forced to mobilize their members through street demonstrations in a number of Chilean towns and to issue public proclamations, such as the Valdivia Proclamation of October 1982, which spoke openly of the breakdown of the national productive apparatus. This is a far cry from the conclusion of Constantine C. Menges (in a preliminary study of Public Policy and Organized Business in Chile in the 1960s) that business associations have a '*direct* role in the formulation of state economic policy – (through) their *voting* and advisory membership in various economic policy-making groups and intimate informal access to both the executive and legislative process' (Menges, 1966: 364, italics Menges).

The 'entrepreneurial revolt' (Campero, 1991) of the early 1980s was not a unified one. It never questioned the fundamental tenets of the economic model and rapidly dissipated in the face of the perceived threat to military and entrepreneurial interests from the wave of street protests which broke out amongst the real victims of the new model: the impoverished and marginalized of Santiago's ever-growing shanty towns. The entrepreneurial groups did now acknowledge, however, that to maintain any influence over government policy they would have to elaborate a more considered programme of economic recovery based on neo-liberal principles. This was discussed in a series of tough confrontations with the government. Their programme as such was rejected by the government, but greater pragmatism became apparent in official policy, including measures to stimulate production, and this eased the tensions between the two sectors. Campero and others have argued that, in the course of these negotiations, the entrepreneurial associations began to articulate a new role for themselves in society, as the 'bearers of the country's modernisation' (Campero, 1991: 145), for which they sought public support by communicating their own set of principles, rather than through the party system as in the past.

> The central theme of the Annual Meeting of Private Enterprise (ENADE) in 1986, was 'The Entrepreneur, Motor of Progress'. That expression sums up the state of mind of a socially protagonistic group. For the first time in its collective history, the entrepreneurs have publicly addressed themes such as the entrepreneurial spirit, entrepreneurial initiative, the economic and social role of the entrepreneur. (Montero, 1993: 53)

Another factor in the rise of this new 'entrepreneurial culture' was the emergence of a new generation of entrepreneurs. This generation was associated particularly with the decade following the crisis of 1982–3. Unlike the 1970s when 'real productive activity was sacrificed to financial activity' (Muñoz, 1988: 44), the 1980s saw macroeconomic policy privilege a productive export sector (in particular fruit growing, forestry and other non-traditional exports), which attracted considerable foreign and domestic investment and proved itself to be highly competitive in the international market. The production of exports per capita increased by 52 per cent between 1981 and 1989. The traditional landed elite disappeared in Chile and gave way to a modern, entrepreneurial class of agro-exporters. Montero (1992) has shown how the entrepreneurs associated with this sector differ from the traditional economic elite of Chile in being 'more professional than patrimonial'. She also found they had 'a spirit of "enterprise" which Chilean business leaders of the past had lacked; an autonomous and cosmopolitan social identity; a more pragmatic conception of the enterprise and (were) less ideological or paternalistic' (Montero, 1992: 122).

Another student of business elites noted the change in entrepreneurial culture in interviews conducted in 1987–8.

> The stereotype of the Chilean business man as a patrimonial, risk-avoiding, rent-seeking, non-maximising property owner, fearful of modern competition, with a short-time horizon and a low propensity to save and invest was no longer representative and certainly not typical of entrepreneurial activity in the dynamic sectors of the economy. Clearly, a new generation of Chilean entrepreneurs was emerging, competitively professional and self-confident and committed ideologically or pragmatically to a liberal model of market economy. (Bartell, 1992: 9)

Interviews by the present author and Professor Ken Medhurst in 1991, 1992 and 1993,[3] confirm that the change in entrepreneurial culture has sustained itself into the post-Pinochet period. The centre-left coalition that won the 1990 elections and formed the first civilian government for 17 years was potentially a threat to the security the private sector had enjoyed under a military government devoted to efficient capitalist development. But the new government showed itself to be devoted to the same cause, and kept virtually intact the neo-liberal model and its emphasis on private-sector-led development. A particularly interesting response (see below) was that of the president of the Confederation of Production and Commerce (CPC) to a question concerning the nature of business interests and the government. While one cannot assume that as a statement it represents conclusive evidence of a permanent shift in this relationship, it nevertheless indicates the perception of a very powerful figure in the business world as to how this relationship was evolving. It is clear that continued informal links exist, but the notion of a separation between the private sphere of the business world and the public sphere of the state is apparent, and the relationship is not dissimilar to the government business links of an advanced capitalist country.

> Curiously, this government is the one that calls most often and most often asks the opinion of the private sector on topics that sometimes entrepreneurs would prefer not to comment on . . . We could say that although at the practical and operative level there have been disagreements, as far as wanting to listen, to get to know and take into account, it's been good . . . we don't have institutionalised arrangements, we have a fluid system of effective work, there are many meetings, many press conferences, telephone calls, consultations, but when it comes to the moment to put into practice, this government operates on its own account and then there are disagreements. In the government there is inertia and, as in almost all governments of the world, it assumes that it knows

more than private groups, and it asks these their opinion but it doesn't let them enter its sphere. (Interview with Professor Medhurst, August 1993)

CONCLUSION

This chapter has focused on one of the most significant features of capitalist development in Chile from the mid-1980s to the 1990s: the changing relationship between the state and the private sector. An evidently more entrepreneurial private sector has enabled the country to tap effectively its significant comparative advantage in natural resource endowment in the international economy. In the early 1960s, the Chilean economist, Anibal Pinto referred to Chile as a case of 'frustrated development'. Three decades later, Chileans are congratulating themselves for having overcome the obstacles to 'take-off'. There are still debates about the future of a model which rests on the export of non-renewable natural resources, in particular how to maintain sufficiently high levels of investment to sustain the high rate of growth and how to 'make growth consistent with equitable distribution' (Ffrench-Davis, 1993: 25), given the persistent inequalities within the society and the effect of the dictatorship in intensifying them. While economic growth has reduced poverty to some extent, well over a third of the population are still officially classified as 'poor'.

But if we assume that the evidence does indeed point to a significant modernization in the structure of the Chilean economy and a change in its pattern of 'behaviour', our concern in this chapter is not to debate the future dynamic these changes have set in motion but *how* the changes themselves have been achieved. Most Chileans prefer, understandably, to recall the democratic traditions which differentiate their country from their Latin American neighbours rather than the period of dictatorship which evokes identification with them. But the fact that the conditions for effective and modernized capitalist development seem to have been established by a ruthlessly authoritarian government has to be confronted.

Chilean success is built upon a clear victory of capital over labour following the growth in power of the latter in the 1960s and early 1970s. That victory was accomplished by a violent *coup d'état* and consolidated during a prolonged period of authoritarian government. Chilean entrepreneurs grew in confidence during these years because their interests were effectively protected and stability guaranteed, even though the government was forcing them to make fundamental and often greatly resisted changes. Even under civilian government today, memories of repression are strong reminders to labour and opposition groups of the costs of dissent.

However, if we leave the story there, it would be too easy to conclude that any country of the South could emulate the Chilean experience simply by eliminating the capacity of the urban and rural poor in general (and organized labour, in particular) to defend their interests. There are no universal lessons available from the Chilean experience about the correlation between dictatorship and capitalist development or democracy and capitalist development. The only general 'lesson' that seems to emerge concerns the importance to that development of clearly defined boundaries between the state and the private sector, in which the state promotes the conditions for capitalist development without being subject to the pressure of particular interests or itself assuming significant agency in the tasks of accumulation. This does not necessarily imply a 'weak' or a 'strong' state *vis-à-vis* the rest of society, but it does require a state with *capacity*.

From the 1930s, Chile's economic elite had been forced to share political power with the middle classes and to recognize the rights of organized labour. This elite accepted a 'cosy' relationship with the state. Industrialists clearly preferred 'protection and monopoly profits', while traditional landowners enjoyed the status and power accorded them in their rural fiefdoms. Chile's 'restricted democracy' rested on the political accommodation which made this possible, until economic stagnation, the ineffectiveness of the state and the rising demands from 'below', irrevocably polarized society. Subsequently, Pinochet transformed the mentality and culture of Chile's ruling class. But those who congratulate themselves on the country's success, should remind themselves that the human and social costs of achieving this have been extremely high and have been borne disproportionately and unacceptably by the poor and the powerless.

NOTES

1 Between 1984 and 1992 the average annual growth rate of GDP was a remarkable 6.1 per cent (Inter-American Development Bank, 1993).
2 Universal suffrage did not come to Chile until 1970, when literacy restrictions were lifted. There had been no secret ballot until the 1958 electoral reforms. In the presidential election of that year only 21.45 per cent of the population was registered to vote (Gil, 1966: 213). Chile is more accurately described as a 'restricted democracy' (Rueschemeyer et al., 1992: 305) until 1970, although levels of literacy were relatively high in Chile by the 1960s. For the purposes of the chapter, the importance of this is that it draws attention to the small size of the politically relevant population, at least until the end of the 1950s, and the importance of the agreements/accommodations which could be reached between the otherwise antagonistic sectors which made up that population.
3 These interviews were conducted as part of a two-year research project on the transition to democracy in Chile, funded by the Economic and Social Research Council (ESRC) of the United Kingdom.

REFERENCES

Angell, A. 1993: Chile since 1958. In L. Bethell (ed.) *Chile Since Independence*. Cambridge: Cambridge University Press, 129–202.
Bartell, E. 1992: *Business perceptions and the transition to democracy in Chile*, Working Paper 184, Helen Kellogg Institute for International Studies, University of Notre Dame, Indiana.
Blakemore, H. 1993: From the War of the Pacific to 1930. In L. Bethell (ed.) *Chile Since Independence*. Cambridge: Cambridge University Press, 33–86.
Campero, B. 1991: Entrepreneurs under the Military Regime. In P. Drake and I. Jaksic (eds), *The Struggle for Democracy in Chile*. Lincoln: University of Nebraska Press, 128–61.
Cavarozzi, M. 1976: *The Government and the Industrial Bourgeoisie in Chile: 1938–1964*. Unpublished PhD thesis, University of California.
Collier, R. B. and Collier, D. 1991: *Shaping the Political Arena*. Princeton, NJ: Princeton University Press.
Collier, S. 1993: From Independence to the War of the Pacific. In L. Bethell (ed.) *Chile Since Independence*. Cambridge: Cambridge University Press, 1–32.
Codevilla, A. 1993: Is Pinochet the Model? *Foreign Affairs*, 72, 127–40.
Cusack, D. 1970: *The Politics of Chilean Private Enterprise Under Christian Democracy*. Unpublished PhD thesis, University of Denver.
De Vylder, S. 1976: *Allende's Chile, the Political Economy of the Rise and Fall of the Unidad Popular*. Cambridge: Cambridge University Press.
Drake, P. 1993: Chile 1930–1958. In L. Bethell (ed.) *Chile Since Independence*. Cambridge: Cambridge University Press, 87–128.
Fagen, R. and Cornelius, W. 1970: *Political Power in Latin America: Seven Confrontations*. Englewood Cliffs, NJ: Prentice Hall.
Ffrench-Davis, R. 1993: *Economic Development and Equity in Chile: Legacies and Challenges in the Return to Democracy*. IDS Discussion Paper 316, Brighton: Institute of Development Studies.
Foxley, A. 1983: *Latin American Experiments in Neo-Conservative Economics*. Berkeley and London: University of California Press.
Gil, F. G. 1966: *The Political System of Chile*. Boston: Houghton Mifflin Company.
Grant, G. 1983: The State and the Formation of a Middle Class: A Chilean Example. *Latin American Perspectives*, 10, 151–70.
Inter-American Development Bank, 1993: *Economic and Social Progress in Latin America, 1993 Report*. Washington: Inter-American Development Bank.
Kiernan, V. 1992: Chile from War to Revolution. *History Workshop Journal*, 34, 72–91.
Lauterback, A. 1965: Government and Development: Managerial Attitudes in Latin America. *Journal of Inter-American Studies*, 7, 201–25.
Menges, C. 1966: Public Policy and Organized Business in Chile: A Preliminary Analysis. *Journal of International Affairs*, 20, 342–65.
Montero, C. 1992: *Chile: Les Nouveaux Entrepreneurs. Problèmes d'Amérique Latine*, 4, Paris: France.
Montero, C. 1993: El Actor Empresarial en Transición. *Colección Estudios CIEPLAN*, 37, 37–68.

Muñoz, O. 1988: El Estado y los empresarios: experiencias comparadas y sus implicaciones para Chile. *Colección Estudios CIEPLAN*, 25, 5–55.

Rueschemeyer, D., Stephens, E. H. and Stephens, J. D. 1992: *Capitalist Development and Democracy*. Cambridge: Polity Press.

Rustow, D. 1970: Transitions to Democracy: Towards a Dynamic Model. *Comparative Politics*, 2, 337–63.

Young, T. M. 1953: *Chilean Parliamentary Government 1891–1924*. Unpublished PhD thesis, Princeton University.

9

South Africa: Democracy and Development in a Post-apartheid Society

TOM LODGE

INTRODUCTION

Until the 1970s, South Africa represented a telling example of a fairly industrialized economy in which growth and development were facilitated by high levels of political repression. Almost from the start, gold mining required a large number of cheap migrant labourers. Gold's fixed price, the low quality of the ore and heavy capital outlays made a coercive labour system a condition of the industry's prosperity until the 1940s. The expansion of secondary industry during the Second World War enabled manufacturing to outstrip mining's contribution to GDP by 1945. This development was accompanied by accelerating urbanization and the establishment in the main cities of a relatively skilled and increasingly well-organized African working class. In certain respects, the apartheid programme of the Afrikaner Nationalist government elected in 1948 was directed at reversing the economic and social gains achieved by urbanized Africans during the previous decade. Reinforced controls on black labour mobility, intensified territorial segregation of blacks and whites, the curtailment of black collective bargaining rights, the removal of Africans' already very limited access to the franchise and the suppression of popular political organizations all helped to ensure massive flows of foreign capital into import-substitution industries which the government helped to boost with walls of protective tariffs. Between 1950 and 1970, annual real GDP growth averaged 5 per cent (Lewis, 1990: 16).

In the 1970s, however, the costs of white supremacy began to outweigh the benefits. The denial of technical training to blacks underlay an alarming skills shortage. Low wages tightly limited the expansion of the domestic market. Increasing resources were required to staff and equip a huge public sector, much of it concerned with the administration of apartheid controls or with expensive economic projects conceived in anticipation of international embargoes on strategic imports. Moreover, controls notwithstanding, economic growth in the 1960s had nurtured a second rapid expansion of the African industrial working class, much of it in the main cities, despite the government's efforts to relocate labour and industries outside the towns. This growth was matched by swelling primary and secondary school enrolments. Between 1970 and 1975 alone, black secondary school attendance jumped from 89,000 to 318,000 (Hirson, 1979: 98). By the early 1970s, black workers still lacked basic rights but, with their skill, their growing literacy and their numerical weight in the industrial economy, their bargaining power had become dramatically enhanced. During the next two decades, a combination of economic recession, labour militancy, localized communal rebellions in black townships, guerrilla insurgency, capital flight, credit restrictions and the spiralling expense of militarized government all combined in 1989 to persuade the government to lift the legal restrictions on the black opposition and to begin a process of negotiated democratization.

This history seems to add confirmation to the contention that 'it is not the structural correspondence between capitalism and democracy which explains the persistence of democracy' but rather 'capitalist development is associated with democracy because it transforms the class structure' (Rueschemeyer et al., 1992: 7). Some theorists may argue that (political) 'participation in the social order' is at certain stages in an economy's development a prerequisite for 'sustained economic growth' (Pougerami, 1991: 10), but if this is the case it does not follow that states and ruling groups concede power and rights voluntarily. In South Africa democratization is taking place because 'pressures from subordinate classes have (become) strong enough to make demands for their inclusion credible' (Rueschemeyer et al., 1992: 259). Historically, high levels of political repression eased capitalist economic development. In time, though, such repression became increasingly difficult to maintain in the face of social changes generated by industrialization.

Pressure from subordinate classes was undoubtedly the crucial agency in determining political transition in South Africa. Any attempt to predict the outcome of this transition must first investigate

the political predispositions of popular classes as well as the institutions with which they will engage, before looking at the developmental tasks which will confront a democratized government. After
considering this, this chapter will go on to ask whether these tasks
can be tackled under democratic conditions.

DEMOCRATIC TRADITIONS, APARTHEID AND THE STATE

How strong are democratic inclinations amongst most South Africans? For most of this century, extremely authoritarian government
co-existed with more or less racially exclusive representative institutions. But although liberal rights and freedoms enjoyed by white
citizens had little impact on the everyday lives of black South Africans, they were not wholly meaningless to blacks either. Under
National Party rule, the judiciary retained a measure of its former
independence, although increasingly it had to apply racist legislation. A privately owned press allowed blacks a few significant channels for the expression of political ideas. Despite censorship, mass
daily newspapers from the late 1960s helped to shape and give voice
to popular feelings. In 1979, labour legislation instituted legal rights
and obligations for black trade unions, giving formal recognition
to their role in a 50-year history of attempting to represent black
workers. Until 1959, a tiny minority of African voters had parliamentary representation in the form of four 'native representatives'
and three 'native senators'. In the Cape until 1936, African participation in the common roll franchise was of considerable symbolic
importance to the African political elite. Popular political organizations, including the African National Congress (the ANC) and the
Communist Party participated in township advisory board elections
until the late 1950s. Coloureds only completely lost their common
roll franchise rights in 1972.[1] It is conceivable, then, that even the
very restricted experience black South Africans had of the rights and
freedoms associated with liberal democracy may have helped to influence their political values.

Black organizations can make claims of varying strength to liberal
and democratic traditions. The ANC until 1960 represented a broad
church accommodating socially conservative and radical nationalists, democratic socialists, liberal constitutionalists and Marxists of
various persuasions. During the 1950s, while its leaders professed a
quite sincere admiration for British political institutions, communists
helped to draft a 'Freedom Charter' with the intention of positioning
the ANC on a non-capitalist path of transition to socialism after the
successful conclusion of a 'national democratic' revolution (Hudson,
1986). The Freedom Charter was adopted at the Congress of the
People, a pageant-like gathering which voted unanimously on each
clause of the draft. The document itself was written after a year-long

campaign in which activists collected popular demands. Whatever the procedural shortcomings of the process, it did dramatically emphasize the ANC's commitment to a populist notion of people's sovereignty.

Until the late 1950s, ANC organization was largely federal in character with each province constituting a fairly autonomous organizational unit, an arrangement which helped to sustain ideological diversity. A new constitution drawn up by Oliver Tambo attempted to create a more centralized hierarchy, making junior leadership echelons subject to the authority of more senior bodies. Leadership at all levels was to be elected at conferences, through a show of hands. In fact, leadership positions were contested less frequently in the 1950s than before, partly because of the ANC's habit of nominating 'caretaker' officials to replace men and women who were legally banned from holding political office but who continued to exercise informal authority behind the scenes. This practice tended to detract from the ANC's constitutional procedures which were intended to safeguard internal democracy. On one occasion when ideological schisms threatened to disrupt a provincial congress, in the Transvaal in 1958, the dissenting faction was forced to withdraw by an assembly of loyalist 'volunteers' armed with sticks and iron bars.

Nonetheless, political disagreements within and between groups in black politics in this period did not generally lead to violence. Quite apart from a strong moral commitment to peaceful conduct by a protestant missionary-trained leadership, black organizations were too weak and small for the stakes involved in their competition with each other to be matters of life and death. Even so, at the time, the ANC attracted fierce criticism from liberal critics, particularly because of the presence of communists in its leadership, who were accused of operating as a manipulative caucus (Duncan, 1959; Ngubane 1963: 162–73).

As an exiled insurgent body, the ANC necessarily acquired a more disciplined and autocratic character. No leadership elections were held between 1959 and 1985, and the participants at the Kabwe conference were presented with a single list of candidates for the national executive, chosen by the president, Oliver Tambo (Ellis and Sechaba, 1992: 150). The organization became less tolerant of ideological diversity, despite its continued protestations of serving as an 'African parliament inclusive of all political persuasions' (Johns and Hunt Davis, 1991: 310). Exile certainly accentuated the influence of the Communist Party whose members appeared to play a preponderant role in defining the organization's intellectual life. The ANC's journal, *Sechaba*, for example, was from its inception edited by communists. Guerrilla warfare in the 1980s helped to militarize the ANC's approach to political and strategic questions. This was especially the case after the formal adoption of an insurrectionary doctrine of people's war at the 1985 'consultative conference'. Harsh treatment of mutineers and suspected traitors in the ANC's detention camps also weakened any remaining democratic impulses within the organiza- tion. The ANC exiles returned home with a well-developed set of authoritarian and bureaucratic reflexes. Back in South Africa, though, they encountered a very different political culture which had evolved during their absence.

In the 1970s and 1980s two successive waves of organization- building had endowed black South African communities with an unprecedented and dense network of voluntary associations. The pioneers in this process were the trade unions set up in the wake of the strikes which broke out in Natal in 1973. The university stu- dents and labour veterans who established the advice centres from which the unions proliferated drew on a critical understanding of South African labour history as well as international models for inspiration. In contrast to earlier communist initiatives, the 1970 unions emphasized tight factory-based organization, highly trained shop-steward leadership and a focus on workplace-related concerns, together with an eschewal of external political links. Leadership accountability, honest finances and shop-floor militancy were key attributes of this new unionism.

These organizations, united from 1978 in the FOSATU (Federa- tion of South African Trade Unions) grouping, concentrated on obtaining management recognition rather than altering state pol- icy. Their militant economism helped to promote and ideology of 'workerism'. This stressed the importance of working-class political autonomy and the dangers of workers joining or forming alliances with socially amorphous nationalist parties (Foster, 1982). Since 1985, with the merger in that year of the FOSATU group with the ANC-aligned 'community' unions, the political posture of the labour movement shifted, with former 'workerists' acknowledging the inter- dependence of shop-floor and community struggles. The new Con- gress of South African Trade Unions (COSATU) rapidly assumed a leading role in the alliance of organizations which broadly acknow- ledged the ANC's moral authority, but trade union loyalty to the ANC was not without qualifications. When COSATU adopted the ANC's Freedom Charter in 1987 it did so with the understanding that the charter provided only a set of 'minimum democratic demands' which did not in any way diminish COSATU's commitment to 'eco- nomic transformation based on working-class interests' (Marx, 1992: 205).

The new unions supplied skills, experience and procedures which could be applied to other forms of organization. In the early 1980s, strategic decisions by activists and deteriorating social conditions in townships both helped to prompt the formation of local 'civic asso- ciations', a movement which mushroomed to embrace even rural settlements in remote homelands. The growth of the civic movement was paralleled by the spread of classroom organization and the subsequent construction of 'Youth Congresses'. Labour militancy, periodic upsurges of school rebellion, the revival of internal ANC networks by 'prison graduates', and the re-ignition in 1978 of 'armed struggle' all helped to stimulate organization-building and to politicize existing associational activity. Much of this organization was intensely localized and participatory in character. Taking its cue from the trade union experience, it attempted to practise a form of direct democracy in which leaders and representatives were simply bearers of popular mandates. In practice, much of the history of the civic movement fell short of this ideal, especially after its deployment as a component in the United Democratic Front (UDF) in the ANC's 'ungovernability' campaign (Seekings, 1992: 233–4). In some locations, though, civic associations managed to establish a network of neighbourhood committees which represented rather impressive efforts at local popular empowerment (Mufson, 1990: 110–13). Their notions of democracy were informed by a conviction that democratic institutions could and should reflect the general will. As a 'UDF Message' put it in *Grassroots* (February, 1986), one of the most successful community newspapers which flourished at the time: 'Our structures must become organs of peoples' power . . . Ordinary people (must) increasingly take part in all the decisions . . . Few people making all the decisions must end.' For a contributor to *New Era*, a publication affiliated to the Cape Town UDF: 'Democracy means, in the first instance, the ability of the broad working masses to participate in and control all the dimensions of their lives. This, for us, is the essence of democracy, not some pluralistic debating society notion of a "thousand schools contending"' (*New Era*, March 1985: 38). In this vein, UDF leaders sometimes said they were opposed to the holding of a round table constitutional conference (*Weekly Mail*, 30 August 1985). Democracy was not negotiable.

Now, whether the UDF and its affiliates succeeded in embodying 'people's power' is a subject of continuing academic controversy (Mayekiso, 1993: 24–37; Jochelson, 1990: 1–32) but this need not detain us here. What is significant is that a participatory democratic ideal was a vital ingredient of the activist culture nurtured in the 1980s and it persists in the minds of many supporters of the civic movement today who remain quite doubtful about the benefits of liberal parliamentarianism. A UDF discussion document reflected this scepticism:

> Not only are we opposed to the present parliament because we are excluded but because parliamentary type representation in itself represents a limited and narrow form of democracy . . . The rudimentary organs of people's power that have begun to emerge in South Africa . . . represent in many ways the beginnings of the kind of democracy we are striving for. (Horowitz, 1990: 21–2)

Even today many activists feel that 'democracy will mean nothing in real terms without the continued struggle of popular movements' (Steinberg, 1993: 15).

If a democratic political culture depended only on high levels of popular political activity, then the habits and attitudes engendered by the township rebellion would hold out considerable hope for the future. Some of this hope would not be misplaced. The communal organizations constructed in the 1980s did help to change popular attitudes to unjust authority, to alter popular expectations from government and to instill more egalitarian political values (Mkhabela, 1994). Any minimal definition of democracy, though, must include freedom of political choice and political association. The participatory bodies developed in the 1980s did not acknowledge the moral legitimacy of political differences; their pyramidal structure reflected a view of the community as an organic unity. Organizations sought to occupy territory and mobilize as many residents as possible within a single locality. Competition between the followers of different black political organizations has become extremely violent, claiming 4,364 lives in 1993 alone and nearly 18,000 victims in the last decade (*The Star*, 17 February 1994). Most of these people died in strife between black political organizations, though police shootings have also been responsible for a proportion of the deaths. Surveys have recorded high levels of politically intolerant predispositions amongst political elites, both white and black (Kotze, 1993: 27–9; Gouws, 1993: 15–31). And to judge from the brutal treatment accorded by township youths to adherents of unpopular political parties in black communities, feelings are just as fiercely partisan amongst the rank and file.

The passions and energies which underlay popular political assertions in the 1980s helped to sustain a rebellion of unprecedented duration and scope. Without an upheaval of this scale it is difficult to see how de Klerk's administration in 1989 could have decided to embark on the road to abdication. It is, however, a long road, and for the government's opponents, it has meant making many concessions. From 1994 until 1999, at least, South Africa's political system will be that of a 'pacted democracy', a power-sharing arrangement which falls well short of the expectations engendered in the years of insurrectionary 'people's power'. Pacted democracies are the result of agreements between contending elites which do not have the capacity to defeat each other decisively. They have been a feature of Latin American transitions from authoritarian rule in which incumbents agree 'to forego appeals to military intervention' in return for their adversaries' undertaking to refrain from 'efforts at mass mobilization' (O'Donnell, Schmitter and Whitehead, 1988: 39). A feature of such transitions are explicit or at least tacit recognitions of the boundaries of policy contention. Such guarantees are obviously easiest to maintain if the incoming leadership has not depended upon widespread popular insurgency to bring about negotiations. Mass mobilization can be decisive in breaking down domination but mobilized masses make a negotiated democratization very difficult to sustain. In South Africa in 1989 a stalemate existed between a regime which could govern only through coercion and an opposition which lacked the coercive capacity to overcome the state.

In recognition of this situation, the government, its allies and its main adversaries negotiated a pacted democratization with seven key features (Rantete and Giliomee, 1992: 515–42). First, elections were to be held on the basis of a proportional representation/party list system. This would enable minority political representation but the list system would strengthen the leadership of the major parties. Elected parliamentarians are prohibited from changing their party allegiance during their terms. Second, an 'interim constitution' would be in force immediately after the elections and for the subsequent five-year term of the transitional government. During this term, parliament will sit as a constituent assembly and will legislate and vote upon a constitution. A two-thirds parliamentary majority must approve the constitution. The interim constitution reflects broad principles to which the final constitution must also adhere. The authority to interpret these principles will rest with a constitutional court whose members will be nominated by the Judicial Services Commission, not the government. The interim constitution provides for an executive president, chosen by a majority in the national assembly and deputy presidents representing those parties with over twenty per cent of the vote. All parties with more than five per cent of the vote are to enjoy cabinet representation. Ministers must be selected by the president after consultation with the deputies. The cabinet will attempt to make decisions through consensus but this is not a constitutional requirement. The House of Assembly is to have 400 members, 200 from the parties' national lists and 200 from their regional lists. Third, nine regional governments and assemblies, composed according to the same principles as the national assembly, will be assigned with specific responsibilities – for example, health, housing and education and they will have the power to raise taxes. Disputes with central government will be resolved by the constitutional court. Each region chooses ten members of a national senate. Fourth, civil service pensions are guaranteed and Mandela has on several occasions publicly promised that there will not be mass dismissals of white public servants (*The Star*, 11 March 1992; 23 March 1992). Fifth, the existing security forces remain in place subject to their reform and amalgamation with the much smaller guerrilla armies, a process already under way. Sixth, a Charter of Fundamental Rights protects conventional liberal freedoms as well as including clauses which safeguard private property, guarantee mother tongue education and endorse affirmative action. Finally, the ANC has committed itself to the retention of large-scale private enterprise and the withdrawal of its historical commitment to nationalize 'monopoly' industries. Moreover, 'private land would not be touched in the process of redistribution' (Mandela quoted in *The Star*, 20 September 1993). These agreements represent significant constraints on the power of the majority party, even if it succeeds in winning the two-thirds of the vote needed for it to decide the final constitution by itself. These will serve to define and limit the ways in which the new government can implement social and economic reform.

The nature of the South African state will be a crucial consideration in any calculation of the success of the new government's programmes. Historically the state has been heavily interventionist, administratively pervasive, bureaucratically complex and extremely large. Counting the homeland civil services, but not the parastatal corporations, the government currently employs 1.2 million people. Salaries alone account for about half the government's expenditure (Wassenaar, 1989: 73). Apartheid helped to cause considerable departmental duplication, for in many fields up to 13 ministries share responsibility. Today the public service is widely acknowledged to be overstaffed. It is also considered to be inefficient. Recruitment to its higher echelons ceased to be competitive in 1948 and employment in its lower reaches was for a long time determined by political and racist principles. The central government civil service remains dominated by whites. White civil servants have for over a decade helped to frustrate reformist initiatives by government; politically and socially they tend to be conservative (Ottaway, 1993: 30–2). The homeland civil services are notoriously corrupt; though they are mainly black in composition, senior white managers have been implicated alongside homeland citizens in a series of financial scandals. Financial incompetence and irregularities are not limited to homeland governments; in particular, government agricultural control boards and developmental agencies have been conduits for the expenditure of huge sums on evanescent projects (Republic of South Africa, 1991; Republic of South Africa, 1992).

Even so, compared to other African states and even states in other semi-industrialized developing countries, South Africa has fairly effective governance, in part a consequence of the state's high degree of social autonomy. For the most part, officials conduct their routine transactions with the public honestly. Tax collection is efficient, as is the financial management of most central government departments. Until the mid-1980s, the government's administrative reach was extensive, despite the breakdown of influx control, the system of passes which attempted to limit black urbanization (Greenberg, 1987). The state's social presence is facilitated by highly developed communications. Until the 1980s, government welfare provision was expanding and its expenditure on health and education today continues to exceed the budgetary allocation to security.[2] State-sponsored research and development, though insufficient, still puts the country in a different league of technological and scientific capacity to the rest of the continent. Notwithstanding its bureaucratic shortcomings and the possible political hostility of many of its personnel, the state still represents quite an effective instrument for the implementation of reformist programmes.

A relatively efficient bureaucracy with its own authoritarian predispositions may be checked by a fractured democratic tradition inherited from liberal and legalistic strains which survived in white parliamentary politics and black resistance. But in both, the historical legacy includes also strong veins of autocracy and intolerance. At best, tradition will offer ambivalent support for a post-apartheid democracy.

THE SOCIAL LEGACY OF APARTHEID

There can be no question that a strong state is a prerequisite for any strategy to lessen South African poverty. By themselves, market forces are unlikely to make good the consequences of decades of state-reinforced material inequality.

In 1989, the Second Carnegie Inquiry into South African poverty published its report (Wilson and Ramphela, 1989). Its findings are helpful in defining the magnitude of the tasks which await a new government. Carnegie's investigators found that South Africa was probably one of the world's most socially unequal societies, with a 'Gini co-efficient' rating of 0.66 in 1971, the highest of 57 countries measured; data for later years were not available. In 1980, 50 per cent of the population was existing below 'minimum living levels'. For a comparatively wealthy country (GNP per capital, US$ 2,340), South African life expectancy was in 1980 unusually low – 54 years.

Amongst the ten million or so economically active Africans in 1985, only one million earned wages above 'supplementary living levels', mostly in manufacturing where real wages rose from 1970 onwards. Mining wages for a million workers improved dramatically in the 1970s but remained below other industrial wages as did the wages of two million agricultural labourers. Domestic servants experienced declining earnings in the 1970s, while 300,000 African state pensioners received pensions which rose 142 per cent between 1970 and 1981 but still remained very modest. All income recipients, though, were relatively privileged compared to the unemployed, estimated in 1981 to be 21 per cent of the economically active population. Sample surveys carried out in cities in the 1980s suggested even higher levels of employment in some: 56 per cent, for instance, in Port Elizabeth in 1985.

Black poverty is reflected in the fact that some 15 per cent of the population experience malnutrition in the homelands and, according to different surveys between 1981 and 1985, African infant mortality was between 94 and 124 per thousand. African children died most frequently from pneumonia, gastro-enteritis and poor nutrition. Compounding these health problems was an increasingly acute housing shortage in the 1980s, reflecting rapid urbanization as well as the unwillingness of the government to build urban housing for blacks in the 1970s. In 1985 the urban housing shortage was estimated to total 583,000 units; in the three years previously 41,000 houses were built in black townships. Average house occupancy in Soweto was between 17 and 20 people.

In education, despite rapid increases in school enrolment in the 1970s, one-third of the African population was found by the 1980 census to be illiterate, though 80 per cent of African children were officially calculated to be attending schools. State expenditure on each black school child in 1980 was one-seventh the per capita allocation for whites. Only one-tenth of black school children managed to pass ten years of schooling with only 5,000 gaining university entrance qualifications in 1978 (Wilson and Ramphela, 1989).

Of course not all of this desperate statistical litany can be attributed solely to the inequalities of apartheid. Near zero growth rates in the 1980s, reflecting global trends, and average demographic increases of the African population of 2.8 per cent help to explain the expansion of poverty. In most respects, though, black poverty has been exacerbated if not caused by government policies, particularly with respect to population removals and racially skewed allocations of expenditure on public health, infrastructure and education.

Recent research suggests a slightly more hopeful situation than the tormented picture which emerges from the Carnegie Report. Between 1985 and 1990, blacks slightly increased their share of personal wealth, from 29 per cent to 33 per cent. 'Gini co-efficient' figures have probably declined since the very dated study cited in the report (Simkins, 1993). Modern research finds that smaller proportions of the black population live below minimum living levels. Demographers believe that African fertility is on the decline and that 'replacement fertility levels could be reached within the next generation' (Mostert, 1990: 73). But though such long-term trends and forecasts may appear comforting, absolute indications of deprivation are likely to remain daunting for a long time to come. Unemployment increased absolutely and proportionately in the 1980s. And merely to stabilize unemployment figures, growth rates would have to exceed 8 per cent (McGraph, 1993: 2). South Africa may be less socially unequal than it was 20 years before, but the absolute numbers of hopelessly poor people have grown despite a measure of redistribution in incomes and government expenditure.

The new government will have to balance the requirements of programmes to diminish poverty with those policies which can help to promote growth. In addition, the government will be influenced by the imperatives of meeting the expectations of its most powerful constituencies and securing the loyalty or, at least, the acquiescence of the former beneficiaries of apartheid. Today, a wealth of prescriptive literature suggests a set of ingredients for a 'social market' compromise between equity considerations and those of growth (Le Roux, 1988). Within the framework of such a compromise the most minimal strategy to address basic needs should include the reallocation of educational expenditure and the reorganization of institutions to benefit African schoolchildren; expansion of primary health care; provision of electricity and clean water through public employment programmes; limited land reform and a redeployment of state agricultural subsidies; the promotion of mass construction of cheap housing; and the creation of safe neighbourhoods through better policing. Such a programme could relieve poverty significantly and might also help to stimulate growth. A few examples can serve to demonstrate what can be achieved on the basis of existing resources.

Current governmental expenditure on education is high, about 7 per cent of GNP, and 24 per cent of the budget; the new government is unlikely to spend much more. White schoolchildren, 10 per cent of the total, absorb about a quarter of the money spent on schools. Equalizing per capita expenditure could release a substantial flow of funds to schools in black neighbourhoods; educational economists believe that this would amount to an increase of 50 per cent in state expenditure on township and rural schools (Donaldson, 1993). It is possible that administrative rationalization of 19 education departments may produce financial savings in the long run but in the short term this is most unlikely. Improvements in African education are more likely to result from a systematic programme to upgrade African teachers, in particular equipping them with science and maths skills, employing the grossly under-used facilities in white teacher training colleges. The ending of class boycotts and teacher strikes in itself represents an important advance; in 1993, African urban schools were disrupted for 40 per cent of the academic year. Resources in tertiary education should be directed at black technical and scientific training. An educational system which can embrace all children of school-going age and which produces larger numbers of matriculants with economically useful skills is not an utopian ideal. After all, most children already receive schooling of some kind or another. But it would require considerable social discipline amongst teachers, many of whom today are affiliated to one of the most militant public sector unions. Whites and black suburbanites would have to pay more for their access to public education if the high quality of the institutions their children attend is to be maintained.

Low-paid public employment schemes might help to reduce the costs of extensions to electrification, piped water and sanitation systems. Policy studies suggest that a doubling of the present rate of connection to the national electricity grid could be financed through administrative rationalization of a byzantine bureaucracy, the revision of tariff charges (and the effective collection of these in townships) and a redirection of municipal expenditure (Morris, 1993). At present white ratepayers are virtually the sole beneficiaries of services which are partly paid for by commercial and industrial rates; townships do not have comparable tax bases to white-governed cities. The racial integration of local authorities will change this. Given the continuing predisposition of the larger municipal governments to spend huge sums of money on unnecessary infrastructure – Pretoria's city

council, for example, recently announced plans to devote R200 million
to digging a lake in the main business district (*The Star*, 1 November
1993) – it is obvious that local government could mobilize considerable sums for more useful projects if it chose to. Mass electrification
in the countryside would represent an especially visible improvement
to people's lives and would of course considerably enlarge the local
market for appliances. This could help to boost employment in a
more substantial fashion than could be achieved by any other public
works programme.

Similarly, a modest programme of land reform and financial assistance for small farmers would not necessarily require a huge outlay
of additional resources to what is presently expended by the government on agriculture. Some state land is available for redistribution
and sizeable expanses of commercial farmland in border areas have
been abandoned by owners (Fenyes and van Zyl, 1990: 495–516).
Money to purchase land and establish black farmers might initially
be derived from the scaling down and redirection of existing government subsidies. In fact white farms, since 1985, have experienced
a sharp reduction of government support, but even so farmers are
still accustomed to receiving generous help at times of crisis. Four
billion rands was spent on drought relief to white farmers in 1992
(Lipton, 1993: 369). White farmers are heavily indebted. Smallholder-
oriented land reform may help to enhance the efficiency of agriculture generally.

The foregoing paragraphs suggest a minimal set of redistributive
measures which would reduce the scope of poverty and inequality
considerably without needing huge leaps in government expenditure
or large flows of external aid. If they are properly directed, such
policies could have a decisive impact on the lives of the present 40
per cent who receive only 5 per cent of total income (Knight, 1988:
491). Skilful political leadership will be vital in any efforts to persuade organized labour to view social investment of this character as
an acceptable substitute for wage hikes. For wage restraint amongst
industrial and public sector workers must be one crucial precondition for growth in an economy in which wages count for 71 per cent
of national income. The renumeration of government employees at
present uses up about half of government expenditure; raising this
proportion would reduce funding available for social expenditure.
Government revenues cannot be augmented by rises in personal taxation; even radical economists recognize that this has already reached
desirable limits (Nattrass, 1992: 40–2). The 100,000 or so managers
and technocrats who run the economy have skills which are easily
marketable elsewhere as current emigration statistics demonstrate.
'Soaking the rich' by reducing their real incomes through higher
taxation would be very risky. Government borrowing cannot be the
main source of development capital. Though South Africa is under-
borrowed internationally, public debt to local lenders is very heavy
and uses up 17 per cent of the budget in interest payments (*The*

Star, 30 September 1993). Though initially economic growth might increase as a consequence of public works programmes, in the long term it will have to be fuelled by the expansion of manufacturing exports and the inflow of foreign investment. Fuller incorporation into the international economy will mean adhering to GATT regulations which stipulate the abandonment of tariffs and import quotas. Not all factories will survive exposure to foreign competition. The textile and transport sectors, together employing 9 per cent of the industrial labour force, are especially likely to lose many jobs. A more liberal trade regime may need to be accompanied by local currency devaluations and hence inflation. An outwardly oriented growth strategy will begin by imposing heavy penalties on urban consumers and industrial workers; effective delivery of social reform will be crucial if the government is to retain its public credibility.

ANC proposals for 'Reconstruction and Development' more or less balance equity concerns with growth imperatives through a strategy of reallocation and rationalization of existing resources. Understandably, in its electoral appeals it placed more emphasis on expenditure than finance; the ANC was not seeking the votes of bankers and stockbrokers. Before the election, though, ANC spokesmen suggested that public expenditure will only increase slightly overall, that social investments will mainly be derived from the redirection of available resources and that the civil service is already too large (*The Star*, 15 March 1992; 29 March 1993). Specifically, the ANC pledged the redistribution of state land, a public works programme to provide clean toilets and water for all within two years, the doubling of electricity connections by the end of the century, the expansion of primary health care, with free access to curative medicine for the aged, the young, the disabled and the unemployed, the reduction of class sizes in schools and the provision of free textbooks and popular extension of private home ownership facilitated by promptings to the private sector to supply finance. Parastatal corporations will be deployed to help the establishment of small businesses and ANC economic policies will seek to promote manufacturing exports. The organization is committed to diversifying ownership, through anti-cartel legislation if necessary. Tariffs and protection will be reduced, though with 'minimum disruption to employment'. The ANC has more faith than most academic economists in the capacity of public sector investment to produce GDP gains. Its programme predicts annual increases of 5 per cent as a consequence of social expenditure. Its policies are not calculated to entice external investors, promising 'no special advantages' for foreign companies. Undertakings to reduce income tax for low-income earners and to collect corporation tax more efficiently are in the same vein. Here the influence of COSATU and SACP advisers may have had a decisive influence in the drafting of the 'Reconstruction and Development Programme' adopted on the eve of the ANC's electoral campaign (African National Congress, 1994a). Even so, for a manifesto in a liberation election, the ANC's vision of 'A Better Life for All' is hardly spend-thrift (African National Congress, 1994b).

THE ANC, DEVELOPMENT AND DEMOCRACY

If surveys are to be believed, the ANC's proposals fall well short of popular expectations. A poll in September 1993 discovered that 80 per cent of its black respondents thought that government should supply free housing (*Sunday Times*, 14 November 1993). Nationaliza-tion was also a popular option preferred in the survey and, indeed, the National Union of Mineworkers recently renewed its commit-ment to public ownership of the gold-mining industry. Specialists debate the extent of land hunger (*Financial Mail*, 5 November 1993), but the ANC's land reform proposals look very restrained when com-pared with those of the PAC which advocate the reduction through confiscation of 'settler'-owned land by two-thirds (Pan-Africanist Congress, 1992: 12).

Moreover an ANC-led coalition will encounter formidable diffi-culties in implementing even a fairly moderate 'growth through re-distribution' programme. A necessary first condition is a streamlined, cooperative and competent civil service. This may be quite difficult to attain. Quite apart from the question of the bureaucracy's present political proclivities, there is the disruption and inefficiency that might result from badly managed affirmative action. The new gov-ernment will be under massive political pressure to create jobs through the expansion of public service. Even maintaining the civil service at its present size will bring additional expenditure on salaries. Equal-izing the renumeration of officials in the former homeland civil ser-vices with those of the better-paid central government might increase the wage bill by as much as 30 per cent, reducing considerably the funding for social expenditure.

Conservative political opposition could also hinder progress. Coa-lition partners may well resist cuts in the quality of schooling and health care available to whites. They might also resist efforts by the state to regulate private patterns of investment. The further removal of commercial agricultural subsidies will further alienate 67,000 white farmers, most of whom have already signalled their opposition to power-sharing. The National Party won the regional elections in the Western Cape partly through persuading Coloured voters that they would be disadvantaged by ANC-promoted employment policies which favoured Africans. Affirmative action is likely to continue to be a contentious issue in the new administration.

Political rivalries which divide the labour movement may assume a more dangerous significance when the ANC attempts to negotiate limits to wage claims with its electoral partner, COSATU. As James Motlatsi, president of the powerful mineworkers union, observed last year: 'An alliance is not a marriage. We have, from time to time, to check that the conditions that require it are still operative' (*The Star*, 11 August 1993). As the afterglow of a liberation election fades, the conditions may seem quite different. Public works schemes, even if they do succeed in creating 300,000 jobs, as the ANC has promised, will hardly dent unemployment statistics. Some three million people between the ages of 16 and 30 have no jobs and more than 80 per cent of the 16- to 19-year-old groups are not working. Surveys demonstrate that nearly half the PAC's support comes from youths aged 17 to 24 (Marketing and Media Research, 1993). The ANC should expect substantial defections of its own young supporters to its more radical rival as expectations of the new government are disappointed over the next five years. Even youth organizations which are nominally affiliated to the ANC have frequently defied ANC attempts to bring them to heel (Nyatshumba, 1993: 20–7).

Can the twin tasks of addressing social injustice and promoting growth be completed under democratic conditions? As already noted, the new constitution embodies a fairly restrictive form of representative democracy with its stipulations for a coalition cabinet and deputy presidents from minority parties. Its Charter of Rights is weighted in favour of 'first generation' freedoms, that is individual civil rights and minority safeguards. As one commentator has observed: 'the push for a bill of rights comes not from the heart of the freedom struggle, but from people on the fringes' (Sachs, 1988: 4). Land reform advocacy groups and trade unions opposed the inclusion of the charter's property clause. Explicit and tacit guarantees of existing property relations are indeed an affront to democratic principles. As Adam Przeworski has argued, 'it is within the nature of democracy that no one's interests can be guaranteed' (Przeworski, 1986: 59). Human-rights lawyers are concerned about what they see as implicit threats to press freedom and academic autonomy in the constitution. Representation by parliamentarians selected by party leaderships removes any element of their accountability to electors.

The ANC's 62 per cent majority in the 1994 election enabled it to appropriate most of the key policy-making portfolios in the new cabinet. If it feels compelled to, it will be able to dictate policies to its partners. Even so, ANC leaders probably know that coalitions function best through consensus. The initial retention of the former finance minister and the governor of the Reserve Bank in their previous posts showed that the new administration has significant commitment to consensual policy-making. In the Transitional Executive Council, a caretaker body established at the end of 1993 to supervise the conduct of government during the elections, ANC representatives demonstrated their willingness to support unpopular policies, backing high pay rises for civil servants and agreeing to the retention of preventative detention. In a similar vein, ANC parliamentarians have indicated support for generously increased renumeration for members of parliament, regional assemblies and national and regional cabinet. These recommendations have already come under fire from COSATU leadership.

In the run-up to the election, the main threats to democratization came from conservative political elites, white and black, and their organized political followings. These were sufficiently formidable for Inkatha and the Afrikaner 'volkstaaters' to extract symbolic constitutional concessions. The conservative politicians have emerged from the election with considerable political strength, having demonstrated their capacity to marshal substantial electoral support.[3] Insurgent white supremacist politics, however, is likely to wane with the re-entry of the Afrikaner nationalist establishment into the arena of legitimate politics and as the more exaggerated fears which animated the partisans of parliamentary and fascist movements prove chimerical.

For the time being, the threat of right-wing military rebellion or terrorism has receded. More serious challenges to democratic stabilization might be mass protests and upheavals requiring authoritarian measures on a large scale and over a long period to contain them. These are more likely to come from the left than the right, especially from organized labour and mobilized youth, if the pace of social reform is too slow. Such challenges are not inevitable; for a while, at least, they can be averted by imaginative leadership and by public faith in the democratic process itself – if people feel that they can make meaningful choices in elections, then they are less likely to contemplate rebellion. Democratic regimes are in certain respects less vulnerable than authoritarian administrations. As Samuel Huntington has pointed out: 'processes and procedures . . . can in substantial measure substitute for the dearth of more deterministic economic and sociological conditions of democracy in Third World nations' (Huntington, 1991: 260). The presence of COSATU representatives in government may help to ensure the loyalty of the better-organized sections of the labour movement and may help to facilitate the establishment of institutionalized forms of corporatism between government, business and labour (Maree, 1993: 25–54). Corporatism, though, may not necessarily result in effective social and economic reform. Indeed, business and labour elites may share a common short-term interest in maintaining protection for socially costly uneconomic enterprises. Labour may not view increased government expenditure on the needs of the rural poor – primary health care, clean water and electrification – as adequate compensation for curbing wage claims of urban workers.

Ironically, the very popularity at the polls of the ANC may be the undoing of democracy. A nationalist movement which can meet the aspirations of the burgeoning African middle class through affirmative action and enforced corporate 'unbundling' and at the same time retain the support of the most powerful labour unions through the deployment of government resources would represent such a formidable political force. It might always be able to out-manoeuvre electoral opponents whose support was derived from more vulnerable or marginal groups. In the recent election, the ANC's principal competitors for the black vote were Inkatha and the PAC, both of which attempted to project their appeal to the least privileged sections of the African population: hostel dwellers, the urban unemployed and the rural landless. If winning the adherence of these people requires decisions which conflict with the interests of middle-class supporters and organized labour, the ANC may prefer to consign them permanently to the ranks of the opposition.

One serious temptation for the ANC in power might be to sacrifice democratic principles and developmental goals to political expediency. The politics of consensus and compromise fostered by pacted transitions is especially conducive to the formation of elite cartels which could seek to include representatives of the most effectively mobilized social forces. In such a scenario, the new government could draw upon strong statist traditions in South African political culture to reconstruct the dominant one-party system under which the country has been governed for so much of its history. Such a system could incorporate the organized working class but still leave many others outside.

This may not be the predominant impulse, though, in determining the future behaviour of the new leadership. As the historical review at the beginning of this chapter suggested, South African political traditions include a fractured liberalism, as much part of the political heritage of opposition as it was an ingredient in the dominant political order. This, together with the commitment to social justice, which is one of the positive legacies of the ANC's relationship with the Communist Party, might help to check the development of an authoritarian corporate oligarchy. The scale of the ANC's electoral victory was a reassuring measure of its popularity. Its leaders may feel sufficiently autonomous to undertake the kind of programme which, rather than representing a response to the most formidable sectional interests, will instead directly address social inequality and promote economic growth. Repeated victories at the polls need not necessarily degrade democracy. To be sure, the ANC's electoral popularity brings with it certain risks, but it also contributes a desperately needed legitimacy to the South African state. Without effective state authority, efforts to secure development will be futile and formal democracy will be meaningless.

CONCLUSION

In South Africa the promotion of economic growth will certainly inflict social costs. These might well be managed better in a political system in which access to political power is quite socially restricted; this may be one of the developmental benefits of South Africa's compromised 'transitional' democracy. The new 'pacted' political order confers upon its executive considerable executive autonomy as well as much-needed legitimacy. The new rulers could use their powers to good advantage to implement those developmental policies which require sacrifices from certain groups. It would be very dangerous, though, if South African political progress followed the path taken by other African countries where democratic commitment has been measured by restrictive government, social austerity and market primacy (Ake, 1991: 37). South Africa's relative industrial strength and economic sophistication have been built by a strong interventionist state, not market capitalism. As this chapter has attempted to demonstrate, that strong state is still needed to foster the conditions for the measure of social justice which will make the sacrifices required by economic advance acceptable.

NOTES

1 Coloureds could vote for special white parliamentary representatives in parliament from 1956 until 1968 and in Cape Town participated on a common roll in municipal elections until 1972.
2 In the 1991/2 budget expenditure on social services represented 38.78 per cent of total government expenditure compared to 19.5 per cent spent on security. Source: *SA Barometer*, March 29, 1991, 89.
3 In the elections the percentages of the national vote received by the parties now represented in the National Assembly were: ANC 62.6 per cent; National Party 20.4 per cent; Inkatha Freedom Party 10.5 per cent; Freedom Front 2.2 per cent; Democratic Party 1.7 per cent; Pan-Africanist Congress 1.2 per cent; African Christian Democratic Party 0.5 per cent.
   The ANC won large majorities in five regions, gained control of the PWV (Witswatersrand) regional assembly with 57 per cent of the vote, won the Northern Cape with a bare minority over the other parties (49.7 per cent) and lost the battles for control of the Western Cape and Natal regional governments to the National Party and Inkatha respectively.

REFERENCES

African National Congress 1994a: *The Reconstruction and Development Programme*. Johannesburg: Umanyano Publications.
African National Congress 1994b: *A Better Life for All*. Marshalltown.
Ake, C. 1991: Rethinking African Democracy. *Journal of Democracy*, 2, 32–44.
Donaldson, A. 1993: Basic Needs and Social Policy. In M. Lipton and C. Simkins (eds) *State and Market in Post-Apartheid South Africa*. Johannesburg: University of the Witwatersrand Press, 271–320.
Duncan, P. 1959: Open Letter to Chief Luthuli. *Contact*, 2 May.
Ellis, S. and Sechaba, T. 1992: *Comrades against Apartheid*. London: James Currey.

Fenyes, T. and van Zyl, J. 1990: The Occupation and Depopulation of White Rural Areas. *Development Southern Africa*, 7, 495–516.

Foster, J. 1982: The Workers' Struggle: Where does FOSATU Stand? *South African Labour Bulletin*, 7, 67–86.

Gouws, A. 1993: Political Tolerance and Civil Society: The Case of South Africa. *Politikon*, 20, 15–31.

Greenberg, S. 1987: *Race and State in Capitalist Development*. Johannesburg: Ravan Press.

Hirson, B. 1979: *Year of Fire, Year of Ash: The Soweto Revolt*. London: Zed Press.

Horowitz, D. 1990: *A Democratic South Africa?* Cape Town: Oxford University Press.

Hudson, P. 1986: The Freedom Charter and the Theory of National Democratic Revolution. *Transformation*, 1, 6–38.

Huntington, S. P. 1991: *The Third Wave: Democratization in the Late Twentieth Century*. Norman: University of Oklahoma Press.

Jochelson, K. 1990: Reform, Repression and Resistance in South Africa: A Case Study of Alexandra Township. *Journal of Southern African Studies*, 16, 1–32.

Johns, S. and Hunt Davis, R. 1991: *Mandela, Tambo and the African National Congress*. New York: Oxford University Press.

Knight, J. B. 1988: A Comparative Analysis of South Africa as a Semi-Industrialised Developing Society. *Journal of Modern African Studies*, 26, 473–84.

Kotze, H. 1993: Political Intolerance: A Survey. *Die Suid Afrikaan*, 43, 27–9.

Le Roux, P. 1988: The Economics of Conflict and Negotiation. In P. Berger and B. Godsell (eds) *A Future South Africa*. Cape Town: Human and Rousseau, 200–39.

Lewis, S. 1990: *The Economics of Apartheid*. New York: Council of Foreign Relations.

Lipton, M. 1993: Restructuring South African Agriculture. In M. Lipton and C. Simkins (eds) *State and Market in Post-Apartheid South Africa*. Johannesburg: University of the Witwatersrand Press, 359–408.

Maree, J. 1993: Trade Unions and Corporatism in South Africa. *Transformation*, 21, 24–54.

Marketing and Media Research 1993: *The First Election: Baseline Survey Report*. October.

Marx, A. 1992: *Lessons of Struggle: South Africa's Internal Opposition, 1960–1990*. Cape Town: Oxford University Press.

Mayekiso, M. 1993: The Legacy of People's Power. *Southern African Review of Books*, 5, 27–9.

McGraph, M. D. 1993: Jobs, Unemployment and Social Mobility. Paper delivered at an Urban Foundation Strategy and Policy Unit Workshop, Johannesburg, 11 May.

Mkhabela, S. 1994: Democratization in Rural South Africa: The Case of Masite, 1986–1993. BA Honours dissertation. Political Studies: University of the Witwatersrand.

Morris, M. 1993: Bringing Power to the People. *The Star*, November 8.

Mostert, W. 1990: Recent Trends in Fertility in South Africa. In W. Mostert and J. Lotter (eds) *South Africa's Demographic Future*. Pretoria: Human Science Research Council, 63–74.

Mufson, B. 1990: *Fighting Years*. Boston, Mass.: Beacon Press.

Nattrass, N. 1992: *Profits and Wages: The South African Economic Challenge*. Johannesburg: Penguin Books.

Ngubane, J. 1963: *An African Explains Apartheid*. New York: Praeger.

Nyatshumba, K. 1993: Bitter Harvest. *Towards Democracy*, 3, 20–7.

O'Donnell, G., Schmitter, P. and Whitehead, L. 1988: *Transitions from Authoritarian Rule, Volume Five, Conclusions about Uncertain Democracies*. Baltimore, Md.: Johns Hopkins University Press.

Ottaway, M. 1993: *South Africa: The Struggle for a New Order*. Washington: Brookings Institution.

Pan-Africanist Congress 1992: The Land Policy of the PAC of Azania. Discussion document, Johannesburg, November.

Pourgerami, A. 1991: *Development and Democracy in the Third World*. Boulder, Colo.: Westview Press.

Przeworski, A. 1986: Some Problems in the Study of the Transition to Democracy. In O'Donnell et al. *Transition from Authoritarian Rule*, vol. 1, Baltimore, Md.: Johns Hopkins University Press, 47–62.

Rantete, J. and Giliomee, H. 1992: Transition to Democracy through Transaction. *African Affairs*, 91, 515–42.

Republic of South Africa 1991: *Special Report of the Auditor General Concerning the Independent Evaluation of the Mossgas Project*. Pretoria: RP/1991.

Republic of South Africa 1992: *Commission of Inquiry into Development Aid: Report to the State President*. Pretoria: RP 73/1992.

Rueschemeyer, D., Stephens, E. H. and Stephens, J. D. 1992: *Capitalist Development and Democracy*. Cambridge: Polity Press.

Sachs, A. 1988: Towards a Bill of Rights in a Democratic South Africa. Paper presented at an ANC seminar on constitutional guidelines, Lusaka, March.

Seekings, J. 1992: Civic Organisations in South African Townships. In G. Moss and I. Obery (eds) *South African Review 6*. Johannesburg: Ravan Press, 216–38.

Simkins, C. 1993: Demography and Income Distribution. Paper delivered at an Urban Foundation Strategy and Policy Unit Workshop, Johannesburg, May 11.

Steinberg, J. 1993: A Place for Civics in a Liberal Democratic Polity. Unpublished paper, Albert Einstein Institution, Civil Society Project, Johannesburg.

Wassenaar, A. 1989: *Squandered Assets*. Cape Town: Tafelberg.

Wilson, F. and Ramphela, M. 1989: *Uprooting Poverty*. New York: W. Norton and Co.

10
Development and Democratization in China

GORDON WHITE

INTRODUCTION

In the aftermath of the 1989 Beijing Massacre and the anti-communist revolutions of central and Eastern Europe during 1989–91, and in the context of the post-Cold-War wave of global democratization, China has become an international political pariah-state for its failure to follow the trend. The Beijing Massacre is seen as a desperate and inevitably temporary abortion of a process of systemic collapse which is the common fate of all Leninist states. Many of the overseas political dissidents who escaped after Tiananmen have advocated rapid democratization as a cure for China's internal ills, and international opinion regards the Chinese regime as a distasteful hold-out which, sooner or later, has to fall into line with the international norm of multi-party liberal democracy. However, to the extent that the newly hegemonic international paradigm of democratization holds that (liberal) democracy is an aid to development and not (as thought earlier) a hindrance, China is an awkward case since its developmental performance over the past 15 years has been outstanding, a fact that does not seem unconnected with its non-democratic form of government.

It is the thesis of this chapter that any view of the Chinese situation which argues for rapid and radical democratization may be fraught with wishful thinking and booby-trapped with inconsistencies which not only weaken its intellectual force, but, if put into practice, could have potentially dire consequences for the welfare of China's population of over 1.1 billion.[1] In particular, confident assertions about the putative complementarity between democracy and socioeconomic progress may be simplistic and misleading. In the contemporary Chinese situation, the relationship between democracy and development – and more specifically between political reform and market-oriented economic reform – is far more tangled and ambiguous than the currently conventional paradigm allows. We need to step outside the paradigm and examine some of its ideas and assertions in a critical and dispassionate way, drawing on comparative international and historical experience to put the Chinese case into context.

In so doing, I would wish to avoid certain unhelpful approaches to the debate over democracy and development. One common tendency is to assert the primacy of 'human rights' in evaluating political arrangements and to advocate democratization to promote these rights, while defining them mainly or exclusively in civil/political terms. When applied to an authoritarian regime of any complexion and record, this approach tends to determine the issue in advance in favour of rapid democratization along liberal lines. Particularly when discussing the relationship between democratization and development, it is important to consider a broader array of rights and freedoms which include social and economic ones as well as civil/political rights and to supplement the language of rights with the language of welfare to enable one to consider the developmental performance of different types of political regime. (For an argument along these lines in the Chinese case which emphasizes the importance of 'subsistence rights', see Kent, 1993) This would allow a reasoned case to be made in favour of a non-democratic regime in certain circumstances.

Another common tendency in debates over democracy and development – found particularly among opponents of rapid democratization – is to take an 'instrumental' view of political systems by evaluating them purely in terms of their capacity to promote socioeconomic development. Thus if authoritarian systems can demonstrably 'do thê job' better than democratic systems, they should be encouraged or tolerated and democracy will have to wait until a later historical stage. (For example, the former prime minister of Singapore, Lee Kuan Yew, uses this kind of argument in evaluating political options in Russia, central and East Asia.)[2] But this approach ignores the importance of promoting civil/political rights and freedoms as unequivocal goods in the here and now, not in some historical *mañana*, and allows one to question the intrinsic political characteristics of a regime regardless of its developmental performance.

A third aid to analysis is to avoid the tendency to make static judgements about hypothesized trade-offs between the nature of a political regime and developmental performance. It may be the case, for instance, that an authoritarian regime may have considerable success in promoting socioeconomic progress, but this does not remove democratization from the agenda. To the extent that democratization is valuable in its own right, it too is a fundamental dimension of 'development' and should be incorporated into thinking and action about the short- and not just the long-term evolution of that regime. This more dynamic approach to the issue requires a view of political regimes which does not draw a hard and fast line between 'authoritarian' and 'democratic' systems, but which regards any particular political system as lying along a continuum from 'totalitarian' through 'authoritarian' to 'democratic' and capable of moving in either direction, even while retaining the same broad generic label.

The last aid to analysis is to avoid a purely normative approach, however much supported by empirical calculations of welfare, by providing a supplementary understanding of the deeper political underpinnings of political regimes and the consequent feasibility of choices between them. However desirable a rapid transition to democracy might be in any particular context, for example, there may be underlying political constraints which make it infeasible. This approach has been elaborated by Dietrich Rueschemeyer and his colleagues (1992: ch. 3), who identify three constellations of power which condition the possibility and nature of democratization in society, the state and the international system.

The analysis which follows will begin by looking at the case for a rapid transition to a liberal democratic regime in China in the context of the specific nature of China as a poor developing society and as a socialist country undergoing radical economic reform in the direction of a 'socialist market economy'. Second, I shall identify the recent changes in contemporary Chinese society during the post-Mao reform era which make some form of democratization both advisable and realizable. Third, I shall investigate the feasibility of democratization in the Chinese context in the light of a number of commonly cited constraints. Finally, I shall outline a notion of 'dual transition' which may be capable of moving China towards democracy without incurring the potential costs arising from a rapid leap to multi-party liberal democracy.

DEMOCRATIZATION, DEVELOPMENT AND ECONOMIC REFORM

The argument for democratization, as advanced by the most vocal elements of the Chinese dissident community and their foreign supporters, takes the following line.[3] First, the particular form of democracy advocated is a full-fledged liberal democratic multi-party system, characterized by an open and competitive political process, periodic free elections and legally guaranteed civil freedoms;[4] second, the transition should be a rapid one, since only an abrupt break with the past can weaken the conservative forces of the previous political and institutional status quo – in effect a political version of the 'big bang' argument for rapid economic reform in the Eastern European context.

Is 'democratization' in this particular sense an essential pre-condition for solving the developmental problems of developing countries in general and China in particular? It is a commonplace to point out here that, in comparative historical terms, liberal democracy, in its full-fledged form, is primarily a characteristic of the advanced industrialized societies and is more a product of socioeconomic modernization than its cause. Moreover, it is the cumulative result of a prolonged and often conflictual process of political development. In the classic case of the United Kingdom, for example, political democratization, in terms of the development of diverse political organizations and the expansion of legalized political participation and representation, emerged very gradually. It lagged behind the pace of economic change and the growth of a capitalist mode of production, and had to be secured through often bloody popular struggles. 'Late modernizers' such as France, Germany and Japan, owed much of their developmental success to long periods of authoritarian rule and their eventual transition to democratic politics rested heavily on the social and economic achievements of the previous era. A similar argument can be made for the most successful 'late late modernizers', the 'four little tigers' of East Asia – South Korea, Taiwan, Hong Kong and Singapore (White, 1988; Wade, 1991).

It would seem reasonable, therefore, to relate the nature of political systems to stages of socioeconomic development. Multi-party liberal democratic systems may well be a prized characteristic of advanced, industrialized societies, but how feasible are they in societies undergoing the traumas of early development, in material terms the transition from a low- to a middle-income country? In this context, China is still a poor country in spite of its impressive developmental performance over the past 15 years, with a per capita income of US$380 by the end of 1992, slightly behind Gambia ($390) and slightly ahead of Guyana ($330); it has yet to make this transition, unlike its East Asian neighbours. The country still faces formidable developmental tasks: to organize a 'regime of accumulation' capable of breaking through powerful ecological and economic constraints and providing strategic guidance over an accelerated process of economic and technological modernization; to generate and redistribute the resources necessary to constrain regional and class-based inequalities and alleviate widespread poverty; to restrain population growth, provide productive jobs for a vast and expanding work-force and to achieve a rapid rise in overall levels of material welfare. These developmental tasks often require the state to make strategic decisions which must be imposed in the teeth of popular inertia, resistance from privileged and powerful social interests and external pressure. Judging from the experience of the East Asian NICs, there would seem to be a need for a strong and 'autonomous' developmental state to do this job in the initial phases of the industrialization process.[5] A strong case can be made to the effect that Chinese experience over the past 15 years represents a socialist version of this phenomenon which has been remarkably successful in terms of both the conventional indices of social and economic development. Not only have high growth rates been achieved throughout the era of post-Mao economic reform, but the benefits of growth have been widely, albeit unequally, shared across the general population, in particular the 75 per cent of the population living in the rural areas.[6] This has taken place under the aegis of a basically unreformed Leninist polity in which the communist leadership has provided strategic guidance throughout, kept the process on course in spite of its inherent tensions and instabilities and attempted to mitigate the potentially serious social costs of rapid economic growth. Given the massive welfare gains achieved thereby, it is reasonable to argue that one should be cautious about recommending radical political change in the short term. Rapid democratization in such a context, particularly a sudden move towards multi-party competition, might well weaken the developmental state by making it vulnerable to the social and regional schisms emerging under the impact of rapid economic growth.

The issue of democratization must also take into account that China faces a double challenge in the 1990s: not merely a developmental task of organizing economic modernization and improving welfare in a large, complex and poor society, but also a systemic task of transforming the previous central planning system into some form of market economy. The experience of Eastern Europe and the Soviet Union suggests that this latter process is economically destabilizing, socially divisive and politically explosive. Markets are disruptive entities in the real (as opposed to the academic) world of economics; even more so in socialist and post-socialist contexts where the populace is accustomed to the provision of non-market benefits, such as job security and subsidized welfare services, which they are reluctant to lose. In the short and medium term, this systemic transformation would appear to require strong, probably authoritarian, controls which operate to set in place an institutional and regulative framework for a market order, to alleviate the concomitant social costs, to counter opposition and to manage social conflicts, not the least between a rising bourgeoisie and an urban working class facing the loss of its former privileges. In this context, a rapid transition to democracy might well exacerbate the political problems of managing the economic transition, problems of which the events leading up to the Beijing Massacre in 1989 provided a foretaste.

On these two counts, therefore, there seems to be *prima facie* historical and comparative evidence to support the case that, in the Chinese context with its specific conditions and challenges, any rapid move towards democracy would pose serious political and developmental problems. However, these and other arguments about the 'dangers of democracy' can lead into a blind alley. For example, they can be used to justify the political abuses of a developmentally effective authoritarian regime, when in fact violation of political rights and abuse of political power by an uncontested political elite are fundamental problems of human welfare which need urgently to be addressed. Democratization of some kind is a potential remedy for these ills. There is also the fallacy of equating a 'firm hand' and a 'strong government' with authoritarianism. The key source of the 'strength' of a regime is its claim to legitimate power and the popular consent and cooperation that this entails. In the Chinese case, however, the reform era has seen a continued, indeed accelerating, erosion of the legitimacy of state socialism and of its core institution, the Chinese Communist Party. As the Beijing Massacre demonstrated, here was a regime increasingly dependent on force, not consent.

Thus the case for political reform along democratic lines in China has two interlinked aspects and must be situated within the rapidly changing dynamics of a Chinese society undergoing economic reform: a normative argument based on a consideration of political rights and welfare, and a practical political argument based on the need to reconstitute the authority of the current regime in a changing societal context as a pre-condition for future developmental success. Since the normative case is well rehearsed in the conventional literature on China,[7] I shall concentrate on the latter considerations of practical politics. I start by examining the pressures operating in Chinese society to put the issue of democratization on the agenda for political action.

POST-MAO ECONOMIC REFORMS AND THE IMPETUS FOR DEMOCRATIZATION

The post-1979 economic reforms have brought major, irreversible political changes to Chinese society and politics. First, the authority and integrity of the hegemonic political institution, the Communist Party, rather than recovering from the ravages of the Cultural Revolution, have continued to decay. This is linked with, and partly explained by, a decline in the authority of the party leadership. The reform era saw an escalating conflict within the post-Mao leadership, partly based on differences in political generations and partly on contending ideological and policy positions. Any semblance of consensus was destroyed by the Tiananmen events. The reformist wing was eclipsed and more conservative elements sought desperately to re-establish an obsolete political rectitude in an environment which they were increasingly neither able to control nor understand. By contrast, the administrative organs of the state machine have been able to retain much of their power; indeed in some ways they have extended it. This is partly because they have been able to exploit new opportunities offered by the economic reforms to amass resources in their own institutional interests, the widespread phenomenon of 'state entrepreneurship' (Blecher, 1991; White, 1991a); and partly because the reforms brought into being a new wave of state institutions tailored to the requirements of an emerging 'socialist market economy' in addition to the 'old' institutions of the centrally planned economic order which strove to retain their previous influence. There has also been a relentless decentralization of power within the governmental apparatus from the central to regional and local levels, which has increased central–local and local–local tensions.

In terms of social structure, Chinese society has become more complex and politically assertive. A gradual shift in the balance of power from state to society has been under way. This has provided greater opportunities for social forces to exert influence over party and state institutions (particularly through informal networks), has opened up greater space for new socioeconomic institutions and interests and has led to increasingly open discontent and friction between the party/state and society. These trends have been more prominent in the cities; the networks of party/state control in the countryside appear to have remained more solidly intact and effective (though this varies widely from area to area). Yet here too the political *status quo* is being increasingly undermined as the rural economy becomes more dynamic, rural society more fluid and rural interests more diverse and articulate.

There have also been important changes in the international political environment. The policy of opening the economy to the outside world has made China more dependent on external economic conditions and more vulnerable to the economic policies of major trading partners.[8] Political vulnerability has been intensified by the demise of state socialism in Eastern Europe and the Soviet Union which left China isolated as virtually the last major remaining bastion of Marxist-Leninist socialism, marooned in a global system in which the balance of power had shifted decisively in favour of the anti-communist camp.

In sum, there have been certain shifts in the basic macro-political balances of power in Chinese society: between centre and localities; between economically more advanced and backward regions; between a weakening party and a still strong administrative apparatus; between the party/state and the economy/society; and between the Chinese state and its international politico-economic environment. It is within the context of these shifting macro-political balances that China's political future should be viewed.

These changes have made the process of economic reforms more difficult to direct and control. They have also intensified the phenomenon of 'shadow pluralism' in the Chinese political process, as the success of official policies depends increasingly on the consent and cooperation of institutions and groups which have their own resources and are less and less dependent on the party-state. Yet the party leadership has so far granted these new social forces little in the way of formal recognition or institutionalized access to the policy process or political system. The overall result is a growing contradiction between the pre-existing political institutions and rules of the game on the one hand, and the pressures of emergent societal pluralism on the other. This situation is not sustainable in the medium or longer term. The events of 1989 showed that the problem could not be solved (except temporarily and superficially) by seeking to suppress these new pressures; in fact, it has made things worse by increasing tensions between state and society and driving alternative solutions underground. There is demonstrable need to seek some form of reconstitution of the polity which will redefine the rules of the political game, reshape the key political institutions and create a new relationship between them and the new political forces arising from a more complex and open society and a more autonomous and free-wheeling economy.

DIMENSIONS OF POLITICAL REFORM

Clearly the pressures for political change are ineluctable, but in which direction and with what institutional consequences? The aims of political reform would be twofold: first, to pave the way for continued economic reforms and set the regulative context for a market-based economy and, second, to reconstitute the Chinese polity on a new normative and institutional basis. What would be the essential components of such a reform? First, a new Communist Party leadership would be needed to break through existing ideological and institutional constraints and it would need to look forward rather than backward politically. Reading between the political lines in Beijing, there is evidence that there is a group of younger leaders waiting in the wings and prepared to accelerate the pace of both economic and political reform. In the sphere of institutions, several changes would seem to be necessary. The role of the Communist Party would need to be reappraised, particularly its currently pervasive and authoritarian relationship with all other political, social and economic institutions. The relationship between central and local governments would need to be renegotiated and put on a more formal basis which defines their specific roles in a new political division of labour and recognizes the realities of local power. In the long run, this renegotiation might lead to some form of constitutional federalism, as several participants in the Chinese debate are arguing. The administrative institutions of the state are also in need of thorough reform: partly by abolishing departments or cutting personnel in the old organs of economic planning; partly through the creation or adaptation of governmental organizations to meet the regulative requirements of a market economy; and partly through an internal administrative reform intended to depoliticize and clean up the bureaucracy and put it on a more professional footing. At the level of social groups, there is a strong case for accommodating their increasing social and political assertiveness by expanding civil liberties, recognizing the legitimate role of emerging organizations in civil society and creating more institutionalized channels of access to the political and policy processes.

This reconstitution of the Chinese state is a dual process, since it involves a recasting of both its political and developmental character and capacity. For the reasons advanced earlier, in the short and medium term there are strong arguments to suggest that a strong and coherent politico-administrative system is required to manage the process of market transition and tackle the still formidable problems posed by poverty, regional inequality and social disruption. These two aspects of the process of reconstitution are mutually dependent; a new form of political system depends on a new form of developmental state and vice versa. Effective handling of the transition to a market economy and of fundamental developmental tasks requires a renewal of the political authority of the regime and a strengthening of its capacity to govern; conversely, progress in political reform rests on an ability to deal with the potential disruptions of market transition and the drags and distortions imposed by socioeconomic backwardness.

All participants in the current Chinese debate on political reform agree that it should lead in the direction of some form of democracy. If this is to be the case, how can the transition to democracy be managed in a way that takes account of the dual nature of a process which attempts simultaneously to achieve both political and developmental progress, systemic change and socio-political stability? Before discussing the possible form such a transition could take, we need to examine the various factors in Chinese society which might stand in its way.

THE FEASIBILITY OF DEMOCRATIZATION IN CHINA

Thinking about the prospects for democratization in China needs to be grounded in an analysis of the factors which are commonly identified as obstacles to democratization there. We can group these factors into four categories: historical, cultural, material and social. The first two, the historical and the cultural, are well known and frequently rehearsed (Huntington, 1991: 301–2), so I shall only refer to them briefly here.

First, there is an historical argument that, unlike some of the former communist countries in Eastern Europe, China has no previous experience of a functioning democracy and that this makes the prospect of any substantive as opposed to formal democratization unlikely in current circumstances. This argument has some validity, as we can see from the cases of Hungary and Czechoslovakia, where the transition to stable multi-party democracy has been facilitated by the ability of post-socialist politicians to draw on the democratic traditions and organizations of the pre-war era. However, the argument has a static quality to it; because x has not been the case in the past, x cannot be the case now. Chinese society has changed in certain important ways since 1949 as a result of successful industrialization and the urbanization and rising levels of education which have accompanied it. As we saw earlier, moreover, the social and economic pluralism resulting from the post-Mao economic reforms have created mounting pressures for political change. These societal trends, which include the emergence of an embryonic urban 'middle class' which many political analysts in China and elsewhere identify as a crucial underpinning for democracy, can support an argument that the social preconditions now exist for a move towards some form of democracy.

A similar evaluation could be made of cultural arguments, particular to the effect that Chinese political culture is not conducive to democracy because it has a deeply rooted tradition of authoritarianism and conditioned popular obedience to authority. While one can question the empirical accuracy of the argument (for example, it is hard to see the popular upsurge of the Cultural Revolution as an expression of conditioned political obedience, the Mao cult notwithstanding), it too can be criticized as overly static. As the floodgates to ideas from abroad have been opened during the reform era, sociopolitical attitudes and aspirations have changed considerably, particularly in the cities and coastal provinces. These changes have not only increased public pressure for democratization, but also provide grounds to argue for its potential feasibility.

There are economic arguments against democratization which would seem to have considerable force and relate to our earlier discussion of the relationship between development and democratization. It can be argued that a democracy worth the name, involving not merely a set of procedures but also widespread popular participation and a high degree of representation of divergent social interests, is difficult in a society in which the vast majority of the population are engaged in a relentless struggle for material existence and lack the time, energy, knowledge and skills to be involved as active political participants (in the national arena at least). Kitching (1983: 49–50) puts the case strongly when he argues that 'it is impossible to construct meaningfully democratic societies . . . in materially poor societies', because of the need for people in poor societies 'to bend both physical and intellectual efforts either to mere survival or to the attainment of a minimal degree of security and upward mobility in a sea of poverty'. In a poor country, he argues, 'the bulk of the population . . . play a marginal or largely passive role in the politics' (1983: 48–9).

If we apply this kind of argument to China, a rapid move to procedural multi-party democracy might have two consequences. On one side, the political process would be dominated by a relatively small number of powerful elites, including elements of the previous ruling stratum, educated and/or organized urban groups, new influentials (notably private business people) and foreigners. On the other side, the bulk of the population, including urban marginals and the vast rural population, would probably be disenfranchised, in reality if not in form. However, this is an argument against a sudden flip-flop to liberal-democratic forms, not an argument against the need to initiate some process of democratization which may take on a more and more substantive democratic character (in terms of public participation and representation of interests) as it proceeds.

Finally, what are the social factors which can constrain or facilitate the transition to democracy? We can discuss this under two headings: consensus (or the lack of it) and the presence (or lack) of a civil society to underpin democratic institutions. As we saw earlier, Chinese society has become more diverse and conflictual during the reform era and has shown increasing signs of becoming ungovernable, even by an apparatus as pervasive as the Communist Party/state. Governmental power has become more dispersed – to bureaucratic institutions and local governments – and the centre's writ has declined. Inter-regional disparities have widened, a new form of market-based class differentiation has begun to emerge, inter-regional and rural–urban migration has led to a vast and potentially disruptive 'floating population' in the cities and there is antagonism between previous political/administrative elites and new social forces emerging in the economic reforms. While these fissiparous tendencies have in no way been comparable to those which emerged in the Soviet Union or Yugoslavia, where national antagonisms have shattered the body politic, they are powerful enough to impose severe strains in the transition to a new set of political arrangements, particularly a multi-party system, which serves to express rather than control social conflicts.

There is a deeper level of concern here, which goes beyond the issue of new political procedures and institutions. The Leninist system which still survives in China has been the main basis of social as well as political integration in Chinese society. If it were to collapse overnight, the task of reconstituting political procedures might (at a superficial level at least) be relatively easy: for example, a new constitution could be drawn up, electoral laws drafted and political parties could be encouraged to emerge as they have in Eastern Europe in large quantities. But what type of institution would be capable of reintegrating society and preventing a potentially destabilizing and costly social anomie? If one looks to 'civil society' to fill the vacuum, though there is evidence of the emergence of new types of social organization (such as associations of enterprises in specific industrial sectors, or of business people and professionals), this process is as yet relatively embryonic and subject to state control (White, 1993a). Moreover, *pace* the current enthusiasm for 'civil society' among Western analysts, we need to be more clear about its composition in post-socialist contexts. For example, as the recent experience of Eastern Europe suggests, a breakdown of the institutions of the state-socialist order sparks a revival of pre-revolutionary social attitudes and organizations, some of which are inimical to democracy and social progress. To make matters worse, some of the most powerful organizations of civil society which had emerged within the bosom of state socialism were illegal or semi-legal. There is a formidable economic 'mafia' in Russia and other former Soviet republics, for example, and in the Chinese case there are powerful underground organizations (such as the secret societies currently based in Hong Kong, but increasingly extending their operations to southern China) which would take noxious advantage of any breakdown of political or social order. In sum, therefore, there seem to be powerful social factors which prompt caution in recommending a sudden dissolution of the current political system.

CHINESE DEMOCRATIZATION: THE TWO-STAGE TRANSITION

If there is a demonstrable need to reconstitute the political order, what form can this take? Does the Eastern European and Soviet scenario of political paralysis and collapse await China? Is it the case that state socialist systems are unable to reform themselves politically and that their only feasible future is a rapid, potentially chaotic and violent transition towards some form of multi-party polity? What, if any, are the political alternatives to this 'collapse scenario'? Is there a form of political transition that can achieve the ultimate aims of political and economic transformation while avoiding the human costs arising from political instability and social anomie?

Any answer to these questions needs to begin by looking more closely at the ideas of 'authoritarianism' and 'democracy'. The Chinese regime, like other Leninist polities, is a particularly dense and pervasive form of authoritarianism in that it aims at, and to a considerable extent achieves, a 'totalistic' control over state, society and economy.[9] In this respect it is unlike those forms of authoritarianism common in the developing world where the intended and achieved scope of political, social and economic control is more limited. For example, the authoritarianism of the 'four little tigers' has varied widely. The Taiwanese regime has been closest to the Chinese, being led by a hegemonic party with Leninist antecedents and with a high degree of ideological, political and social control, at least until the mid-1980s. But even here, the economy was 'free' in the sense that private entrepreneurs and managers were able to pursue profit relatively unencumbered by an interventionist state (though the same freedom did not extend to workers, who were prevented from organizing their own unions and using strikes or protests to advance their own interests). Compared to the Chinese mainland, moreover, there was more intellectual and cultural freedom, even though both these spheres were subject to political manipulation and control. There was also greater space for 'civil society', the formation of relatively autonomous social organizations, and for competitive politics, albeit in non-party form and largely at the local level (Tien, 1989; Winckler, 1984). Though there is little doubt that the Taiwan regime was, until the mid-1980s at least, coercive and oppressive, not without its own 'totalistic' aspects, there is a qualitative difference when compared with the Chinese mainland. This difference allows us to follow convention by classifying such regimes into two basic ideal-types, the authoritarian and the totalistic, distinguished by the extent of their intended and achieved scope of control, mobilization and ideological, social, economic and political engineering.

This familiar distinction allows us to pose the question of China's short-term future political evolution in a different way – not in terms of a hypothetical move from Marxist-Leninist socialism to liberal democracy, but as a dual transition: first, from a totalistic to an authoritarian form of state socialism and, second, from the latter to a liberal-democratic polity presiding over a largely private-enterprise economy. In the first stage, the Chinese Communist Party would retain a dominant (though diminished) position, rather like its counterpart in Taiwan, the Kuomintang, until the late 1980s, or the Lee Kuan Yew regime in Singapore. This is not such an unthinkable prospect. A large number of China's reformers, particularly within the country, are willing to admit, even after Tiananmen, that it may be advisable for the Communist Party to retain its hegemonic role in the near and middle future, since there is no credible political alternative at this stage and there is a real prospect of anarchy, even civil war, should the party be toppled in East European fashion. The rapid implosion of the Soviet Union is a sobering lesson here, and the Chinese themselves do not have to look very far backward into their own recent national history to fear the break-up of the nation into inter-regional strife and warlordism. In developmental terms, moreover, the transition to authoritarianism would be compatible with, and could well facilitate the introduction of, a full-fledged market economy. It could also preserve the capacity of the regime to define and implement strategic programmes to tackle key developmental problems.

A first stage of 'transition to authoritarianism' is all the more significant as a real political option because that is the direction in which the Chinese reforms were evolving before Tiananmen. In practical terms, steps were being taken to limit the power of the party by separating it from the state administration (by abolishing leading party groups in government bodies and reducing the incidence of 'interlocking directorates', whereby the same person held both party and government posts). The power of party secretaries and committees was being reduced in relation to professional managers in state enterprises; official 'mass organizations' were gaining more autonomy and other political institutions (notably the National People's Congress) were acquiring additional powers to act as a partial check on the party. This reform thrust was given impetus by the Thirteenth Party Congress in 1987, when the then party General Secretary, Zhao Ziyang, spelled out these and other measures in his official report (1987). Moreover, state power had also been undermined by the economic reforms – by the impact of the Open Policy, the increasing operational autonomy of state enterprises and the rapid emergence of a dynamic non-state sector through small-scale industrialization. This process may have been interrupted temporarily by Tiananmen, but it has long since regained its momentum, accelerating from the beginning of 1992 onwards.

This gradual process of political liberalization was accompanied by the emergence of the political theory of 'new authoritarianism' (*xin quanweizhuyi*), which received some support from senior party reformers, most importantly Zhao Ziyang, though it was never given any official recognition (Du Ruji, 1989; Rong Jian, 1989; Wang Hao, 1989). The theory draws on the experience of the 'four little tigers' of East Asia and on the work of US political scientists, notably Samuel Huntington (1968). Theorists of 'new authoritarianism' argue that China's political arrangements must reflect its current cultural and economic constraints as an underdeveloped country. In such a context, a rapid transition to some form of full-fledged democracy is neither politically feasible nor economically advisable. Full democracy is an ultimately desirable state which must await the establishment of social, economic and political pre-conditions, notably the separation of political and economic life, the spread of markets, the formation of a diversity of socioeconomic groups and interests in civil society and a concomitant growth in political awareness and skills. According to its advocates, the role of the 'new authoritarian' regime which is to emerge from the matrix of Marxist-Leninist state socialism is to guide this transition, establishing the social and economic basis for a longer-term, second transition towards democracy, in particular by introducing a market economy which changes the balance of power between state and society, expands the space available for the organised expression of socioeconomic interests, and gradually increases pressures for democratic participation, representation and competition.

THE TRANSITION TO THE 'NEW AUTHORITARIANISM'

Any possibility for developing 'new authoritarianism' as a theoretical matrix for political reform was dashed by the Beijing Massacre of 4 June 1989. Though its approach to the issue of democratization is similar to that taken in this chapter, as a practicable proposition it raises certain problems. First, there are serious obstacles to be faced in moving from a 'totalistic' to a 'new authoritarian' polity, notably the institutions and vested interests of the *ancien régime*. Second, there is the question of who is to hold power in such a system. On the one hand, it is likely that previous political and bureaucratic elites would retain the whip-hand (indeed, 'new authoritarianism' provides a convenient theoretical cloak for their continuing dominance). On the other hand, they would probably be sharing their power with certain elements of the politically active intelligentsia, many of whom retain the elitist attitudes of their imperial predecessors. Thus in social terms, the 'new authoritarian' system would be highly elitist, matching its elitist project of political tutelage, and there is no inherent impetus to incorporate important mass constituencies such as industrial labour and the peasantry. Third, while the political rationale for 'new authoritarianism' was based on an attempt at hard-headed Huntingtonian realism about the need for political order and stability to tackle the difficulties of development, it would have to be 'translated' into something which was ideologically more palatable to politically assertive and influential constituencies both within and outside China. Fourth, once authoritarian systems are established, they tend to calcify and prove hard to remove. Without some form of enforceable constitutional and institutional guarantees from the outset, underwritten by a political compact of forces able to maintain pressure on the political elite to give them substance, the result might be yet another form of despotism.

How could a first-stage 'transition to authoritarianism' be crafted to avoid the pitfalls of 'new authoritarianism' and how can this be linked to the second stage of transition to democracy?

Let us begin by considering the prerequisites for the first stage of political liberalization. The first of these is a change in the leadership of the party and state. The nature of the party leadership is crucial in assessing the feasibility of political reform since it still forms the central nucleus of political power in China. The balance between different political elements in the leadership has been shifting gradually during the 1980s and early 1990s. Every day that passes brings an imperceptible weakening of the conservative old guard and a strengthening of younger, more reform-minded political generations. As for potential opposition from the stratum of party/government officials embedded in the institutions of the *ancien régime*, many have already benefited financially from the opportunities offered by a spreading market economy, and this increasingly gives them a vested interest in continuing the economic reforms and reduces their vulnerability to political reforms. The armed forces could play a pivotal role, but current (albeit fragmentary) evidence tends to suggest that the People's Liberation Army is not wedded to the political *status quo* and may not have a political project of its own, being prepared to accept the status of a professional army outside or above politics (Cheung, 1990).[10]

A second prerequisite of political change is an accommodation between reformers within the party and representatives of other influential political forces, notably activists in the Democratic Movement, regional and institutional interests within the state machine and representatives of important social groups such as business and labour. This accommodation would not be easy to achieve given conflicts of interest and perspective between groups and it would require skilful and authoritative leaders able to command support across these political divides. It is at cardinal moments of political transition such as this that the quality of political leadership becomes crucial.

The purpose of the 'grand accommodation' would be to work out a programme of political reform and establish a coherent alliance of disparate forces to provide the political basis to carry this out. The basic function of this political pact would be to design and engineer the dual transition: to complete the short-/medium-term transition from totalism which is already well under way in the direction of some form of circumscribed authoritarianism, and a longer-term transition to a political democracy worthy of the name. I use the term 'circumscribed authoritarianism' because the diverse character of the alliance of political forces underlying the pact would lead towards a degree of dispersion of political power and moves towards democratization in the *short*, not merely the long term. The breadth of the initial coalition would condition the force of this impetus towards democratization.

Steps towards democratization could take place in at least three spheres: the constitutional, institutional and social. *Constitutional* changes would require legal changes to guarantee basic civil and economic rights, to define the legal and institutional mechanisms necessary to establish and enforce them and to set the rules of the game for a new system of political institutions. *Institutional* changes would involve a redefinition of the position of the dominant party (even though in the short and medium term the party might remain hegemonic); and encouragement of more institutional pluralism by ceding power to other political organizations, such as the People's Representative Congresses, the non-communist 'democratic parties', the Chinese People's Political Consultative Conference or local communities in both cities and countryside. These institutions already exist, having been set up in an earlier era of 'New Democratic' accommodation in the 1940s as the CCP came to power. Their lifeless bodies could have fresh political air breathed into them. *Social* democratization would involve an expansion of social space to allow for the organization of group interests in 'civil society', greater freedom of ideological and cultural expression and the establishment of more autonomous mass media. The political bases of the regime could be widened by 'corporatist' means involving institutionalized consultation with, and representation of, key social groups such as industrial labour, business sectors and agriculture, some of which is already under way (Unger and Chan, forthcoming).

Ideally, such a 'grand accommodation' would attempt to set a timetable and define a process whereby these initial moves towards democratization, which might still guarantee the party's hegemonic position, albeit in attenuated form, would be followed by successive further moves leading towards some ultimate end-state of 'mature' democracy, such as a fully functioning multi-party system in which the Communist Party would no longer play a guaranteed hegemonic role. Participants in the 'grand accommodation' would certainly wish to define the concrete policies necessary to achieve the first stage of reform: the separation of the party from the state administration, the removal or weakening of party organizations within enterprises, the radical reduction of direct state controls over economic activity, measures to bring about the internal restructuring of the party itself, reform of existing 'mass organizations', and greater space for social organizations in 'civil society'. These specifically political measures would be reinforced by the continuation of politically significant changes in the economy, notably changes in the ownership system which, through privatization or some alternative reform, would continue to undermine the economic dominance of the state.

In the short and medium term, the resulting political system would be hybrid, comparable to counterparts in countries such as Singapore or Taiwan where elements of single-party dominance have co-existed with elements of institutionalized competitive democratic politics. To the extent that political reform is accompanied by continued transformation of the economic system, the balance of power between state and society would continue to shift in a direction favourable to pluralist politics and this would strengthen the impetus for further change in the political system. This impetus could be further strengthened by the post-Cold War era of international politics in which it is more difficult than before for authoritarian regimes of any political colour to withstand external pressures for political reform. It is these trends in the real world of power – both domestic and international – which give one some confidence that a sustained transition of this nature is feasible as well as desirable.

CONCLUSIONS

A political accommodation of this kind could prove capable of breaking the deadlock in Chinese reform, the depressing cycle of elite conflict and policy oscillation which we witnessed during the 1980s. While there is still a possibility of an Eastern European-style collapse, there are substantial political differences between the Chinese and Eastern European political situations. While most of the East European parties were foreign transplants, representing the hegemonic interests of a hated imperial neighbour, the Chinese Communist

Party has its own independent history and is much more deeply rooted in society, particularly in the countryside where the vast majority of the population still lives. China also lacks a tradition of a strong civil society and any experience of democratic governance, both of which have facilitated the displacement of the ruling parties of Eastern Europe. In spite of the fissiparous forces present in Chinese society, these cannot compare in intensity with the nationalist hostilities which have torn apart the Soviet Union and Yugoslavia. Moreover, the economic impact of the reforms in China has been impressive, unlike Eastern Europe and the Soviet Union where they came too little or too late.

The two-stage process of political transition would face powerful constraints, but there are some reasons for optimism. Ideological obstacles may prove less damaging than might be expected, since the traditional ideology of Marxist-Leninist socialism has lost most of its appeal and could be supplanted by the kind of 'developmental nationalism' which has played an important role in other East Asian success stories. Social tensions and conflict are a natural concomitant of the transition process, such as clashes between urban and rural interests and between a rising bourgeoisie and a strongly entrenched urban working class. Successful management of these conflicts would require a prudent and flexible leadership with a credible ideology and sufficiently firm base of support, both inside and outside the party. Indeed, the key constraints are political: the availability of skilled and progressive leaders, the coherence of any political alliance forged between reformist elements inside and outside the party and their ability to neutralize opposition from the older generation of party leaders and or discontented regional elites. However, even if the 'political pact of transition' is able to overcome these obstacles, it will need to live by its results. If it cannot deliver what it promises in terms of political stability and economic improvement, it faces a fate similar to its predecessor and the prospect of a radical, possibly violent, political rupture would become more likely.

It is clear that the Marxist-Leninist-Maoist version of socialist politics has become increasingly irrelevant and unacceptable in China. As in the Soviet Union and Eastern Europe, moreover, no credible alternative vision of 'socialist democracy' has arisen to take its place. In politics as in economics, liberalism will most likely be the guiding force for change, though this will probably incorporate elements of the previous system (not only Chinese state socialism but also its 'traditional' imperial precursor). The most likely scenario for the longer-term future is along East Asian lines (comparable to Japan and South Korea), combining a competitive political system that may still be dominated by a hegemonic political institution with a capitalist economy involving a high degree of state involvement.

While such a combination promises to be economically dynamic, it also carries the potential for the kinds of socioeconomic exploitation and inequalities characteristic of such societies. While some elements of Chinese state socialism – such as basic welfare services, job security and relatively egalitarian income distribution – might have reflected the actions of a paternalistic party-state and posed problems from the point of view of economic efficiency, they are also valued attributes of a human society. Indeed, it is the hope of some contemporary political theorists in China that there are elements of the old which can be made complementary with the new in the form of some kind of social democracy which could combine social welfare with economic dynamism. The likelihood of such an outcome depends on the specific constellation of political forces organizing the political transition.

ACKNOWLEDGEMENTS

The author would like to thank Anita Chan, Jude Howell, Hua Sheng, David Kelly, Barrett McCormick, Peter Nolan, Tony Saich, Shang Xiaoyuan, Jon Unger and Yang Mu for their productively critical comments on this paper.

NOTES

1 The problem of scale is important. While I would not argue that events in China are likely to parallel those in Bosnia, even potentially milder repercussions of systemic collapse in China would be magnified by the vastness of its population (the population of Bosnia is only about four million).
2 For a clear presentation of views, see the interview with Lee reported by Branegan (1991).
3 The internal Chinese debate about political reform and democratization actually contains a variety of positions, some of which as we shall see in our discussion of 'neo-authoritarianism', are closer to the position advanced in this paper. For a review of different Chinese approaches to democracy, see He Baogang (1993: part 1).
4 Huntington (1991: 7) gives a 'procedural definition' of democracy as follows: a nation's political system is democratic 'to the extent that its most powerful collective decision makers are selected through fair, honest, and periodic elections in which candidates freely compete for votes and in which virtually all the adult population is eligible to vote'.
5 The notion of 'autonomy' is a slippery one but it refers to the ability of a political/governmental leadership to define and implement a coherent strategy of national development, either in the absence of a positive 'development coalition' of specific socioeconomic interests capable of organizing the developmental transition, or without being prey to powerful vested interests which may seek to impede or distort the process of national development. For discussions of the notion of the 'autonomous' developmental state, see the Introduction by myself and Robert Wade in White (1988), White (1984) and Evans et al. (1985).

6 This positive judgement is shared across a wide political spectrum, however galling the vision of an economically successful socialist state. For a useful review of socioeconomic progress during the reform era, see Nolan (1990), and for an overview of the political dynamics involved, see White (1993b).

7 For an effective presentation of the case, see McCormick (1994).

8 For a valuable analysis of the political dynamics and impact of the 'Open Policy', see Howell (1993).

9 For an analysis of this system, see Tang Tsou (1986: ch. 5). Tang Tsou uses the term 'totalitarianism' in his analysis.

10 The evidence is too weak to make a firm judgement on the potential political role of the PLA. Even if it lacks a political project, it may be compelled to step in if social and political chaos occurs. The key issue then is whether it would act as a midwife for democratic change or stay in office in ways redolent of the military in African polities such as Nigeria.

REFERENCES

Blecher, M. 1991: Developmental State, Entrepreneurial State: the Political Economy of Socialist Reform in Xinji Municipality and Guanghan County. In White (ed.) 1991b, 265–94.

Branegan, J. 1991: Interview with Lee Kuan Yew, in *Time*, 4 November, 44–5.

Cheung, Tai Ming 1990: The PLA and its Role between April-June 1989. Mimeo, paper presented at the Third Annual Workshop on PLA Affairs, National Sun Yat Sen University, Kaohsiung, Taiwan.

Du Ruji 1989: Reflections on New Authoritarianism. *Zhengzhixue Yanjiu* (Political Studies Research), Beijing, 3:1989, 21–5.

Evans, P. B., Rueschemeyer, D. and Skocpol, T. 1985: *Bringing the State Back In*. Cambridge: Cambridge University Press.

He Baogang 1993: Three Models of Democracy: Intellectual and Moral Foundations of Liberal Democracy and Preconditions for its Establishment in Contemporary China. Unpublished D.Phil. thesis, Canberra: Australian National University (July).

Howell, J. 1993: *China Opens Its Doors: The Politics of Economic Transition*. Boulder, Colo.: Lynne Rienner.

Huntington, S. P. 1968: *Political Order in Changing Societies*. New Haven, Conn.: Yale University Press.

Huntington, S. P. 1991: *The Third Wave: Democratization in the Late Twentieth Century*. Norman: University of Oklahoma Press.

Kent, A. 1993: *Between Freedom and Subsistence: China and Human Rights*. Hong Kong: Oxford University Press.

Kitching, G. 1983: *Rethinking Socialism: A Theory for a Better Practice*. London: Methuen.

Liu Jun and Li Lin (eds) 1989: *Xin Quanweizhuyi: Dui Gaige Lilun Ganglingde Lunzheng* (Neo-Authoritarianism: A Debate on the Theoretical Reform Programme). Beijing: Beijing Economics Institute Publishing House.

McCormick, B. 1994: Democracy or Dictatorship: a Response to Gordon White. *The Australian Journal of Chinese Affairs*, 31 (January).

Nolan, P. 1990: Introduction. In P. Nolan and Dong Fureng (eds) *The Chinese Economy and its Future: Achievements and Problems of the Post-Mao Reforms*. Cambridge: Polity Press, 1–37.

Petracca, M. P. and Mong Xiong 1990: The Concept of Chinese Neo-Authoritarianism: an Exploration and Democratic Critique. *Asian Survey*, XXX:11 (November), 1099–117.

Rong Jian 1989: Is New Authoritarianism Feasible in China? *Shijie Jingji Daobao* (World Economic Herald), Shanghai, 6 January.

Rueschemeyer, D., Stephens, E. H. and Stephens, J. D. 1992: *Capitalist Development and Democracy*. Cambridge: Polity Press.

Tang Tsou 1986: *The Cultural Revolution and Post-Mao Reforms: A Historical Perspective*. London: University of Chicago Press.

Tien Hung-mao 1989: *The Great Transition: Political and Social Change in the Republic of China*. Stanford University, California: Hoover Institution.

Unger, J. and Chan, A. forthcoming: China, Corporatism, and the East Asian Model. In B. McCormick and J. Unger (eds) *The Future of Chinese Socialism: Eastern Europe or the Four Little Dragons?* Armonk, NY: M. E. Sharpe.

Wade, R. 1991: *Governing the Market: Economic Theory and the Role of Government in East Asian Industrialization*. Princeton, NJ: Princeton University Press.

Wang Hao 1989: A Theory of Transitional Democratic Authoritarianism. *Political Studies Research*, 3, 16–20.

White, G. 1984: Developmental States and Socialist Industrialisation in the Third World. *Journal of Development Studies*, 21(1), 97–120.

White, G. (ed.) 1988: *Developmental States in East Asia*. London: Macmillan.

White, G. 1991a: Basic-level Government and Economic Reform in China. In White (ed.) 1991b, 215–42.

White, G. (ed.) 1991b: *The Chinese State in the Era of Economic Reform*. London: Macmillan.

White, G. 1993a: Prospects for Civil Society in China: a Case Study of Xiaoshan City. *The Australian Journal of Chinese Affairs*, 29 (January), 63–87.

White, G. 1993b: *Riding the Tiger: The Politics of Economic Reform in China*. London: Macmillan.

Winckler, E. A. 1984: Institutionalization and Participation on Taiwan: from Hard to Soft Authoritarianism. *China Quarterly*, 99 (September), 481–99.

Zhao Ziyang 1987: Advance Along the Road of Socialism with Chinese Characteristics (25 October) *Beijing Review*, 30:45 (9–15 November).

11

Democracy without Development in the South Pacific

PETER LARMOUR

INTRODUCTION

In the early 1990s, Western Samoa extended the franchise from heads of household (*matai*) to all adults (Tagaloa, 1992: 131). A pro-democracy movement was formed in the Kingdom of Tonga (Helu, 1992: 145–9). Fiji held its first general election since the 1987 military coups, but on a racially biased constitution. A *Fiji Times* editorial of 3 September 1992 asked if democracy might be a 'foreign flower' unable to take root in South Pacific soil. This chapter answers the question comparatively by looking at conditions for democracy in the 22 island states of the South Pacific. It concludes that small is not necessarily democratic; that democracy is sensitive to where the boundary between 'domestic' and 'external' politics is drawn; and that democracy may flourish at relatively low and relatively high levels of economic development, but is threatened by the process of development itself. However, since only a few states in the South Pacific have prospects of development, existing democracy is, to that extent, safer.

METHOD

Comparison can work in four ways (Tilly, 1984: 82–4). First, it can highlight the features of a particular case, for example understanding democracy in one country by comparing it with its neighbours. Second, it can use the country as an example of a more general phenomenon, such as 'democratization' or 'development'. Third, comparison can analyse democracy, or its absence, as an effect of a more encompassing system, such as the country's dependent position in a colonial or global economic system. Fourth, as in this chapter, a set of countries can provide evidence for the relationship between variables such as 'development' and 'democratization'. The presence of both these variables in one country, and their joint absence in another, suggests they may be causally linked. This variation-seeking form of comparison does not require that the countries be otherwise similar. It may be more convincing to find that democracy and development are co-present, and co-absent in countries otherwise quite different, and in spite of these differences (Przeworski and Tuene, 1970: 34–8).

The argument of the chapter is in two steps. The first is inductive, looking for patterns in democracy, as defined below, and Gross Domestic Product (GDP) per capita, and comparing the conclusions with the results of wider and more sophisticated surveys summarized by Lane and Ersson (1990: 68–73, and their chapter in this volume). The second is deductive, applying a recent theory of the social conditions for democracy that aims to reconcile quantitative cross-national studies with comparative history (Rueschemeyer et al., 1992).

EVIDENCE

Table 11.1 ranks the 22 island members of the South Pacific Commission according to their per capita GDP. Nauru has about the same GDP per capita as Australia's, but is based on dwindling phosphate revenues. Comparisons are difficult because of the large non-monetary sectors in most of the islands, and the importance of aid and remittances for the smaller islands. Urbanization is included as a structural indicator of development and ranges from 100 per cent in Nauru to 13 per cent in the larger Melanesian countries. Resident populations range from Pitcairn's 100 to Papua New Guinea's 4 million, with an average of 120,000.

The economic conditions in which the *Fiji Times*'s 'foreign flower' might grow are determined by the small size of the island economies, which makes them dependent on a narrow range of exports and raises the unit costs of services. Their remoteness imposes high freight charges. Rates of economic growth during the 1980s have been 'uniformly bad' (Thirlwall, 1991: 19). Watters argues that in the smaller economies, characterized by high levels of migration, remittances, foreign aid and public expenditure, the prospect of 'autonomous economic growth' sustaining an acceptable standard of living is simply 'false' (1987: 33). Evidence given to an Australian parliamentary inquiry identified only two of the independent states (Papua New Guinea and Fiji) as 'capable of independent and self-sustaining growth', while Kiribati, Cook Islands, Tuvalu, Nauru and Niue were considered as 'not having prospects of viability' (Australia, 1989: 60).

Only nine, capitalized in table 11.1, are constitutionally independent. Tonga alone was never colonized. There is a large intermediate category of 'associated' states which have renegotiated their colonial relationships with New Zealand or the United States. Association allows Cook Islanders and Niueans to retain New Zealand citizenship. The Compact of Free Association with three of its former colonies allows the United States to retain military access to them, while negotiations continue with a fourth, Palau.

DEMOCRACY

Democracy is a broad and contested idea that may not travel well to, or within, a region as diverse as the South Pacific (Lawson, 1991; Crocombe et al. 1992; Durutalo, 1993). Indigenous political traditions vary between, and within, the three major culture areas: Polynesia, to the east of the region; Melanesia, to the west; and Micronesia to the northwest. Sahlins (1963) famously distinguished Polynesian 'chiefs', who inherited leadership, from Melanesian 'big men', who achieved it, though in practice the sons of big men tended to have a better chance than others of succeeding them, and there are many examples of inherited chieftaincy in Melanesia (Chowning, 1977: 41–6). Micronesia includes chiefly and non-chiefly systems.

The average population of a South Pacific state, excluding Papua New Guinea, is 105,000 – about the same, if non-citizens were included, as the Greek city-states which provide Western political theory with its images of democracy (Held, 1987: 23). Traditional political systems were even smaller, with the largest political unit in Polynesia numbering only 40,000 (Kirch, 1984: 37), and in Melanesia 'several thousand' (Chowning, 1977: 41). While a small population provides opportunities for direct democracy, it does not necessarily lead to it. Small-scale systems in the South Pacific were direct, in the sense of face to face, but not necessarily democratic in the sense of political equality. However, the Melanesian systems described above did provide equality of political opportunity for men. Polynesian systems also varied in their degree of stratification, and at the most egalitarian extreme, chiefs shared decision-making in village meetings with other adult males (Kirch, 1984: 35). There are strong traditions of equality between adult men speaking in village meetings in parts of

Micronesia (Tabokai, 1993: 26–7). However, everywhere, women, foreigners (variously defined) and young people tended to be side-lined, as they were in the Greek city-states. In any case all but the two smallest territories (Tokelau, population 1,600, and Pitcairn, population 100) now have systems of representative government, superimposed upon, and partly supplanting, smaller-scale face-to-face traditional systems.

Political parties are weak throughout the region, while turnout of voters in elections and turnover of representatives are high (Ghai, 1988: 71). As in other communally oriented societies (Parekh, 1992: 169–75), South Pacific democracy is not necessarily liberal or indi-vidualistic. For example, a national survey of voters in Papua New Guinea (PNG) found 39 per cent did not regard casting their vote as an individual matter, deferring instead to community meetings, clan heads, councillors or church leaders (Saffu, 1989: 21). Popular opinion is often found to be in favour of tighter controls on young people, women, migrants or (in Kiribati) 'non-conformist people' (Larmour, 1985: 316).

Here I use three conventional, formal indicators of representative democracy: universal suffrage; a responsible executive; and non-gov-ernment news media. Responsible executives include prime ministers responsible to parliaments, and directly elected presidents and gov-ernors (high commissioners in the French territories, by contrast, are appointed from Paris). Private media, particularly TV, may be as docile as their official counterparts, but newspapers such as PNG's *Times*, Solomon Islands' *Star* and Tonga's *Kele'a* have been such sig-nificant critics of government that the presence of such media seemed a useful indicator of freedom of speech and legitimate opposition. Comparative data on human rights is not available for the smaller countries, though Fiji has come under criticism since the 1987 coups, and PNG for the actions of its security forces in suppressing a rebellion in Bougainville.

Table 11.1 shows that 12 of the 22 countries have all three of these indicators. The exceptions to universal adult suffrage are the very small colonies of Tokelau and Pitcairn, governed by village meetings and intermittent visits by New Zealand or British officials. Neither Tonga's king, nor his cabinet, are responsible to parliament, though reformers are trying to make ministers more accountable. Fiji's parliament was usurped by the army in 1987. A new parlia-ment was elected on racially defined constituencies that gave greater value to the votes of indigenous Fijians than to others.

Table 11.1 shows three exceptions to a broad pattern of universal suffrage (typically achieved in the 1960s) and responsible executives (typically achieved in the 1970s). The exceptions are the French ter-ritories, without completely responsible executives; Fiji, where demo-cracy has been interrupted; and Tonga, where democratization is incomplete. Non-government media tend to be absent in the smaller territories.

THE PATTERN OF DEMOCRACY AND DEVELOPMENT

Per capita GDP and urbanization seem to be more closely related to constitutional status than to any of the three indicators of democracy. The associated states fall between the richer colonies and the poorer independent states. Fiji is the exception: independent, but with per capita GDP more like an associated state, and an interrupted record of democracy.

Patterns of variation involving democracy, rather than constitutional status, are at best faint. The richer French and US territories seem to have achieved universal suffrage slightly earlier than the others (in the 1950s rather than the 1960s), but there seems to be no correlation with responsible government. The presence of nongovernment media seems as much to do with population size, and presumably market potential, as GDP.

Fault may lie in the units of analysis and the region chosen. High per capita GDP and early suffrage in the French territories had as much to do with conditions in France as conditions in the South Pacific, so the proper unit of analysis for comparison with the independent states might have been 'France' itself. Similarly, our historical measures of 'representative democracy' refer mostly to events that took place while the territories were, or still are, colonies. So what is being compared are the colonial policies of Britain, France etc., as much as circumstances in the territories. If that is so, then the significant comparisons are narrowed to independent states (capitalized in table 11.1) or even further to democratic events since independence: Western Samoa's adoption of universal suffrage in 1991, Fiji's coups, and the rise or demise of non-government media (Tonga, never colonized, would have a longer comparable history). However, no stronger patterns seem to emerge from comparing the subset of independent states, and events since independence seem too few to generalize about: it may simply be that it is too soon after independence for any pattern to emerge.

The choice of the 'South Pacific' as a region was based on geographical proximity, common historical experiences and cultural background (particularly in Polynesia) and the availability of standardized data from regional organizations. But the line drawn around it is inevitably arbitrary: Indonesia's Melanesian province of Irian Jaya and New Zealand and Hawaii with their Polynesian populations might well have been included. The countries listed are also members of other non-geographical regions, within which they might be compared: the region of small states (including those in Europe); or island states (including those from other oceans); or third world states.

In a sense table 11.1 is just the top left-hand corner of a table with a finite number of rows (the 160 or so countries in the world) and an infinite number of columns (factors which might determine the presence or absence of democracy) (Rose, 1991: 453). More elaborate analysis would be required to tease out relationships between other subsets of these columns and rows, and whether 'the South Pacific' was an analytically significant region in understanding the relationship between development and democracy.

Meanwhile, the rather muffled conclusions that can be drawn from table 11.1 are consistent with many of the conclusions Lane and Ersson drew from their review of research on the conditions for democracy (1990: 68–73). Consistent with their finding that a strong association between the democracy and per capita GDP held only among OECD countries (ibid.: 69), table 11.1 reveals no relationship between the two in the South Pacific countries. Lane and Ersson found that GDP per capita also correlated strongly with more structural indicators of modernization, such as industrialization and urbanization, and there is a rough correlation between urbanization and per capita GDP in table 11.1. Lane and Ersson concluded that while there were correlations between democracy and cultural factors (such as ethnic heterogeneity) and political factors (such as persistence of institutions), these were 'of such moderate strength' that more research was needed to arrive at a theory of the conditions for democracy, while deviant cases would continue to require explanation. One such theory is applied to the region of cases in table 11.1 in the second part of this chapter.

THE RELATIONSHIP BETWEEN DEMOCRACY AND DEVELOPMENT

Table 11.1 shows the current pattern of representative democracy in the region, but it does not explain how it was achieved. Nor can it predict whether it will persist. The argument of the *Fiji Times* editorial, quoted at the start of this chapter, was that democracy is a 'flower', rooted in particular social and economic conditions, and perhaps unable to flourish without them. Liberals have argued that a minimum level of property ownership, or education, was necessary for effective democracy. Marxists have argued that in societies riven by conflict between capital and labour, democracy must be a sham.

Following Barrington Moore's *Social Origins of Dictatorship and Democracy* (1969), Rueschemeyer et al. (1992) start with labour-repressive systems of agriculture which, they argue, make landlords hostile to democracy. They show that the push for democracy tends to come from the new working classes, which (being small) need allies. Thus they disagree with those who see the middle classes as bearers of democracy: the middle classes may jump either way, based in part on their perception of longer-term threats from the working class. Parties play an important role in moderating perceived threats. Perceived class interests and allegiances are socially constructed, and what happens in one place may provide a model for others. Once a

Table 11.1 GDP, population, urbanization and democracy

	GDP/ capita ($A)	Population	Urbanization (%)	Constitutional status	Universal suffrage achieved	Responsible executive achieved	Non-govt media
NAURU	22,418	9,600	100	independent	1957	1976	NO
French Polynesia	19,745	201,400	59	French territory	1953	(Paris)	YES
New Caledonia	16,350	173,300	80	French territory	1957	(Paris)	YES
Northern Mariana Islands	12,851	49,100	94	US commonwealth	1965	1975	na
Guam	12,374	137,000	91	US territory	1931	1971	YES
American Samoa	6,660	49,000	40	US territory	1957	1976	YES
Cook Islands	4,837	17,400	27	associated (NZ)	1957	1965	YES
Palau	3,564	15,600	68	associated (US)	1965	1981	na
FIJI	2,312	742,000	39	independent	1963–87, 1992	1970–87,* 1992	YES
Federated States of Micronesia	1,717	111,600	26	associated (US)	1965	1986	YES
Niue	1,553	2,200	21	associated (NZ)	1960	1974	NO

Table 11.1 cont.

	GDP/ capita ($A)	Population	Urbanization (%)	Constitutional status	Universal suffrage achieved	Responsible executive achieved	Non-govt media
Marshall Islands	1,514	48,000	66	associated (US)	1965	1986	YES
VANUATU	1,379	151,900	18	independent	1975	1980	YES
PAPUA NEW GUINEA	1,302	3,963,000	13	independent	1964	1975	YES
TONGA	1,297	96,900	26	independent	1960	(king)	YES
TUVALU	1,245	9,100	30	independent	1967	1978	NO
WESTERN SAMOA	936	161,100	21	independent	1991	1962	YES
SOLOMON ISLANDS	734	328,000	13	independent	1967	1978	YES
KIRIBATI	696	73,500	33	independent	1967	1979	YES
Tokelau	478	1,600	na	NZ territory	NO	(Wellington)	NO
Wallis & Fortuna	16	13,900	na	French territory	1961	(Paris)	NO
Pitcairn	na	100	na	British territory	NO	(London)	YES

*Military coups in 1987; semi-military rule till 1992 election
Sources: South Pacific Commission, 1993; Robie, 1990; Bryant, 1993

particular pattern is established, it may be hard to shift, so conditions for the establishment of democracy may be different from those for its maintenance.

Rueschemeyer et al. thus explain the correlation between democracy and development in terms of relative class power. Development tends to open up spaces for democracy and creates new groups which press for its realization or frustration. These democratic opportunities are also determined by the degree of state autonomy from society, and transnational structures of power.

RELATIVE CLASS POWER

In the analysis by Rueschemeyer et al., landlords resist giving up the power they held under 'agrarian feudalism'. They will be more anti-democratic 'the more they rely on state-backed coercion rather than on the working of the market' to control their labour force (1992: 60). They are also under threat from peasants with small or no landholdings 'because they demand land more frequently than workers insist on control of the means of production' (ibid.). There are two usual suspects for 'labour-repressive' landlords in the South Pacific: chiefs and big plantation owners.

Chiefs

Chiefly traditions are often considered hostile to democratization in Fiji, Western Samoa and Tonga. Pre-contact chiefly systems have also persisted in parts of Micronesia, and there is a general revival, or reinvention, of chieftaincy in the region, including parts of Melanesia (White, 1992).

The typical form of pre-contact land tenure in the South Pacific was by kinship group. However, in the more extreme forms of pre-contact Polynesian chieftaincy, particularly in Hawaii, chiefs did dispossess kinship groups and claim the land themselves. Stratification was also taking place in Tonga. Elsewhere in Polynesia, kinship, the need for popular support in competition with other chiefs and the possibility of popular rebellion kept relationships between chiefs and commoners more reciprocal. Tribute was repaid in various ways, and chiefs could not in practice dispossess those who failed to pay (Kirch, 1989: 39).

The Hawaiian monarchy did not survive, but the emerging Tongan monarchy redeployed itself. The king claimed to own all the land, but granted hereditary estates to a group of nobles. Traditional rights of use were codified and later expressed as an entitlement for each adult male of a block of land and a house site. Adult males got the right to vote for representatives to a parliament dominated by the king's nominees and representatives of the nobles. So, paradoxically, the earliest form of adult male suffrage emerges from one of the more stratified traditional systems. Clearly it is part of a (continuing) struggle in which the king must often appeal for popular support against the nobles who might challenge him again. Such a need for popular support is more present in places like Western Samoa and Fiji, where contenders and chiefly titles are both more numerous.

In the terms of the argument of Rueschemeyer et al., these chiefly systems are only partly labour repressive, and have not actually dispossessed the producers from the land. They are thus not fully 'feudal' in the sense, say, implied in the Labour Party's criticism of the chiefly system in Fiji (National Federation Party and Fiji Labour Party Coalition, 1991: 34–5). Chiefs may, of course, be trying to become more feudal. In Fiji, chiefs get state help in ensuring tribute from the use of land in the 22.5 per cent of rents reserved for them by the Native Land Trust Board (NLTB) (Kamikamica, 1987: 231). Though they may claim some of its product, they do not own the land. They cannot dispossess people from it nor alienate the land itself.

However, if chiefs are generally unable to dispossess their kin, kinship groups may be able to act as 'landlords' in relation to outsiders. For example in Fiji, land is registered in the name of kinship groups (*mataqali*) and some of it leased by the NLTB to non-members, some to members of other *mataqali*, but mainly to descendants of Indian settlers. Though not directly 'labour repressive', such landowning groups do have political interests opposed to those of their tenants, who presumably want lower rents, more secure tenure or, ideally, conversion of their leases to freehold.

Big plantation owners

The second possible candidates for anti-democratic landlords are the big plantation owners: Unilever in Solomon Islands, the Colonial Sugar Refining Company in Fiji, the Société Française des Nouvelles Hebrides and so on. Their political power was based not on feudal hangovers but on their centrality in the early colonial political economy, particularly as a source of government revenue. However, like feudal landlords, they had little interest in expanding democracy to include representatives of labour, the landless or smallholders.

In that case, democracy might have been more likely before plantations were established, or in places where there was less alienation of land. Table 11.2 shows the extent of land alienation, by freehold or leasehold, in countries for which figures are available. Land ownership is important because it was fear of its loss that was supposed to drive landlords' hostility to democracy. Table 11.2 also includes dates for responsible executives and universal suffrage, taken from table 11.1.

Table 11.2 suggests a faint relationship between the extent of

Table 11.2 Land alienation and representative democracy

	Private freehold or leasehold (as % area)	Responsible executive (year)	Universal suffrage (year)
Tuvalu	0	1978	1967
Niue	0	1974	1960
Cook Islands	1	1965	1957
Papua New Guinea	1	1975	1964
Solomon Islands	3	1978	1967
Tonga	4	NO	1960
Western Samoa	5	1962	1991
Vanuatu	15	1980	1975
New Caledonia	23	NO	1951
Guam	24	1971	1931
Fiji	35	1970, 1992	1963

Sources: Larmour, 1994 and table 11.1

alienation and the lateness or failure of responsible government. Generally, the countries with less alienated land (at the top of table 11.2) achieved universal suffrage in the 1960s and responsible executives in the 1970s. In four of the five countries with more than 3 per cent alienated land, responsible executives are either absent (Tonga, New Caledonia), relatively late (Vanuatu) or interrupted (Fiji, which also has the most alienated land). However, two of the latter also achieved universal suffrage relatively early: Guam in the 1930s and New Caledonia in the 1950s.

Tonga also had the earliest adult male suffrage with relatively little land alienation or equivalent indigenous plantation agriculture. The causal flow might in fact be the other way: wider suffrage creates the possibility of resisting consolidation, enclosure and alienation of land. At the least, we can say that there seems to be some correlation between agrarian structure and democracy.

Guam might be the exception that proves the rule. Its Spanish plantation history is more like that of Latin America. It won universal suffrage under US control in 1931, but half of the alienated land is now used for military rather than plantation purposes.

The working class

The other side of 'relative class power' is the working class, presumably defined in terms of its reliance on selling its labour to subsist and without the guarantees of subsistence provided by membership of a landholding group. This working class grew in plantations and mines which provide both the circumstances and opportunity to organize for narrowly industrial and wider political goals, such as democracy (which may then be instrumental in promoting 'industrial' goals like minimum wages, or health and safety legislation). Many of its members are migrants, and about half of the labour force of the smaller islands is working in metropolitan countries, particularly New Zealand and the United States (Watters, 1987: 35). Some 44 per cent of Cook Islanders, for example, and 61 per cent of Niueans now live in New Zealand (ibid.: 36). South Pacific trade unions have promoted democratic principles, such as a non-racial common electoral roll in Fiji, and political parties, such as the Solomon Islands General Workers Union and the Nationalists' Party in Solomon Islands (Frazer, 1992: 28–31). Frazer (1990: 191–2) shows how the *Maasina Ruru* movement in Solomon Islands, previously analysed as an early nationalist movement, can be reinterpreted as an early expression of 'industrial consciousness'. He argues that early forms of industrial action necessarily take a wider democratic form.

STATE AUTONOMY

It is not easy to reduce the relationship between state and society to a single dimension of autonomy. On the one hand introduced states seem – in Hyden's phrase – 'suspended in mid air' above the societies they claim to govern (1983: 7). On the other hand, by arbitrarily drawing boundaries around indigenous political systems, they constituted what became national societies, and play a particularly active role in the economy (Larmour, 1992: 108–12). Table 11.1 does provide a simple scale of constitutional autonomy, ranging from colony through associated state to independence. Redeployments of the relationship between state and society are likely to have an impact on prospects for democracy. Taxation is one such relationship: the introduction of income tax in colonial PNG provoked a reaction that led to the democratization of the legislative council (Downs, 1980: 186–95), while the introduction of a value added tax provoked a realignment of politics in post-coup Fiji, briefly aligning the Labour Party with the coup leader who had deposed them.

TRANSNATIONAL STRUCTURES OF POWER

The UN promoted decolonization and supervised elections, for example in PNG, and the US Trust Territory of the Pacific Islands (which became Palau, the Northern Marianas, Marshall Islands and the Federated States of Micronesia). The process of decolonization that began with Western Samoa's independence in 1962 seems to be faltering in the face of French determination to retain its three South Pacific colonies.

Transnational strategic and military factors have also determined the prospects for democracy. The US military presence on Guam limits the scope of action of the local legislature, for example over land use matters. The end of the Cold War has not diminished the United States' desire to retain military access to its former colonies in Micronesia, particularly Palau, nor the non-nuclear strategic interests of Australia and New Zealand in the region. Military factors are not necessarily or entirely anti-democratic. The Second World War had a generally democratic effect. It showed that colonial governments could be defeated by non-Western people. It provided liberating and well-paid experiences of working with the Americans, inspiring the *Maasina Rule* leaders described above. Through the Atlantic Charter and trusteeship provisions it made the colonial governments give post-war priority to development and welfare.

Foreign aid has had a similarly ambiguous effect on democracy. Since the end of the Cold War, the World Bank and aid donors have begun to make aid conditional on democratic reforms (Leftwich, 1993). Australia, New Zealand and the United States did the same in relation to Fiji after the coups. International non-government organizations are taking up environmental and human rights issues in ways that create opportunities for groups within the islands to question, challenge and resist their own governments. Amnesty International, for example, has strongly criticized the PNG government for human rights abuses in the secessionist island of Bougainville (Melbourne *Age*, 20 November 1993).

ETHNICITY, INDIGENOUSNESS AND GENDER

Rueschemeyer et al. found that racial and ethnic divisions become important 'when they are linked to class and/or where racial and ethnic groups are differentially linked to the state apparatus' (1992: 48). At the limit, 'these divisions may constitute social segments that must be treated much like classes themselves' (ibid.). There has been a bitter but inconclusive academic debate whether the 1987 crisis in Fiji was 'really about' class or ethnicity (Robertson and Tamanisau 1988 and Sutherland, 1992 for class; Scarr, 1988 and Ravuvu, 1991 for ethnicity). The formulation by Rueschemeyer et al. reasserts the role of politics in organizing around social divisions and notices the way that the state can organize, and disorganize, potentially collective actors such as class, ethnic or gender groups.

In Fiji, New Caledonia and Guam democracy as majority rule comes into conflict with claims for indigenous rights. A leading civilian supporter of Fiji's 1987 coup denounced democracy as 'that crazy demon' threatening the racial survival of indigenous Fijians, who then amounted to 46 per cent of the population (quoted in Sutherland, 1992: 192). Indigenous people make up a similar proportion of the population in New Caledonia, and election results and referendums tend to oppose independence from France. Another referendum is promised by France for 1998. In Guam, some indigenous people claim that only they, rather than immigrants from the United States and the Philippines, should be able to vote in referendums on self-determination (Cristobal, 1987: 123).

Rueschemeyer et al. argue that, historically, class inclusion has preceded gender inclusion, and has been more violently resisted, perhaps because class relations 'are more intimately linked to state interventions in society' (1992: 48). In nineteenth-century Tonga, while adult men were the first in the region to get the vote, women – particularly non-chiefly women – lost the influence they had held through kinship, particularly as sisters, and as producers of traditionally valued goods, such as fine mats (Gailey, 1987). They did not get the vote until 1960. Elsewhere, women also tended to be the last in a sequence of European men, indigenous chiefs and the indigenous commoners to be enfranchised, but Rueschemeyer et al. found that when women did get the vote, 'their voting participation did not significantly change the political spectrum in any country' (ibid.). This conclusion is confirmed in the most recent extension of the franchise to women in Western Samoa, where the Human Rights Protection Party was returned to power after universal suffrage substantially raised the proportion of women in the electorate (*Samoa Sunday Observer*, 7 April 1991).

CONCLUSIONS

In the South Pacific, the domestic balance of class power seems even – but weakly so. On the anti-democratic side, chiefs lack the power of dispossession, while the power of big plantation owners has been reduced by nationalization and division of plantations into smallholdings. However where indigenous landowners become landlords, as in Fiji, they have interests opposed to those of tenants and will resist the extension of democratic rights to them, or try to prevent tenants using democratic rights to improve their tenure. The pro-democratic side of the balance is weakened, particularly in the smaller states, by the absence overseas of a working class who have nothing to lose from democracy.

State autonomy from society is relatively high in the colonies and associated states, and in the independent states that rely on foreign aid rather than domestic taxation. The transnational circumstances have been pro-democratic since the end of the Cold War.

The theory propounded by Rueschemeyer et al. can therefore

account for the prevalence of democracy in the South Pacific in terms of transnational circumstances, state autonomy and the absence of strong domestic enemies and supporters. It confirms the *Fiji Times's* perception that democracy is a 'foreign flower' without prejudging democracy's chances for growth, which will continue to depend on the transnational climate as well as the domestic soil.

In the longer run, assuming the transnational circumstances and degree of state autonomy remain constant, the prospects for democracy will depend on 'relative class power' within each territory, and in some circumstances racial and ethnic groups may act as if they were classes (Rueschemeyer et al. do not extend class-like status to gender groups). This relative class power will be transformed by economic development, which may strengthen the supporters of democracy, or its opponents, or both.

Fiji's flawed democratic record and unusually high position, for an independent state, in the GDP league table are thus related. Development typically involves labour migration, which changes the domestic balance of political forces, for example by creating an absent working class not voting at home, or an immigrant working class which may be denied the full benefits of citizenship. Migration brings different populations together, so that conflicts arising from development, and conflicts over democracy itself, often come to be framed in ethnic or racial terms. For example, the nativistic reactions against 'Indians' in Fiji are an extreme example of such responses to any people moving from the highlands and outer islands to find work in mines, plantations and towns throughout the region. Fiji may be less an exception than a precursor for other developing states.

For democratic theory, the South Pacific evidence suggests three conclusions. First, while smallness of scale may permit direct democracy it does not ensure it. In the South Pacific direct forms of village-level government coexist with representative forms of democracy, which were introduced towards the end of colonial rule (or, as in Tonga, devised in order to stave off foreign intervention). While direct, these village-level governments are in many cases inegalitarian (among men) and exclusive (of women).

Second, the South Pacific cases reinforce the argument of Rueschemeyer et al. that democracy arises at the intersection between domestic and transnational circumstances. Assessments and explanations of democracy are thus sensitive to the boundary between 'domestic' and 'external' and to the 'unit of accounting' for the presence or absence of democracy. The French territories are democratic if counted as 'part of France', but not on their own. Migrant workers from the smaller territories may strengthen pro-democratic forces where they work in New Zealand and the United States, but their absence leaves the field open to potentially anti-democratic forces at home (a tension which the Cook Islands sought to resolve by creating a special parliamentary seat reserved for overseas voters). The descendants of migrant workers have been at the forefront of democratic politics in

Fiji but one of the consequences of the 1987 coup has been their relative disenfranchisement in a new constitution that gives more value to the votes of indigenous Fijians. Labour migration across existing political boundaries (and the construction, or dissolution, of political boundaries that interrupt flows of labour) thus play an important part in the growth of democratic politics, and reactions against it.

Third, if the transnational circumstances are held constant, then the prospects for democracy seem best at very high levels of domestic development (as in the OECD countries and their colonies and associated states) or very low levels (the independent South Pacific, excluding mineral-rich Nauru). It is the process of development that puts existing systems of government – democratic or undemocratic – at risk, creating opponents as well as supporters of change, but not guaranteeing the outcome. If existing systems are undemocratic, then development may create opportunities for democracy, but cannot guarantee the outcome. In the early 1980s, moves towards democracy were more successful in Western Samoa (relatively poor, see table 11.1) than in Tonga (marginally better off). In both cases the result has depended more on domestic political circumstances than foreign government pressure (though Western Samoans and Tongans abroad have been involved on both sides of the debate).

The results of conflicts over democracy are contingent. If the political system is already democratic, as in all but a handful of South Pacific countries, then further development may simply put democracy at risk. However, few have prospects for development in any case. Their lack should mean that already established democracy is not put at risk. Countries with the greatest potential for development – PNG and Fiji – are, for that reason, most at risk of democratic reversal.

ACKNOWLEDGEMENTS

Research was funded by grants from the Macmillan Brown Centre for Pacific Studies, University of Canterbury, New Zealand, and the Department of Political Science, University of Tasmania.

REFERENCES

Australia, 1989: *Australia's Relations with the South Pacific*. Joint Committee on Foreign Affairs Defence and Trade, Canberra: Australian Government Publishing Services.
Bryant, J. 1993: Development Below? Aspects of Urban Poverty in the Pacific. *Development Bulletin*, 27, 16–20.
Chowning, A. 1977: *An Introduction to the Peoples and Cultures of Melanesia*. 2nd edn, Menlo Park, Cal.: Cummings Publishing Co.
Cristobal, H. 1987: The Organization of People for Indigenous Rights: A

Commitment Towards Self Determination. In L. Souder-Jaffrey and R. Underwood (eds) *Chamorro Self Determination: the Right of a People.* Guam: Chamorro Studies Association and Micronesian Area Research Center, University of Guam, 7–32.

Crocombe, R., Neemia, U. Ravuvu, A. and Vom Busch, W. (eds) 1992: *Culture and Democracy in the South Pacific.* Suva: Institute of Pacific Studies.

Downs, I. 1980: *The Australian Trusteeship: Papua New Guinea 1945–75.* Canberra: Australian Government Publishing Services.

Durutalo, S. 1993: Democracy in the South Pacific Context. *Review*, 13(10), 1–12.

Frazer, I. 1990: Solomon Islands Labour History and Maasina Rule. In C. Moore, J. Leckie and D. Munro (eds) *Labour in the South Pacific.* Townsville: James Cook University of Northern Queensland, 191–204.

Frazer, I. 1992: Trade Unions and the State in Solomon Islands. *New Zealand Journal of Industrial Relations*, 17(1), 23–37.

Gailey, C. 1987: *Kinship to Kingship: Gender Hierarchy and State Formation in the Tongan Islands.* Austin: University of Texas Press.

Ghai, Y. 1988: Systems of Government I. In Y. Ghai (ed.) *Law, Politics and Government in the Pacific Island States.* Suva: Institute of Pacific Studies, 54–75.

Held, D. 1987: *Models of Democracy.* Cambridge: Polity.

Helu, I. 1992: Democracy Bug Bites Tonga. In R. Crocombe et al., (eds) *Culture and Democracy in the South Pacific.* Suva: Institute of Pacific Studies, 139–52.

Hyden, G. 1983: *No Shortcuts to Progress: African Development Management in Perspective.* London: Heinemann.

Kamikamica, J. 1987: Fiji: Making Native Land Productive. In R. Crocombe (ed.) *Land Tenure in the Pacific.* 3rd edn, Suva: University of the South Pacific, 226–39.

Kirch, P. 1984: *The Evolution of the Polynesian Chiefdoms.* Cambridge: Cambridge University Press.

Lane, J.-E. and Ersson, S. 1990: Comparative Politics: from Political Sociology to Comparative Public Policy. In A. Leftwich (ed.) *New Developments in Political Science.* Aldershot: Edward Elgar, 61–81.

Larmour, P. 1985: Kiribati. In P. Larmour and R. Qalo (eds) *Decentralisation in the South Pacific.* Suva: Institute of Pacific Studies and Institute of Social and Administrative Studies, University of the South Pacific, 309–30.

Larmour, P. 1992: States and Societies in the South Pacific. *Pacific Studies*, 15(1), 99–121.

Larmour, P. 1994: A Foreign Flower? The Social Bases of Democracy in the South Pacific. *Pacific Studies*, 17, 45–77.

Lawson, S. 1991: *The Failure of Democratic Politics in Fiji.* Oxford: Clarendon Press.

Leftwich, A. 1993: Governance, Democracy and Development in the Third World. *Third World Quarterly*, 14(3), 605–24.

Moore, B. 1969: *The Social Origins of Dictatorship and Democracy.* Harmondsworth: Penguin.

National Federation Party and the Fiji Labour Party Coalition, 1991: *The Fiji Constitution of 1990. A Fraud on the Nation.* Nadi: Sunshine Press.

Parekh, B. 1992: The Cultural Particularity of Democracy. *Political Studies*, XL, 160–75.

Przeworski, A. and Teune, H. 1970: *The Logic of Comparative Social Inquiry.* New York: Wiley.

Ravuvu, A. 1991: *The Façade of Democracy: Fijian Struggles for Political Control.* Suva: Institute of Pacific Studies.

Robertson, R. and Tamanisau, A. 1988: *Fiji: Shattered Coups.* Leichhardt, NSW: Pluto Press in association with Australian Council for Overseas Aid.

Robie, D. 1990: Pacific Media Ownership – the Voice of Neocolonialism. *New Zealand Journalism Review,* 27–9.

Rose, R. 1991: Comparing Forms of Comparative Analysis. *Political Studies,* 34(3), 446–62.

Rueschemeyer, D., Stephens, E. H. and Stephens, J. D. 1992: *Capitalist Development and Democracy.* Cambridge: Polity.

Sahlins, M. 1963: Poor Man, Rich Man, Big-Man, Chief: Political Types in Melanesia and Polynesia. *Comparative Studies in Society and History,* 5, 285–303.

Saffu, Y. 1989: Survey Evidence on Electoral Behaviour in Papua New Guinea. In M. Oliver (ed.) *Eleksin: The 1987 Election in Papua New Guinea.* Port Moresby: University of Papua New Guinea, 15–36.

Scarr, D. 1988: *Fiji: The Politics of Illusion. The Military Coups in Fiji.* Kensington, NSW: University of New South Wales Press.

South Pacific Commission, 1993: *South Pacific Economies: Statistical Summary.* Noumea, New Caledonia: South Pacific Commission.

Sutherland, W. 1992: *Beyond the Politics of Race: An Alternative History of Fiji to 1992.* Canberra: Department of Political and Social Change, Research School of Pacific Studies, Australian National University.

Tabokai, N. 1993: The *Maneaba* System. In H. Van Trease (ed.) *Atoll Politics: the Republic of Kiribati.* Christchurch and Suva: Macmillan Brown Centre for Pacific Island Studies and Institute of Pacific Studies, University of the South Pacific, 23–9.

Tagaloa, A. 1992: The Samoan Culture and Government. In R. Crocombe et al. (eds) *Culture and Democracy in the South Pacific.* Suva: Institute of Pacific Studies, 117–38.

Thirlwall, A. 1991: The Performance and Prospects of the Pacific Island Economies in the World Economy. Research Report Series No 14. Honolulu: Pacific Islands Development Program, East–West Center.

Tilly, C. 1984: *Big Structures, Large Processes, Huge Comparisons.* New York: Russell Sage Foundation.

Ward, R. G. 1985: Land Use and Land Availability in Fiji. In H. C. Brookfield, F. Ellis and R. G. Ward, *Land, Cane and Coconuts: Papers on the Rural Economy of Fiji.* Canberra: Research School of Pacific Studies, Australian National University, 15–64.

Watters, R. 1987: Mirab Societies and Bureaucratic Elites. In A. Hooper et al. (eds) *Class and Culture in the South Pacific.* Suva and Auckland: Institute of Pacific Studies and Centre for Pacific Studies, 32–55.

White, G. 1992: The Discourse of Chiefs: Notes on a Melanesian Society. *Contemporary Pacific,* 4(1), 73–108.

12

Has Democracy Failed Russia?

PETER RUTLAND

INTRODUCTION

The collapse of the Soviet Union caught almost everybody by surprise, West and East. This unexpected development was taken as a vindication of Western values and proof of the superiority both of market economics and a democratic system of government. The United States had 'won' the Cold War, and it was assumed that there was no need to debate what was meant by such terms as 'market economics' or 'democracy'. The problem was immediately conceived, almost without reflection, as one of 'transition' – of getting Russia from point A (an authoritarian socialist political system with a state-run command economy) to point B (a democratic polity with a market economy).

There hardly seemed to be the time (or the inclination) to ponder the special problems which the concepts of democracy and market might encounter in the post-socialist landscape. On the contrary, most Western commentators assumed that the processes of building a democracy and a market economy were compatible, mutually complementary and universal in application. This assumption is aptly illustrated by President Clinton's adoption of the economical phrase 'market democracy' to refer to the end-point towards which Russia is assumed to be headed.

This chapter explores three central issues. First, it examines and questions the concept of democracy which is being propagated by the bulk of Russia's Western advisers and well-wishers. The component elements of the liberal consensus on the democratic transition in Russia are critically assessed, and some alternative explanations discussed. Second, the chapter summarizes the unresolved problems of state- and nation-building in Russia, which overshadow the niceties of selecting this or that democratic system. Finally, the linkages between flawed democratization and market reform are explored.

The key point to bear in mind is that Russian politics is still on the downward path of disintegration rather than on the upward march of transition. The unexpectedly abrupt collapse of the Soviet state unleashed turbulent processes of fragmentation which are still coursing through the political, economic and social fabric of Russia. Eltsin and the democratic movement managed to mobilize sufficient political forces to destroy the old system, but in the process they created transitional political institutions which have proved a shaky foundation upon which to build a new democracy. Russia has not yet had the luxury of facing the trade-off between social justice and economic growth, or even between democracy and economic development. Social inequality has been increasing, economic output has plummeted, and the struggle to build a viable democracy is still far from over. Thus the analytical structure of this essay will of necessity differ from the other chapters in this volume.

The democratic opening of 1988–90 created two new political actors: a shallow but broad democratic movement, geared to election campaigns, signature gathering and mass protests, and a ramshackle elected parliament with minimal legislative power, which was temporarily graced with political legitimacy as the symbol of democracy. Ranged in opposition to the democratic movement and the parliament were the serried ranks of the old elite: the military, the bureaucrats, the factory managers, the secret police and the professional party politicians.

The two major characteristics of this transitory political regime have been presidentialism and regionalism. Presidentialism refers to the pivotal role played by Boris Eltsin in mediating the conflict between the old and new political groupings. The term 'presidentialism' is something of a misnomer, since the authority wielded by President Eltsin is, for the most part, neither defined by law nor checked by institutional structures. The power adheres more to his person than to the office he holds. Regionalism surfaced because, with the collapse of the old command economy, there was a shift from functional to territorial representation of political interests. This is probably good for democracy in the long term, but it makes the national leadership's task much more difficult in the short term.

MODELS OF DEMOCRACY AND THE RUSSIAN CASE

Most discussions of the spread of democracy to Russia share similar assumptions about the elements which constitute a democratic political system. There is a robust liberal consensus about the characteristics of democracy, which was simply extended to the Russian case. The model includes the following elements:

1 the holding of free and fair elections;
2 legislative and executive branches with clearly defined powers;
3 a fair and independent judicial system;
4 a free and inquisitive press;
5 the widespread sharing of democratic values in society at large;
6 respect for human rights, at least individual rights, and possibly collective rights (for example, for ethnic minorities);
7 the presence of civil society, that is, a plurality of social organizations (Gastil, 1993).

Few liberal democrats would find fault with this list of features. The characteristics enumerated therein are primarily those of values and institutional procedures. What is absent is any consideration of politics *per se*: of the struggle for resources between different social and political groups. There was no concordance among Western liberals as to who exactly would make up the new ruling elite (should it include former communists?) or where the new political parties would come from. Democracy was seen primarily as a source of political legitimation rather than as a forum for policy resolution. The implicit assumption seems to have been that if these values and institutions were in place, political parties would emerge to compete for the popular vote, and good government would follow as a matter of course.

Imagine, then, the surprise of observers upon finding that Russia's faltering steps down the road toward democracy have been accompanied by economic disintegration, rampant crime, the collapse of public morals, rising death rates, ecological catastrophe, loss of international influence and the continuation in power of fragments of the old communist-era elite. Rather than interpreting these phenomena as challenging the validity of the model of democracy being espoused, the issue is typically seen solely in terms of Russia's unique problems. That is, we are told that Russia has failed democracy, and not that democracy has failed Russia.

If one works down the checklist of characteristics of liberal democracy, one finds that they are all more or less present in the Russian case, albeit in distorted form. (To paraphrase Trotsky, it is democracy reflected in a samovar.) The problem lies not so much in the absence of some of the standard features of democracy, but in the hostile environment within which they have been planted.

Free and fair elections

The first partially free elections in Soviet history were held in March 1989, to the USSR Congress of People's Deputies. The Communist

Party was the only political party allowed to take part, and despite being largely excluded from the mass media, independent candidates were able to defeat Communist Party nominees in about 25 per cent of the seats. A curious two-tier legislature was introduced, with a small Supreme Soviet being chosen from the directly elected congress, which met only three or four times a year. In 1990 new legislatures were elected in each of the 15 Soviet republics, and a loose democratic coalition ascended to power in the Russian Republic Supreme Soviet (Kiernan, 1994). Boris Eltsin became chairman of the Russian parliament, and in June 1991 he was chosen as president in direct popular elections. (Vladimir Zhirinovsky, a virtual unknown, came third, with 6 per cent of the vote.) Gorbachev, appointed president of the USSR by the Soviet Congress, refused to put himself up for popular election. Eltsin came to be seen as the true, legitimate voice of the Russian people.

This experience showed how dangerous it can be for authoritarian regimes to toy with elections – no matter how unfair the electoral process or how pusillanimous the powers of the legislature. Gorbachev's experiment with elections set in train a dynamic of democratic legitimation which undermined the authority of the Communist Party in a few brief years. So far, so good for the liberal democratic model. The trouble was that after the failed coup of August 1991, which led to the unravelling of the Soviet state, Eltsin proved strangely reluctant to pursue the electoral path. In all the Eastern European countries, free elections were held within weeks or months of the cracking of the socialist regime. However, Eltsin decided not to hold elections to the Russian parliament in late 1991 (the Soviet parliament was disbanded). He was too fully engaged with the struggle to dislodge Gorbachev from power and dismantle the centralized Soviet state. Perhaps also he feared the victory of communists, or of centrists and democrats not loyal to him. The parliamentarians themselves, having been elected the previous year, were in no hurry to submit themselves to re-election.

The irony is that if elections had taken place in late 1991 the democrats would probably have won handsomely. After the price liberalization of January 1992, however, the economic decline accelerated – and the democrats could no longer blame all the economic woes on the former communist leaders. In spring 1992, Democratic Russia activists were eagerly collecting the one million signatures needed to call for a referendum demanding fresh elections and a new constitution. Eltsin torpedoed this campaign with a speech in which he casually announced that he would not be calling for early elections. Even Eltsin's closest admirers freely concede that the failure to hold fresh, multi-party elections in late 1991 or early 1992 was a fundamental error.

1992 and 1993 were consumed by political struggles between Eltsin and the Supreme Soviet (of which more below), and it was not until December 1993 that free, multi-party elections were held in Russia. The problem was that in the intervening two years no fully developed party system had emerged.

In general, political parties come from one of two sources (or some combination of the two). They either originate as mass social movements which grow 'upwards' through participation in elections, or they begin as parliamentary factions which grow 'downwards' into society. In the course of the elections of 1989 and 1990 a loose coalition of voters' clubs emerged, which came together as the Democratic Russia movement in October 1990. In 1992–3 there was no opportunity for Democratic Russia and the other fledgling parties to develop through electoral campaigning. Instead their leaders had to engineer crises and confrontations around which to mobilize their followers (Brudny, 1993). The only party which tried to create an 'American-style' network of regional organizations was Nikolai Travkin's Democratic Party, with limited success. The Communist Party, of course, still had a nationwide organization, although factions broke off to the left and right.

The top-down route of party formation was also weak. The Inter-regional Deputies Group which democratic deputies formed in the USSR Supreme Soviet in 1989 never coalesced into a coherent political party. It was riven by personal jealousies and divided over the national question. The parliament was relatively powerless, and all decision-making authority rested in the presidential apparatus. This meant that there was nothing of substance to bargain over in parliament, and thus no incentive to forge lasting political coalitions. There was instead an endless succession of small parties which were created as potential launching pads for politicians seeking entry into government. They were known as 'taxicab parties', because their members could fit into a single car, and they periodically changed passengers. Like the democrats, the Russian nationalists also suffered from a plethora of midget parties, and it was not until the violent demonstrations they organized in February and May 1993 that they showed themselves able to get people into the streets.

Communists and nationalists aside, it was hard to differentiate between the various parties on the policy spectrum. The key distinguishing characteristic of politicians after 1991 was whether they were loyal or hostile to Boris Eltsin ('ours or theirs'). The political map of Russia did not consist of a left–right policy spectrum, but a series of concentric circles of diminishing access, radiating outwards from the Kremlin. Much to the annoyance of the democrats, Eltsin refused to take over the leadership of Democratic Russia, arguing that the president should be 'above politics'. He instead chose to forge a new ruling elite out of old and new politicians by doling out individual jobs and favours.

Thus when fresh elections were finally held, on 12 December 1993, in the wake of Eltsin's crushing of the old parliament, there was a frantic scramble among the democrats to come up with viable parties.

Unable to agree among themselves, the democrats and centrists split between Russia's Choice, led by Egor Gaidar; two smaller parties led by Gaidar's rivals Grigorii Yavlinsky (Yabloko) and Sergei Shakhrai (Russian Unity and Accord); Travkin's Democratic Party; and the industrialists' lobby, Civic Union. Russia's Choice was the party closest to Eltsin, but it never developed a network of regional organizations and was a party in name only.

The parties only had some six weeks to prepare for the elections, and the campaign turned into an American-style media blitz. The three leading democratic parties spent an estimated $85 million on their media campaign, while Zhirinovsky spent $14 million. The US National Democratic Institute issued a handbook on the art of campaigning, with detailed instructions on handling the press and the role of the 'sked'yuler' in managing the candidate's time (USNDI, 1993). The atmosphere in the elections is illustrated by the following story, told by the head of a public relations firm in Moscow. 'One candidate walked into our office and said he wanted to be elected to the Duma. When we asked him which ticket he was planning to run on, he said that it was up to us to decide such questions' (*Financial Times*, 25 November 1993).

It was hard to tell the parties apart on policy grounds: everybody was in favour of stopping inflation, halting the economic decline, protecting the rights of Russians abroad, ending subsidies to the other republics, stopping crime and so forth. The election coincided with a referendum on Eltsin's controversial new constitution (see below) and the dominant factor shaping behaviour of voters seems to have been their attitude towards Eltsin's crushing of the parliament in October. This, together with discontent over the economic crisis and political chaos facing the country, meant that the democrats did much worse than expected. The Communist Party and their rural allies, the Agrarians, did well by mobilizing their traditional constituencies, while the Liberal Democrats topped the party list thanks to the nationalist rhetoric of their charismatic leader, Vladimir Zhirinovsky (Lentini and McGrath, 1994).

Thus when Russia finally had its first free election, it produced a propaganda victory for an eccentric neo-fascist whose campaign pledges included irradiating Lithuania and seizing Alaska. The democrats had little choice but to cooperate with the Communists and Agrarians in order to keep Zhirinovsky well away from power.

The election had come two years too late. By the end of 1993 the voters had lost faith in politicians from all sides of the political spectrum. Even in Moscow, the most democratic of all the cities, there was no sign of any trust in political institutions and leaders. In an October 1992 survey, Muscovites were asked who ran their city. Only 11 per cent named the mayor, and 3 per cent the council, while 32 per cent named 'corrupt bureaucrats', and 43 per cent 'the mafia'.[1]

Table 12.1 Results of the 12 December 1993 election

	Party list votes (%)	seats	Single seats	Total seats
Russia's Choice	15.04	40	56	96
Liberal Democrats	22.9	59	11	70
Communist Party	12.4	32	33	65
Agrarians	7.9	21	26	47
Yabloko	7.8	20	13	33
Russian Unity	6.8	18	9	27
Women of Russia	8.1	21	4	25
Democratic Party	5.5	14	7	21
Civic Union	1.9	–	18	18
Future of Russia	1.6	–	1	1
Independents	–	–	30	30

Source: V. Tolz, Russia's parliamentary elections. *RFE/RL Research Report*, 3, 2, 14 January 1994, 1–14

Separation of powers

Eltsin made two crucial political errors after August 1991. The first was the delay in calling elections, and the second was procrastination in drawing up a new constitution. The two errors were connected. Eltsin was reluctant to see a freshly elected parliament, since this would challenge his right to design the new constitution. However, without elections the political log-jam over the constitution could not be cleared. The delay in drawing up the new constitution caused intense feuding between president and parliament, and exacerbated the rise of assertive regionalism, discussed in a separate section below.

Eltsin's advisers urged him to model the Russian political system around a US-style presidency, with a constitutional court policing the allocation of powers between the presidency and the legislature. There were several problems with this approach, however.

First, Eltsin was in no rush to create a strong legislature which could rival his power. Despite the fact that the Russian Congress of People's Deputies was the vehicle which propelled Eltsin into power, Eltsin felt himself to be an independent political actor after his direct election in June 1991 and his pivotal role in facing down the August coup.

Second, while the idea of a strong executive had plenty of parallels in Russia's past, the other elements of the American model – an independent constitutional court and a powerful legislature – were totally absent from Russia's historical record. Tradition dictated that there would be a built-in tendency for excessive power to gravitate to the presidency.

Third, there are grounds for arguing that the US-style separation of powers is less universally applicable than is often assumed. (It is worth recalling that the Founding Fathers themselves were all too aware of the uniqueness of the model they were devising.) For example, the US system assumes civilian control over the military and a reasonably wide dispersion of economic power in society – neither of which pertain in Russia or in countries like Brazil, which opted for a strengthened presidency in April 1993. Valenzuela notes that presidentialism in Latin America has typically resulted in deadlock with a hostile congress. Of 33 presidents elected in Latin America in the past 10 years, only six enjoyed a friendly majority in parliament throughout their period in office (Valenzuela, 1993: Shugart and Carey, 1992).

Between the coup of August 1991 and the signing of the Minsk agreement which ended the USSR five months later, Eltsin focused his energies on removing Gorbachev from power. His second priority was to halt the country's economic collapse. In October 1991 he persuaded congress to grant him emergency power to rule by decree for one year. He then appointed a team of young technocrats, led by Deputy Prime Minister Egor Gaidar, to implement a programme of radical economic reform. The shock therapy launched in Poland in January 1990 seemed to be succeeding, and both the International Monetary Fund (IMF) and the US government urged Eltsin to follow Poland's example. Price liberalization was launched in January 1992 and was immediately attacked by parliamentary critics.

The stage was set for two years of increasingly tense political confrontation between a truculent congress and an independent president determined to pursue his own political and economic agenda. In the process Eltsin alienated his former political allies: Ruslan Khasbulatov, chairman of the congress, and Aleksandr Rutskoi, Eltsin's running mate as vice-president in 1991.

It is not clear to what extent the rivalry between Eltsin and the congress was really a dispute over policy, or simply a struggle for political power. Eltsin did not seem strongly committed to following through with shock therapy, to the extent of cutting subsidies to ailing industries – but nor did his parliamentary opponents really have any credible alternative to fiscal stringency. The social background of the two groups was also broadly similar. While the Eltsin faction may include more academics and former outsiders, its core consists of former Communist Party officials and industrialists. Gaidar himself, for example, was a former economic editor of *Pravda* from an elite family. Thus, rather than being animated by alternate conceptions of Russia's future, or the interests of different social groups, the political struggles were really just a manifestation of the old Leninist principle of 'who against whom?'.

Bolstered by his emergency powers, Eltsin tried to rule the country directly, with scant regard for the opinions of the congress. However, in April congress was able to force Eltsin to postpone plans to free energy prices, and to release more funds to clear unpaid wages. He suffered a crucial political defeat in June 1992 when he failed to gain control over the Central Bank. The Central Bank continued to obey congress, issuing inflationary credits to Russian enterprises and to her CIS trading partners.

The presidential apparatus grew rapidly to more than 20,000 officials, and took over the former Central Committee building in addition to the Kremlin. The presidential machinery included the office of prime minister, which was only established separately in January 1993. Unfortunately, this hastily assembled bureaucratic leviathan operated in a very inefficient manner. A table of organization was not drawn up for a year, and senior officials found it hard to keep track of all Eltsin's decisions (Petrov, 1993).

Eltsin was in no great hurry to move ahead with a new constitution. (Russia continued to operate under the 1978 constitution, which had been amended more than 300 times.) He made half-hearted efforts to forge a coalition with centrist forces in the second half of 1992 (such as the industrialists' group, Civic Union), but these endeavours fell apart at the seventh congress in December 1992, which forced the resignation of Gaidar. Eltsin appointed as prime minister Viktor Chernomyrdin, a conservative former oil industry official who was acceptable to congress and to Eltsin (but not to his young economic reformers). However, most of the reformist ministers stayed in office.

Eltsin then toyed with the idea of calling a special assembly to approve a new constitution. On 2 March 1993 he proposed a referendum on the issue, and declared that he no longer felt bound by the existing constitution. Congress met in extraordinary session and voted to revoke Eltsin's emergency powers. Eltsin declared 'special rule' in a television address, but subsequently backed down. Both sides agreed to hold a referendum on 25 April. On the first two questions – trust for him personally and for his economic policies – Eltsin won a ringing endorsement from 58 per cent and 53 per cent of voters. The next two questions – calling for elections for president and congress in 1993, instead of 1995–6 as scheduled – failed to win the support of 50 per cent of the electors, which was required to be binding.

Eltsin failed to follow up on his referendum success. On 5 June he presented his draft constitution for discussion at a constitutional assembly, a gathering of 750 of the great and the good, which was only empowered to discuss the constitution, not to adopt it. Khasbulatov and 70 of his followers left on the first day, after his opening speech was booed. The draft constitution adopted by the assembly would have to be approved in a referendum.

Throughout 1993 there was political trench warfare between the congress and the president. Eltsin used television addresses and calls for referendums to appeal directly to the people. He continued to play the anti-communist card which he had used against Gorbachev – accusing the parliamentarians of seeking the restoration of Soviet socialism. He also skilfully lured parliamentary deputies into jobs in his administration. Both sides accused the other of corruption on a lavish scale (most of which was probably true, but none of which was legally proven).

Eltsin decided to lance the boil by disbanding the parliament by decree on 21 September and calling for fresh elections for president and congress (neither of which were within his legal powers). Parliamentary deputies occupied their building, the White House, and refused to budge. Street violence broke out on 3 October, and Eltsin sent in troops to take over the parliament building.

It was politically unwise for Eltsin to put himself in a situation where he had to resort to violence. The television images of tanks shelling the White House would cost him dear in the December election. The use of force against the White House was approved by only 14 per cent of respondents in a November poll, while 44 per cent considered it a 'political mistake' and 37 per cent considered it 'totally unacceptable' (Grushin, 1994). It was also a high-risk venture. It was not clear until the morning of 4 October, 48 hours into the crisis, that Eltsin would be able to find army units willing to storm the parliament. In 1991 Eltsin had to convince the army *not* to storm the White House – and it is always easier to persuade someone to do nothing than to do something.

In the wake of the October events, Eltsin disbanded all the regional councils, suspended the constitutional court and banned eight political parties and their newspapers (although most of these bans were subsequently lifted). Eltsin also dropped his pledge to hold early presidential elections (not due till 1996).

The draft constitution went through several more revisions, which served to weigh it even more heavily in favour of presidential rule. For example, the president nominates the prime minister, and can dismiss parliament after three refusals of his candidate. Parliament has the power to pass a vote of no confidence in the government – but it only comes into effect after a three-month delay, and the president can still choose to dismiss the parliament. The constitution created a bicameral legislature. The upper chamber, the Federation Council, consisted of 178 deputies, two from each of the country's 89 regions. The lower house, or Duma, had 450 popularly elected deputies (half from single constituencies and half from national party lists, with a 5 per cent cut-off).

The constitution was approved in a referendum on 12 December, the same day as elections to congress. Despite initial reports that 51 per cent of the electorate had endorsed the constitution, it was revealed three months later that the actual figure was 46 per cent. Technically, this meant that the constitution was invalid, but in Russia people had long since stopped paying attention to technicalities.

An independent judicial system

The emergence of an independent judiciary has been one of the weak spots in the Russian transition to democracy. On one hand, the old system of political controls over the judicial system collapsed with the banning of the Communist Party after the August coup. However, political leaders at all levels continue either to ignore or manipulate the judicial system as they see fit, and the rule of law remains an elusive goal. Popular respect for the law is at a low ebb: few would turn to it for redress of grievances with any expectation of a just and speedy outcome.

Perhaps most disappointing of all has been Eltsin's unwillingness to acknowledge the importance of judicial autonomy. This has been evidenced by his reliance on rule by decree, his reluctance to recognize the authority of the constitutional court and his centralization of control over the judiciary within the presidential apparatus (usurping the ministry of justice) (Sharlet, 1993).

Liberals hope that marketization will promote the rule of law, by creating a plurality of economic interests with an incentive to have their rights respected. However, thus far Russia's free economy has turned into a free-for-all economy, in which businessmen turn to private enforcement regimes (that is, 'the mafia') to ensure contract compliance.

A free press

Russia's democratization began, of course, with Gorbachev's *glasnost* campaign, and over the past decade it has acquired a combative and broadly independent press staffed by a core of dedicated journalists. A broad spectrum of opinion is available, from the far right (*Den/ Zavtra*) and far left (*Pravda*) to a clutch of pro-government newspapers. However, there are a number of deficiencies in the Russian media which make it difficult to talk of a completely free press. Financial constraints have caused a catastrophic decline in the circulation of national newspapers. Only papers which have gone completely tabloid, such as *Argumenty i fakty*, have been able to remain profitable. The others all depend on business sponsorship and/or government assistance (through the allocation of subsidized newsprint).

President Eltsin and his leading adviser Gennadi Burbulis have proved all too keen to use their financial and political leverage over the press to serve their own partisan agenda. Two bureaucracies were set up for the purpose – the federal information centre and the ministry of information. President and parliament repeatedly locked horns in their struggle for control over the media (in particular the newspaper *Izvestiya* and the television channels). The television networks tend to be subservient to Eltsin's political position, and in some respects are less objective than they were back in 1991. The situation in the provinces is even worse. The liberal national newspapers are often difficult to obtain, and the local press, with a few exceptions, remains under the control of provincial political bosses.

Popular support for democratic values

The presence or absence of a 'civic culture' in Russia has been a topic of fierce controversy among Western political scientists. A number of large surveys were conducted, whose findings appeared to show that democratic norms were widely respected in Russian society (for example, the view that free speech should be granted even to those holding opposing political views) (Gibson and Duch, 1992). However, many Sovietologists have challenged these findings. In most cases the questions were taken straight from US surveys, where the political context is quite different. Moreover, it was argued that Russian citizens were not used to opinion polls and would tend to give what they supposed to be the 'right' answer (even more so than in the West).

This implied that their apparent commitment to Western values might only be skin deep. If the Russian political leadership changed tack and began suggesting that Western freedoms were a luxury Russia could not afford, then the citizens' commitment to civic values might evaporate. Also, these surveys consistently showed a clear preference for strong political leadership and law and order if anarchy threatened. For example, in a November 1993 poll a 'strong hand to enforce order' was favoured by 63 per cent and opposed by 25 per cent (Grushin, 1994). The results of the December 1993 elections did little to bolster those who argued that democratic values had taken root in Russia.

Respect for human rights

Human rights has been one of the areas most closely monitored by Western governments, and there has been dramatic progress. Just about all the political prisoners inherited from the communist era have been released, although some people remain in prison for 'economic crimes' which would not feature on Western statute books. Freedom to travel and emigrate are enjoyed by all, and although the lack of due process raises concerns in the West, on the criterion of human rights Russia has moved decisively towards democracy. Russia is keen to be accepted as a normal member of the international community and sees respect for human rights as part of this process.

In a curious twist of fate, the use of human rights as a political tool has switched sides. It is now the Russian government who is invoking the principles of the Helsinki Accords, to protest the denial of citizenship and language rights to Russians living in Estonia, Latvia and elsewhere. And Western governments are worried not about the right to emigrate, but at the prospect of a flood of impoverished migrants heading west.

The growth of civil society

De Tocqueville argued that the strength of US democracy lay in the dense network of social organizations characteristic of American society. If citizens organized themselves on a voluntary basis to solve the challenges of their daily lives, they would develop the culture of tolerance and responsibility which would enable them to rule their country and their nation. Such a pattern seemed to emerge in Poland, where powerful interest groups such as the Catholic Church and Solidarity, which refused to be absorbed by the socialist state, eventually brought the whole system crashing down. US aid for democratization in Russia has focused on the promotion of associative behaviour, from independent trade unions to environmental action groups, in the belief that this is the best long-run foundation for democracy.

In the 1980s several observers of the Russian scene began to argue that elements of a plural, civil society were sprouting up under the surface of Brezhnevite stagnation (Saivetz and Jones, 1994). They pointed out that the USSR was a highly educated, urbanized industrial society with an articulate and self-conscious intelligentsia. Political repression was reserved for outright dissidents, and did not intrude upon the daily life of 95 per cent of Soviet citizens. They were relatively free, within the confines of their private lives, to pursue their own interests, to construct their own identities and to develop a dense network of social ties. This vibrant private sphere was hidden beneath the surface of an ossified public domain, in which the dead language of Marxism-Leninism was the only tolerated means of expression.

The implication was clear. There was a vibrant civil society lurking behind the shell of Soviet socialism which could burst forth at any time. This Tocquevillian vision seemed to be coming true during the Gorbachev era, when there was an explosion in the activity of informal groups (*neformaly*). The informals, estimated to number 60,000 by 1987, ranged from Buddhists to body-builders, from anti-Semites to amateur theatricals.

The informals played an important political role, chiselling away at the mortar holding together the monolith of communist society. However, once *glasnost* gave way to democratization, the pluralism of the Russian informals did not make the transition from the social to the political sphere. This was not true in the non-Russian republics, where large mass movements grew up around the kernel of informal organizations. The most common pattern (seen in Armenia, Lithuania and Latvia) was for green movements (usually protesting nuclear power) to mount increasingly large demonstrations which then turned into Popular Fronts with a nationalist political agenda.

No such pattern appeared in Russia itself, however. Environmental groups were active and achieved some popular support, but did not create any significant nationwide organizations. They remained small, isolated groups of local enthusiasts. As political and economic change gathered pace, the informals were left behind. Many of their activists were elected to regional councils or to the national parliament, and abandoned their groups. The dislocations that accompanied the break-up of the USSR undermined the basis for the activism of many of the groups: there was no longer a Communist Party to protest against, or all-powerful ministries to lobby. Many of the informals fed into the democratic movement, but, as described above, this failed to prove a sound enough base for a multi-party system to emerge. In the Russia of 1993 and 1994 it was still hard to find voluntary associations at sub-national level which could be cited as incubators of democratic values and experience.

Thus the hypothesis that a nascent civil society was incubating within Soviet society does not seem to have been vindicated by the subsequent course of events. Some would argue that it is unfair to expect the informal groups to have been able to create order out of the chaos of the collapsing Soviet system. However, it provides further ammunition for critics of the civil society hypothesis, who argue that its advocates were guilty of a conceptual error. While Marx followed Hegel in portraying civil society as arising in opposition to the state, the originators of the concept (Adam Smith and Adam Ferguson) saw civil society as superior to and inclusive of the state (Cohen and Arato, 1992). For them the essence of civil society was private property and the rule of law, both of which served to limit the growing state. If one accepts the latter interpretation, then it is premature to talk of civil society in the former USSR or in present-day Russia, since private property and the rule of law are still essentially absent. The adoption by democratic activists of a model of civil society in opposition to the state may also have backfired in political terms. By campaigning on the basis of 'anti-politics' they fuelled popular distrust of politicians and made it hard for the newly elected leaders to overcome popular cynicism and build legitimacy.

ALTERNATIVE PERSPECTIVES ON DEMOCRATIZATION IN RUSSIA

Liberal constitutionalism is not the only approach to studying democratic transitions. This section discusses three other theories (elite theory, Marxism and rational choice) which see politics not solely as a matter of institutions and values, but as a struggle for control over resources by rival social groups. The orthodox consensus on Russian

democratization is surprisingly silent on the question of *cui bono*.
In principle, *everybody* is supposed to benefit from democratization (the political equivalent of Pareto optimality). There is at most
a grudging recognition that some unsavoury social groups have been
doing rather well from 'market democracy', such as old *nomenklatura*
officials and new mafia businessmen. But this is seen as a tragic and
temporary distortion of the process. A change of analytic perspective
may help understand why democracy has had such a hard time taking root in Russia.

1 *Elite theory* argues that the success of democratization hinges
upon direct negotiation between key strategic groups. 'Strategic' is
defined as having sufficient political power to derail the democratization process despite the efforts of pro-democracy groups (Higley
and Field, 1980). Social values or the constellation of representative institutions formally in place matters less than the fact that an
explicit pact is struck between elite groups. Elite theory argues that
democracy is introduced when elite groups stop trying to use non-
democratic methods to eliminate their rivals and agree to channel
their political competition into periodic elections. It is only when
pressure from below is met by flexibility among ruling elites that
democratization occurs.

This model seems to fit the democratic transitions in southern
Europe and Latin America fairly well (Higley and Gunther, 1992).
Direct meetings between elite groups did take place, and deals were
struck. Similarly, the model seems applicable to the Eastern European
transitions (Banac, 1992). Reformist communist leaders sat down
with sundry intellectuals, dissidents and social organizations at 'round
tables', and agreed to create a democratic political system. The communist leaders initially tried to secure some guarantees for their own
future political role, but in most countries they were swept aside by
the wave of popular distaste for the *ancien régime*. However, after
suffering initial electoral defeat, several of the region's reformed communist parties staged electoral comebacks, and many of the old managerial cadres managed to retain a privileged position in the economy.
The Eastern European cases do of course differ from the Latin American transitions in some crucial respects, such as the weakness of
organized social interests and the urgent need for radical economic
transformation (Schmitter and Karl, 1994).

What does the elite theory approach tell us about the Russian
case? At no point in the Russian transition did elite groups sit down
and forge a consensus. Rather, the political process lurched forward
from crisis to crisis, until the Soviet system collapsed. The old Communist Party structure had served as an institutional forum for the
brokering of elite interests, but progressively disintegrated from 1989
onwards, as it was forced to share power with the elected Congress
of People's Deputies and to cede more autonomy to the regions. Unfortunately, the elected parliaments which emerged in 1989–90 never
achieved sufficient political authority to serve as the location for a

negotiated transfer of power. This was because power was split between the Russian and Soviet parliaments – and between them and the still influential Communist Party and ministerial bureaucracies.

The nearest one can find to a transition pact in Russia is Gorbachev's negotiations at Novo Ogarevo in 1991 with the republic leaders for a new Union treaty (the '9 plus 1' process). However, this deal was based on the false premise that the USSR was still a viable entity. It was this putative pact which caused the August coup, which in turn triggered the break-up of the Soviet Union. The 'pact' which created the Commonwealth of Independent States (CIS), signed in Minsk in December 1991 between Eltsin, Shushkevich and Kravchuk (the presidents of Belarus and Ukraine), was not really a pact at all but a *fait accompli* presented to the other republic leaders by Eltsin. Note the absence of the Central Asian leaders at the initial Minsk meeting: there was not even a pretence that they were consulted. Moreover, the pact did not establish any terms for the future relations between the members of the CIS, and no stable set of relations has yet emerged.

In the absence of an explicit political deal between elite groups in Russia, elite theory's prognosis for democratization in Russia is rather gloomy. However, the absence of a strong working-class or peasant mobilization is a plus as far as the elite theory is concerned, and leaves open the possibility that a new elite consensus may yet be forged. The most likely forum for such a pact is, of course, the much-abused parliament where, as of mid-1994, communists and democrats seemed to be cooperating effectively. In February 1994 the Duma granted an amnesty to the hardliners charged with participation in the August coup and October insurrection. In April 1994 Eltsin persuaded the various political and social leaders to sign a civic accord, promising to respect the constitution and to suspend political attacks on each other for two years. The Communists, Agrarians and Yabloko refused to sign, as did three regional leaders.

2 *Marxism*, which is in certain ways similar to elite theory, sees democracy as a compromise forced on capitalist elites by working-class mobilization (Rueschemeyer et al., 1992). In return for granting the workers the right to vote and a chance to share in political power through the lottery of periodic elections, the capitalists get to keep private property and most of their economic power. Crucially, democracy does not extend to the international arena – where the laws of capitalist economics continue to reign supreme (Gills and Rocamora, 1994).

In some respects, the Marxist model fits the Soviet case fairly well (Arato and Feher, 1989). Working-class mobilization and the internationalization of the economy have been important features of the Russian transition. The coalminers' strikes of July 1989 were critical in persuading Gorbachev to abandon the idea of mass repression as a tool for clinging to power. Prior to the miners' strikes, the only mass unrest had been in non-Russian regions such as Armenia and the Baltic. However, the miners never developed a nationwide organization, and were always rather vague as to their political and economic agenda (Rutland, 1990). Unlike labour unions in South Africa or Argentina, they did not emerge as a permanent political player at the national level. By the end of 1992 economic collapse and the spectre of mass unemployment had completely emasculated the Russian working class.

The main problem with applying Marxist analysis to the Russian case is, of course, the absence of a self-conscious capitalist class. Marxists can argue that the managers of state industry are 'object-ively' carrying out the functions of capitalism, by guaranteeing the continuation of accumulation. They can also point to the managers' manipulation of the privatization process to convert their political power as a bureaucratic stratum into economic power as a property-holding class (Clarke et al., 1994). However, this is a lengthy pro-cess, and in the meantime no one could plausibly argue that the ex-*nomenklatura* are acting cohesively as a class-for-itself. The evid-ence for the existence of such a class as a national political actor is simply not there at present (Rutland, 1992). If there were such a class, one can imagine that there would not be such political and administrative chaos in Russia. In the meantime, the processes of democratization and market reform are proceeding in a very hap-hazard fashion.

3 *Rational choice theory* helps explain the sluggish progress to-wards democracy in Russia. Rational choice shares with orthodox liberalism a recognition of the importance of institutions. However, it stresses the importance of strategic behaviour by self-interested actors within these institutions.

One of the central tenets of rational choice theory is the indetermin-acy of majority voting (the Condorcet paradox). The composition of the majority-winning coalition is not necessarily fixed in advance: the precise sequence in which a series of decisions are voted on can decisively influence the final outcome. This means that control over the institutional structure and procedures which determine agenda-setting is absolutely crucial (Hardin, 1989). In a democracy there is always the possibility that certain groups may be permanently ex-cluded from the ruling majority coalition (for example, an ethnic minority, the poor or women). Indeed, just such an exclusion is virtually unavoidable.

This means that the very first steps of constitutional design in a new-born democracy can have a pivotal and lasting impact on the subsequent course of politics in that society. A group which loses its ability to influence the agenda, to ensure its place in the ruling coali-tion, may have little or no incentive to accept the new political sys-tem as legitimate. Rational choice theory alerts us to the likelihood that such key groups as the military and defence industry can see little to gain from the introduction of democracy in Russia unless there are some institutional guarantees protecting their interests.

The rational choice approach generates some interesting insights which tend to favour the elite theory account of democratization in Russia over the standard liberal interpretation. However, a neo-institutional approach is difficult to apply to contemporary Russia: the situation is so unstable that institutions come and go with bewildering rapidity. It is also worth remembering the Potemkin village phenomenon. On Russian soil, institutions are not what they seem, and the functions of political actors are generally not reflected in formal structures.

All three of these alternative approaches converge on a common conclusion: that democratization cannot simply be reduced to the question of constitutional design. (For instance, does the country possess democratic institutions or not, on a 1 to 10 scale?) One must analyse the political trade-offs between different social groups which are necessary to get the democratic show on the road.

STATE AND NATION-BUILDING IN RUSSIA

The antinomies of Russian nationalism

One of the major differences between the transitions to democracy in Russia, on the one hand, and in Eastern Europe and Latin America on the other hand, is that in Russia one is dealing with the break-up of a multi-national empire. This raises profound questions about the existential nature of the state which most other nascent democracies have not had to face (although India and South Africa are comparable in some respects).

Democracy presupposes that there is agreement on the boundaries of the *demos* (the people) that is to rule itself. Western political theory has little to say on the subject of where nation-states come from and what are the principles upon which they should be constituted. The Western experience with nation-building – even including the United States – is a long and painful one, extending over several centuries and invariably involving warfare. There are grounds for doubting whether the process has yet reached its conclusion in Russia. In Russia there was and is no agreement on the shape of the political community which is to be the subject of self-determination. Russia must choose not merely what sort of political system it desires, but also *what* Russia is as a cultural entity, and *where* it is in terms of physical borders. The young American democracy faced similar challenges – and came up with some answers (such as Manifest Destiny) which the international community would obviously not accept in Russia today.

The multi-national nature of the USSR was the factor which eventually caused its dissolution. It proved beyond Gorbachev's ability to devise a political system which could incorporate the 48 per cent of the Soviet population who were not of Russian nationality. The same disintegrative logic which undermined the USSR is continuing to eat away at the coherence of the Russian Federation.

Russia had never been constituted as a nation-state in the conventional sense. Under the Russian empire the population was even more ethnically diverse than in the USSR, and it was only in the last decades of tsarism's existence that halting efforts were made to mobilize Russian nationalism. The fact that the Russian empire spread for 350 years across contiguous territory meant that it was difficult for Russians to perceive where the Russians ended and the foreigners began. The idea of a Russian nation-state became even more elusive during the Soviet period. Although ethnic Russians dominated the Soviet state, many aspects of Russian culture were suppressed, and the Russians had to rule not in their own name but in the name of multi-national socialism. Russian nationalists faced an agonizing dilemma – whether to give their loyalty to the Soviet state, as the historic inheritor of Russian statehood, or to denounce the USSR as a usurpation and distortion of Russia's heritage. This quandary persisted from the 1920s, when the 'National Bolsheviks' reluctantly swung behind Lenin, to the 1980s, when the nationalist right split into defenders and opponents of the Soviet order.

Nationalism emerged as the crucial factor in the demise of the USSR. Gorbachev found to his horror that the political reform process of *perestroika* was swiftly dominated by debates over the Armenian–Azerbaijani dispute, and over Baltic demands for independence. Many Western observers had expected that the main challenge to Moscow would come from the exploding Muslim populations of Central Asia. However, their leaders stayed loyal to the USSR to the bitter end, and it was only in the Baltics and west Ukraine (regions annexed during the Second World War) that one saw mass mobilization along nationalist lines.

However, one can argue that it was Russian nationalism, rather than the nationalism of the non-Russian peoples, which ultimately played the decisive role in the destruction of the USSR. Gorbachev was unable to appeal to Russian popular interests, for fear that this would antagonize the non-Russian republics still further. Gorbachev's commitment to the Soviet state created an opening for Eltsin's political comeback (after his dismissal from the Politburo in 1987). Eltsin began articulating the interests of the Russian people, and was able to turn the institutions of the Russian Federation into a power-base to rival that of Gorbachev in the federal Communist Party and government. In the crucial political showdown of August 1991, the core institutions of the Soviet state – the army and the KGB – abandoned the USSR and switched their loyalty to Eltsin's Russia.

However, having freed itself from the confines of the Soviet Union, Russia's problems in defining itself as a nation-state are far from resolved. The challenge to Russia's cohesion has both an external and an internal aspect. The former refers to Russia's relations with its ex-Soviet neighbours – what the Russians now refer to as the 'near abroad'. The internal aspect is the fact that 19 per cent of the Russian Federation's population are non-Russians, mostly living in 21 autonomous republics.

The largest ethnic minority within Russia is the 5.5 million Muslim Tatars, and Tatarstan is the most powerful of the republics, thanks to its oil industry. For most of the ethnic republics, however, secession is not a feasible option. They are too geographically isolated for independent statehood (most of them surrounded on all sides by Russian territory), and in many cases the titular nationality is outnumbered by the Russian inhabitants. The one region which seems bent on secession, and which has achieved *de facto* independence, is Chechenya in the northern Caucasus. The non-Russian republics are part of the broader problem of the fragmentation of central authority, discussed below.

The external aspect of Russian identity is a more serious cause for concern. The problem manifests itself in three dimensions: the Russian diaspora, economic relations and military issues. The collapse of the USSR left 25 million Russians living beyond the boundaries of the Russian Federation – 11 million in Ukraine and 7 million in Kazakhstan – whose interests Moscow is determined to protect. It also left the anomaly of Ukraine, which many Russians persist in regarding as a 'little brother' without the right to national self-determination. Many Ukrainians – a majority in the eastern provinces – speak Russian as their first language, and their political loyalty to an independent Ukraine has yet to be tested.

As far as economic relations are concerned, the new members of the CIS soon discovered that their economies were heavily dependent on Russia even after they had won their formal political sovereignty. Price liberalization revealed that each country was being subsidized by Russia to the tune of 10 to 20 per cent of their GDP, mostly through the delivery of oil and gas at prices below world market levels. However, this was a two-way dependency: many Russian factories were tied to customers in the newly independent states. They formed a powerful lobby within Russia arguing for continued (subsidized) trade with the CIS. The outflow of roubles to the other republics was an important factor undermining Gaidar's efforts to achieve monetary stability in 1992. The level of subsidies was drastically reduced with the termination of the 'rouble zone' in July 1993 – but continued even after that date.

The security dimension has not yet surfaced as a pivotal factor in Russian domestic politics, but it could explode onto the scene at any time. What military policy should a democratic Russia adopt towards its neighbours? Should it stand by while Tadzhikistan is torn apart by civil war? Should it intervene to try to stop the six-year-long conflict between Armenia and Azerbaijan? Should Russia do nothing if Ukraine uses force to prevent the secession of Crimea (75 per cent Russian, and part of the Russian Federation until 1954)? Democratization does not provide an answer to any of these dilemmas, yet

Table 12.2 Typology of national–regional political relations

		At local level	
		Old elite makes deal with new elite	Old and new elites do not make deal
Relations with centre	Province makes deal with centre	*Nizhegorod*	*Mordovia*
	Province does not make deal with centre	*Saratov*	*Sakha*

these are the very questions at the forefront of Russian politics, around which battle lines are being drawn.

It is this external aspect that is the most unstable element in the Russian political equation at the present time. Most Russian politicians are still seeking some sort of special relationship with the near abroad and are not content just to build a conventional nation-state within the boundaries of the Russian Federation. It is unlikely that they will come up with a formula for confederation which will tempt their neighbours to join, but the mere act of trying will continue to distract Russian statesmen for the foreseeable future.

It should be remembered that even the European empires, which had the benefit of an ocean between their homeland and their colonies, all underwent political identity crises after the end of empire. The Russian post-imperial dilemma is far more wrenching, and will overshadow the democratization process for years to come. The way Russia perceives its relations with its neighbours will crucially influence the character of the democracy which emerges within its borders.

Moscow and the regions

Even taking the national boundaries of Russia as given, the crucial issue in Russian domestic politics is state-building rather than democratization. Russia remains an unwieldy giant of a country, spread over 7,000 miles and with atrocious means of communication between its component parts. The collapse of the Soviet state apparatus, the spread of democratization and the failure of the new elites to build nationwide political parties all served to weaken Moscow's ability to manage the country.

The key challenge facing Eltsin is the recreation of central bureaucracies and the reassertion of Moscow's control over the provinces. He may fail in this task, but it would be a misnomer to describe the resulting decentralized, unstable political system as 'democratized'. Throughout its history the Russian state has followed a repeated cycle of centralization and decentralization. What we are seeing now may not be democratization *per se*, but another transient 'Time of Troubles' (as the period 1598–1613 is known), which will be followed by the re-emergence of a powerful state.

As a student of Russian history, Eltsin was no doubt acutely aware of the dangers of anarchy and of the need to restore a centralized chain of command. The trouble was that his efforts to re-establish central authority were inextricably connected with his feuding with his political opponents, both before and after 1991.

Russian politics between 1990 and 1994 unfolded as a messy struggle for power between two broad sets of elites: national and regional. Politicians in Russia's 21 ethnic republics and 68 regions fall broadly into three groups: those inclined to go along with reform, those trying to maintain the old system and those prepared to join whichever group wins the contest (Hahn, 1993; Friedgut and Hahn, 1994). Regional politics can be analysed along two axes: (1) whether the old elites (Communist Party officials and industrial managers) made a political deal with the new elites (new politicians elected into office from the democratic movement, the new businessmen, etc.); or (2) whether the patronage connections of regional leaders fed into Eltsin's presidential apparatus, or into that of Eltsin's rivals in congress.

Applying these criteria to each of Russia's 89 regions would produce a two-by-two typology along the lines of table 12.2 (with a few regions listed as examples).[2]

In 1990–1 Eltsin encouraged the regions 'to take as much sovereignty as they wanted' in his bid to undermine Gorbachev's political authority. He encouraged them to set up their own foreign trade deals, to stop paying taxes to the federal government and so on. After his goal of dislodging Gorbachev was accomplished, he moved to rein in the provinces. Eltsin argued that the regional Soviets elected in 1990 were large, unwieldy bodies (often with 200–300 deputies), dominated by old communist elites, and were chronically unable to administer effectively. On these grounds, in October 1991, he persuaded congress to suspend regional elections for one year, during which he would directly appoint governors in the regions (Wishnevsky, 1994). In addition to appointing governors, Eltsin set up a network of presidential envoys in each region, in emulation of the central control network run by the old Communist Party. (Eltsin had no legal authority to establish presidential envoys, and the institution was repeatedly denounced by congress.) The elected regional councils receded to a decorative role, as real political power shifted into the executive organs. On several occasions governors dismissed elected city and district mayors.

The 21 ethnic republics within the Russian Federation, which had already started declaring their 'sovereignty' in 1990, were exempted from Eltsin's direct rule and were allowed to select their own leaders. Following the lead of Tatarstan and Chechenya, they forced Eltsin to sign a new Federation Treaty in March 1992, which seemed to recognize their sovereign authority over everything except military affairs. Eltsin poured large subsidies into the ethnic republics in 1992 to wean them away from supporting Khasbulatov and congress.

These concessions to the ethnic republics angered the leaders of the other regions. As the political battles in Moscow intensified, the regions were able to carve out more and more autonomy as Eltsin and the congress competed for their loyalty. In 1992 the economic reformers in the central government were willing to ally with conservative leaders in the provinces in order to isolate the conservatives in the centre. By 1993 local budgets were raising roughly as much revenue as the federal authorities (although thanks to deficit financing the latter were still spending twice as much) (Hanson, 1994).

However, the balance shifted in early 1993, as Eltsin started to prune regional subsidies and sought stronger powers. Regional leaders blocked Eltsin's efforts in March 1993 to establish presidential rule and to have a referendum on the new constitution. Several regions began electing their own administrators, who were no longer answerable to Eltsin, and Sverdlovsk even declared its own 'sovereignty'. In the constitutional draft which finally emerged in July 1993 the ethnic republics did win recognition of sovereignty, dual citizenship and official language rights. Each republic and region would be granted two seats (one for the governor and one for the head of the council) in the upper chamber of parliament, the Federation Council. After the October events, however, Eltsin felt stronger politically and moved to curtail the regions' political autonomy, while expressing his willingness to allow them to keep their economic autonomy. All regional councils were dismissed, and the final constitutional draft revoked many of the republics' special rights. Tatarstan was able to hold out for a special bilateral treaty with Russia, which Eltsin signed on 15 February 1994. This preserved some privileges (for example, exemption from military service), but made no mention of sovereignty (Teague, 1994).

It is unrealistic to suggest that the Russian Federation may go the way of the Soviet Union, and break up into independent states. Russians share a strong sense of cultural homogeneity, and have four centuries' experience of life in a common state. The central regions of Russia are totally dependent upon European Russia for access to the outside world, while the Russian Far East is in danger of colonization by China and/or Japan and will look to Moscow for support. Thus one should not count on the disintegration of the Russian state. However, in the short term the political struggles between the centre and the regions have derailed the process of democratization at both local and national level.

DEMOCRACY AND ECONOMIC DEVELOPMENT

It is somewhat premature to raise the question of the connection between democracy and economic development in Russia, since the government is still struggling to halt the collapse of the economic system. In the past four years officially recorded GDP has fallen by some 40 per cent, a slump greater than that experienced by the Western countries during the Great Depression. However, the roots of this economic collapse lie in the old system of central planning, rather than with the decisions taken by politicians since August 1991 (Rutland, 1994).

The command economy allocated resources with scant regard to demand or production costs. Already, by 1990–1, the system of central control was breaking down, as inflation took hold and firms found that planned deliveries failed to arrive. Complete disintegration occurred with the break-up of the USSR and the dismantling of the Communist Party's hierarchy of political control of the economy.

Thus, in 1991, Russia experienced the demise of an economic system that had been in place, in violation of the basic laws of market economics, for 70 years. There was little the government could do in the face of such monumental changes. The 'shock' came from 70 years of the misallocation of economic resources, and not from the government's decision to liberalize prices. In the sense that democratization helped accelerate this collapse, then democracy has been bad for economic development. But nobody would seriously argue that the old system could have been sustained indefinitely.

That said, however, one can criticize the Gaidar team for being too optimistic in their conviction that freeing prices and opening the Russian economy to foreign trade would sweep away the inherited inefficiencies of the past. Price liberalization without the presence of competing producers was a recipe for massive inflation, as monopoly suppliers cut output and raised prices. Opening up foreign trade led to a fire sale of natural resources, with much of the earnings staying outside the country. In 1992–4 capital flight from Russia was $12–15 billion a year (Ellman, 1993; Murrell, 1993; Aslund and Layard, 1993).

In spring 1992, with support for reform eroding in the face of a 300 per cent rise in consumer prices, Eltsin started backing away from the reform agenda, releasing inflationary credits to state enterprises and postponing the liberalization of energy prices. A memorandum of agreement was signed with the IMF in February 1992, but Russia repeatedly failed to meet its targets for fiscal and monetary stringency. Russia stopped repayments on the $70 billion of foreign debt which it had inherited from the USSR. Given the political and economic challenges facing Eltsin, Russia's Western creditors were powerless to enforce conditionality. Despite repeated promises of aid from the G7 countries, actual aid disbursements were a small fraction of the $28 billion promised in April 1993.

In their enthusiasm to apply shock therapy, the Gaidar team overlooked the fact that building a market economy in Russia would require a state capable of providing the minimum public goods which even Adam Smith recognized as essential (freedom from crime, a stable currency, the rule of law). Rebuilding an effective Russian state would have required political compromise with the key political elites inherited from the Soviet past – the parliament, the industrial managers and others. The Gaidar team eschewed such efforts. Instead they believed in the possibility of a 'technocratic fix' – the swift implementation of economic reforms before a coalition of interests opposed to reform could be assembled. Economic reform came to be seen as a substitute for political reform. However, while the Polish reformers had enjoyed nine months of unchallenged authority to implement their programme, Gaidar had come under attack as soon as the parliament reconvened, on 13 January 1992, and the congress managed to force Eltsin to delay key elements of the programme. As a result, the shock therapy was still-born.

Over the course of 1992 Eltsin became more and more politically dependent on the success of the economic reforms. The theory was that Eltsin's political prestige would carry through the economic reforms. In practice, the polarity was reversed, and Eltsin's political authority came to hinge on his controversial economic programme. Anatoly Chubais persuaded Eltsin to go ahead with a mass distribution of privatization vouchers in July 1992, in the hope that this would build a popular base of support for economic reform – as occurred in the Czech Republic. The Supreme Soviet was persuaded to adopt the privatization law by including a provision which allowed workers and managers to buy 51 per cent of the shares. Privatization became a vehicle for the consolidation of managerial control over the old state enterprises, but was nevertheless trumpeted by the government as the most successful element in the reform programme.

Given the rapidity of the changes in the Russian economy, interest groups found it difficult to come together and exert influence over the political process. One can observe two different types of nascent economic interest groups: the old and the new.

The traditional industrialists still control many of the resources in the country. While often powerful in the cities and provinces, they have not been able to articulate a collective interest at national level. They have sought influence through a mixture of confrontation tactics (encouraging their workers to strike, for example) and personal lobbying, rather than through an open process of political bargaining. The reforms are forcing these industrialists to behave in a more market-like manner, but they still rely heavily on tapping their old patronage network for favours from the state.

The new capitalism which is emerging in Russia revolves around short-term rent-seeking behaviour. There is no money to be made in manufacturing, whereas rich profits can be had speculating in foreign currency, exporting raw materials and importing foreign consumer durables. Success in gaining access to foreign trade hinges on one's political contacts. The old and new elites compete for access to the political decision-makers who can allocate export quotas or bank credits.

It is hard to see how this raw, predatory capitalism can be justified to a democratic electorate. On the other hand, this is just what many Russians, raised on Upton Sinclair, expected a market economy to look like. Given the partial character of Russian democratization, there is currently little sign of this popular discontent translating into an effective political movement. Also, for most Russians the 'market' is a political abstraction, a symbol of change which must be accepted as inevitable, and not a question of choosing this or that economic policy.

In its haste to embrace 'capitalism', the Gaidar team did not dwell on the fact that there is no standard Western model for the construction of capitalism. The emphasis on trade liberalization as a key to integration with the world economy is particularly puzzling. First, the majority of capitalist countries saw their economies grow behind protective barriers for decades. Most had non-convertible currencies right up until the 1970s. Second, there is China, which has enjoyed spectacular economic growth without implementing almost any of the prescriptions of the Russian reform programme. Chinese exports have boomed, but exchange controls are still in place, and trade barriers keep out foreign imports. Private property rights are not clearly defined, still less protected, in law, and most firms are still owned by local state authorities. The existence of a range of options within the capitalist path did not deter the Russian reformers from presenting their programme as the only alternative which could save Russia. This accords well with the ideological mindset inherited from the Russian past, in which politics is reduced to a choice between right and wrong, between obedience and dissent.

CONCLUSION

It is difficult to write about the Russian example in a comparative context, since so much about the case is unique. Unlike the East Europeans, there was no clean break with the old political and economic system. Instead of a wholesale turnover of the political elite, there was a protracted political battle between the executive and legislative branches of government, each claiming to be the true guardian of democracy. Unlike the other countries in transition to democracy, Russia is a former empire that has still not defined its relations with its neighbours and its character as a federal state. The transition to a post-communist political order is far from over. According to one November 1993 poll, respondents described the political situation as follows: anarchy 42 per cent; don't know 20 per cent; old order under new names 17 per cent; democracy 14 per cent; and dictatorship 7 per cent (*Economist*, 11 December 1993, 23).

Sceptics will use the Russian experience to argue that an attempt to build simultaneously a market economy and a democracy achieves neither. Radical economic reform imposed huge strains on the bureaucratic and democratic systems, and left little room for the forging of political consensus so essential to democracy. However, it is premature to come to such a judgement. At least a five- or ten-year perspective will be required to evaluate the character of the Russian transition. As of mid-1994 there were signs of a consensus forming around the political centre, and inflation was slowing, even though the GDP continued to decline.

On the other hand, very few countries with a living standard of less that $5,000 a year have been able to operate as a democracy. Russia is less than half way to this target, and has few of the cultural traditions (such as a history of British colonialism) which have enabled countries like India and Botswana to buck the trend. Thus one's prognosis for the future of democracy in Russia must be rather grim.

This is not at all to suggest that Russia would have been better off with some sort of authoritarian regime. For all its flaws, the democratization of Russia was the only conceivable way to rid the country of the Soviet system and set it on course towards a more civilized society. The critique laid out in this chapter is meant to show that democratization still has a long way to go, not that it was a mistake to go down that road. The most specific criticism which is made in this chapter is that the attempt to adopt a separation of powers model exacerbated the political feuding at national level and encouraged the fragmentation of central authority. A parliamentary system, with an executive president selected from the congress, would have been more likely to produce political stability – and would not necessarily have made radical economic reform any less feasible.

ACKNOWLEGEMENTS

The author wishes to thank Nikita V. Zagladin and Yitzhak M. Brudny for thoughtful conversations on the issues raised here.

NOTES

1 Data provided by Andrei Dekhtyarev from *Mossoviet*, 2 February 1994.
2 This typology was derived from the work of Kate Stoner Weiss of Princeton University.

REFERENCES

Arato, A. and Feher, F. (eds) 1989: *Gorbachev: the Debate.* New York: Humanities Press.

Aslund, A. and Layard, R. (eds) 1993: *Changing the Economic System in Russia.* New York: St Martin's Press.

Banac, I. (ed.) 1992: *Eastern Europe in Revolution.* Ithaca, NY: Cornell University Press.

Brudny, Y. M. 1993: The Dynamics of Democratic Russia. *Post-Soviet Affairs,* 9, 141–70.

Clarke, S., Fairbrother, P. and Borisov, V. 1994: The Privatization of Industrial Enterprises in Russia. *Europe/Asia Studies,* 46, 179–214.

Cohen, J.-L. and Arato, A. 1992: *Civil Society and Political Theory.* Cambridge, Mass.: MIT Press.

Di Palma, G. 1990: *To Craft Democracies.* Berkeley: University of California Press.

Ellman, M. 1993: Shock Therapy: Failure or Partial Success? *Harriman Institute Forum,* 6.

Friedgut, T. and Hahn, J. (eds) 1994: *Local Power and Post-Soviet Politics.* New York: M.E. Sharpe.

Gastil, R. (ed.) 1993: *Freedom in the World.* New York: Freedom House.

Gibson, J. L. and Duch, R. M. 1992: Democratic Values and the Transformation of the Soviet Union. *Journal of Politics,* 54, 329–71.

Gills, B. and Rocamora, J. (eds) 1994: *Low Intensity Democracy.* Boulder, Colo: Westview Press.

Grushin, B. 1994: Public Opinion in Russia. Lecture at Harvard University, 4 February.

Hahn, J. 1993: Attitudes towards Reform among Russian Provincial Politicians. *Post-Soviet Affairs,* 9, 66–85.

Hanson, P. 1994: The Center versus the Periphery in Russian Economic Policy. *RFE/RL Research Report,* 3, 17, 29 April, 23–9.

Hardin, R. 1989: Why a Constitution? In A. Lijphart and B. Grofman (eds) *The Federalist Papers and the New Institutionalism.* New York: Agathon Press.

Higley, J. and Lowell Field, G. 1980: *Elitism.* London: Routledge.

Higley, J. and Gunther, R. (eds) 1992: *Elites and Democratic Consolidation in Latin America and Southern Europe.* Cambridge: Cambridge University Press.

Kiernan, B. 1994: *The End of Soviet Politics.* Boulder, Colo.: Westview Press.

Lentini, P. and McGrath, T. 1994: The Rise of the Liberal Democratic Party and the 1993 Elections. *Harriman Institute Forum,* 7.

Murrell, P. 1993: What is Shock Therapy? *Post-Soviet Affairs,* 9, 111–40.

Petrov, Y. 1993: Eltsin's Policies. Talk by Eltsin's former chief of staff, Duke University, 24 April.

Rueschemeyer, D., Stephens, E. H. and Stephens, J. D. 1992: *Capitalist Development and Democracy.* Chicago: Chicago University Press.

Rutland, P. 1990: Labor Unrest and Movements in the USSR, 1989–90. *Soviet Economy,* 6, 345–84.

Rutland, P. 1992: *Business Elites and Russian Economic Policy.* Occasional paper, Royal Institute of International Affairs, London.

Rutland, P. 1994: The Rocky Road from Plan to Market. In White, S.,

Pravda, A. and Gitelman, Z. (eds) *Developments in Post-Soviet Politics*. Durham: Duke University Press.

Saivetz, C. and Jones, A. H. (eds) 1994: *In Search of Pluralism*. Boulder, Colo.: Westview Press.

Schmitter, P. C. and Karl, T. L. 1994: The Conceptual Travels of Transitologists and Consolidologists. *Slavic Review*, 53, 173–85.

Sharlet, R. 1993: Russian Constitutional Court: The First Term. *Post-Soviet Affairs*, 9, 1–39.

Shugart, M. S. and Carey, J. M. 1992: *Presidents and Assemblies: Constitutional Design and Electoral Systems*. Cambridge: Cambridge University Press.

Slater, W. 1994: Russia: The Return of Authoritarian Government? *RFE/RL Research Report*, 3, 1, 7 January, 22–31.

Teague, E. 1994: Russian and Tatarstan Sign Power-sharing Treaty. *RFE/RL Research Report*, 3, 14, 8 April, 19–27.

USNDI (US National Democratic Institute) 1993: *Kak pobedit' na vyborakh*. (INDEM) Handbook, Moscow.

Valenzuela, A. 1993: The Crisis of Presidentialism. *Journal of Democracy*, 4, 3–16.

Wishnevsky, J. 1994: Problems of Russian Regional Leadership. *RFE/RL Research Report*, 3, 19, 13 May, 6–13.

PART III
Conclusion

13

Two Cheers for Democracy? Democracy and the Developmental State

ADRIAN LEFTWICH

INTRODUCTION

A book of this kind calls for a conclusion, one that seeks to pull together some of the strands that have been so carefully woven by the individual authors and yet which goes beyond their distinguished specialist contributions by generalizing in a comparative fashion. To this extent a conclusion is partly parasitic and partly not: it feeds off what has been written, but also goes further and uses the contributions as a platform for something broader. In this chapter I set out to do that.[1]

A number of overlapping questions have been present throughout the book. Amongst the central ones are the following. Is political democracy a condition for sustained economic development, as is now asserted in official Western orthodoxy? Or is a certain level of prior economic development the necessary platform upon which democracy can become established and flourish, as was once widely believed? Put slightly differently, is it possible to combine both political democracy and rapid sustained economic growth? In short, is successful democratic development a serious option? If so, can this commence at any point in the developmental process or is democratic development

Table 13.1 **Average annual rates of growth (%) in GNP per capita, 1965–1990**

Sustained democracies	
Jamaica	−1.3
Venezuela	−1.0
Gambia	0.7
Costa Rica	1.4
India	1.9
Mauritius	3.2
Malaysia	4.0
Singapore	6.5
Botswana	8.4
Non-democracies	
Zaïre	−2.2
Bolivia	−0.7
Argentina	−0.3
Peru	−0.2
Haiti	−0.2
Nigeria	0.1
Philippines	1.3
Pakistan	2.5
Thailand	4.4
Indonesia	4.5
China	5.8
Taiwan	7.0
S. Korea	7.1

Sources: Council for Economic Planning and Development (1992); World Bank (1992a)

only possible after certain economic *and* political conditions have been established?

It will be clear from the evidence in previous chapters and from table 13.1 that while negative average annual rates of economic growth have been recorded under some democratic regimes, as in Jamaica and Venezuela, it is also the case that slow growth rates have been achieved under formally democratic conditions, as in India and Costa Rica. But the problem here is that such sluggish rates of growth have left very substantial numbers of the population in poverty and ignorance; they have effectively remained outside development and the inequalities have been gross. Much more important, and central for the concerns of this chapter, some democratic regimes (as in Botswana, Malaysia and Singapore) have achieved exceptional rates of growth. And the main thesis of the chapter will be that only in *democratic developmental states* is it possible for the political arrangements which we generally call democracy (even in its simplest form) to be combined with sustained and strong economic growth in the crucial early stages of development. I will suggest that this type of state, the democratic developmental state, is a subtype of the broader category of developmental state and I will define the essence of such states, outline their conditions and characteristics and illustrate their forms and features. In doing so, I shall hope to highlight some of the important issues which emerge from the previous chapters. But I shall also hope to underline the point made in the first chapter concerning the primacy of politics in development and the centrality of the state.

DEMOCRACY AND DEVELOPMENT: MEANINGS AND ISSUES

Any discussion about the relationship between democracy and development, and whether the two can profitably go hand in hand, depends on what we mean by these terms.

For example, if democratic processes are held to be an intimate component of a wide conception of social, economic *and* political development, as Nehru and other leaders of the Indian Congress held (see Kaviraj in this volume), then it does not make sense to try to explore the relationship between them. On such a view, rapid economic growth under non-democratic conditions is flawed development because political development (that is progressive democratization) is stunted. But if, on the other hand, one considers (as I do) that it is both possible and desirable for analytical purposes to differentiate between, and compare, different kinds of political arrangements and the patterns of socioeconomic growth to which they do or do not give rise, then it is also both possible and necessary to explore the democracy–development relationship, as one example of this wider polity–economy question.

For the purposes of my argument here, therefore, I start by assuming that democracy and development can be treated as analytically separate social phenomena with largely distinct and measurable empirical referents. Typically, in the case of 'development', the data we use for purposes of measurement and contrast includes conventionally 'hard' economic data such as GNP per capita, average annual rates of its growth over a 20-year period (as in table 13.1), levels and forms of industrialization, and so forth. But we would also look for crucial cognate indicators of *social* development such as life expectancy, literacy, distribution of income and many others of the kind which the UNDP has been seeking to quantify on a world-wide basis in order to measure 'human development' (UNDP, 1992). Using such indicators as these one can identify those societies where rapid and sustained socioeconomic development has taken place, such as Korea, Botswana, Malaysia, Mauritius and Thailand, and those where development has been sluggish (India and Nigeria) or, as has often been the case in the third world, negative (as in both Bolivia and Jamaica and many countries in sub-Saharan Africa) (World Bank, 1992a).

Likewise, in the case of democracy, there are a number of straightforward indices that help one to decide whether a political system may be said to be democratic or, perhaps, measure the degree of democratization (as Lane and Ersson have shown in this volume). For example, these would include such obvious features as whether there are regular and fair elections, whether the political parties accept the rules of the game, whether human rights are well respected and whether the press is both free and independent of the state. The UNDP as well as other authors and organizations have developed means for measuring these phenomena on a comparative basis (Gastil, 1986; Humana, 1987; Derbyshire, 1989; Freedom House, 1992; UNDP, 1992).

Using such rough definitions and indicators of democracy and development, one can construct a simple classification of democratic and non-democratic polities, as well as determining where there has been sustained and rapid economic development and where not. Using recent World Bank data for average annual rates of growth in GNP per capita over the period between 1965 and 1990 (table 13.1), one might suggest that those societies with negative, virtually stagnant or very slow rates of growth have not developed, while those with, say, average annual rates of growth of 4 per cent or more have clearly experienced rapid and sustained development and that this is reflected in critical social indicators like life expectancy. For instance, table I shows that Botswana, Malaysia, Korea and Indonesia have experienced rapid and sustained levels of average annual growth in GNP per capita of 8.4 per cent, 4 per cent, 7.1 per cent and 4.5 per cent, respectively. Conversely, the same data show that Jamaica, Costa Rica, Haiti and Zaïre have had stagnant or negative rates of growth over the same period at −1.3 per cent, 1.4 per cent, 0.2 per cent and −2.2 per cent, respectively (World Bank, 1992a: 218–19).

Using a simple two-by-two table of democracy and non-democracy, development and non-development, there are four ways in which these variables may be combined, as below, each of which is illustrated with examples based on the available data about their economic and political characteristics.

1 democratic development (Botswana, Malaysia)
2 non-democratic development (Korea, Taiwan, China, Indonesia)
3 democratic non-development (Jamaica, Gambia, Costa Rica)
4 non-democratic non-development (Haiti, Zaïre).

Of course such a classification is simplistic and the much more detailed analysis of data provided in this volume by Jan-Erik Lane and Svante Ersson offers a much more robust and rigorous basis for exploring the democracy–development relationship. Moreover, there are many societies which could not be easily placed within any of the four categories. India, for instance, has for most of its independence sustained a functioning (albeit extremely shaky) democracy, but its average annual rate of growth in GNP per capita has been slow (at 1.9 per cent). This cannot be described as non-development, but equally it does not qualify as rapid and sustained development. Pakistan has had periods of both democracy and military rule, so it is not clear into which political category it falls (but it has certainly not been a sustained democracy), and has averaged a 2.5 per cent average annual rate of growth in GNP per capita, somewhat better than India's, but still not 'rapid and sustained', being well short of the 4 per cent mark. Mauritius, also a functioning democracy, has generated an annual average rate of growth in GNP per capita of 3.2 per cent which is not far off Malaysia's excellent record of 4 per cent, but does not – at least on the statistical definition used here – qualify as a developmental democracy. Yet it is approaching that, since it has clearly been democratic and has generated a very respectable rate of growth.

Despite the obvious limitations of the approach, the point is to show that while many, if not most, third world societies have had slow, stagnant or even negative records of development, some of them have done exceptionally well in terms of their socioeconomic development. Amongst these, a few have been democracies. And it is these which must be the focus of our interest, for they stand out clearly as having transformed, or having begun to transform, the material lives of their people, while protecting human rights far better than the majority of third world societies, especially the other non-democratic developmental states. Few as they may be, the question is why and how have they been able to succeed as developmental democracies?

Before dealing with that question, there are a few further assumptions to clarify. I assume that, given a choice, most people would favour *both* democracy and development. And I therefore assume further that some form of democratic development (for instance as in Malaysia or Botswana) which combines the fundamental aspects of political democracy with sustained socioeconomic growth is preferable to non-democratic development (as in Korea, 1960–87), and that both are preferable to democratic non-development (as in Jamaica) on the one hand, and to non-democratic non-development (as in Zaïre) on the other hand. I suspect that most authors in this volume and most readers of it would agree. More to the point, I assume further that this is what a poor peasant farmer or urban worker would prefer, if asked, and if such simple choices were available.

If this is so, the central question then is: under what circumstances may political democracy be combined with socioeconomic development of a sustained and vigorous kind? My answer is that this combination is only likely to occur in democratic developmental states.

But before looking at the characteristics of such states, it is necessary to introduce the notion of the developmental state more fully.

THE IDEA OF THE DEVELOPMENT STATE

Although the provenance of the term 'developmental state' is relatively recent, the idea of a state capable of promoting sustained and rapid economic growth and development goes back a long way – at least to the writing of Friedrich List (1885) in the mid-nineteenth century – and may be found in a variety of contexts since then, as I have outlined in more detail elsewhere (Leftwich, 1995). While such states have not yet been fully theorized, the important recent tradition of analysis of these states has its origins primarily in the work of the distinguished American political scientist, Chalmers Johnson. His work on Japan, South Korea and Taiwan (Johnson, 1981, 1982 and 1987) has set the framework for most subsequent studies of the developmental state as a state form and of specific developmental states, such as Taiwan (Wade, 1990).

For the purposes of present discussion, I define developmental states in preliminary terms as: those states whose internal politics and external relations have served to concentrate sufficient power, authority, autonomy, competence and capacity at the centre to shape, pursue and encourage the achievement of explicit developmental objectives, whether by establishing and promoting the conditions of economic growth, or by organizing it directly, or a varying combination of both.

Although Johnson's paradigm case, post-war Japan, was formally democratic (a point I shall return to later), most developmental states have not been. In particular, Korea and Taiwan, the closest parallels to Japan and the most cited examples of the species, have had very stern records of authoritarian rule, and democratization has come only recently to them. The same can be said for Indonesia and Thailand. All have produced sustained and rapid rates of growth under often harsh political conditions. Historically, post-Meiji Japan and Bismarckian Germany may be said to fall into the same category of non-democratic developmental states. And it is certainly arguable that the key period of capital accumulation and economic transformation even in Britain (between 1750 and 1850) occurred under political circumstances which would not be regarded as even remotely democratic today (Rueschemeyer et al., 1992).

For Johnson, the developmental state was essentially a capitalist developmental state. One of its distinguishing features has been the manner in which it has been able to persuade or cajole the private sector to do its bidding, but also to work closely with that sector to achieve national developmental goals set primarily by key elements in the state bureaucracy (see below). But other theorists, such as

Gordon White (1984), have identified three types of developmental state – state capitalist, intermediate and state socialist – and he has explored the role and prospects of the latter in third world industrialization. However, with the world-wide demise of these socialist states, with the interesting and important exception of China,[2] the only extant type of developmental state appears to be the capitalist developmental state, of which there have been two main types: democratic and non-democratic. Before looking at the particular features of *democratic* developmental states, it is necessary to outline the main features of the species in general.

CHARACTERISTICS OF THE DEVELOPMENTAL STATE

Bearing in mind the definition of developmental states outlined above, what characteristics do they have?

Developmental elites

First and foremost, all developmental states have been led by determined developmental elites, which have been relatively uncorrupt, at least by comparison with the pervasive corruption so typical of, say, Haiti, Zaïre and the Philippines under Marcos. These elites have often been associated with founding figures, such as Lee Kwan Yew in Singapore, Sir Seretse Khama in Botswana, General Park Chung Hee in Korea and President Soeharto in Indonesia. Often, the core policy circle surrounding the leadership has been quite small. For instance, even in Indonesia, with a vast population of 170 million, it was estimated for the 1970s that the small ruling group responded primarily to the values and interests of less than a thousand persons in the bureaucratic, technocratic and military elite of the country (Jackson, 1978: 3–4). What seems to characterize developmental elites such as these is their developmental determination, their commitment to economic growth and transformation and their capacity to push it through. This contrasts starkly with, say, the incompetent and 'predatory' state of Haiti (Lundahl, 1992) or the corrupt 'cronyism' of the Marcosian Philippines (Hawes, 1992), or even the relative developmental immobilism of the Indian state, given its control by three dominant 'proprietary classes' (Bardhan, 1984: 54).

A further feature of these developmental elites has been the dense traffic between top levels of the civil and military bureaucracies and high political office, something which is very rare in Western liberal democracies. Such elites have in general also been highly nationalistic – a major impetus for economic development – often responding to internal or regional security threats and thus underlining and extending Tilly's thesis (for Europe) about the importance of warmaking in state formation (Tilly, 1975).

Relative state autonomy

Second, a shared aspect of all developmental states has been the relative autonomy of the elites and the state institutions which they command. By autonomy is meant that the state has been able to achieve relative independence (or insulation) from the demanding clamour of special interests (whether class, regional or sectoral, where they exist) and that it can and does override these interests in the putative national interest (Nordlinger, 1987: 369–71). It is important to note that 'autonomy' in this sense does not mean isolation from the society. On the contrary, as Evans (1989) describes it, the reality is more like 'embedded autonomy'. This means that the autonomy of the well-developed bureaucracies is embedded in a dense web of ties with both non-state and other state actors (internal and external) who collectively help to define, re-define and implement developmental objectives. Indeed in the capitalist developmental state, on the Japanese template, it is this intimacy between the key bureaucracies and the economic agents in the private sector which makes the combined public-private drive to attain development goals so powerful and effective. Here, state and market are, in theory, pulling in the same direction, though in Wade's terms it is the state which is the senior partner, actively involved in 'governing the market' (Wade, 1990).

Bureaucratic power

Third, both the developmental determination of the elite and the relative autonomy of the state have helped to shape very powerful, highly competent and insulated bureaucracies with authority to direct and manage the broad shape of economic and social development. MITI, in Japan, might be thought of as the ideal example of this, but in all developmental states comparable institutions may be found, such as the Economic Planning Board in Korea, the Economic Development Board in Singapore and the Ministry of Finance and Development Planning in Botswana. What differentiates these economic high commands (or 'pilot agencies', as Johnson calls them) in developmental states from the generality of planning institutions in so many developing countries is their real power, authority, technical competence and insulation in shaping the fundamental thrusts of development policy.

Weak civil society

Fourth, in all developmental states, civil society has experienced weakness, flattening or control at the hands of the state. Either the institutions of civil society have been negligible at the inception of the developmental state, as in Botswana (Molutsi and Holm, 1990: 327), or they have been smashed or penetrated by it as in Korea, Indonesia and China (Moon and Kim in this volume; Sundhaussen, 1989: 462–3; Gold, 1990: 18–25). And it seems that this weakness or weakening of civil society has been a condition of the emergence and consolidation of developmental states. Later (for instance in Korea in the 1980s) as the pressures for democratization have emerged, they have often come from those groups in society – students, professionals, managers – who would normally have formed the core of civil society institutions and who, when democracy arrives, move quickly to do so.

The developmental state and economic interests

Fifth, the power, authority and relative autonomy of these states was established and consolidated at an early point in their modern developmental history, well *before* national or foreign capital became important or potentially influential. This is interestingly demonstrated in China, now, when foreign capital is beginning to become important and, no doubt in due course, as will local capital. The power and authority of the state appears well enough established to deal with this. It is for this reason, as well as many others, that China since 1979 may be seen as having begun to move clearly in the direction of a typical developmental state (White, 1991 in this volume) or a 'market-facilitating' state, as some call it (Howell, 1993: 2), a process which will accelerate if economic liberalization continues.

This consolidation of state power and authority before national or foreign capital has begun to grow in importance has greatly enhanced the capacities of developmental states *vis-à-vis* private economic interests, whether internal or external. It has enabled these states to have much greater influence in determining the role which both foreign and national capital has played in development and has also enabled the state to set the terms for this. All developmental states have established a battery of instruments which they have been able to use to bend capital to their developmental purposes (Mardon, 1990). The important comparative point to note here is that this situation sharply differentiates these developmental states from the generality of Latin American states where historically powerful landed interests, an emerging bourgeoisie and foreign capital were deeply entrenched (Evans, 1987). This seriously compromised the capacity and restrained the autonomy of Latin American states to achieve balanced national industrial modernization.

Developmental states and human rights

Whether democratic or not, there is little doubt that developmental states have not been particularly attractive states, at least not by

Table 13.2 Human rights records of developmental states (1987)

Botswana	71%
Singapore	59%
South Korea	59%
Thailand	57%
Malaysia	53%
Taiwan	47%
Indonesia	30%
China	23%

Source: Humana (1987)

either Western liberal or socialist standards. This is especially true for the non-democratic developmental states, where human rights records have been very poor and, sometimes, appalling. Opposition has not been tolerated and, as would be expected from the earlier point about civil society, any organization or movement which looked as if it would challenge the state and its developmental purposes has been swiftly neutralized, penetrated or incorporated as part of the ruling party. But despite this, most developmental states have had better records (which may not be saying much) than many non-developmental states, as table 13.2 shows. It is based on Humana's work (1987) which offers a percentage mark for human rights records. It is worth noting that Humana calculates that the world average is 55 per cent.

While the human rights records of Taiwan, Indonesia and China have been very poor, the others are about average, or better, on a global basis, and (in 1987) were better than South Africa, the former Soviet Union, Iran, Albania and the Central African Republic.

Developmental states: legitimacy and performance

Legitimacy is notoriously difficult to measure, especially under non-democratic conditions. Nonetheless, despite often poor human rights records, case studies suggest widespread support for the regimes and considerable legitimacy, even in Indonesia (Liddle, 1992: 450). This is not to say that these states have been without internal opposition. On the contrary, they all have experienced often persistent (and sometimes violent) opposition, as in Korea, Indonesia and Thailand. Despite this, few developmental states appear to have had their fundamental constitutional or political legitimacy seriously threatened.

It is probable that this strange mixture of repression and legitimacy is best explained by the manner in which these states have been able to distribute the benefits of rapid growth, at least in terms of schools, roads, health care, public housing and other facilities, to an expanding circle of people. Using the Human Development Index (HDI) of the United Nations Development Programme (UNDP, 1992: 2), it would seem that most developmental states have done remarkably well. The HDI measures progress in human development by combining indicators of per capita income, life expectancy and educational attainment, and it ranks countries from best (1) to worst (160). In this ranking, Korea, Singapore and Malaysia fall in the top 30 per cent, while the others are all in the top 60 per cent – way ahead of, say, India, Pakistan, Vietnam, Egypt, Kenya or Bolivia. For instance, in the developmental states referred to here, life expectancy as a key social indicator is nowhere lower than 62 years of age (Indonesia) and is as high as 74 in Singapore. In the others, it is as follows: Korea 71, China 70, Malaysia 70, Botswana 67 and Thailand 66. This compares favourably with, say, Tanzania 48, Zaïre 52, India 59, Peru 63 and Bolivia 60 (World Bank, 1992).

Summary of developmental state characteristics

This brief account suggests that the developmental state, as a subtype of state in the modern world, is not confined to Confucian East Asia, as is sometimes suggested (Onis, 1991: 124). It is found in Islamic and Buddhist Southeast Asia as well as in Africa. Developmental states are dominated by strongly nationalistic and determined developmental elites. Combining varying degrees of repression and legitimacy, where civil society is weak or weakened, these states concentrate considerable power, authority, autonomy and competence in the central political and especially bureaucratic institutions of the state, notably their economic bureaucracies, and they generate pervasive 'infrastructural capacity' (Mann, 1986) to achieve their developmental objectives. This has enhanced the capacity of these states to deal authoritatively and not dependently with both domestic and especially foreign economic interests in pursuit of national developmental objectives.

What is crucial to recognize here, to pick up the central theme of the first chapter in this book, is that all this is not simply the result of the application of the principles of 'good governance' (World Bank, 1992b) by these states; nor, in most respects, does the model of the developmental state even approximate the World Bank model of good governance (Leftwich, 1994). The developmental state is primarily a function of the internal political dynamics of these societies and their external relations, which have together acted to shape the form and features of state power and hence its administrative capacity. With the considerable developmental momentum which these states have generated, they have been able to drive through some of the most remarkable transformations in socioeconomic conditions seen since post-Meiji Japan, thereby liberating the bulk of their people from some of the worst features of poverty, disease and material insecurity. In short, the distinguishing characteristic of developmental states is that their political purposes and institutional structures have been driven by developmental needs, while their developmental objectives have been politically driven.

THE DEMOCRATIC DEVELOPMENTAL STATE

These characteristics and capacities have been shared by democratic and non-democratic developmental states alike. What then differentiates them and what are the salient features of the democratic development state?

Using Botswana, Singapore and Malaysia as the prime examples of democratic developmentalism, the first thing to note is that they qualify in most basic respects as political democracies, in that political parties are free to organize and that regular and essentially fair elections have been held under conditions of adult suffrage. Governments are essentially accountable to representative political institutions, the judiciary is independent and the rule of law is more honoured than not. While they clearly have good records in civil and human rights by comparison with most of the third world, this is not to suggest that they approximate typical Scandinavian standards in this respect: they do not (as table 13.2 shows). For instance in both Malaysia and Singapore, tough internal security legislation exists and these states have not been averse to using it for political purposes. Official attitudes to opposition and dissent have hardly been tolerant, as Lee Kwan Yew indicated in 1982:

> Every time anybody starts anything which will unwind or unravel this orderly, organized, sensible, rational society, and make it irrational and emotional, I put a stop to it and without hesitation. (Cited in Harris, 1986: 61)

Democratic developmental states may thus be thought of as authoritarian democracies.[3] But despite these and other aspects of these states which mean that they fall short in certain respects of the full requirements of *liberal* democracy, their political characteristics differentiate them fundamentally from authoritarian regimes (whether developmental or not) on left, right and centre, such as the former Soviet Union, South Africa under apartheid, Indonesia or the hopeless and venal patrimonialism of Zaïre.

But if these states qualify as democracies, why have they been able to achieve such remarkable developmental successes, when other democracies, such as Venezuela, Costa Rica, Jamaica and India, have lagged so far behind? I suggest that in all three cases the necessary power, authority, autonomy, continuity and political capacity which developmental states and their elite require if they are to achieve sustained and rapid economic growth have been achieved because they are all dominant-party democracies. That is to say, in all three cases, one party has dominated the political scene and remained in power, being returned in each successive election since independence, roughly 30 years ago. In Botswana it has been the Botswana Democratic Party (BDP) (see Holm's chapter in this volume), in Singapore it has been the People's Action Party (PAP) (Cone, 1988) and in Malaysia the United Malays National Organization (UMNO) has been the dominant party controlling the national coalition in the Alliance Party and, later, the Barisan National (Ahmad, 1989). It should also be pointed out that in the paradigmatic case of the democratic capitalist developmental state, Japan, one party – the Liberal Democratic Party – held power without a break for almost 40 years from 1955 to 1993.

This contrasts sharply with other democratic but non-developmental states, such as Jamaica or Sri Lanka where no dominant party exists. It also contrasts with India where the initial post-independence pre-eminence of the Congress Party has been disintegrating in the last 20 years. But even before that, the prospects for developmental state autonomy under the earlier hegemony of Congress were negligible, given the dominant coalition of proprietary classes in party and state (Bardhan, 1984) and, perhaps, the ideology of Nehruvian democracy (as Sudipta Kaviraj shows in his subtle chapter in this volume).

In short, dominant-party rule in a competitive pluralist political environment over a long period has both defined and facilitated the emergence of developmental democratic states, just as authoritarian and military-backed regimes have done so in non-democratic developmental states. These democratic developmental states command our attention because they have taken major steps in transforming the general welfare in their societies in ways that democratic non-developmental states (and others) have not been able to do. None of the common features of all developmental states which I sketched above would have been possible in these democratic developmental states without this central condition of long-term, dominant-party rule. Without it, their developmental elites would have been divided or paralysed; relative state autonomy would have been impossible and the badgering demands of special interests would have come to predominate; bureaucratic continuity and capacity would have been compromised; and either local or foreign economic interests, or both, would soon have become entrenched in ways that would be unlikely to serve national developmental goals.

CONCLUSION

The concluding points are not particularly comfortable ones, but they seem hard to avoid.

First, as Huntington has pointed out (1987) there are many goals of development which include not only democracy and economic growth but also equity, stability and national autonomy. It is unreasonable to believe that they can be attained simultaneously, at least if the prior experience of developed countries is anything to go by. But dominant-party democratic developmental states, on the model outlined above, hold out some prospect for at least achieving respectable levels of growth and the distribution of its benefits that will make a real difference to the majority of the population under essentially democratic conditions.

Second, to illustrate the point in a slightly different way, it is worth emphasizing that the ANC government in South Africa (as Tom Lodge points out in his insightful chapter) has Herculean tasks before it, not only in terms of post-apartheid state-building, but also in basic developmental terms. For not only must it correct past inequalities but it must also promote the much-needed and sustained economic growth that will both help to fund this restructuring and raise the average level of human welfare, *while also* maintaining democratic rule. This is not an uncommon situation in the developing world. If it can be regularly re-elected with substantial majorities in open competition over the next 25 years at least, it will be able to establish the kind of democratic developmental state which alone stands a fair chance of achieving these goals. If not, endemic instability and insecurity will engulf the country, and both democracy *and* development will be overwhelmed.

Third, these considerations underline the main point of the first chapter in this volume: the primacy of politics in development and the centrality of the state. Wherever one looks, it is the political context, the political dynamics and the political purposes which shape the structure of the state, fashion its developmental aims and determine their outcomes. Sustained and effective development can never be reduced to administrative arrangements, or managerial considerations evacuated from politics. For this reason, democratic developmental states may not be had to order. In their absence, the second best is likely to be non-democratic developmental states but they, too, have a complex political provenance in conditions which do not always exist. As we slide down the list of preferences, the third best will probably be democratic non-development. Last of all, one must expect many third world societies to revert to non-democratic non-development as unsecured democracies collapse. But in each instance, as recent experience world-wide has shown, the particular outcome will depend on politics.

Finally, democratic developmental states of the kind I have outlined here may not satisfy all the first principles of liberal or social democracy. But they are certainly preferable to non-democratic developmental states. Of course there are risks. Any dominant-party regime that remains in power for long is in danger of becoming complacent and corrupt. The hope is that electoral discipline will contain this, as in Botswana, Malaysia and Singapore, and that the fear of electoral defeat will compel such regimes to work hard to deliver the developmental goods as those regimes clearly have done. But if eliminating the continuing misery of hunger and poverty remains the real objective, then the democratic developmental state, or authoritarian democracy, may be the only way of combining the basic elements of democracy with the continuity and coherence of policy that is required for sustained development.

If democratic developmental states can then proceed to establish the political *and* economic conditions in which a less authoritarian democracy can later flourish, they will have fulfilled a historic mission of modernization and will have worked themselves out of a job. Until then, unrestrained liberal democracy on the Fukuyama model may be the last thing that those at the sharp end of poverty need.

NOTES

1 The first part of the title of this chapter is taken from the essay of that title by E. M. Forster (1972).
2 The case of Cuba, as a socialist developmental state in White's terms, requires careful attention. While it has not achieved the kind of economic growth and structural transformation characteristic of other developmental states, its record in terms of human development has been impressive. Perhaps, in the post-Soviet era, as Cuba finds it necessary to liberalize its economy and its external economic relationships, the developmental potential of the state in a less hostile international environment will become clear.
3 I am grateful to Margaret Lamb for the point.

REFERENCES

Ahmad, Z. A. 1989: Malaysia: Quasi-Democracy in a Divided Society. In L. Diamond et al. (eds) *Democracy in Developing Countries,* vol 3, Asia. London: Adamantine Press, 347–82.
Bardhan, P. 1984: *The Political Economy of Development in India.* Oxford: Basil Blackwell.
Cone, D. K. 1988: State, Social Elites and Government Capability in Southeast Asia. *World Politics,* 40, 252–68.
Council for Economic Planning and Development, 1992: *Taiwan Statistical Data Book.* Taipei, Republic of China: CEPD.
Derbyshire, D. and I. 1989: *Political Systems of the World.* Edinburgh: Chambers.
Evans, P. B. 1987: Class, State and Dependency in East Asia: Lessons for Latin Americanists. In F. C. Deyo (ed.) *The Political Economy of the New Asian Industrialism.* Ithaca, NY: Cornell University Press, 227–47.
Evans, P. B. 1989: Predatory, Developmental and Other Apparatuses: A Comparative Political Economy Perspective on the Third World State. *Sociological Forum,* 4, 561–87.
Forster, E. M. 1972 (1951): *Two Cheers For Democracy.* London: Macmillan.

Freedom House Survey Team, 1992: *Freedom in the World. Political Rights and Civil Liberties, 1991–1992.* New York: Freedom House.

Gastil, R. D. 1986: *Freedom in the World: Political Rights and Civil Liberties 1985–1986.* New York: Greenwood Press.

Gold, T. 1990: The Resurgence of Civil Society in China. *Journal of Democracy,* 1, 18–31.

Harris, N. 1986: *The End of the Third World.* Harmondsworth: Penguin.

Hawes, G. 1992: Marcos, His Cronies and the Philippines' Failure to Develop. In R. McVey (ed.) *Southeast Asian Capitalists.* Ithaca, NY: Cornell University Southeast Asia Program, 145–60.

Howell, J. 1993: *The Poverty of Civil Society. Insights from China.* Discussion paper 240. Norwich: University of East Anglia, School of Development Studies.

Humana, C. 1987: *World Human Rights Guide.* London: Pan.

Huntington, S. P. 1987: The Goals of Development. In M. Weiner and S. P. Huntington (eds) *Understanding Political Development.* Boston, Mass.: Little Brown, 3–32.

Jackson, K. D. 1978: Bureaucratic Polity: A Theoretical Framework for the Analysis of Power and Communications in Indonesia. In K. D. Jackson and L. W. Pye (eds) *Political Power and Communications in Indonesia.* Berkeley: University of California Press, 3–22.

Johnson, C. 1981: Introduction: The Taiwan Model. In J. S. Hsiung (ed.) *Contemporary Republic of China. The Taiwan Experience, 1950–1980.* New York: Praeger, 9–18.

Johnson, C. 1982: *MITI and the Japanese Miracle.* Stanford, Cal.: Stanford University Press.

Johnson, C. 1987: Political Institutions and Economic Performance: the Government–Business Relationship in Japan, South Korea and Taiwan. In F. C. Deyo (ed.) *The Political Economy of the New Asian Industrialism.* Ithaca, NY: Cornell University Press, 136–64.

Leftwich, A. 1994: Governance, the State and the Politics of Development. *Development and Change,* 25, 363–86.

Leftwich, A. 1995: Bringing Politics Back In: Towards a Model of the Developmental State. *Journal of Development Studies,* 31, 400–27.

Liddle, R. W. 1992: Indonesia's Democratic Past and Future. *Comparative Politics,* 24, 443–62.

List, F. 1885: *The National System of Political Economy.* New York: A. M. Kelley.

Lundahl, M. 1992: *Politics or Markets? Essays on Haitian Underdevelopment.* London: Routledge.

Mann, M. 1986: The Autonomous Powers of the State: Its Origins, Mechanisms and Results. In J. A. Hall (ed.) *States in History.* Oxford: Basil Blackwell, 109–36.

Mardon, R. 1990: The State and the Effective Control of Foreign Capital. The Case of Korea. *World Politics,* 43, 111–38.

Molutsi, P. and Holm, J. D. 1990: Developing Democracy When Civil Society is Weak: The Case of Botswana. *African Affairs,* 89(356), 323–40.

Nordlinger, E. A. 1987: Taking the State Seriously. In M. Weiner and S. P. Huntington (eds) *Understanding Political Development.* Boston, Mass.: Little Brown and Co., 353–93.

Onis, Z. 1991: The Logic of the Developmental State. *Comparative Politics,* 24, 109–26.

Rueschemeyer, D., Stephens, E. H. and Stephens, J. D. 1992: *Capitalist Development and Democracy*. Cambridge: Polity Press.
Sundhaussen, U. 1989: Indonesia: Past and Present Encounters with Democracy. In L. Diamond et al. (eds) *Democracy in Developing Countries*, vol 3, Asia. London: Adamantine Press, 423–74.
Tilly, C. 1975: Reflections on the History of European State-making. In C. Tilly (ed.) *The Formation of National States in Western Europe*. Princeton, NJ: Princeton University Press, 3–83.
UNDP (United Nations Development Programme), 1992: *Human Development Report 1992*. New York: Oxford University Press.
Wade, R. 1990: *Governing the Market: Economic Theory and the Role of Government in East Asian Industrialization*. Princeton, NJ: Princeton University Press.
White, G. 1984: Developmental States and Socialist Industrialization in the Third World. *Journal of Development Studies*, 21, 97–120.
White, G. 1991: *Democracy and Economic Reform in China*. Discussion paper 286. Brighton: Institute of Development Studies.
World Bank, 1992a: *World Development Report 1992*. New York: Oxford University Press.
World Bank, 1992b: *Governance and Development*. Washington: The World Bank.

Index